INTER-AMERICAN DEVELOPME

ECONOMIC AND SOCIAL PROGRESS IN LATIN AMERICA

2008 REPORT

Outsiders?

THE CHANGING PATTERNS OF EXCLUSION IN LATIN AMERICA AND THE CARIBBEAN

GUSTAVO MÁRQUEZ
ALBERTO CHONG
SUZANNE DURYEA
JACQUELINE MAZZA
HUGO ÑOPO
COORDINATORS

OUTSIDERS?
The Changing Patterns of Exclusion in Latin America and the Caribbean

©2007   Inter-American Development Bank
1300 New York Avenue, NW
Washington, DC 20577

Co-published by
David Rockefeller Center
for Latin American Studies
Harvard University
1730 Cambridge Street
Cambridge, MA 02138

Distributed by
Harvard University Press
Cambridge, Massachusetts
London, England

To order this book, contact:
IDB Bookstore
Tel: 202-623-1753
Fax: 202-623-1709
E-mail: idb-books@iadb.org
www.iadb.org/pub

ISBN: 978-1-59782-059-2
ISSN: 0095-2850

The IDB's Office of External Relations was responsible
for the design and production of this report.

Publisher	Rafael Cruz
Production Editor	Michael Harrup
Graphic Designers	Leilany Garron and Dolores Subiza
Editorial Assistant	Cathy Conkling-Shaker
Proofreader	Joanne Blake
Translator (Chapter 4)	Gabriel Dobson
Indexer	Breffni Whelan
Additional Typography	Word Express, Inc.

Contents

CHAPTER 10

CHAPTER 11

CHAPTER 12

PART III ADVANCING INCLUSION

CHAPTER 13

CHAPTER 14

Annotated Table of Contents

PART I THE CHANGING PATTERNS OF INCLUSION AND EXCLUSION

CHAPTER 1

Social exclusion evolved and changed as much as societies did with the re-establishment of democracy in the mid-1980s. Exclusion has become more urban and visible and is at the source of
a growing sense of disengagement and dissatisfaction that affects wide segments of the population, creating a fertile ground for populist experiments that erode the economic, social, and
political institutions of democracy.

CHAPTER 2

The outcomes of exclusion have traditionally been understood as the product of stigma and
discrimination that target groups easily identifiable by their racial, ethnic, and gender identity.
This chapter reviews an extensive body of literature that documents the relative and multidimensional deprivation that the excluded suffer as a consequence of their lack of access to the
institutions and resources with which those in the mainstream obtain outcomes valuable in a
market economy.

CHAPTER 3

Conventional wisdom holds that the multiple deprivations suffered by traditionally discriminated-against groups (indigenous peoples, Afro-descendants, and women) are the product of
overt discrimination. The results of a set of highly controlled economic experiments suggest
that substantial differences in endowments associated with race, ethnicity, or gender, rather
than discrimination, explain these differential outcomes. Recognizing the difference between
these two concepts is crucial for the design of effective antidiscrimination policies.

Democratization, macro stabilization, and globalization have drastically changed the way the state functions and have altered the channels of social, political, and economic inclusion that a truncated version of the welfare state provided to a fortunate few. These modern forces of inclusion and exclusion interact with traditional excluding forces and have made larger and more diverse segments of the population more vulnerable to social exclusion.

The labor market is one of the social loci where modern exclusionary forces (largely economic and social in origin) have expanded, both in magnitude and scope, the impact of social exclusion. Rising unemployment, mediocre levels of growth, and an increasing demand for education have increased the share of low-wage employment in the region in the last decade and a half.

Latin America and the Caribbean has the greatest income inequality of any region in the world. Individuals at the bottom of the income distribution are unlikely to see significant improvement in their social position or that of their children, regardless of effort or ability. Conversely, those fortunate few in the upper echelons of the income distribution show little downward mobility, again regardless of effort or ability.

The results of a set of highly controlled social experiments in six Latin American capital cities suggest that Latin Americans do trust and cooperate, but that exclusion, by increasing social distance and heterogeneity, reduces incentives to cooperate. Welfare losses of between 22 and 72 percent relative to what could have been obtained under full cooperation were observed in the experimental setting. Though these values should not be interpreted as actual GDP losses, they are indicative of the important economic consequences of social exclusion.

Privatizations have a bad reputation with Latin Americans, mostly because of the exclusionary outcomes they represent for employees fired from privatized firms. However, they may have an inclusionary effect as well, by expanding the scope of the population served and improving the quality of services produced. High-quality public regulation is crucial for determining which of these two impacts is greater.

In spite of the formal equality of political rights guaranteed in national constitutions, the democratic systems in the region often limit the formal channels of influence of some groups within the population. Social mobilization has the potential to increase the voice of the excluded and to make the formal political system pay attention to their demands. This suggests that social movements can be more part of the solution than part of the problem for the region's evolving democracies.

CHAPTER 10

The judicial and law enforcement systems of countries in the region have only weakly adapted to the dramatic changes that Latin American and Caribbean societies have experienced in the last twenty-five years. The excluded, who face increasing violence and insecurity in their daily lives, lack adequate access to justice and economic and physical security.

CHAPTER 11

Financial inclusion holds important benefits for excluded groups of the population, facilitating savings, helping families smooth consumption, and reducing the limitations of dependence on volatile cash flows. In spite of these advantages, empirical studies have found that the fraction of poor households with savings accounts is much lower than that of nonpoor households.

CHAPTER 12

Lack of civil registration documents makes entire segments of the population "invisible." Interestingly, modern forms of social program delivery often make possession of official identification documents a strict requirement for program participation. This suggests that more sophisticated targeting needs to be complemented with civil registration campaigns to avoid excluding targeted groups from the benefits of these programs.

PART III ADVANCING INCLUSION

CHAPTER 13

Social inclusion is a process aimed at actively promoting social, economic, and cultural equality. Inclusive public policies affect not only the results of public policy and the outcomes obtained by excluded groups, but also how these results and outcomes are achieved. Inclusive public policy changes the basic normative framework, the institutions that operationalize the basic norms, and the policies and programs that these institutions implement. Political leadership and an active civil society are essential drivers of this process.

CHAPTER 14

Progress towards inclusion in the region requires efforts both to comprehend the forces that create exclusion and to understand how the public policy process can significantly advance inclusion. Public policy knowledge and experience in regard to attacking exclusion is very limited, but elements of public policies and programs being implemented in the region today can help guide the needed rethinking of the problems and possibilities of inclusion processes. Ultimately, however, policy recommendations in this area must be the product of civic participation and democratic processes that are at the core of any set of national initiatives for inclusion.

Preface

The 2008 edition of the *Report on Economic and Social Progress* deals with the changing patterns of social inclusion and exclusion, one of the most pressing concerns faced by policymakers in Latin America and the Caribbean. In fact, much of the lively debate on the economic and social policies needed to attain sustainable and equitable growth hinges on the issue of social inclusion. What this report shows is that attaining social inclusion demands not only redressing past injustices with resource transfers and affirmative action programs, but also, and more importantly, changing the way decisions are made, resources are allocated, and policies are implemented.

Social exclusion is the most dangerous threat that democracy faces in Latin America and the Caribbean. The advent of democracy in our region was the result of a dramatic social struggle that engaged the majority of the population under the banner of creating more modern, more prosperous, and fairer societies. Indeed, the past quarter century has witnessed significant progress that made our political systems more democratic, confronted the corrosive effects of rampant inflation, and integrated our economies into the world market. Yet progress has not been limited to politics and economics: life expectancy, health, literacy, and other indicators of well-being have improved and continue to improve. But poverty, inequality, and lack of good jobs and opportunities to facilitate social mobility for the majority represent areas in which a great deal of work remains to be done—and in which Latin American and Caribbean societies are more than ever demanding results.

At the same time, social exclusion cannot be addressed by short-term or simple "fixes" because it is a complex phenomenon with many interrelated and mutually reinforcing features. Violence, crime, social protests, lack of integration into the financial system, and lack of access to the health and education systems, among other limitations, can condemn members of excluded groups to lives of poverty and squalor. Transforming societies into ones in which the color of a person's skin or the wealth of a person's parents does not determine the fate of present and future generations is a complex process aimed at promoting the integration of the majority into the mechanisms and institutions that allow included groups to work, do business, and prosper.

Promoting social inclusion requires well coordinated and carefully considered actions on the part of both governments and civil society to advance the rights of excluded groups. This includes changing both the wider rules by which societies operate and the specific ways in which programs and policies are implemented. The Inter-American Development Bank, as an international financial institution, can aspire to collaborate in this process in multiple ways. The Opportunities for the Majority initiative, in which the

Bank is investing significant resources and effort, aims at expanding the opportunities of the excluded majority and improving their access to the institutions and resources that can empower them to take charge of their destiny and to prosper in an economy and a society in which success depends on effort and ability, and not on one's circumstances at birth.

I sincerely hope that this report contributes to our understanding of the complexities of social exclusion and of the potential of public policy to promote social inclusion and combat social exclusion.

Luis Alberto Moreno
President
Inter-American Development Bank

Acknowledgments

E*conomic and Social Progress in Latin America* is the flagship publication of the Inter-American Development Bank. This issue was a joint production of the Bank's Research Department and the former Sustainable Development Department coordinated by Alberto Chong, Suzanne Duryea, Jacqueline Mazza, and Hugo Ñopo, as well as Gustavo Márquez, who was the overall leader of the project. The team benefited from the useful and insightful comments and supervision of Eduardo Lora, who was Chief Economist a.i. during the preparation of the report. Rita Funaro, Michael Harrup, and John Dunn Smith edited the report in its entirety. Carlos Andrés Gómez-Peña, research and technical assistant, was in charge of coordinating the report's production process. Overall research assistance was provided by Ana Carolina Izaguirre Corzo.

The principal authors of each individual chapter are presented below, along with their acknowledgments for assistance they received:

Chapter 1   Gustavo Márquez

Chapter 2   Néstor Gandelman, Hugo Ñopo, and Laura Ripani
      Santiago Amieva, Sebastián Calónico, Ted Enamorado, Gabriela Flores, Diana Góngora, Georgina Pizzolitto, and Holger Siebrecht provided valuable research assistance, and Nnenna Ozobia offered welcome comments.

Chapter 3   Alberto Chong and Hugo Ñopo
      Lucas Higuera, Gianmarco León, and Sebastián Calónico provided valuable research assistance.
      The authors drew on papers produced by the participants in the Discrimination and Economic Outcomes Research Network project: Víctor J. Elías, Julio J. Elías, and Lucas Ronconi; David Bravo, Claudia Sanhueza, Sergio Urzúa, Dante Contreras, Diana Kruger, Daniela Zapata, and Marcelo Ochoa; Juan-Camilo Cárdenas, Alejandro Gaviria, Rajiv Sethi, Sandra Polanía, and Natalia Candelo; Ximena Soruco, Giorgina Piani, and Máximo Rossi; Marco Castillo, Ragan Petrie, and Máximo Torero; and Néstor Gandelman, Eduardo Gandelman, and Julie Rothschild. Andrea Moro was the academic advisor of the network.

Chapter 4   Juan Camilo Chaparro and Eduardo Lora

Chapter 5   Gustavo Márquez and Carmen Pagés-Serra
      María Fernanda Prada provided valuable research assistance.

Chapter 6   Viviane Azevedo and César Bouillón

Chapter 7   Sebastián Calónico, Natalia Candelo, Juan-Camilo Cárdenas, Alberto Chong, Hugo Ñopo, and Sandra Polanía

   Lucas Higuera provided valuable research assistance.

   A collaborative effort like this requires the support of many colleagues. Among them we would like to thank Martín Benavides and Juan José Díaz, Néstor Gandelman, Saúl Keifman, Nathan Lederman, Giorgina Piani, and Arodys Robles and their fieldwork teams in the different cities of our project. The insightful comments of Jeffrey Carpenter and Orazio Attanasio were very much appreciated.

Chapter 8   Alberto Chong, Gianmarco León, and Hugo Ñopo

   Vanessa Ríos provided valuable research assistance.

   The authors would like to thank Máximo Torero and Florencio López-de-Silanes for their inputs and comments.

Chapter 9   María Mercedes Mateo and J. Mark Payne

Chapter 10   Heather Berkman

   The author would like to thank Gustavo Béliz and Andrew Morrison for their comments on previous versions of this chapter.

Chapter 11   Suzanne Duryea

   The author thanks Luis Tejerina and Ernesto Schargrodsky for their input and comments.

Chapter 12   Suzanne Duryea

   The author thanks Amanda Glassman and Leslie Stone for their input and comments. Victoria Rodríguez Pombo provided valuable research assistance.

Chapter 13   Jacqueline Mazza

Chapter 14   Jacqueline Mazza

   The author would like to thank Zakiya Carr-Johnson (boxes on Jamaica and Brazil), Nnenna Ozobia (box on Ecuador), André Médici and Gabriela Vega (box on reproductive health), Juliana Pungiluppi (box on Colombia), and Fernando Carrillo-Flórez (box on justice) for their valuable contributions.

   Marco Ferroni provided substantial review and substantive input.

Benedicte Bull, Martín Benavides, Cristina García, Claudia Jacinto, and Alejandra Solla contributed to a seminar in Washington, DC, in October 2006 that served as an early discussion about this report. Fernando Carrillo-Flórez and Ricardo Santiago organized a very useful seminar in Madrid with the participation of Joan Prats, Rosemary Thorp, José Antonio Sanahuja, Alain Touraine, and Rodrigo Contreras.

PART I

The Changing Patterns
of Inclusion and Exclusion

Outsiders?

L atin America and the Caribbean has undergone immense societal transformations in the past twenty-five years. The re-establishment of democracy during the mid-1980s changed both politics and policies in the region and gave rise to fresh expectations about a future of more modern, more prosperous, and fairer societies.

As sweeping as these changes have been, however, they have yielded only mixed results. The region is today more prosperous and modern than it was twenty-five years ago, after languishing for years under the watch of dictatorial, sometimes messianic, and often corrupt generals. Macroeconomic stability has been achieved and still prevails in spite of repeated adverse financial shocks. The combined impact of economic liberalization (a national decision) and globalization (a global phenomenon) has allowed the region to integrate itself into the world economy, an inexhaustible source of riches in the best circumstances, and at worst a shackle on distortionary domestic policies. The interventionist and centralized states whose fiscal crisis marked the decade of the 1980s have gone through a "silent revolution" that has transformed beyond recognition the way they relate to the population (Lora, 2007). On the other hand, poverty and highly skewed distributions of assets (including human capital) and income are an obstacle on the path to fairer societies in the region. Social exclusion, historically rooted in different forms of stigmatization of groups traditionally identified by race, ethnic origin, or gender, has changed as much as the region itself has changed and is now affecting much more diverse and growing groups among the population, especially those who eke out a living in precarious jobs without any prospect of improvement. Their exclusion does not result from being "outside," isolated, left out, but rather from their interactions with more modern and prosperous societies.

These changes in the dynamics of inclusion and exclusion do not lend themselves to simplistic interpretations. There have been advances in the inclusion of some groups, at least in some dimensions, and there have also been regressions that have deepened exclusion. For instance, women have been included in some dimensions (formal political representation and education) but are still segregated in worse jobs than men. Contrastingly, entire sectors of the population have been excluded from formal jobs and their associated social insurance protection by slow growth and unemployment. Then again, the dynamism of civil society and the rise of social movements have made certain excluded groups (like landless peasants in Brazil, the unemployed in Argentina, and indigenous peoples in Bolivia) important actors in the political arena.

Exclusion and inclusion are complex and dynamic processes that operate in every dimension of social life. Exclusion in one dimension (for instance, lacking identity documents) leads to exclusion in multiple other dimensions (for instance, from opening a savings account or participating in formal politics). Social exclusion manifests itself in multiple social maladies (poverty, informal employment, political unrest, crime, and lack of access to health and education, to mention just a few), all of which limit the ability of large sectors of the population to participate fruitfully in a market economy and therefore diminish their well-being.

A look at society through the eyes of the excluded themselves offers a sobering lesson about the interrelated and complex nature of the deprivations they suffer and the ways they find to face them. The microdocumentaries "Faces of Exclusion" that complement this report (www.iadb.org/res/ipes/2008/videos.cfm?language=en) attempt to provide the reader with such a vision. They offer a striking illustration of lives that are lived not somewhere else, but on the streets through which we walk and by people with whom we interact in the pursuit of our daily chores.

The "outsiders" of yesterday (marginalized, rural, ill-nourished, poor, and isolated) were safely out of sight. Exclusion among these groups has not disappeared. Modern forms of servitude, often bordering on slavery, still thrive in rural areas of the region. Gaspar, the subject of one of the microdocumentaries, is a 78-year-old rural worker in Brazil who lacks identity papers, has never been registered with Brazilian labor authorities, and is therefore excluded from a government-financed old-age pension for rural workers (Aposentadoria Rural). In another of the microdocumentaries, indigenous Matsiguenga communities' lack of access to health facilities stands in striking contrast to the riches produced by the Camisea gas field, which is located on their ancestral lands in the Peruvian Amazon. These stories offer stark illustrations of the mechanisms and consequences of traditional forms of exclusion.

But social exclusion today has become more urban and visible, its victims people who are not "outside," but whose exclusion results from their disadvantaged interactions with the institutions and resources that enable the mainstream to prosper in a market economy. The stories depicted in the "Faces of Exclusion" microdocumentaries are a testimony to these disadvantaged interactions. Peddling candy or cellular minutes or performing circus acts on street corners while the red light stops traffic becomes a source of income when one cannot find a decent, well-paying job. Collecting recyclables from garbage cans, squatting in abandoned buildings, sleeping on the same streets that their more affluent neighbors use to go to work and play are some of the survival strategies of these urban excluded. The inhabitants of poor, crime-ridden areas of the region's cities, excluded from the protection of police and the judiciary, create their own forms of organization to contain violence and protect victims, providing, as they do so, a lesson in dignity and compassion.

In the midst of all these multiple deprivations the excluded struggle to make a living with their limited resources. Their daily life is hampered by institutions that are unresponsive to their needs and rights as citizens and by their lack of access to resources as mundane as telephones to receive a call for a job interview, or as dramatic as medical services denied to them by overwhelmed public health facilities. They are left out of the paths towards inclusion that more privileged members of society enjoy, yet they are not outsiders, as their exclusion arises from their participation in social life with limited resources and within rules that are often biased against them by embedded discrimination and prejudice.

Exclusion is at the source of the growing sense of disengagement and dissatisfaction that affects the population of countries in the region and creates a fertile ground for populist experiments that erode the economic, social, and political institutions of democracy. This disengagement has grown in spite of reasonable progress over the medium term on life expectancy, health, literacy, and other indicators of well-being, as shown by the United Nations Economic Commission for Latin America and the Caribbean (ECLAC) in its recent (2007) report on social cohesion. Politicians all along the political spectrum now mention the fight against social exclusion as the main task of development and substantive democratization. As Goodin (1996: 343) points out, "'Social exclusion' is a catchy phrase, and it catches much of what is substantively of concern to us. Indeed, the great value of the concept lies in its promise to link together so many of our other social concerns, tracing them to common (or anyway cognate) causes and prescribing identical (or anyway integrated) cures."

For all the political nuances and overtones with which the term has been used, the notion of social exclusion provides a powerful political rallying cry for anybody who worries about the plight of the worst off in society. However, as normally happens with effective mobilizing notions that need to mean different things to different groups, there is no clarity regarding what is meant by social exclusion. Even if the ambiguity of the concept of social exclusion is useful as a mobilizing tool, the design and adoption of inclusive policies is hindered by the lack of conceptual clarity about the nature of exclusion and the forces that produce and reproduce it.

THE CONCEPT OF SOCIAL EXCLUSION

Social exclusion is an inefficient and dysfunctional dynamic social, political, and economic process whereby individuals and groups are denied access to opportunities and quality services to live productive lives outside poverty. Following Sen (1999), this report argues that those social, political, and economic processes of societies limit the functionings of certain individuals or groups, resulting in their diminished well-being.[1] Those processes might affect the behavior, command of resources, or access to institutions of the excluded individuals or groups in ways that limit their ability to function and, therefore, to acquire or use capabilities that are valuable in a market economy.

Functionings take place in a social space in which individuals and groups engage in "transactions" through behaviors that express their choices based on their command of resources under the set of formal and informal rules that regulate those transactions. Social capital, norms, and collective action deserve special mention within this set of formal and informal rules. They improve collective welfare, especially in circumstances in which the state is weak and cannot respond appropriately to people's needs. Exclusion, in contrast, erodes trust and hinders collective action. When trust among economic

---

[1] The notion of "functionings" comes from Sen's *Development as Freedom* (1999). It is different from the concept of opportunities, in that functionings refer to the social interactions and exchanges in which individuals or groups engage in order to achieve a certain outcome, rather than to the ability (exercised or not) to engage in those interactions; it is different from the concept of capabilities in that functionings refer to a particular realization of the (unobservable) set of capabilities.

agents is not at its fullest, transactions costs inflate, and the scope for economic trades is reduced. As a result, society suffers a welfare loss. Public policies can shape formal and informal institutions that promote (or hinder) the intrinsic motivations of individuals and the self-management possibilities within civil society, thereby affecting trust, reciprocity, and willingness to cooperate.

The term "social exclusion" was coined in the 1970s in France to describe the situation of those groups excluded from the benefits of employment-related safety nets and other groups locked in social ostracism by drug use and other forms of dysfunctional behavior (Lenoir, 1974). However, social exclusion applied to the Latin American and Caribbean context is both a larger (in terms of scale and type of people affected) and more multidimensional concept.

Exclusion is by nature a multidimensional, dynamic social process and therefore is not the "consequence" of some particular "cause" (in the sense of an event that precedes an outcome, without which the outcome would not have happened) (Burchardt, Le Grand, and Piachaud, 2002). We all participate in multiple interactions in our daily social life in which we exchange our labor for a salary with an employer, use that salary in transactions with producers and sellers to buy goods and services, vote in elections, recur to the police and the justice system to solve economic and noneconomic disputes, pay (or evade) taxes, participate in community organizations and churches, go to a government office to obtain licenses and permits, and do innumerable other things. All of these exchanges occur within a certain set of social, economic, and political institutions (formal and informal) that provide opportunities and services required to obtain outcomes valuable in a democratic market society. Social exclusion arises when a set of those formal and informal rules constrain the functionings of certain individuals or groups.[2]

Social exclusion has been used to conceptualize the restrictions that hindered the functionings (Tsakloglu and Papadopoulos, 2001) and access to opportunities (Behrman, Gaviria, and Székely, 2003) of certain specific groups (women, indigenous peoples, Afro-descendants, the handicapped). Buvinić and Mazza (2004: 6) state that "exclusion is produced if belonging to a certain group has a considerable impact on the individual's access to opportunities, and if the interactions between social groups happen in the frame of an authority/subordination relationship." Exclusion in this view is considered to be a group phenomenon and therefore leads to the development of inclusion policies geared towards increasing the opportunities and access of specific groups of the population. An example within this family of policies is the 2002 Brazilian National Program of Affirmative Action (Programa Nacional de Ações Afirmativas), which introduced, beginning in that year, affirmative action quotas for Afro-descendants and indigenous peoples in a range of different areas, including public sector hiring and contracting, higher education, and parliamentary seats.

More recently, social exclusion in Latin America and the Caribbean has come to be seen as either an (undesirable) outcome of the economic reforms of the 1990s or a mechanism that prevents important segments of the population from benefiting from the

---

[2] The report departs here from the notion of "no participation" as the criterion of exclusion. In fact, the intent is to highlight that the excluded do participate, albeit in disadvantaged circumstances, or with rules biased against them, or both.

macroeconomic prosperity that the region has recently been experiencing. Therefore, it has become a recurring theme in alternative economic policies that place a high value on income and asset redistribution. Under this view the focus of inclusion policies moves to fundamental changes in economic and social policies that seek to redress inequality and poverty for all people, whether part of an excluded group or not.

Material deprivation is one of the crucial outcomes of exclusion but is just one aspect of the deprivations suffered by the excluded. Furthermore, material deprivation is highly correlated with other dimensions of deprivation that affect the capacity of the excluded to obtain outcomes desirable in a market economy. Lack of (or low-productivity) employment results in low incomes and poverty, but also restricts the participation of those unemployed and in low-productivity jobs in social institutions, such as unions and other forms of worker organizations geared at improving their working conditions. Political and electoral systems that exclude disadvantaged groups of the population diminish these groups' ability to influence government actions and thus reduce investment in the provision of high-quality services (such as schools) needed by the excluded to improve their lot. Geographical segregation increases the exposure of disadvantaged groups to crime and violence, both because the rich retreat into gated communities with private security and because the disadvantaged lack the social, economic, and political resources needed to access the preventive and corrective forces of the judicial system and the police.

Focusing on social exclusion aims at expanding the analytical and policy focus from poverty specifically into a broader range of concerns. Poverty focuses on outcomes such as measurable income; is based on the analysis of cross-sectional, static data; and looks at individuals and households. Exclusion, instead, focuses on processes, sheds light on the multidimensional nature of deprivation and the interactions between those dimensions, understands deprivation as a dynamic phenomenon, and looks at individuals and households in the framework of a community (Burchardt, Le Grand, and Piachaud, 2002).

Multidimensional deprivation is one outcome of exclusion, but as such needs to be distinguished from the process that produces and reproduces the exclusionary outcome. Poverty, unemployment, informality of employment, lack of political engagement, and dysfunctional forms of social interaction are outcomes of exclusion but should not be confused with the process that generates them. Compensatory policies such as income transfers or subsidized public employment can reduce poverty, and the ensuing reduction of material deprivation will, it is hoped, affect all the other outcomes of exclusion. However, to the extent that such transfers do not have an impact on the forces that constrain the functionings of the excluded, the process of exclusion will continue unabated.

The excluded do not inhabit a social universe devoid of interactions and exchanges from which they are to be rescued by inclusion. Rather, the outcomes of exclusion are the product of particular interactions and exchanges through which the excluded are denied access to resources that would enable them to participate actively in the market economy and the formal and informal institutions that provide social services and opportunities to others. Neither are the excluded passive objects of exclusion; instead, they organize and develop individual and collective actions to change the social features that generate exclusion. Often this results in an "alternative" set of behaviors and institutions that serve to replace the outcome (access to the financial system) denied by exclusion. Exclusion is also at the root of contentious politics and street protests that draw attention to issues important to groups excluded from political representation.

AN OVERVIEW OF THIS REPORT

The outcomes of exclusion (unemployment and underemployment, poverty, disengagement from the state, and "bad" integration with the community) have traditionally been understood as the result of decades, if not centuries, of discrimination and stigma. Discrimination is crucial as a force of exclusion because it lies at the heart of individuals' "transactions."

Traditionally, particular attention has been paid to the role of ethnic origin as the main culprit in discrimination. It has been documented that indigenous peoples and Afro-descendants have less capacity to generate income because of their lower levels of human capital (i.e., formal education or training), lower remuneration in the labor market, and less access to high-quality jobs. This leads to a notoriously higher incidence of poverty among these groups, which persists despite the overall improvement of other groups in society, and lower returns to assets (physical and human capital, public assets, and social capital) that affect income generation strategies.

Latin Americans do believe that discrimination is alive and well, but do not believe that it operates only, or mostly, against traditionally discriminated-against groups (indigenous peoples, Afro-descendants, women). Recent opinion surveys such as Latinobarometer report that most people in the region believe that the poor, the uneducated, and those who lack social connections are the groups that suffer the most discrimination.

Beliefs, however, are informative only to the extent that they influence the economic decisions and outcomes of individuals engaged in market transactions. The fact that different individuals obtain different outcomes in their economic transactions could be explained by differences in the observable productive characteristics of the individuals, and by various factors that are unobservable for the researchers (such as entrepreneurial attitudes, motivation, and work ethic) but that can easily be "seen" by an employer or another relevant actor in the markets in which these individuals participate. Recent advances in the economic literature using highly controlled experiments geared towards obtaining information on unobservable traits show that stereotyping (which vanishes when information flows reveal the "true" productive capabilities of individuals) and self-discrimination (which does not vanish) largely explain discriminatory outcomes. This is not to deny the evident differences in human capital and financial and social assets associated with gender, race, ethnic origin, and class distinctions. What this literature reveals is that these differences do not necessarily reflect overt discrimination; rather, they may result from differences in endowments of various groups within the population. Markets may simply act as resonance boxes that reflect these differences in endowments. This suggests that the automatic attribution of differential outcomes to discrimination may be misleading and a pernicious departure point for the design of remedial policies.

But there is much more to exclusion than discrimination. Focusing on interactions and exchanges makes it possible to move beyond group affiliation (e.g., according to gender, race, ethnicity, religion) towards a more general understanding of exclusionary outcomes as a product of constraints on the functionings of the excluded that do not arise from discrimination alone. From this point of view, exclusion is a moving target. Looking at exclusion through the lenses of groups that have persistently been excluded from the benefits of social services or the opportunities of political participation would obscure multiple other forms of exclusion that affect the disadvantaged, even if they do not belong to stigmatized groups.

The long period of sustained growth and modernization in Latin America and the Caribbean from 1930 through the debt crisis of the 1980s resulted in substantial growth in productivity (Thorp, 2007). The contemporary expansion of public employment and the industrialization process served to create paths for integration of a lucky few, mostly through employment in public or manufacturing jobs that gave them access to social security and other benefits of a truncated version of the welfare state. In this context, basic citizens' rights became attached to formal sector jobs, rather than developing independently of place of employment (Gordon, 2004). The debt crisis in the region in the 1980s and the economic policy reforms of the 1990s disrupted those paths of integration and made those left behind (in unemployment, job informality, or simply poverty) more vulnerable to the traditional forces of exclusion.

Globalization, democratization, and macroeconomic stabilization changed the capabilities of the state to propel and sustain social integration and the mechanisms for doing so, thus altering the patterns of inclusion and exclusion. Democratization has exposed corruption and waste in the public sector, but a new equilibrium between political legitimacy and administrative efficiency has yet to be reached. Stabilization has restricted the capability of the state to fund excessive public expenditure through inflationary financing, whereas globalization (through both trade libereralization and technological change) has threatened employment and tested the limits of income protection and social security policies. These forces have not only changed the nature of the state, but also made a larger part of the population vulnerable to the traditional forces of exclusion.

Although the effect of these societal changes encompasses multiple dimensions of social life, the labor market is a crucial place where these new forces of exclusion manifest themselves. The labor market has been one of the social loci where "modern" exclusionary forces (largely economic and social in origin) associated with globalization, democratization, and economic stabilization have expanded, both in magnitude and scope, the impact of the traditional forms of exclusion that persist unchecked in the region. Under these conditions, having a job is not necessarily a means of escaping material deprivation and poverty, and in most cases it does not offer access to mechanisms of social protection, insurance, and participation that could create a path towards social inclusion for workers who have jobs and their families.

As labor is the main, if not the only, source of income for most of the population, low wages mean material deprivation for workers and their families. A worker in a low-productivity job is likely to be excluded in at least two dimensions (from consumption because of a low wage and from access to social security because of job informality) but is not in this state of exclusion necessarily as a result of discrimination in the labor markets. An economy growing slowly and generating more bad jobs than good is likely to have a substantial number of people from the mainstream (i.e., those not traditional victims of discrimination) in bad jobs. Not having a job or having a precarious job severs the connection between workers and the provision of social services linked to formal wage relations. Having a formal job makes workers subject to payroll taxes, and their tax contributions entitle the workers and their families to insurance against medical problems, old age, disability, and death risks. Because bad jobs "do not exist" as far as the region's labor authorities are concerned, there is no possibility for workers in these jobs to present grievances or to form or belong to a union, thus making them vulnerable to exploitation and unsafe working conditions.

Exclusion resulting from nonemployment or employment in the informal sector has grown in importance in urban areas during the last decade and a half and has resulted in an increase in the percentage of the population excluded from the benefits associated with formal employment. Such exclusion is more acute for groups traditionally considered vulnerable (women, youth, the unskilled), but is increasingly affecting prime-age, educated males normally considered part of the mainstream. The dynamics behind this growth in bad jobs have been shaped by at least two sets of factors. On the one hand, the region's lackluster economic performance since the late 1990s, which has shown itself in rising unemployment in some countries, mediocre employment growth in most, and rising demand for education (associated with larger imports of capital goods and technology), has increased the share of low-wage employment in total employment. On the other hand, the change in the sectoral structure of employment and the increase in women's participation have had small effects and have sometimes (as in the case of a declining share of agriculture in total employment) gone in the direction of reducing the share of low-wage work.

Individuals excluded from good jobs for reasons unrelated to their qualifications and effort are likely to see their interests as diverging from those of society at large. This feeling is bound to be stronger if hopes and expectations for the future, both for the present and for subsequent generations, are low. Two societies with identical income distributions may have different levels of welfare depending on their degree of social mobility. In societies with very low mobility, the family in which one is born and the education level of one's parents are more important than one's own effort in determining one's present income and welfare and those of one's descendants.

The picture that emerges from measurements of social mobility in Latin America and the Caribbean is not that of a region advancing towards equality of opportunities for all, independent of social origin. Most individuals in the region feel that they are unlikely to see significant improvement in their income or social position or that of their children, regardless of effort or ability. It therefore should not be surprising that under these conditions, incentives to work, to acquire skills, and to participate fully in social and political activities are weak. In contrast, the small group of the population belonging to the middle and upper classes of income and welfare, who have income and opportunities comparable to those in the developed world, are very unlikely to see their situation deteriorating. This excess of security stunts innovation and risk taking and leads to the perception that public officials and entrepreneurs are more interested in the status quo than in the public welfare.

Social capital and trust levels across society are one of the most notorious victims of this grim panorama of exclusion, immobility, and inequality of opportunities. Cooperating with other individuals or groups in society and trusting them involves significant personal risks given the uncertainty regarding the actions of the other parties involved and the characteristics of the institutional context in which these interactions occur. Social exclusion may increase these risks both because the stakes are higher (making uncertainty more important) for those who are excluded, and because exclusion decreases the ability of the institutional context to channel to each individual involved in a particular transaction valuable information about the behavior and incentives of other individuals engaged in the transaction.

In order to fully gauge the burden that social exclusion imposes on social capital and trust, the researchers involved in this report turned to the tools of experimental economics. A representative sample of individuals in six capital cities in the region were engaged in a series of games in a tightly controlled setting that allowed for an understanding of what incentives and mechanisms affect the possibility of group formation for different social groups. The researchers found that Latin Americans are as willing to cooperate as individuals in other parts of the world, but that their willingness to cooperate decreases as the gap in social traits (class, income, education) increases among individuals. This has an important economic cost in terms of foregone opportunities to engage in mutually beneficial transactions. The actual gains that accrued to players in the games fell short of their full potential in magnitudes that vary between 22 and 72 percent, indicating the enormous welfare losses that exclusion produces for everyone, not just the excluded, as a consequence of the associated erosion of trust and incentives to cooperate.

As noted previously, exclusion is multidimensional, and deprivation in one sphere interacts with deprivation in other areas to deepen the limits on the functionings of the excluded. Understanding exclusion as a process that constrains the functionings of everybody, not only the excluded (rather than looking at the outcomes of excluding features of society, as the traditional deficit-focused analysis does), makes it possible to integrate a wide variety of social phenomena within a unified conceptual framework that highlights social interactions as sources of exclusion.

Yet this report does not pretend to offer a conclusive, much less a complete, enumeration of the functionings of individuals and groups engaged in the social, political, and economic exchanges that shape social exclusion, its determinants, and its dynamics. Rather, the chapters in Part II of this report attempt to develop some examples of the ways that looking through the lens of exclusion enables one to question a number of acquired beliefs about the impact of policies and social phenomena. It is hoped that these examples will help other researchers and the policy community to deepen the collective understanding of the mechanisms of social exclusion and the remedies on which to rely in order to advance towards a more inclusive and fair society.

State actions such as privatizations, regulations to increase access to financial services, and provision of identification documents to the population look quite different in the eyes of the excluded, because their access to resources and institutions is more restricted than that of those in the mainstream that policymakers have in mind when designing policies. Privatizations, which have an exclusionary impact on employees who are laid off from the privatized public enterprise, might at the same time have an inclusionary effect by expanding service to previously unserved sectors of the excluded population. Programs aimed at inclusion, such as conditional cash transfers, may nevertheless have an exclusionary impact on those members of excluded groups who do not have the proof of identity required to register for the programs. On the other hand, those programs might still produce an inclusive outcome for their beneficiaries by giving them access to the financial sector via the debit card through which program disbursements are made.

Street protests and other forms of contentious politics that disrupt the normal operation of the political system can be seen both as a sign of a deficit and as a source of increased democratic representation. When looked at through the lens of exclusion, contentious politics highlights both the absence of channels of influence through which the excluded can obtain changes in resource allocation from the political system and the opportunities for inclusion when the political system integrates street demands into its own programmatic agenda. Crime and violence, which have a destructive impact on the social environment in which the excluded live and work, make daily life more difficult for the excluded, who do not have the access to political influence, justice, and police services that the mainstream has.

The multiple angles of social exclusion examined here, and the multiplicity of dimensions that have not been addressed or even mentioned, show quite clearly that social inclusion is a moving and very complex target. An inclusive society is not necessarily devoid of poverty and social ills but is a society where the color of one's skin or the wealth of one's parents are not key determinants of whether one is poor or receives a quality education or proper medical care. Equality of opportunities, increasingly representative political representation, and high mobility are characteristics of inclusive societies.

Inclusive policies are not just a matter of outcomes, but more fundamentally a matter of processes that affect who makes decisions and how they are made. Inclusion is central to democracy, and greater inclusion deepens democracy. For this reason the inclusion process is dynamic and interrelated across the many dimensions of social life. Inclusion in one aspect (such as the inclusion and high achievement of women in education) can very well coexist with exclusion in another one (such as a high degree of occupational segregation for women in domestic and clerical work).

For these reasons inclusion is not an end point or an objective in the usual sense of the word. Inclusive public policies result from a dynamic policy process aimed at actively promoting social, economic, and cultural equality of opportunities, at addressing the impact of past discrimination and exclusion, and at achieving diversity. Inclusive policies need to address the changing nature of societies that continually alter the pattern of exclusion and inclusion for different groups.

Advancing inclusion requires changes in the normative framework that governs the fair treatment of citizens on a nondiscriminatory basis, in the operation of the institutions that design and administer laws, policies, and programs, and in the programs and policies that ensure greater equality for excluded populations. Inclusion processes encompass both governments and societies at large in the quest for a fairer, more equitable, and more dynamic society that can offer equal opportunities and access to all of its members independent of the privilege of their birth or the color of their skin.

MAIN MESSAGES

Exclusion is a dynamic, changing process that interacts with social, cultural, economic, and political societal changes.

Exclusion is neither the consequence of dysfunctional economic policies nor a fringe phenomenon that growth and modernization are going to eliminate. The changing patterns of exclusion and inclusion in the region are part of the deep social, cultural, economic, and political transformations that democratization, economic stabilization, and integration with the world economy have brought to Latin American and Caribbean societies.

Exclusion affects changing and more diverse groups of the population.

Stigmatization of and discrimination against groups easily identifiable by observable characteristics such as ethnicity, race, gender, or disability have been the traditional sources of exclusion in the region. Modern forces of exclusion, largely economic and social in origin, are currently affecting more diverse and visible groups within the population defined not by their ethnic or racial identity, but by the processes (such as unemployment or lack of access to land) that produce and reproduce their exclusion.

Exclusion is a multidimensional phenomenon, and those multiple dimensions are interrelated.

Material deprivation is one of the salient outcomes of exclusion but is just one aspect of the deprivations suffered by the excluded. Material deprivation is highly correlated with other types of deprivation (lack of access to justice and high-quality education, disengagement from political participation, and reduced feelings of safety resulting from higher crime, among others), and each of these aspects of deprivation interacts with the others (as, for example, when legitimate business or employment opportunities are very scarce in a crime-ridden neighborhood), augmenting the limitations on the functionings of the excluded.

Exclusion reduces social capital and welfare for the entire population.

Trust and cooperation are reduced by social distance. A set of experiments conducted in six large cities in the region found that the larger the social distance (measured by differences in income or education) within a group, the less individuals in the group cooperated with one another. This lack of cooperation in an experimental setting diminished the welfare of the whole group (not just the disadvantaged) in magnitudes between 22 percent and 72 percent relative to the potential welfare that could have been obtained with full cooperation. Though these figures should not be literally interpreted as GDP losses, they are an indication of the social welfare that Latin American societies fail to generate as a result of limitations on trust and willingness to cooperate associated with social exclusion.

Historically, inclusion processes have been driven by an active social and political leadership.

History shows that inclusion drives (such as the civil rights movement in the United States in the 1960s or Malaysia's New Economic Policy in the 1980s; see Chapter 14) have been accomplished through the interaction between an active civil society and its organizations and a sympathetic political leadership. Inclusion does not happen "naturally" as a consequence of economic growth or institutional modernization but requires decisive social and political leadership.

Inclusion is not just about changing outcomes, but crucially about changing the processes that produce and reproduce exclusionary outcomes.

Inclusive policies represent a significant transformation regarding the way resources are apportioned, political institutions are governed, and opportunities are accessed. Inclusion aims to achieve equality of access and opportunities for the excluded by bringing them into the social, institutional, and political structures that make decisions regarding access and opportunities. Inclusive policies are thus not merely a matter of creating new ministries or designing new programs; rather, they are about changes in the ways social, economic, and political decisions are made.

Inclusive public policies involve more than changes in the protection of rights of excluded groups.

Changes at the normative level are needed to protect and advance the rights of excluded groups. But the institutional framework needs to overcome embedded discrimination and stigmatization of excluded groups that has arisen from and continues as a result of these institutions' own past practices. In order to make normative changes effective, institutions must change the ways in which they operate, hire employees, and enforce laws and regulations. This in turn materializes as changes in the implementation of programs and policies, which hopefully produce more inclusive outcomes that feed back into the process, strengthening the position of excluded groups to induce changes at the normative, institutional, and policy levels.

Traditional Excluding Forces:
A Review of the Literature

L atin America and the Caribbean is the region with the most unequal income distribution in the world. This income inequality is linked to the unequal distribution of human and physical assets and differential access to key markets and services. Poverty, deficient access to health care, poor educational outcomes, poor working conditions, and lack of political representation are more the norm than the exception for substantial pockets of the region's population. Inequalities in these areas are a major factor in the social tensions that have wracked the region throughout its history. Nonetheless, another key ingredient in these social tensions is the existence of traditional excluding forces that worsen outcomes for the excluded groups. The pockets of the population that are typically on the "unfavored" side of the distribution of outcomes are largely identified by observable characteristics such as ethnicity, race, gender, and physical disability. This chapter reviews what is known about these traditionally excluded groups.

Everyone participates in multiple exchanges in his or her daily life, and these exchanges occur within a certain set of social, economic, and political institutions (formal and informal) that provide opportunities and services needed to obtain valuable outcomes in a market society. Social exclusion arises when those formal and informal institutions constrain the functioning of some groups of agents: the excluded. These institutions are the *transaction points*, which are connected to outcomes (namely, discrimination, housing segregation, lack of access to education, etc.) that reflect the exclusion suffered by these groups. These outcomes have been described in the academic literature on excluded groups. This survey attempts to (a) identify the transaction points where different actors in Latin American societies suffer exclusionary processes, (b) document the outcomes that arise from those processes, and (c) describe the literature that has addressed these issues for traditionally excluded groups.

Who are the traditionally excluded sectors that this survey will address? Social exclusion in Latin America and the Caribbean predominantly affects indigenous peoples, Afro-descendants, persons with disabilities, and those living with the stigma of HIV/AIDS. Given the paucity of studies on HIV/AIDS-infected people, this analysis deals with only the first three of these traditionally excluded populations. The literature on gender differentials is given only cursory treatment and is reviewed only to the extent that it simultaneously addresses differentials in other individual characteristics (indigenous peoples, Afro-descendants, etc.). In the section "Labor Markets and Exclusionary Outcomes," the survey devotes special attention to migrants, who confront particularly daunting barriers for labor market insertion.

The markets or transaction points considered have been clustered into three categories: (a) relative deprivation in terms of income, education, land and housing, physical infrastructure, and health; (b) labor markets as a transaction point that both produces exclusionary outcomes and serves as a resonance box for inequities in other markets; and (c) other transactions in the political and social arena (political participation, social protection, and security/crime). As in any classification effort, the boundaries between these clusters are not clear-cut, and some pieces (or ideas) were harder to classify than others.

Because of the importance of the matter, the literature on this topic has been vast and diverse, with contributions from an interesting variety of disciplines. However, this survey limits itself to presenting the main ideas discussed in academic economics papers that address the issues of traditionally excluded groups from a quantitative perspective. An extensive bibliography that encompasses the sources for these ideas appears at the end of this report, and the online version of this chapter (www.iadb.org/ipes) contains hyperlinks to the electronic versions of the references cited within. Box 2.1 provides basic definitions for some of the terms used in this chapter.

RELATIVE DEPRIVATION AND EXCLUSION

Multidimensional deprivation is one outcome of exclusion, but to thoroughly understand it demands knowledge of the process behind the exclusionary outcome. The transaction points addressed in this section include the processes of accessing sources of income, educational opportunities, a place to live, health services, and physical infrastructure. The papers on which this section is based form part of the literature on outcome differentials that derive from exclusionary processes functioning in these transaction points.

Income Deprivation

Income deprivation is only one of the outcomes of exclusion, but it is clearly one of the most crucial. Furthermore, material deprivation is highly correlated with other dimensions of deprivation that affect the capacity of the excluded to obtain desirable outcomes in a market economy. Lack of employment (or employment at low productivity) results in low incomes and poverty but also restricts the unemployed and those in low-productivity jobs from participating in social institutions such as unions and other worker organizations geared toward improving working conditions (Gaviria, 2006).

Poverty and limited access to income are probably among the most-studied topics in the social exclusion literature on Latin America. There are at least three reasons for this focus. First, the literature dealing with these topics for Latin America tends to replicate, with some lag, previous applications in developed countries. Second, data on income are widely available through household surveys in most countries. Finally, and most importantly, many of the problems of limited access reviewed in this chapter (e.g., health, education) may actually arise from lack of income generation opportunities. If this is indeed the case, policies targeted to solve differential access to income sources may also help to improve other aspects of segregated groups' living conditions.

The literature reveals at least two approaches to defining poverty: one with poverty measured as low income and the other focusing on unsatisfied basic needs (e.g., running water, education). Nonetheless, there is also the view that poverty among indigenous peoples varies according to the perceptions, actual conditions, and priorities of each indigenous group. Indigenous peoples are aware and proud of their cultural and ethnic identities, languages, social organization, and ancestral knowledge, and none of these aspects are captured by the traditional measures of human poverty (Coba, 2005).

Whether basic income statistics are presented alone or the impact of a specific exclusionary characteristic (e.g., ethnicity or disability) on income is estimated, the results are largely the same: the poverty statistics for indigenous peoples and Afro-descendants reveal a worse situation than that of the rest of the population in almost the entire region (Costa Rica and Haiti are two important exceptions). When poverty rates are estimated by race, Afro-descendants constitute 30 percent of Latin America's population but represent 40 percent of the region's poor. In general, indigenous peoples and Afro-descendants, in different magnitudes, have lower income levels compared to the rest of the population (Machinea, Bárcena, and León, 2005; Busso, Cicowiez, and Gasparini, 2005; Bello and Rangel, 2002; Dade and Arnusch, 2006).

When income statistics are considered over time, overall there has been a reduction in poverty in the region, but the share of indigenous and Afro-descendant poor is still larger than the share of nonindigenous non-Afro-descendant poor. Interestingly, indigenous peoples have largely been unaffected by either increases or declines in national poverty rates in Mexico, Bolivia, Ecuador, and Peru. The conclusion is that the income sources of indigenous peoples are less affected by macroeconomic shocks, whether positive or negative. Moreover, analysis of data for Ecuador and Mexico during their last crisis-and-recovery episodes has shown that indigenous peoples were less affected by the crises as they unfolded, but their recovery was so slow that the net impact on them was worse than for nonindigenous populations. When two basic ways of reducing poverty to attain the Millennium Development Goals—growth in the mean and reduction in inequality—were evaluated, it was found that even small income redistributions from wealthy individuals to nonwhites would be equivalent to relatively large annual growth rates through 2015 (Busso, Cicowiez, and Gasparini, 2005; Espinosa, 2005a, 2005b; Gacitúa Marió and Woolcock, 2005b; Hall and Patrinos, 2005; Patrinos and Skoufias, 2007; Escobal and Ponce, 2007; Benavides and Valdivia, 2004; Borja-Vega and Lunde, 2007; Borja-Vega, Lunde, and García-Moreno, 2007; Contreras, Kruger, and Zapata, 2007).

Overall, there is agreement in the literature that the lack of access to income on the part of excluded groups is a widespread phenomenon in Latin America and the Caribbean (Ponce, 2006; Telles and Lim, 1998; Montaño, 2004; Hall and Patrinos, 2005; Dudzik, Elwan, and Metts, 2002; Hernández-Jaramillo and Hernández-Umaña, 2005; Sánchez, 2006).

Education Differentials

Income deprivation, as reviewed in the previous subsection, can both cause and be caused by deprivation in other dimensions, most notably education. The opportunity cost for low-income families of sending their children to school may preclude them from investing in schooling and condemn these youngsters to low productivity, low wages, and poor-quality jobs. Income deprivation is partially the cause of differentials in educa-

Box 2.1 Glossary

In this box we provide basic definitions for some of the terms used in this chapter. Recognizing that many of these terms have evolved (to use Pinker's [2002] term, they have been running the "euphemism treadmill"), we provide, wherever needed, the different names under which the same concept is known. Of course, we have made our best attempt to use the *current* politically correct terms (although sometimes it is not an easy task to stay current on the treadmill).

Afro-descendants, Afro-Latinos, people of African descent. In Latin America, people of African descent are citizens of Latin American countries who are descended from African slaves brought to America as part of the slave trade.

Conditional cash transfers. Conditional cash transfer (CCT) programs are a type of poverty alleviation intervention in which poor families receive cash subsidies conditional on specific actions, such as sending some of their family members to preventive health care centers and sending their children to school.

Displaced individuals. Displaced individuals are those who have been forced at some point to leave their city, region, or country.

Indigenous, indigenous peoples. The indigenous peoples of the Americas are the pre-Columbian inhabitants, their descendants, and many ethnic groups who identify with those historical peoples.

Labor segmentation. Labor segmentation refers to the fact that individuals of certain groups face obstacles to finding good jobs (in terms of access to social security, benefits, paid vacations, job security, and, in general, formality) that are not related to their ability or productive characteristics.

Mestizos, mestizo population. *Mestizo* is a term of Spanish origin used to designate people of mixed indigenous and European ancestry.

Millennium Development Goals. The Millennium Development Goals (MDGs) are eight goals that United Nations members have engaged to work together to achieve by the year 2015: (1) eradicate extreme poverty and hunger, (2) achieve universal primary education, (3) promote gender equality and empower women, (4) reduce child mortality, (5) improve maternal health, (6) combat HIV/AIDS, malaria, and other diseases, (7) ensure environmental sustainability, and (8) develop a global partnership for development.

---

tion, but these differentials in education also perpetuate disparities in income. In order to integrate excluded groups, it is necessary to break this vicious circle. The exclusion phenomenon in its purest form is evident when, even after different income levels are controlled for, there are still differences in education outcomes, or the converse, when even after education levels are controlled for, there are still differences in income levels. The transaction points in these cases are the school system and the labor market.

The literature has analyzed various aspects of the education experience for different groups. Some authors argue that the key differentials are at the initial steps in formal

Minorities, excluded groups, discriminated-against groups. These terms include people of African descent, indigenous peoples, and displaced individuals, as well as people with disabilities, migrants, and those suffering with the stigma of HIV/AIDS. Nonetheless, note that, in some countries of the region, those who suffer exclusion are not numerical minorities.

Oaxaca-Blinder decomposition. The Oaxaca-Blinder decomposition is an econometric technique for measuring the extent to which the differences in outcomes between two groups can be explained by differences in their average observable characteristics (and for determining what is left unexplained by these differences).

Occupational segregation. Occupational segregation refers to the fact that individuals of certain groups tend to cluster in certain occupations. The most common example is the existence of male-dominated and female-dominated occupations.

Statistical discrimination, group-based discrimination. Statistical discrimination arises when there are differences in the amount or quality of information available about the characteristics of groups. For instance, suppose a manager who belongs to, say, an indigenous group is more culturally attuned to the applicants from her group than to applicants from others and therefore has a better idea of the likely productivity of the applicants of her own group. Even in the absence of preference-based discrimination, such a manager will rationally bid more for an applicant of her own group. This concept, as well as that of taste-based discrimination, is explored more deeply in Chapter 3.

Taste-based discrimination, preference-based discrimination. Taste-based discrimination takes place when some people simply dislike a particular group of people and are willing to pay a cost to avoid interactions with them.

Unsatisfied basic needs. Census and household surveys typically report a number of welfare statistics (access to health care, access to running water, etc.). The term *unsatisfied basic needs* refers to a situation in which there are insufficient levels of at least some of these indicators.

Western societies, occidental societies. The definition of Western societies is of a somewhat subjective nature, depending on whether cultural, economic, or political criteria are used. From a cultural and sociological approach, the term *Western societies* encompasses all cultures that are derived from those of European countries.

education, reporting evidence of lower probabilities of attending school as well as lower graduation rates for primary school. Others estimate differences between Afro-descendants and indigenous peoples and the rest of the population and find that restricted participation in the secondary education system is one of the main exclusionary factors interfering with the development of these groups. Higher education levels have received less attention. Scattered evidence does show that the disabled have less access to education than the rest of the population (Filmer, 2005; Sánchez and García, 2006; Beckett and Pebley, 2002; García-Aracil and Winter, 2006; World Bank, 2005; Lémez, 2005).

Several authors document differences in test scores, grade repetition, and other traditional educational indicators for disabled people, indigenous populations, and different racial and ethnic groups (Hernández-Zavala et al., 2006; Patrinos and Psacharapoulos, 1992; Porter, 2001; Solano, 2002; Ñopo, Saavedra, and Torero, 2004).

Illiteracy is the most blatant form of education deprivation. Its evolution does not seem to be homogeneous in the region, with reports of decreasing illiteracy rates and literacy gaps for indigenous peoples in Bolivia but no significant changes over time for Afro-descendants in Ecuador. Differences in literacy rates between indigenous men, indigenous women, and the general population are also reported for Panama (Mezza, 2004; Ponce, 2006; Coba, 2005).

Returns to education in the form of differences in job opportunities are the key transmission mechanism that perpetuates education and income differentials. Since excluded groups have lower education levels than the rest of the population, in order for them to close the salary gap, the quality of schools available to excluded groups must be improved and access to them must be increased. But if returns to education vary among groups, as seems to be the case,[1] that will not be enough (Patrinos and García-Moreno, 2006).

Providing a broader picture of the challenges in the area of education, studies show that language barriers seem to be an important factor behind continued social exclusion. The lower educational performance of indigenous children in Mexico is mostly due to the lower outcomes of those who are monolingual, whereas bilingual indigenous children perform almost equivalently to their nonindigenous counterparts. In rural Peru, after economic and linguistic differences between students are adjusted for, the disparity in performance between rural and urban schools disappears. Similarly, between one-half and two-thirds of the differences in grades between indigenous and nonindigenous students in Bolivia and Chile can be attributed to variations in school quality; also, between one-fourth and two-fifths of the same gap can be attributed to family characteristics (Parker, Rubalcava, and Teruel, 2005; Cueto and Secada, 2004; McEwan, 2004).

Policy-oriented papers highlight the need to improve educational opportunities for excluded groups. For the problems of access and attendance rates, the issue of pedagogic pertinence of school curricula to students' needs and environment is of considerable importance, and the challenges of designing a multicultural approach (e.g., bilingual schools) are significant as well. The region needs to improve strategies for promoting bilingual/multicultural practices in areas with higher proportions of indigenous populations (Hopenhayn and Bello, 2001; Bello and Rangel, 2002; Peredo, 2004).

Breaking the intergenerational transmission of disadvantages has to do with, among other things, better access to education for excluded groups. It is urgent to reduce inequalities in primary school. In general, there has been substantial progress towards the Millennium Development Goals in primary education, but indigenous peoples and Afro-descendants have lagged behind (Buvinić, 2004; Ocampo, 2004; IDB, 2003b; Bouillon and Buvinić, 2003; Buvinić and Mazza, 2005).

---

[1] See "Labor Markets and Exclusionary Outcomes" in this chapter.

Health Disparities

The concept of health in Western societies often varies from that for indigenous peoples or Afro-descendants in Latin America and the Caribbean. In the Western tradition, the right to health can be defined as being able to achieve the highest possible level of physical and mental health and access to public health services (Sánchez and Bryan, 2003). By contrast, for many indigenous peoples, for example, health is an integral concept associated with emotional, spiritual, and physical elements in people's relationship with their surroundings. In other words, health is understood as having a good relationship with Mother Nature. The difference in concept is not only academic. The cause of poor health conditions among indigenous peoples may reflect differences between occidental medicine and traditional ancestral treatments, and there may be an analytical bias against traditional medicine in favor of Western medicine (Sánchez and García, 2006; World Bank, 2005; Bernal and Cárdenas, 2005; Peredo, 2004).

The research on access to health care and health outcomes often ignores the fact that different personal and group characteristics, rather than race or ethnicity, may be behind differential health outcomes. In particular, the rural-urban dimension explains a sizable part of the health gap between ethnic minorities and whites. Even though the literature has not presented formal, indisputable evidence of discrimination against indigenous peoples or Afro-descendants with respect to health outcomes, many papers argue that such discrimination does exist. In Guatemala, characteristics of the indigenous population (geographic location, education, household size, etc.) have been found to be unable to account for lower height-for-age scores and to point to unobserved factors, including discrimination (Dade and Arnusch, 2006; Sánchez and Bryan, 2003; Marini and Gragnolati, 2003; Hopenhayn and Bello, 2001; Coba, 2005; Ribando, 2005; Peredo, 2004; Bello and Rangel, 2002; Robles, 1999).

When infant mortality rates for indigenous-urban, nonindigenous-urban, indigenous-rural and nonindigenous-rural are disaggregated, two important conclusions emerge. First, indigenous populations in urban areas have lower infant mortality rates than indigenous (and nonindigenous in some cases) populations in rural areas. Second, indigenous populations have higher infant mortality rates than nonindigenous populations living in their same area (urban or rural). Thus, the larger share of indigenous populations living in rural areas is an important determinant of worse indigenous health outcomes but cannot account for the entire differential. It is an open question whether including other factors (education, income level) could close the gap and preclude a discrimination interpretation (Machinea, Bárcena, and León, 2005; Coba, 2005).

Finally, there is an incipient literature on stigmatization and access to health care for people with physical or mental disabilities. This literature argues that failure to ensure that people with disabilities receive effective educational services results in exclusion from the labor market and contributes to poor health (Dudzik, Elwan, and Metts, 2002; Acuña and Bolis, 2005).

Land and Housing Differences

Geographical segregation increases the disadvantage of excluded groups because both quality of housing and access to public services tend to be deficient in the areas where these groups are concentrated. Although there is an old and broad literature on housing differentials, researchers interested in Latin America and the Caribbean have only recently begun to focus on these issues and discuss them in two dimensions: access to land or housing, and housing quality, which includes many health-related issues like running water, garbage disposal, and adequate sanitation (Gaviria, 2006).

International organizations have pushed the idea of providing access to land titles for the poor as a cost-effective poverty alleviation policy. However, the case of Mexico shows that although access to land can raise household welfare significantly in rural areas, it would not be enough to lift most of the indigenous population out of poverty. Moreover, Afro-descendants have been much less successful in obtaining collective land rights than indigenous peoples. Only the constitutions of Brazil and Colombia (and then only since 1988 and 1991, respectively) mention the cultural and agrarian land rights of their Afro-descendant populations (Finan, Sadoulet, and de Janvry, 2005; Dade and Arnusch, 2006; Ribando, 2005).

Most Afro-descendants have been integrated into the mestizo culture and therefore do not possess the racial/cultural group identity or specific relationship to the land that would allow them to receive privileged access to land. A notable exception is the Garifuna community, descendants of escaped slaves from St. Vincent, which won communal land rights in Honduras and Nicaragua by proving that its language, religious beliefs, and traditional agriculture techniques are inextricably linked to its notion of land (Ribando, 2005).

With respect to ownership ratios, indigenous peoples and Afro-descendants seem to be at least as well off as the rest of the population. In addition to issues regarding ownership, significant housing quality problems (e.g., overcrowding, unsatisfied basic needs) exist among the indigenous populations in Costa Rica and Panama. The evidence shows that the housing conditions of the indigenous population living in rural areas are not very different from those of the nonindigenous living in the same area. The differences in the aggregates are strongly affected by the different percentages of individuals from indigenous and nonindigenous groups living in urban and rural areas. Similarly, in the Limon province of Costa Rica (home to most Costa Rican Afro-descendants), Afro-descendants and non-Afro-descendants live in similar housing conditions. This does not imply the absence of housing problems for the indigenous or Afro-descendant population. Rather, given where they live, Afro-descendants and members of indigenous groups live in conditions similar to those of their neighbors; the question of why they live in these areas and why these areas lack access to public services remains unanswered (Benavides, Torero, and Valdivia, 2006; Ponce, 2006; González, 2006; Solano, 2002; Coba, 2005; Putnam, 2002).

According to the literature, there are three main issues with respect to land access for indigenous peoples: (a) gender-differential treatments, (b) the impact of major development projects (e.g., oil drilling in Colombia and Venezuela, hydroelectric and other types of power stations in Chile, deforestation in the Venezuelan and Brazilian Amazon), and (c) migration to cities.

A few decades ago, the majority of the indigenous population lived in rural areas. There are still sizable "ancestral" lands, but the migration of individuals from indigenous populations to the cities has created new problems. It has been argued that the liberal reforms of the nineteenth century that introduced the idea of private land ownership are the cause of indigenous poverty. Most countries overlook the common law rights traditionally used by indigenous peoples to allocate land use. The relationship of indigenous peoples with the land is not only economic; it includes many social, cultural, and religious aspects as well (Bello and Rangel, 2002).

Many times the combination of a country's legal framework with major development projects forces indigenous migration to the cities. There are two reasons why such migration places indigenous women in a particularly vulnerable situation. First, they are traditionally specialized in the management of natural resources, and after migration they face stronger challenges adapting to urban environments. Second, according to indigenous customs, land ownership is typically passed to male family members in the understanding that women will get married and gain access to land through their husbands. Because indigenous women cannot work in their traditional specialities in cities and dissolution of families is more common among those who migrate to cities, migrant indigenous women are at greater risk for being cut off from assets. For instance, this is the case for the Aymara and Quechua communities in Bolivia (Peredo, 2004).

As with the indigenous populations, the Afro-descendant population of Colombia is also undergoing an important urban migration process. These migrants (many forcefully displaced) end up living in lower-quality houses in neighborhoods with poor access to public utilities. Similar results have been found for Honduras, Ecuador, and two locations in Argentina. However, the evidence in Peru points in the opposite direction. Afro-descendants there have better building quality and better access to public utilities than the general public (Sánchez and García, 2006; González, 2006; Ponce, 2006; Universidad Nacional de Tres de Febrero, 2006; Benavides, Torero, and Valdivia, 2006).

How important is access to land for indigenous and Afro-descendant populations? According to a World Bank report (2005), although its cultural connotations are not the same for indigenous peoples and rural Afro-descendants in Colombia, territory seems to be the essential element for improving well-being. Afro-descendants in rural areas perceive access to land as a guarantee of subsistence and continuity of cultural traditions. Indigenous peoples see in territory the basic pillar of quality of life, and collective ownership of territories implies the recognition of ancestral rights.

Disparities in Access to Physical Infrastructure

The literature reports that Afro-descendants and indigenous peoples have lower access to public utilities and that investment in infrastructure in areas populated by these groups is below "ideal" levels. As emphasized previously, the differences in access reported among ethnic and racial groups are not attributed to ethnic discrimination. Rather, these are the consequence of other characteristics of the ethnic groups (e.g., urban vs. rural) (Ponce, 2006).

According to most sources, Latin American governments invest very little or do not invest at all in infrastructure and services in areas mostly populated by Afro-descendants. This has negative consequences for the marketing of agricultural products and ecological resources. Sample statistics for the Afro-descendant population in Brazil and Colombia are telling. For instance, the municipality with the highest percentage of Afro-descendants in Colombia has the lowest per capita level of government investment in health, education, and infrastructure. Moreover, the lack of access to infrastructure is not gender neutral. As a result of the traditional gender-based division of labor in the region, rural female workers and indigenous women live under harsher conditions because of deficiencies in access to running water, electricity, and transportation (Sánchez and Bryan, 2003; Ribando, 2005; ECLAC, 2000).

In Colombia, access to and quality of public services are the main determinants of the lower levels of well-being among the Afro-descendant population. However, Afro-Peruvians have significantly greater access to public infrastructure than the average citizen and the indigenous population. In Ecuador, in terms of sewerage system coverage, access to running water, and telephone, electricity, and garbage disposal services, the indigenous population systematically has the worst statistics, followed by Afro-descendants and the white population (e.g., 10.9 percent of indigenous households have telephones at home compared to 17.7 percent of Afro-descendant households and 42.1 percent of white households). Consideration of whether these ethnic differences reflect different shares of urban and rural settlements among ethnic groups leads to the conclusion that the condition of the Afro-descendant population cannot be explained by geographic location alone (Sánchez and García, 2006; Benavides, Torero, and Valdivia, 2006; Ponce, 2006).

LABOR MARKETS AND EXCLUSIONARY OUTCOMES

In terms of exclusion, labor markets act as resonance boxes for inequities or for exclusion mechanisms already exercised in other social spheres. Labor markets convert into earnings differentials variations in access to health care services, educational quality, and basic living conditions. These earnings differentials are, in turn, the main channel through which differences in health, education, and basic living conditions persist. Differences in human capital characteristics such as education and health, discussed earlier in this chapter, are also a major determinant of the labor market performance of traditionally discriminated-against groups. Labor markets are not necessarily the culprits of exclusion, but the extent to which they work as catalysts for the execution of exclusion mechanisms is an issue that must be addressed.

Limited Access to Labor Markets

Much of the literature on limited access to labor markets focuses on migrants and people with disabilities. Although today's world is characterized by high global mobility and fewer restrictions on migration of high-skilled workers, international labor markets remain segmented in a way that limits the international migration of poor and unskilled workers. People migrate in the hope of attaining better working and living conditions in their new home. However, other variables—including racial, social, and cultural discrimination—interfere when immigrants try to find a job in their country of destination.

Migration occurs both within Latin America and the Caribbean and, more predominantly, from this region to more developed countries. Migration effectively reduces the labor supply in the home country. Self-selection by skill appears to be very important. Migrants suffer many difficulties in labor markets that locals do not, ranging from economic to cultural, social, psychological, and linguistic problems. Gender, for instance, is often a limitation on migrants' access to labor markets. In Chile, Peruvian immigrants are mainly women and greatly concentrated in the domestic service and the informal sectors, despite their educational attainment. While the educational level of immigrants varies widely, this heterogeneity is not reflected in their occupations. Extensive labor segmentation limits the access of trained people to jobs suitable to their preparation. However, a study of gender differences among cross-border migrants in Argentina found no differences between males and females in occupational status, earnings, and unemployment levels (Clark, Hatton, and Williamson, 2003; Pellegrino, 2002; Bello and Rangel, 2002; Stefoni, 2002; Cacopardo and Maguid, 2001; Mazza, 2004).

Access to labor markets is also limited for people with disabilities. Disabled people participate less in the labor market than the rest of the population because of transportation obstacles and the costs they face in reaching the workplace and in being productive once there. From the point of view of labor demand, sometimes employers view a disability as a sign of lower productivity (or additional workplace costs), triggering "statistical" discrimination. In general, the disabled participate in low-skill jobs, agriculture, and service-related industries. In the developing world (although data in this area are scarce), people with disabilities are much less likely to be economically active (either employed or unemployed) than the population overall. Policy changes to combat labor market discrimination against those with disabilities require access to better data as a first step. Improved accessibility for the disabled and greater rehabilitation technology would also increase the possibilities of social and economic inclusion of these people (Hernández-Licona, 2005; Elwan, 1999; Montes and Massiah, 2002; Álvarez, 2000).

In principle, an efficient labor market with perfectly rational players is largely "race blind." However, statistics suggest that this is not the reality. An examination of factors that influence workplace decisions suggests that race and ethnicity play significant roles in determining job placement and career opportunities. A report on an IDB (2001b) conference summarizes key facts about differentials in economic opportunity among different ethnic groups in Argentina, Brazil, Peru, and Bolivia. It concludes that the mechanisms through which such differentials may arise are persistent educational gaps and discrimination in the labor market. In Guatemala, ethnicity has been found to have a surprisingly small effect on female labor force participation. However, non-Afro-descendant workers earn more than double the income of Afro-descendants (male and female) in Brazilian metropolitan areas. Unemployment is also drastically higher among Brazilian Afro-descendants than among Brazilian non-Afro-descendants. In rural Mexico, indigenous men are substantially less likely to be wage earners than nonindigenous men, and wage gaps between the two groups are around 15 percent in agricultural wage jobs and 35 percent in self-employment, both favoring nonindigenous individuals over their indigenous peers (Arends, 1992; Roland, 2001; de Janvry, Finan, and Sadoulet, 2005; Fazio, 2007).

Limited Access to Formal Jobs

The literature on formality and traditionally excluded groups has not been abundant. In Peru, even though the percentage of Afro-descendants outside the economically active population is higher than the national figure, the percentage of Afro-Peruvians working in the formal sector is higher than that of the rest of the population. Also, the average labor earnings of Afro-Peruvians are not different than the average for the rest of the population (although the average per capita income is significantly lower). There is, however, a high degree of occupational segregation, as 40 percent of Afro-descendants work in low-skill jobs (requiring low levels of qualifications) (Benavides, Torero, and Valdivia, 2006; Duryea and Genoni, 2004).

Interestingly, an individual's migratory condition is a characteristic that overlaps with ethnicity and gender. The gender and migratory condition of laborers were found to determine the seasonal labor recruitment patterns of plantations in Guatemala. Large plantations preferred hiring migrants over cheaper female laborers because hiring migrants inhibited the development of workers' solidarity. In general, migrants work under poor conditions. Guatemalan migrant workers in the Chiapas area are mostly males (90 percent) and dedicated to agricultural labor (98 percent); almost one-third of them are illiterate, and hence they are limited in the working conditions they can achieve. Bolivians working abroad, particularly in neighboring countries, are predominantly undocumented and illegal immigrants in the countries where they reside; thus, they are subject to abuse and exploitation, working under precarious conditions (Bossen, 1982; Angeles and Rojas, 2000; Farah and Sánchez, 2003).

Segregation and Discrimination

The literature on segregation of and discrimination against traditionally excluded groups in Latin American labor markets has been abundant. The dramatic increase in female labor force participation in the region is perhaps the most notorious change in labor markets since the 1970s. On the other hand, segregation of indigenous peoples and Afro-descendants within occupations related to domestic service has not changed substantially. Similarly, indigenous populations, especially indigenous women involved in agricultural production, still work under very precarious conditions (Peredo, 2004; Coba, 2005; Solano, 2002).

A family of papers using wage decompositions à la Oaxaca-Blinder reveals a noticeable wage gap between the public and private sectors in Brazil. There is also a wage gap by skin color and an even greater one by gender in the public sector. Earnings differentials that cannot be attributed to differences in human capital increase with job responsibilities, regardless of the skill level (Marconi, 2004; Arias, Yamada, and Tejerina, 2002; Contreras et al., 2006; Barrón, 2006; Leite, 2005; Campante, Crespo, and Leite, 2004; Guimarães, 2006).

Among the disabled, earnings and employment gaps in Chile and Uruguay are substantial. Depending on the intensity of the disability, the earnings penalty ranges between 18 percent and 26 percent in Uruguay and between 20 percent and 37 percent in Chile. On the other hand, the employment rate gaps are between 30 percent and 57 percent in both countries.

Another body of research studies earnings gaps in the region. In Lima's labor markets, discrimination has been found to play almost no role in wage differences between locals and migrants. In Bolivia and Peru, discrimination is estimated to account for 28 percent of the ethnic wage gap observed, whereas in Guatemala and Mexico it represents up to 50 percent of the overall earnings differential. In Brazil, the income gap between indigenous and nonindigenous workers widens with increased schooling. Noticeable gaps were found to exist in employment and earnings between Afro-descendants and other workers in six metropolitan areas in Brazil in the late 1990s; in São Paulo and Salvador, it reached as high as 100 percent (non-Afro-descendants earning, on average, twice as much as Afro-descendants). In Ecuador, about half the earnings gap between indigenous and nonindigenous workers as well as between women and men is explained by educational attainment and half by discrimination. The main determinants of a child's enrollment in school are the educational level of the mother, the father's profession, the household's wealth (for boys), child labor, and the opportunity cost for indigenous children. There is a significant difference in returns to schooling by ethnicity but not by gender. In another kind of market, the Uruguayan soccer market, there is evidence of racial discrimination against Afro-descendant players in the national league but not with respect to international promotions (Barrón, 2005; Ñopo, 2004; Patrinos, 2000; Roland, 2001; García-Aracil and Winter, 2006; Gandelman, 2006).

As far as the relationship between earnings and racial differences is concerned, in Peru there is a statistically significant premium for whiteness on earnings among wage earners, but not among the self-employed, suggesting the existence of employer discrimination (Ñopo, Saavedra, and Torero, 2004).

SOCIAL AND POLITICAL EXCLUSION

Political and electoral systems that exclude disadvantaged groups reduce the ability of those groups to influence public policies and programs, which results in lower investments in precisely the services they need to prosper (i.e., high-quality educational and health services). Most of the literature reports underrepresentation of indigenous peoples and Afro-descendants, but the results are not unanimous. For instance, one study finds that there are statistically significant differences among ethnic groups in socioeconomic status and subjective well-being but not in political participation, social capital, or social mobility (Gaviria, 2001). However, this result differs from those of the remaining studies, which find differences by ethnic group in political participation.

Latin America has a good track record in the area of educational quotas and quotas to increase women's participation in representative government bodies. By 2005, eleven countries had adopted such quotas. However, there are still only incipient efforts to incorporate quotas for excluded populations such as Afro-descendants and indigenous peoples. According to data from Nicaragua and Brazil, Afro-descendants are very poorly represented politically. In 2003, only 27 of 594 Brazilian congressmen (roughly 5 percent) identified themselves as being of African descent, even though 45 percent of Brazil's population is of African descent. Furthermore, there is not a single Afro-descendant in Nicaragua's national assembly, even though Afro-descendants make up 9 percent of the country's population. In general, excluded groups have very little political representation in the region (Buvinić, 2004; Dade and Arnusch, 2006; Peredo, 2004; Benavides, 2006; Bouillon and Buvinić, 2003).

Little has been written about the access of excluded groups in Latin America to social protection programs such as social security, conditional cash transfers, and other poverty reduction strategies. One study has found that Afro-descendants in Honduras have greater access to basic social services than indigenous peoples, perhaps because they tend to live in more economically prosperous regions than indigenous peoples, who are being left behind geographically. The study's recommendation is for more efficient spending on public services, in particular, education and health; the introduction of evaluation programs for public services; and economic incentives for school attendance (e.g., lunch programs, transportation). A policy-oriented analysis argues that social exclusion manifests itself in Latin America mostly through the high level of income inequality; this should be combated, according to the analysis, with a long-term social policy that addresses inequality and promotes inclusion through more educational opportunities, labor policy, and social security rather than using segmented protection and social policy as a compensatory tool. A review of the situation of Afro-descendants in the region reveals a vicious circle in which limited access to goods, services, and opportunities plus low education levels lead to educational and labor market discrimination. Lack of government intervention in this area exacerbates the problem (Bouillon and Buvinić, 2003; ESA Consultores, 2005; Ocampo, 2004; Sánchez and Bryan, 2003).

Another important aspect of exclusion is whether it can lead to political instability and social conflict. Attempts to explain social disorder and inequality in Peru find that social exclusion (defined here as limited access to human capital), but not discrimination (defined here as unequal pay for the same levels of human capital), promotes the existence and persistence of horizontal inequalities (inequalities among culturally defined groups), leading to further inequality. Ethnicity does not seem to be the prime mover of social disorder in Peru. In Ecuador, however, both social exclusion and discrimination play a role, and ethnicity appears to be a prime mover of social disorder. Neither migration, intermarriage, collective actions nor government policies constitute mechanisms of social equalization in either country (Figueroa and Barrón, 2005; Figueroa, 2006; Sánchez, 2005).

In terms of security and violence, most of the literature about vulnerable groups concentrates on gender-related violence (mostly domestic violence). Regarding the excluded groups referred to in this study, the literature focuses mainly on the case of displaced individuals in Colombia, who are largely Afro-descendants and indigenous peoples. In a new kind of study of patterns of discrimination against indigenous populations in war, with evidence from the civil war in Peru during the 1980s and 1990s, there is evidence of taste-based discrimination in war crimes (World Bank, 2005; Castillo and Petrie, 2005).

CONCLUSION

This chapter has attempted to summarize the prolific production of the last three decades in the area of economic analysis of exclusion in Latin America and the Caribbean. As in any inventory effort, this survey may suffer from omission problems, although the research team has attempted to minimize that possibility. The review of the literature presented here suggests that the academic community has not devoted equal attention to all dimensions of exclusion in the region. Lack of access to income and education and labor market outcomes have received much more attention than political representation, social protection, and security.

In terms of excluded groups, Afro-descendants and indigenous peoples have been the most studied, while migrants and the disabled have been relatively neglected. In part because of the lower proportion of Afro-descendants and indigenous peoples in their populations, a few countries (e.g., Uruguay and Argentina) are largely absent from the analysis, while Colombia and Panama have been the most studied countries in regard to exclusion of specific groups.

From a data perspective, it is rewarding to observe that all countries in Latin America and the Caribbean conduct periodic surveys of their populations (household surveys, censuses, etc.) with standards that guarantee valuable and useful inputs for research. Unfortunately, however, in some cases these surveys do not properly identify tradition- ally excluded groups. Overall, there is a need for more and better data on traditionally excluded sectors of Latin American and Caribbean society. This is particularly important when one considers that a full understanding of exclusion requires an analysis that, beyond outcomes, must explore the processes and channels through which exclusion occurs.

From a methodological point of view, the quality and approaches of the academic production are rather heterogeneous. Given the data supply that the academic commu- nity faces, the emphasis has naturally been on the documentation of differentiated out- comes for traditionally excluded groups. Only recently has the emphasis begun to shift, in at least two dimensions. On the one hand, the emphasis on documenting differences in average outcomes between the excluded and the nonexcluded has moved to document- ing variations in the distributions of such outcomes. On the other hand, the emphasis on differences in outcomes has shifted to differences in processes. In terms of the latter, the advances in the experimental literature have been of extreme importance. The next chapter focuses on recent methodological developments as it seeks an understanding of a particular and extremely important aspect of exclusion: discrimination.

Discrimination in Latin America: The Proverbial Elephant in the Room?

Discrimination is believed to be a powerful force for exclusion, because it limits the ability of individuals to engage in transactions and access institutions that allow non-discriminated-against groups to achieve socially valuable outcomes. It is quite obvious to any casual observer of the region that there are substantial differences in economic and social outcomes that are associated with gender, racial, ethnic, and class distinctions. Understanding how much of these differences is due to discrimination, as well as the channels through which such discrimination operates, is a crucial first step in our analysis of social exclusion.

According to conventional wisdom, Latin American societies are highly discriminatory. This belief is hardly surprising given the prevalence of ethnic and class conflicts in the region that are rooted in history and the plethora of anecdotal information that reinforces this notion. However, whereas it cannot be argued that many societies in the region do not, in fact, discriminate, crucial questions have barely been broached. Understanding the extent of such discrimination as well as the channels through which it operates deserves special attention.

How widespread is discrimination in Latin America? The quintessential opinion survey of the region, the Latinobarometer, explores perceptions of discrimination for representative samples of eighteen countries.[1] As shown in Figure 3.1, when individuals were asked in 2001 who they think suffers the most from discrimination, they consistently—and overwhelmingly—highlighted the poor. Indigenous peoples and Afro-descendants were ranked second and third, respectively, on the same question. Interestingly, this pattern is consistent across countries of the region. In all the countries surveyed, poverty is perceived as being the main driver of discrimination. In particular, the responses vary from 14 percent in the case of Panama to 49 percent in the case of Nicaragua. Figure 3.2 illustrates these results for the countries surveyed.

However, these results are not entirely consistent with the answers to a similarly worded question asked only a few years later. Starting in 2004, the same Latinobarometer survey asked Latin Americans why they think people in their country are not treated equally. Echoing the 2001 survey results, one out of every three Latin Americans pointed toward poverty as the culprit in unequal treatment. However, in a departure from the earlier poll, individuals did not identify ethnic and racial characteristics as the second and third top reasons for discrimination. Rather, in 2004, lack of education and connec-

---

[1] The countries surveyed by the Latinobarometer are Argentina, Bolivia, Brazil, Colombia, Costa Rica, Chile, Dominican Republic, Ecuador, El Salvador, Guatemala, Honduras, Mexico, Nicaragua, Panama, Paraguay, Peru, Uruguay, and Venezuela.

Figure 3.1
Most Discriminated-Against Groups in the Region, 2001

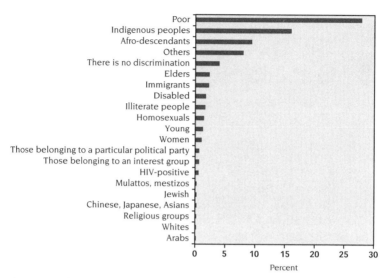

Source: Latinobarometer (2001).
Note: Figure presents responses to the question "Which groups do you think are the
most discriminated against, or do you think that there is no discrimination?"

tions were blamed for unequal treatment. One interpretation of these results is that Latin Americans now consider "economic" factors more important than "social" factors in explaining unequal treatment. Figure 3.3 shows the ranking of reasons for the whole region in 2004 and 2005. Figures 3.4a through 3.4e show how five reasons for unequal treatment vary in terms of perceived prevalence or importance from one country to another. Whereas the Dominican Republic and Nicaragua top the list of countries reporting poverty as the number-one cause of discrimination, Guatemala is the country with the highest percentage of respondents citing lack of education as the most prevalent reason for discrimination. Mexico, Colombia, and Panama head the list of countries in which not having connections is given as the main factor leading to discrimination. Skin color raises important concerns in Brazil and to a lesser extent in Bolivia. The percentage of respondents who answered, "Everyone is treated equally in (country)" varies from 16 percent in Peru to 2 percent in Mexico, Paraguay, and Chile. The cases of Paraguay and Chile are interesting, as they do not rank near the top of the lists for any of the discriminatory factors depicted in Figure 3.4 (with Paraguay even appearing last in the list for unequal treatment resulting from skin color), yet very few people in these countries state that everyone is treated equally there. Thus, it would appear that the survey does not capture well the subtleties of discrimination in these two countries.

The most recent Latinobarometer survey, for 2006, further complicates the picture. In addition to the reasons for unequal treatment cited in the survey for 2004 and 2005, a new alternative allowed individuals to state that they don't feel discriminated against at all. Interestingly, nearly 24 percent of the surveyed individuals chose this response,

Figure 3.2
Percentage of People Who Think Poverty Is the Main Reason People Are Not Treated Equally

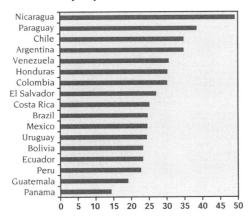

Source: Latinobarometer (2001).

Figure 3.3
Reasons for Discrimination That Most Affect Population, 2004 and 2005

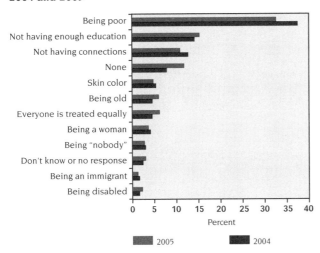

Source: Latinobarometer (2004, 2005).
Note: Figure reflects responses to the question "Out of all the reasons for which people are not treated equally, which one affects you most?"

making it the new top answer (Figure 3.5). The relative ranking of the rest of the reasons for unequal treatment remained almost unaltered. The only difference, if any, is that being old ranked ahead of not having connections for the first time in 2006. As before, skin color, gender, and disabilities were not ranked high as characteristics causing individuals to suffer from discriminatory behaviors on the part of others.

In Europe, as opposed to Latin America, the characteristics that the population perceives as being the drivers of discrimination (or disadvantaged treatment) are more "social" than "economic" in nature. Eurobarometer, the European opinion survey, dedicated a recent special issue (European Commission, 2007) to exploring discriminatory perceptions in the EU25. The four groups ranked by surveyed respondents as the most disadvantaged were the disabled, the Roma (i.e., Gypsies), those over age 50, and those of a different ethnic group than the majority of the population. These results come closer to what conventional wisdom would dictate in terms of characteristics of discriminated-against groups.

The fact that the characteristics typically linked to discrimination register low on the opinion surveys in most countries in Latin America is in itself quite remarkable. Perhaps societies in the region do not discriminate on the basis of ethnicity, race, or gender as much as conventional wisdom suggests. Perhaps the individuals surveyed are being "politically correct" and thus are reluctant to reveal their true beliefs for fear of retaliation. Or

Figure 3.4
Reasons for Unequal Treatment, 2005

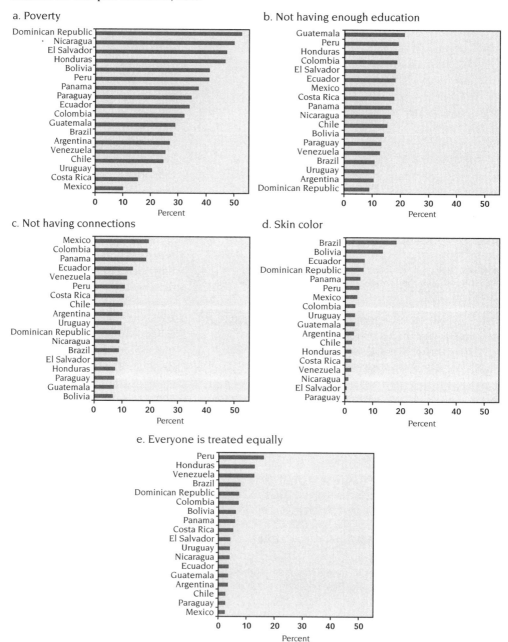

a. Poverty

b. Not having enough education

c. Not having connections

d. Skin color

e. Everyone is treated equally

Source: Latinobarometer (2005).
Note: Percentage of people who responded that poverty (panel a), lack of sufficient education (panel b), lack of connections (panel c), or skin color (panel d) is the reason why people are not treated equally, or that everyone is treated equally (panel e).

Figure 3.5

Reasons for Unequal Treatment That Most Affect Population, 2006

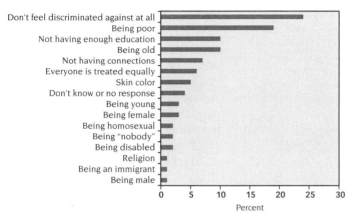

Percent

Source: Latinobarometer (2006).
Note: Figure reflects responses to the question "Of all the reasons for which people are not treated equally, which one affects you most?"

the problem may be that the factors that opinion polls indicate lead to the highest levels of discrimination are those that, indeed, capture not poverty per se but characteristics that respondents associate with poverty. In fact, perhaps the perception of discrimination on the basis of poverty may be highly correlated with other variables such as the general economic condition of the population or with categories that are more traditionally linked with variables that influence discriminatory practices. In countries that are relatively homogeneous in terms of race, the perception of poverty as a key discriminatory problem is relatively low. For instance, this is the case in Uruguay, where only about 20 percent of Latinobarometer respondents link discrimination with poverty. By the same token, in countries that have more racial diversity, Latinobarometer respondents indicate that poverty is a crucial discriminatory issue. This is the case of Peru, for example, where nearly 41 percent of Latinobarometer respondents cite poverty as the most important reason for unequal treatment. Figures 3.6 and 3.7 show scatter plots of simple correlations between basic economic variables and perceptions of discrimination. Figure 3.6 shows that the perception of discrimination on the basis of poverty is accentuated in poorer economies. Conversely, Figure 3.7 suggests that people in societies that are less unequal in terms of income are more apt to view their environment as nondiscriminatory.

Given the above, select countries in the region have recently made efforts to improve on previous methodologies to gain more precise knowledge about the perceptions of discrimination. For example, researchers in Peru adapted the discrimination scales of the Detroit Area Study of 1995 (National Survey on Exclusion and Social Discrimination; DEMUS, 2005) and found that 88 percent of a representative sample of Peruvians had experienced at least one instance of discrimination. In Mexico, the results of the First National Survey on Discrimination in Mexico (SEDESOL, 2005) show that nine out of every ten individuals with disabilities, an indigenous background, or homosexual orientation or who are elderly or members of religious minorities think discrimination exists in their country. The Survey of Perceptions of Racism and Discrimination in Ecuador (Secretaría Técnica del Frente Social, 2004) reveals that 62 percent of Ecuadorans accept that there is racial discrimination in their country, but only 10 percent admit to being openly racist. Afro-descendants are the group perceived to suffer the greatest discrimination in

Figure 3.6

Perceptions of Discrimination on the Basis of Poverty Are Stronger in Poorer Countries

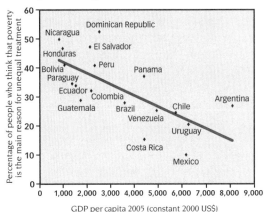

Sources: Latinobarometer (2005) and World Bank (2007).

Figure 3.7

Perceptions of No Discrimination Are Stronger in Less Unequal Societies

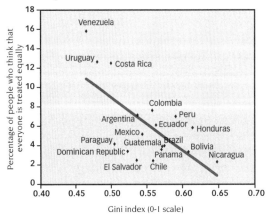

Sources: Latinobarometer (2005) and World Bank (2007).

Ecuador. These are three prominent examples of approaches in the region to measuring perceptions of discrimination using ad hoc surveys. However, these surveys and most related ones, while specialized, suffer from potentially confusing biases similar to those described previously (Bertrand and Mullainathan, 2001).

Interestingly, Latin Americans' perceptions of discrimination are also reflected in the public discourse. Soruco, Piani, and Rossi (2007) document the intricacies of discriminatory attitudes toward migrants (or their families) present in the media in Cuenca and San Fernando, Ecuador. In analyzing the content of newspaper articles referring to migration during September 2005 and February 2006, they find much discriminatory discourse. According to these authors, the traditional discrimination against peasants and the indigenous population has taken a new form as discriminatory attitudes against migrants who, after returning home, bring back from abroad "Westernized" attitudes and behaviors.

This panorama of perceptions and public discourses about discrimination in Latin America is an important step towards understanding the magnitude of the problem, but it is still only relatively useful in understanding the mechanisms through which discrimination occurs and its welfare costs. Nonetheless, as Figures 3.6 and 3.7 suggest, perceptions of discrimination (or the lack of it) may be associated with economic outcomes such as the size of the economy and income distribution. An economic analysis of discrimination, beyond perceptions, is much needed. An appropriate understanding of the mechanisms through which discrimination takes place as well as the economic implications of the related processes becomes a must for the appropriate design of policies.

BEYOND OPINION POLLS

In order to analyze discrimination from an economic perspective, it is not enough to use information on the perceptions of individuals. Such data are informative only to the extent that these perceptions may exert influence on individuals' economic decisions, actions, and outcomes. It is precisely in relation to outcomes that the economic literature has advanced the understanding of discrimination. As a preface to the subsequent discussion of efforts to identify discrimination and its channels, it is worth outlining a few working definitions of discrimination from the international economics literature. This will aid in expositional clarity and put into perspective the studies that this section will describe.

Discrimination is a process that may take place under different circumstances (or, using economic language, in different markets; or, using this report's language, at different transaction points) and based on different characteristics that give rise to discrimination (race, ethnicity, gender, disability, and migratory status, to name a few). Altonji and Blank (1999: 3168) provide a definition of discrimination as it applies to labor markets:

> a situation in which persons who provide labor market services and who are equally productive in a physical or material sense are treated unequally in a way that is related to an observable characteristic such as race, ethnicity, or gender. By "unequal" we mean these persons receive different wages or face different demands for their services at a given wage.

This is the *unequal treatment for the same productivity* definition, which outside of labor markets would read *unequal treatment for the same characteristics*. Some characteristics, of course, are harder to observe than others. One avenue to better understanding discrimination along these lines would be to design studies aimed at uncovering the unobservables as much as possible. Before delving into this further, it is useful to distinguish between *preference-based discrimination* (people treating members of certain groups differently simply because they do not like them) and *statistical discrimination* (people using group membership as a proxy measure for unobserved characteristics). The latter corresponds to the popularly held notions of stigmatization or stereotyping.

An example clarifies the idea. Assuming that a given group has abilities to perform certain manual tasks and not necessarily others of an intellectual nature, some employers may not offer the same opportunities for white-collar jobs to members of that group. This could be a situation in which a group member does not even get in the door for an equal comparison of observable human capital characteristics between himself or herself and somebody else. Stigmatization in this sense constitutes a form of discrimination that complements the notion of unequal treatment for the same characteristics.

Enriching the discussion, the National Research Council's Panel on Methods for Assessing Discrimination (2004: 39), although confined to racial discrimination, complements the previous definition by extending it beyond labor markets. The panel

> use[s] a social science definition of racial discrimination that includes two components: (1) *differential treatment on the basis of race* that disadvan-

> tages a racial group and (2) *treatment on the basis of inadequately justified factors other than race* that disadvantages a racial group (differential effect). Each component is based on behavior or treatment that disadvantages one racial group over another, yet the two components differ on whether the treatment is based on an individual's race or some other factor that results in a differential racial outcome. (italics in original)

This second component serves to scrutinize certain hiring and promotion practices, for example, as elements that unintendedly introduce (or accentuate) discriminatory outcomes. Under the lens of this distinction, economic attempts to measure and disentangle discrimination have focused on the first component, unequal treatment.

The literature for the region has tried to quantify discriminatory outcomes in different ways, beyond opinion polls. The topics of interest have been diverse, ranging from income differences to limited participation in labor markets (limited access to human capital, segregation, differences in returns to human capital characteristics, limited access to jobs, and informality); limited access to health care services, education, and physical infrastructure and housing; and lack of political representation, social protection, and security (victimization). Chapter 2 surveyed the literature that addresses differences in the topics mentioned above with respect to race, ethnicity, migratory status, disabilities, and gender (as a cross-cutting category).

To put things in context, it is worth discussing a typical example of the literature: studies of discrimination in labor income generation. In this case, efforts have focused on documenting earnings differentials between females and males, or between indigenous and nonindigenous populations, or between Afro-descendants and whites. Comparisons of hourly labor earnings (wages or self-employment income) suggest the existence of notorious gaps. Depending on the estimates, nonindigenous workers earn between 80 percent and 140 percent more than indigenous ones. However, nonindigenous workers also exhibit human capital characteristics that are, on average, more desirable than those of indigenous workers. The most notorious of these characteristics is education (schooling), but differences have also been found in labor market experience and field of specialization. In a panorama like this, to attribute the whole earnings gap to the existence of labor market discrimination in pay would be misleading. At least one component of the gap involves differences in observable human capital characteristics that the labor market rewards and, hence, cannot be attributed to the existence of discrimination. With econometric techniques the literature has been able to identify, to some degree, the magnitude of this component. For the example of racial earnings gaps, the literature has shown that these differences in human capital characteristics account for more than one-half of the documented earnings gaps.[2]

The evidence of discrimination (or, more precisely, earnings gaps that cannot be explained by differences in productive characteristics of individuals) that this type of study has found is notoriously smaller than what a simple comparison of earnings would

---

[2] For more details surrounding these issues, see Chapter 2, which exhaustively documents the studies that have conducted this type of analysis for the region, considering different transaction points and different social groups.

suggest. Nonetheless, these studies have been subject to criticism. The most common has been their failure to truly identify discriminatory behaviors as a result of the presence of "unobservable characteristics." That is, these studies can typically analyze only those human capital characteristics that are easily observable (years of schooling, labor market experience, field of specialization, sector choice, etc.), but there are others, not as easily observable, that also help to explain earnings gaps. Good examples of these unobservable characteristics would be education quality, entrepreneurship attitudes, motivation, work ethic, commitment, and assertiveness. A researcher typically cannot capture these characteristics in a survey (and in that sense, cannot "observe" them), but an employer, or more generally, the relevant actors in the labor market can see them and act accordingly. If there are regular differences between the indigenous and nonindigenous populations in some of these "unobservable characteristics," the components of the earnings gaps attributable to discrimination will be overestimated. The literature has moved then towards different attempts to "observe the unobservables," that is, towards trying to capture, through research methods, the richest possible set of information to which the relevant actors in the markets have access in making their decisions.

CAN UNOBSERVABLES BE OBSERVED?

Recent research focusing on Latin America and the Caribbean has found mixed evidence for the unequal treatment definition of discrimination. There have also been attempts to disentangle preference-based and statistical discrimination, and the evidence suggests that Latin Americans do not engage in discrimination of the former type. One interesting attempt to assess social class discrimination with a rich set of data is a study by Núñez and Gutiérrez (2004). These authors utilized administrative records of alumni of a university in Chile where they had access to school performance variables in addition to the human capital variables that studies have traditionally used. This allowed them to uncover some elements of individual productivity previously considered to be unobservable. To assess class differences, they asked a pool of individuals to rate, using a five-point scale, the extent to which they believed a surname belonged to a high-class or a low-class category. Their results suggest the existence of some sort of "classism" in Chile. Individuals with surnames perceived as being part of the upper class had earnings significantly above those of individuals with surnames perceived as being from the lower class, even after human capital characteristics, including school performance indicators, were controlled for. Bravo, Sanhueza, and Urzúa (2006b), following the same approach of scrutinizing college alumni, studied gender differences in labor market earnings among graduates from programs in business/economics, law, and medicine at the same university. They found evidence of unjustified gender differences in earnings, though only in the law profession. The gender differences they found in the business/economics profession vanished after family conditions were controlled for. Gender differences among alumni of the medical school vanished after hours worked, firm size, and geographic region were controlled for.

Along a different line, Bravo, Sanhueza, and Urzúa (2006a) replicated in Santiago, Chile, the standard hiring audit study by mail (see Riach and Rich, 2002). They sent resumes of fictitious applicants to the job postings that appeared in the Santiago newspapers of wider circulation. "Synthetic" resumes were created such that for each job posting, they sent resumes for female and male applicants, with high-class and low-class surnames, and from wealthy and poor municipalities (neighborhoods). With these variations by gender, surname, and municipality, they randomly created human capital characteristics as well as labor market histories for their fictitious applicants. Between March and August 2006, they sent 6,300 resumes in response to job postings and recorded the callbacks received by their fictitious applicants. They found no systematic differences in callback rates by gender, surname, or municipality. This surprising result contrasts with the other results obtained by Bertrand and Mullainathan (2004), who originally applied this methodological approach and found substantial differences in callback rates for fictitious applicants with "black-sounding" and "white-sounding" names to job advertisements in Chicago and Boston. The result suggests that Chilean employers, or at least those who post their job vacancies in the newspapers, do not act discriminatorily in regard to applicant gender, surname, or municipality in the first rounds of their process to fill their vacancies.

Moreno et al. (2004), inspired by the same audit study methodology, designed a field experiment to detect discrimination in hiring in Lima. Instead of creating a sample of synthetic resumes to be sent in response to job postings, they monitored the functioning of the job intermediation service of the Ministry of Labor. The enriched design improved on traditional audit studies by measuring actual job offers and not just callbacks. In assessing discriminatory outcomes in job hiring by race and gender, they found no significant differences across groups. Males and females as well as white-looking and indigenous-looking applicants were equally likely to get job offers in the three occupations of the study: salespersons, secretaries, and (administrative and accounting) assistants. The design of the study also allowed the authors to interview the applicants before their job interviews. In these interviews, the researchers were able to capture a rich set of human capital characteristics that were used as controls for the results of the study. One of the aspects explored in the researchers' interviews, expectations/motivations, led to an interesting result. When the researchers asked individuals, "How much would you like to earn at this job for which you are applying?" they found no race differences but significant gender differences. Females asked for wages that were between 6 percent and 9 percent lower than those asked for by their male competitors, even after a rich set of observable characteristics were controlled for. This reveals some sort of self-discrimination or self-punishment in labor markets (for similar evidence in the United States, see Babcock and Laschever, 2003).

A study by Cárdenas et al. (2006) provides another example of an application of the experimental economics literature to understanding discrimination. Cárdenas and his colleagues had their research participants (a sample of people involved in the provision of social services, on both sides of the counter: beneficiaries and public officials) complete a survey that asked about their values, then engage in a series of games (dictator, distributive dictator, ultimatum, trust, and third-party punishment).[3] To properly measure the behavior of public officials, they also gathered information on non–public

---

[3] A full description of these games, as well as the field protocols and precise operative definitions of the concepts studied (altruism, trust, and social punishment), can be found in Cárdenas, Chong, and Ñopo (2007).

officials in order to be able to generate the appropriate counterfactuals of interest. Within this setup, they tried to measure the extent to which individuals who work in the provision of social services to the poor discriminate against the beneficiaries of the services. Across the board, they found an interesting paradox in study participants' prosocial behavior. Public officials claimed to have higher levels of fairness—in the areas of altruism, trust, and social punishment—compared to non–public officials. However, when facing real monetary incentives to put in action the preferences they stated in the values survey, they acted in less prosocial ways than their non–public official peers. Both public officials and the control group favored women and households with lower education and more dependents (especially if the dependents were children). On the other hand, ex-combatants, street recyclers, street vendors, and individuals cohabiting (without being formally married) received less favorable treatment.

Castillo, Petrie, and Torero (2007), in another experimental setup, detected some stereotyping of fellow participants among a representative sample of young Lima residents; this stereotyping vanished, however, after information about their fellow participants' performance on certain tasks was publicly revealed. Using a repeated public goods game, the researchers measured the extent to which people trust each other and engage in reciprocal behavior.[4] In this game, each participant was given a twenty-five-token endowment and asked to decide how to divide it between a private and a public investment, which had different returns that depended not only on the individuals' decisions but also on the decisions of their peers. They found that people do consider personal characteristics of others when given the opportunity to choose partners, with study participants showing evidence of stereotyping in favor of women and tall and white-looking people. However, when the participants were given information about the past performance of other players, the information that was previously used to stereotype no longer seemed to matter. The information inflow about performance of individuals overrode participants' previous beliefs. Or, more technically: in the presence of an information shortage, performance-optimizing individuals relied on observable characteristics as proxy measures of performance, stereotyping their peers accordingly. When such stereotyping proved to be suboptimal for their performance-maximizing objectives (in this case, as the result of an additional information inflow), these same individuals stopped using it.

Along similar lines, within a simplified setup, Elías, Elías, and Ronconi (2007) performed a study of group formation and popularity among adolescents in Argentina. In experiments conducted in a sample of same-gender and mixed-gender classrooms in Buenos Aires and Tucumán, they asked students to rank their classmates according to their preferences in forming a team. The students were also asked to assess the attractiveness of their classmates. This subjective information about students was then complemented with information, gleaned from administrative records, about grades, disciplinary actions, participation in scholarship programs, and tenure at the school; school administrators were also interviewed as a source for further information. Interpreting the aggregate rankings of the students as measures of popularity, they found no role for

---

[4] This public goods game and three other related games are explored further in Chapter 7, within the context of a broader experimental project undertaken in six capital cities of the region.

ethnicity, skin color, parental wealth, or nationality as explanatory factors. The only factor they found to be important in determining popularity was academic performance. Attractiveness was found to be important only in mixed-gender schools. Interestingly, they also found preferences for assortative mating in that there was a strong correlation between the students' academic performance and that of their corresponding top choice in the rankings. Similarly, preferences for assortative mating were also found for attractiveness, parents' level of education (as reported by the students), and gender.

Along a different line, testing the hypothesis of differential treatment in the courts on the basis of gender, Gandelman, Gandelman, and Rothschild (2007) went into the field to document cases of housing-related discrimination in Uruguay. Using data for 2,437 cases involving foreclosure proceedings, annulment of purchase agreements, actions in rem (actions for the delivery of a possession), annulments of promissory purchase agreements, and evictions, they analyzed the role of the gender composition of the defendant household in the duration of the process. They found, after controlling for a set of covariates, a strong correlation between the presence of women in the household and the granting of time extensions in the processes. Judges were found to be more lenient with women across the board.

CONCLUSIONS

Discrimination is well-rooted in the Latin American collective subconscious. Most of the individuals in the region think there is some sort of discrimination. Nonetheless, when asked about the reasons for this discrimination, most people in the region do not believe that it operates in regard to the traditionally discriminated-against groups (indigenous peoples, Afro-descendants, and women, to cite the most prominent historical examples), but that the poor are the ones who suffer the most from discrimination. After the poor, Latin Americans believe that the uneducated and those who lack significant social connections are those who suffer discrimination the most. These perceptions about the identity of the discriminated-against groups pose interesting and challenging questions for the research agenda. They point towards the existence of some sort of discrimination on the basis of economic reasons, rather than others of a biological or sociological nature.

But an economic analysis of discrimination requires more than information about perceptions. It is necessary to explore economic decisions and their outcomes. The economic literature in regard to the region has advanced towards an understanding of discrimination by analyzing outcomes. Examples of discrimination have been demonstrated in the labor market (wages/earnings, occupations, formality), in access to public goods and services (education, health, security), and in political representation, among other areas. There are now well-documented differential outcomes in most of the region's markets according to gender, race, and ethnicity, with an emphasis on the unfavorable situation of minority groups. However, documentation of differentiated outcomes is not necessarily a proof of discrimination. The presence of unobservable factors limits researchers' ability to assess discrimination along these avenues. As it is very difficult to properly identify discrimination (as there are too many unobservable elements), it is even more problematic to attempt to quantify its economic impact.

This chapter has shown the results of recent empirical research towards the goal of understanding discrimination in the region and its channels, using tools that emphasize efforts to "observe the unobservables." Interestingly, many of the results obtained from controlled experimental setups seem to contradict the idea that today's Latin Americans act discriminatorily. The evidence points towards the existence of stereotyping that vanishes when additional information is revealed about those at whom the stereotyping is directed. To some extent, there is also evidence that some sort of self-discrimination partially explains discriminatory outcomes. Both stereotyping and self-discrimination are behaviors that may simply be outcomes resulting from equilibrium situations in which agents in markets show up with substantial differences in endowments. Under these kinds of circumstances, labor markets (or the other transaction points analyzed in this section) simply operate as resonance boxes that amplify differences that exist in other spheres. These are areas in which more research needs to be conducted in order to enable us to understand the mechanisms underlying these behaviors.

How can these generalized perceptions about discrimination coexist with the lack of evidence of discriminatory behaviors? Is there a way to reconcile this apparent mismatch? This chapter closes with two proposed explanations to the puzzle. On the one hand, it could be that in many other transaction points, not yet analyzed by the experimental literature, there is evidence of discriminatory behavior. Along these lines it should be emphasized that for the experimental literature, in order to develop a deeper understanding of the functionings and to be able to "observe the unobservables" as much as possible, there is a cost to be paid. The gains in specificity achieved by such studies come at the cost of bounds on the possibilities of generalizing the results (reduced external validity). The sample of studies outlined here does not exhaust either the set of relevant transaction points or the intergroup interactions. Hence, more research is needed.

On the other hand, it is absolutely true that what most Latin Americans observe in their daily activities are substantial differences in human, physical, financial, and social assets that are associated with gender, racial, ethnic, and class distinctions. However, these differentiated outcomes do not necessarily emerge as a result of the discriminatory practices of Latin Americans today. Unfortunately, the confusion of differentiated outcomes with discrimination has been commonplace in the academic discussion. This, in turn, has automatically been transferred to public discourse and to collective memories. The extremely unequal distribution of wealth and assets in the region reinforces the generalized notion that there is discrimination in Latin America. An important step towards understanding the issues and the proper design of policies that will effectively address discrimination is recognizing the differences between these two concepts, as they require different responses from governments, states, and societies. It is important to clarify the discussion in order to move forward.

CHAPTER 4

State Reform and Inclusion: Changing Channels and New Actors

The nature of exclusion changes over time. Some social groups, such as racial minorities and women, have faced persistent exclusion or discrimination in education and labor opportunities or have been deprived of the possibility of influencing political decisions in their communities or countries. But analyzing patterns of social inclusion and exclusion only from this point of view would be a mistake, because it leaves out many other forms of exclusion that mainly affect the poor—whether or not they are racial minorities or women—and that have an impact on the way Latin Americans of all economic classes perceive how society, the economy, and politics work.

This chapter analyzes the impact on patterns of inclusion and exclusion of three enormously important phenomena that have affected most Latin American countries in the last three decades: democratization, macroeconomic stabilization, and globalization. Obviously these are not the only phenomena that have influenced the constantly changing patterns of inclusion and exclusion in the region. They have been chosen because they have emerged relatively recently and involve a sufficiently large number of countries, making it possible to deduce their most important effects.

One important consequence of these three phenomena has been that they have altered the way the state functions, as well as many of the channels of political, economic, and social inclusion. To a large extent, democratization, economic stabilization, and participation in international trade and financial flows revealed the crisis into which Latin American states had fallen in the early 1980s. The crisis of the state in Latin America was not only fiscal, but also a crisis of administration and legitimacy. It made a decisive contribution to the collapse of autocratic governments, to the reduction of inflation and control of the immense associated fiscal disorder, to the opening to international trade, and to the exposure to international capital flows following the dismantling of controls on external financing and barriers to foreign direct investment. The crisis also set in motion a large number of state reforms, ranging from the way the three branches of government function and relate to one another to the institutions and policies of economic intervention and provision of social services. This "silent revolution" in the Latin American state (Lora, 2007), which is still under way, has changed and will continue to change the patterns of political, economic, and social inclusion and exclusion.

The three sections that follow this introduction analyze how democratization, macroeconomic stabilization, and globalization have expanded the economic, social, and political possibilities of some groups in Latin America and reduced those of others. The last section focuses on the fiscal expressions of the three phenomena, emphasizing the importance of taxation and public expenditure for patterns of inclusion and exclusion in the region.

DEMOCRATIZATION AND POLITICAL REFORMS

In 1977 only four Latin American countries (out of nineteen presidential countries) could be considered democratic (or semidemocratic), with leaders elected in free (although not necessarily fair or clean) elections. Thanks to the wave of democratization that began in the late 1970s and continued through the 1980s until the mid-1990s, all countries in the region can now be considered democratic or semidemocratic (Smith, 2005, chap. 1). Democratization processes and the political reforms of the last three decades have opened channels of political participation for a variety of social groups and altered the balances of political power, which is now less socially and regionally concentrated, although very permeable to the influences of special interests and economic power.

Working Classes and Indigenous Populations in the Democratization Process

The democratization processes in the region were driven by social pressure from groups with growing economic and political power, mainly the organized working and middle classes. Strikes and demonstrations by the working classes in Peru and Argentina were decisive in ousting military governments in 1977 and 1983, respectively. In Chile a multiparty alliance was formed that defeated President Augusto Pinochet in the historic plebiscite of 1988. In Brazil, the famous metalworkers' strike of 1980 and the formation of the Workers Party aligned the working class with the business sector to form a common front that eventually led to the removal of the country's military government in 1985. Latin America's middle classes gave their support to these antiauthoritarian fronts and broadened demands to include human rights, freedom of social organization, and corruption control. The varied forms of expression and organization of "civil society" were crucial in replacing armed confrontation with electoral competition in El Salvador, Guatemala, and Nicaragua in the 1990s and in the Mexican democratic opening in 2000. Consequently, democratization processes essentially sprang from pressure from previously excluded groups under the risk of being left out of political power.[1]

Although the working classes played a decisive role in democratization in the region, in the long run they did not maintain their political influence. Surprisingly, many of the economic reforms contrary to the interests of the organized working class were adopted by governments led by parties traditionally allied with them, such as the Justicialista Party in Argentina, the Liberal Party in Colombia, and Acción Democrática in Venezuela. The liberalization of international trade, privatizations, and certain labor reforms, which were part of a strategy of economic liberalization and participation in the world economy, weakened the power of the working classes and contributed to the general feeling of disillusionment and frustration with traditional political parties.

---

[1] The role of the elites in democratic transitions should be mentioned. Karl (1990) found that the most common form of democratic transition in Latin America in the twentieth century was activated and agreed to by the elites. This pattern is associated with the democratic transitions in Colombia, Costa Rica, and Venezuela between 1948 and 1958; in contrast, the elites played a very minor role in the democratic transitions of the last thirty years in Argentina, Nicaragua, and Peru. See also Burton, Gunther, and Higley (1992) for a discussion of this subject.

Democratization also opened spaces for political activism by indigenous popula-tions in some countries.[2] Indigenous movements faced a dilemma of identifying politi-cally with campesino (small farmer) or worker social segments or uniting around their own indigenous identity (see Chapter 10). This is a crucial disjunction that leads, in the first case, to emphasizing social justice for reasons of equality with other groups or, in the sec-ond, to emphasizing their differences from the rest of society. Faced with this dilemma, it is not surprising that in countries with relatively small indigenous populations, these groups have mostly taken the first option, whereas the purely indigenous option has been adopted in countries—like Bolivia, Ecuador, and Guatemala—where indigenous populations are relatively sizable (see Box 4.1). But the second option has been a costly conquest, which is still in progress, and not the automatic product of democratization.

Gender Quotas in Legislatures

Between the 1920s and 1960s universal suffrage spread to all of Latin America. In 1929, Ecuador was the first Latin American country to permanently give the vote to women, and Paraguay was the last in 1961 (Smith, 2005: 186). Women's right to vote was fully rec-ognized in the democratization processes beginning in 1977. However, this has not been sufficient to guarantee the vigorous influence of women in the region's political life. It was not until the 1990s that measures were taken to increase the political inclusion of women in Latin American countries, specifically guaranteeing their participation in legislatures (see Figure 4.1). About half of Latin American countries adopted gender quota laws in the 1990s, partly for domestic reasons to attract votes among women, as in the case of Argentina in 1991, and partly as a result of international pressure resulting from the Fourth World Conference on Women held in Beijing in 1995, which decided to promote the adoption of quotas to reduce the systematic underrepresentation of women in legis-lative bodies. As a result, in Argentina, women's participation in the Chamber of Depu-ties (lower house) rose from 5 percent to 27 percent, exactly in line with the standard, and in the Senate (upper house) from 3 percent to 36 percent. Costa Rica's 1997 law was also very effective in increasing women's participation in the country's single chamber, from 14 percent to 35 percent (although the quota specified by the conference was 40 percent). For the region as a whole, the adoption of quotas in the 1990s raised women's participation in legislative bodies by eight percentage points. Quotas are more effective in countries where they are compulsory, where the position of candidates is specified on the electoral list (so that women candidates' names are not relegated to the end), and where noncompliance (such as loss of the party's seats in the legislative body) is penal-ized (see Smith, 2005: 249–53, and Htun, 2004).

Perhaps more significant than the number of women members of congress is par-ticipation in cabinet and senior government posts. In 1990 women held only 9 percent of ministerial positions in the region; ten years later their share had risen to 13 percent. In some of the region's countries—Chile, Colombia, Costa Rica, El Salvador, Honduras, Panama, Venezuela—between a fifth and a quarter of cabinet posts are currently filled

---

[2] This section is based on Smith (2005: 254–62). See also Peeler (2003).

Box 4.1 Political Inclusion of Indigenous Populations in Bolivia, Ecuador, and Guatemala

In Bolivia, during the transition to democracy (1978–1982), indigenous groups began to explore new forms of organization, splitting from the National Revolutionary Movement (Movimiento Nacional Revolucionario, or MNR), which represented campesino interests. The Tupac Katari Revolutionary Liberation Movement (Movimiento Revolucionario Tupac Katari de Liberación, or MRTKL), which emerged in the 1980s as an arm of the Katarista movement of indigenous inspiration, formed alliances with the country's traditional parties and actively participated in government between 1993 and 1997 in coalition with MNR. In 1999, the MRTKL split into Quechua and Aymara factions. The latter gave rise to the Movimiento al Socialismo (MAS) in 2001 under the leadership of Evo Morales, one of the few indigenous presidents in Latin America, who was elected in 2005. His administration has been marked by a dilemma similar to that of the indigenous populations themselves: whether to identify with a dispersed and conflictive set of interests and national identities or with the indigenous populations. Because of this dilemma, the social demands of Bolivia's indigenous populations have not been channeled through the formal institutions of the central government.

With many decades of activist tradition, but split by the agrarian reform policies of the 1960s and 1970s, the indigenous campesinos of Ecuador succeeded in reunifying in 1986 under the Ecuadorian Confederation of Indigenous Nationalities (Confederación de Nacionalidades Indígenas del Ecuador, or CONAIE). Using its capacity for organization and protest, in the 1990s CONAIE transformed national politics in the country, with the transformation culminating in the overthrow of President Jamil Mahuad in 2000. Through the Pachakutik Plurinational Unity Movement (Movimiento de Unidad Plurinacional Pachakutik, or MUPP), created by CONAIE, which has participated in congress since 1996, the Ecuadoran indigenous movement has combated discrimination in social policies and employment and gained importance as a decisive force and not simply as a force with veto power.

The indigenous peoples of Guatemala, who were brutally repressed in the 1970s and 1980s, have gained political influence since democratization. As in Bolivia and Ecuador, they moved from identifying with campesinos to uniting around their own indigenous identity. Under the Nueva Granada Democratic Front in 1995, and still in the midst of repression, members of indigenous groups won six seats in Congress, including two Maya women. In 1996 during the Álvaro Arzú administration, which was supported by other Maya groups, indigenous peoples reached several peace agreements with the Guatemalan government. However, Guatemalan society has not yet fully adopted the indigenous cause. In a 1999 referendum, a majority (53 percent versus 47 percent) of the population rejected recognition of Guatemala as "a multicultural, ethnically plural and multilingual state." Some of the peace agreements have not been implemented, especially those relating to increasing the tax burden to allocate more resources to social expenditure. The full political and social inclusion of indigenous peoples in Guatemala remains a task for the future.

Source: Based on Smith (2005).

by women. In Chile, Colombia, and Mexico, women have held the positions of foreign affairs and defense ministers. And of course, in Argentina, Nicaragua, Panama, and currently in Chile, the presidency has been in women's hands (although, strictly speaking, only in the last case on their own political merits rather than by extension of their husbands' power) (Smith, 2005: 249–53).

Patterns of Electoral and Political Inclusion and Exclusion

Regular elections are the key component of democracy, although they do not by themselves guarantee its proper working. Effective exercise of the right to vote in Latin America is far from being total, although it is very high in presidential elections, in which over 70 percent of registered voters usually participate in most

Figure 4.1

Participation by Women in the Legislative Branch, 1990 and 2000

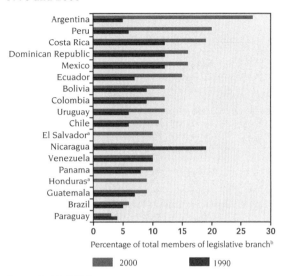

Source: Smith (2005).
[a]No data are available for El Salvador and Honduras for 1990.
[b]In the case of countries with bicameral legislatures, the percentage relates to members of the lower house.

countries. Uruguay, Peru, Bolivia, Chile, and Brazil are, in that order, the countries with highest voter turnout, whereas Colombia and Guatemala are at the opposite extreme (see Figure 4.2). Empirical evidence shows that the first elections to establish (or re-establish) democracy in a particular country generate an electoral enthusiasm that later tends to fade. Compulsory voting increases turnout by ten percentage points, although it is difficult to define the impact because its effectiveness depends very much on the sanctions attached to the requirement. Moreover, the percentage varies from one election to another. In general, presidential elections attract more voters than parliamentary or local elections. Turnout is also higher when election campaigns are hard-fought or when elections are dominated by a single issue. It does not seem to be linked to institutional factors (civil rights, political stability, development of parties, political fragmentation), demographic factors (age distribution of the population), or education levels (literacy rates or percentage of the population that has completed secondary studies). In short, turnout patterns in elections remain largely unexplained. It is probable that they are closely related to cultural or historical factors that influence patterns of economic and social inclusion. In this respect, turnout does not seem to be very different from interpersonal trust or any other form of social capital (IDB, 2000, chap. 4).

Since voter turnout in the region is far from total, the question is: Do voter turnout patterns differ systematically from one social group to another? If they do, this will determine whether the groups' interests are taken into account by the political system.

Figure 4.2
Voter Turnout in Presidential Elections in Latin America,
Various Years

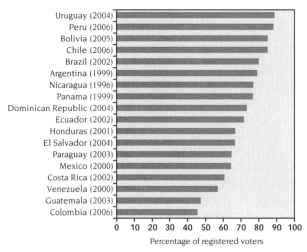

Percentage of registered voters

Source: International Institute for Democracy and Electoral Assistance (IDEA).

However, the fact that channels of political influence are not limited to the act of voting also has to be considered, since casting a vote is only one form of political participation. Other forms are also important: citizens who are better informed or have more direct contact with parties and candidates are more likely to influence decisions. It could be that turnout and other forms of political participation mutually reinforce each other, which means that the groups that are not heard or have no channels of influence in the political system are the same as those excluded from the act of voting, forming a vicious circle of political exclusion that is difficult to break.

Patterns of political participation by education and economic group were studied in a previous edition of this report based on the Latinobarometer opinion polls in seventeen countries in the region (IDB, 2000, chap. 4). It is worth summarizing the report's conclusions in regard to these patterns. By education level, differences are small for turnout but large for other forms of participation, such as watching and listening to political news, talking about politics with friends, trying to influence other people's political opinions, or working for a political candidate. For example, people with at least some college-level education are twice as likely to talk about politics as people who have had only primary school, but the probability of voting among the former group is only slightly higher than among the latter. The trend is somewhat similar for patterns of political participation by income group. There are no discernible differences in voter turnout according to income, but there are for other forms of participation, which tend to increase with income levels. The IDB study also analyzed participation patterns by age group. Surprisingly, participation in the region varies only slightly from one age group to another, although it is found to be slightly lower in younger groups.

It is important to note the relationship between voter turnout patterns and the weakness of political parties. If parties do not represent interests that unite broad sections of the population, then the link between turnout and political inclusion is weak.[3] In countries where political parties are programmatic—such as Chile, El Salvador, Nicaragua, and Uruguay—the population can expect to feel included as a result of the act of voting

---

[3] This is closely linked to the degree of institutionalization of political parties (see IDB, 2005: 34).

for the party that most represents their political interests. In contrast, in countries where parties are more prone to clientelism—such as Bolivia, Colombia, Guatemala, Peru, and Venezuela—voting is not sufficient to achieve broad political inclusion, because close links have to be maintained with politicians to obtain the benefits of participation (IDB, 2005: 34).

Patterns of political participation in Latin America do not differ substantially from those in other regions of the world, except perhaps that political participation is distributed more uniformly in Latin American countries than in the United States. In European countries participation patterns are practically identical to those in Latin America. Consequently, based on differences in voter turnout or the other forms of political participation mentioned, it cannot be said that there are very pronounced biases in favor of certain social or economic groups and against others. However, no definite conclusions should be drawn from this analysis because of the difficulty in determining the relative effectiveness of the various forms of participation and because perhaps the most important channels of political influence in Latin America are not captured by opinion polls. In particular, small but economically powerful groups with well-defined interests can have a disproportionate influence on political decisions in the region, since they can organize more easily than larger groups with less economic power and more dispersed interests.

Whether these powerful interest groups can effectively displace other less-organized social groups in a country depends on whether the country's political system creates incentives for politicians to respond to regional, sectoral, or class interests. For example, soft regulations on election campaign finances facilitate the influence of powerful groups. The same can be said of electoral institutions that oblige politicians to overrespond to geographical interests, because this opens the way for the influence of geographically very concentrated economic sectors. Likewise, some voting systems create incentives for politicians to cultivate personal groups of supporters instead of following their party directives, which presumably represent broader national interests.

According to an index that quantifies the incentives created by voting systems for politicians to cultivate relations with voters or with their party leaders, in Latin America politicians have more incentive to stay on good terms with party leaders than in any other part of the world (IDB, 2000: 193–95). As a result, regional interests generally have little influence on the working of Latin American political systems. Political systems are more susceptible to influences from interest groups that organize nationally in order to reach party decision-making centers directly. Consequently, powerful economic groups with very defined and concentrated national interests can exclude the regional, sectoral, or social interests of groups that do not have national organizing capacity. However, this conclusion has to be balanced with at least three considerations.

First, the electoral systems of some countries do create incentives for cultivating personal relations with the electorate rather than with party leaders. The best-known case is Brazil, where candidates do not have to be nominated by their parties to run election campaigns using the party name and voters can express their preferences for individual candidates on the proposed lists. Second, the election systems of some countries have undergone major reforms. The general trend has been to exchange closed lists for open lists in which voters may choose among candidates of the same party, which increases incentives for politicians to respond more to voters and less to party hierarchies (Payne and Perusia, 2007). Third, the most important change in the channels of influence of regional interests has been political decentralization.

Political Decentralization

Previously, Latin American central governments named officials at lower levels of government and controlled a significantly higher proportion of total public expenditure (Wiesner, 2003). Under this system, local authorities had more incentives to respond to the demands of the central government than to the preferences of the people of their locality. The central government was the body that made most decisions on expenditure, even in local cases. This arrangement reinforced the bias in favor of agents that had national capacity to organize and exert pressure. Public sector labor unions, particularly in the areas of health and education, are a clear example (IDB, 2005; Daughters and Harper, 2007).

The deepening of decentralization in Latin America in the 1990s had two special features that changed the patterns of inclusion and exclusion associated with decentralization. First, the rate of decentralization was not equal among all public expenditure items. The services decentralized between 1996 and 2004 were largely nutrition, public hospitals, maintenance of interurban highways, urban transport services, and regional universities. The second significant characteristic of the recent decentralization process in the countries of the region (with the exception of Brazil) is the local taxation lag. Local authorities now have a series of expenditure responsibilities, but their capacity to levy taxes is very limited, because of very small local tax bases or legal restrictions on designing an independent tax policy (Daughters and Harper, 2007).

Both transformations have had a dual effect on inclusion of the population. Although it is true that election of local authorities and devolution of certain expenditure decisions have involved previously excluded segments of the population, it is also true that this process has been limited because of the low level of local tax collection in the region. In other words, inclusion of the population in local public policymaking in Latin America has been partial: people can now influence the spending decisions of mayors and governors, but there is little concern about the sources of revenue needed to cover such expenditure.

An additional effect of political decentralization has been the strengthened role of nongovernmental organizations and community organizations. (Angell, Lowden, and Thorp, 2001, document this phenomenon very well for Colombia and Chile.) Under centralist schemes, local governments had no need to develop independent administrative capacity; with political decentralization the need exists, particularly on issues related to institutional strengthening and community development. The result is that nongovernmental organizations and community organizations are now participating in the execution and design of local public policies.

STABILIZATION AND MACROECONOMIC POLICIES

Inflation and Economic Populism

In the 1970s and 1980s, Latin America was characterized by persistently high inflation and quite a few cases of hyperinflation (conventionally defined as monthly inflation rates over 50 percent). Populism was the characteristic of the macroeconomic policies of a number of administrations, such as those of Juan D. Perón in Argentina between 1973 and 1974, Salvador Allende in Chile between 1970 and 1973, and Alan García in Peru between 1985 and 1990 (Kaufmann and Stallings, 1991). The economic policies typical of populism produced very marked patterns of exclusion and inclusion of the population, as described below.

In general, populist governments in Latin America during this time assumed power with strong electoral support from the middle classes of formal urban workers in both public and private sectors. These governments argued that the low level of economic activity was a problem of repressed demand. Raising wages was expected to create a virtuous circle of high demand, higher production, and higher wages. For this reason, the starting point of populist measures was significant wage hikes for public and private sector employees (Cardoso and Helwege, 1991). To contain inflationary pressures, governments froze prices and, in some cases, fixed the exchange rate. In the short term, these measures benefited the urban middle classes at the cost of other segments of the population. Higher real wages in the cities—a consequence of nominal wage increases, frozen prices, and appreciation of the real exchange rate—had a counterpart in their impact on agricultural producers, both suppliers of the domestic markets and exporters (Kaufmann and Stallings, 1991). Up to this point it can be said that populist governments kept their political promises in the short term: what they intended and achieved was to favor the social class that supported them politically.

However, monetization of fiscal deficits and the depletion of international reserves revealed the unsustainable nature of these policies. Inflationary pressures put an end to price controls and reversed the trend in real urban wages. The initial economic boom fueled by these measures was followed by deep economic crises, which rapidly wiped out the increase in real income. For example, the real wage of industrial workers in Chile rose 20 percent in real terms between 1970 and 1971, then plunged 11 percent in 1972 and 38 percent in 1973. Real wages in the manufacturing sector did not return to their 1970 level until 1981 (Larraín and Meller, 1991).

The pattern of inclusion and exclusion induced by populist measures responds to criteria of political economy. The poorest population segment in Latin America is concentrated in rural areas, but this group did not have sufficient voice or organization to exercise political pressure and was excluded from public policy decisions. In contrast, the middle class, characterized as urban with formal employment in the public and private sectors, had the organization and voice required to demand measures in its favor, although these measures had only short-term effects (Cardoso and Helwege, 1991).

Another way of interpreting the segmentation produced by economic populism is as a political struggle to determine the social distribution of the inflation tax (which results from the loss of purchasing power of the currency held by the public, as a result of excessive increases in money supply). This tax was very important in Latin America in the 1970s and 1980s: on average 4.4 percent of gross domestic product (GDP) between 1973 and 1983 and 10.8 percent between 1983 and 1987 (Edwards and Tabellini, 1991). In a situation in which a country's monetary authority can grant unlimited credit at no cost to the central government, how the inflation tax is distributed is decided by those in power. The costs are possibly shared regressively, because the poorest segments of the population and small businesses have no access to financial instruments to protect them from this tax.

These populist experiments financed by inflation taxes seem to be a thing of the past. At the end of the 1980s, eleven Latin American countries had inflation rates over 20 percent, and four suffered price increases of more than 1,000 percent annually. In contrast, over the 2001–2005 period, no Latin American country had an average inflation rate over 20 percent, and only five reported inflation above that figure in any one of these years (with a 41 percent maximum in Argentina in 2002).

A decisive factor in the macroeconomic stabilization processes in Latin America was the granting of independence to central banks to make their own decisions on monetary policy, with the predominant objective (and in some countries the only one) of reducing inflation. Between 1988 and 1996, the central banks of twelve Latin American countries were reformed by law or constitutionally, being granted more independence in the design and conduct of monetary policy as a guarantee of price stability. In this process, governments gave up their discretionary power to finance themselves directly from the central bank, which eliminated the main cause of the inflation tax. As will be shown in the following section, the independence of countries' monetary authorities also had important effects on the patterns of inclusion and exclusion associated with credit and exchange rate policy.

The End of Directed Credit

Prior to the macroeconomic stabilization of the 1990s, the central governments of Latin America had considerable ability to direct credit to influential economic sectors or groups. This was feasible because public banks were very important within the financial system, because the central bank was an important intermediation agent, or because the government strictly regulated allocation of credit by private banks. In the late 1980s, a significant percentage of total lending in Latin America was directed by the government using one of these three mechanisms: around 30 percent in Colombia, 35 percent in Mexico, and 40 percent in Argentina, and up to 80 percent in Brazil (Morris et al., 1990). In these financial systems in which the government played a central role, access to credit was determined by the ability of economic agents to exert political pressure. Agents that were unable to exert pressure were excluded and had to pay high financing costs (Edwards, 1995).

Brazil represented the region's most extreme case of discretionary directed credit. First, public banks were and still are central players in the country's financial system: in 2002, 43 percent of the total assets of the Brazilian financial system were held by public banks (Galindo, Micco, and Panizza, 2007). Moreover, in the 1970s and 1980s, national development banks, particularly the Brazilian National Development Bank (Banco Nacional de Desenvolvimento Econômico e Social, or BNDES), allocated a large amount of funds to the industrial sectors, which were protected at that time. In general, credit was granted to the most powerful sectors in the economy, especially heavy manufacturing, finance, and large-scale agriculture (Frieden, 1991). Under the argument that these sectors were fundamental for national development, these policies excluded highly profitable projects in other sectors.

In recent years, the trend toward directed credit in the region has been reversed, and market mechanisms have been given a greater role. Privatization of public banks, the independence granted to central banks, and deregulation of private lending have cut off old, vocal industrial groups from cheap or subsidized credit. At the same time, new credit options have emerged, such as microcredit or lines of credit for small- and medium-sized enterprises, including sectors previously excluded from the financial system (IDB, 2004). Another recent phenomenon in Latin America has been the development of local bond markets. Here two opposing forces have come together, because there is evidence that growth of public debt bonds has stimulated bonds of private origin. However, an excessive level of domestic public debt is simultaneously crowding out the borrowing capacity of the private sector (IDB, 2006b, chap. 7), which excludes formal companies from this nonintermediated financing mechanism.

Exchange Rate Policy

Exchange rate policy has undergone a transformation similar to that of credit policy, and the patterns of exclusion and inclusion that it generates have also changed. To understand this transformation, it should be borne in mind that a country's exchange rate system affects each population group differently. Regimes with fixed or fairly inflexible exchange rates can be expected to produce low inflation rates and real appreciation, which benefits the urban middle and upper classes by increasing their purchasing power. This scenario, however, harms agro-exporters and other producers of tradable goods. A flexible exchange rate regime, accompanied by moderate inflation and real appreciation, produces the opposite effect (Blomberg, Frieden, and Stein, 2005).

Some empirical works have found that trade liberalization has been a breaking point in the relation between exchange policy and the interests of different sectors in Latin America (Frieden, Ghezzi, and Stein, 2000). In the previous context of high tariffs, the protected economic sectors had no interest in pressuring for an exchange rate policy in their favor. After losing their tariff protection as a result of trade liberalization, the sectors were interested in compensating for the loss by pressuring for more flexible exchange rate policies with a trend toward real depreciation. Frieden, Ghezzi, and Stein (2000) found a positive relation between the weight of manufacturing industry in output and the probability that a country had a flexible exchange rate system. This relation has strengthened in recent years as barriers to international trade have been removed.

In conclusion, before the effects of globalization, the objective of exchange rate policy in Latin America was to protect the real income of the urban middle and upper classes, without taking into account the economic sectors protected by trade policy. As trade protection declined, these sectors' power to determine exchange rate policy increased, and the interests of the urban middle and upper classes lost ground.

Transformation of Industrial Policy

Public ownership of companies and privatization processes are one aspect of relations between the state and the productive base; another is industrial policy, which has changed drastically, particularly as a public policy response to the globalization process. The transformation of industrial policy in Latin America and the impact of the change on social exclusion and inclusion are briefly described below.

Industrial policy prior to the globalization process was very uniform among the countries of the region in the framework of import substitution policy (Melo, 2001). As mentioned earlier, its main instruments were tariff protection, directed credit, direct subsidies, and exchange rate controls. Its center of attention was the manufacturing sector, especially heavy industry, and its objective was to develop previously nonexistent economic activities to supply domestic markets.

Under the old industrial policy, the main beneficiaries were business owners and formal employees linked to the protected sectors. Urban in origin, both segments of the population succeeded in protecting companies and formal jobs at the cost of high domestic prices, valuable fiscal resources, and a bias against the agricultural and export sectors (Melo and Rodríguez-Clare, 2007).

The transformation of this industrial policy into that which exists today in the countries of the region was not a gradual or linear process. Structural adjustment policies in the late 1980s and early 1990s led to temporary abandonment of the type of intervention represented by the old industrial policy in most Latin American countries. Later, in the mid-1990s, industrial policy in the region began a slow recovery that is still evident (Peres, 2005). However, unlike those under the import substitution model, the new industrial policies are characterized by (a) being much more heterogeneous across countries and (b) having the clear purpose of stimulating potential export sectors. In other words, there has been no return to the previous industrial policy model (Machinea and Vera, 2006; Ramos, 1996).

Melo (2001) and Peres (2005) offer a typology of the new spectrum of industrial policies in the region.[4] A group of countries, among which Brazil is a good example, have focused on supporting the economic activities in which they have clear dynamic comparative advantages (for example, biotechnology) or have technological externalities that could be very valuable for the national productive base (for example, information technology in Costa Rica). In both cases, the ultimate objective is not to supply the domestic market, but to develop new exports. Another group of countries, of which Mexico and Colombia are good examples, support existing clusters of productive activities. The objective is to raise competitiveness and embrace the international competition that these activities face without granting direct subsidies to the companies involved. A third and last group, of which Chile is the outstanding example, has applied horizontal or neutral industrial policies across sectors. The objective is to stimulate the productivity of the largest number of economic activities without interfering in factor markets for allocation of resources.

---

[4] Garay (1998) describes in detail the new industrial policies in place since the mid-1990s in Argentina, Brazil, Mexico, and Venezuela.

The diversity of current industrial policymaking in the region is reflected in the resulting change in patterns of exclusion and inclusion. Neutral policies and policies to promote sunrise sectors, unlike cluster policies, are less likely to be captured by business groups and can be more equitable in sectors that did not previously receive public support. Nonetheless, cluster promotion policies are much more inclusive than the old industrial policies because they are targeted at sectors other than manufacturing and because they are not based on protectionist measures such as tariffs or market quotas. Even so, current industrial policies, particularly those targeted at clusters, have very few elements that promote investment in human capital in the sectors that receive support. It could be said, then, that modernization of the labor force is the great challenge for modern industrial policy in Latin America.

Although it is true that Latin America's new industrial policies are more inclusive than the ones they replaced, it is also true that old patterns of exclusion persist as a result of the concentration of economic power. Such is the case of the business class in Guatemala, which, thanks to its voice and cohesion, has succeeded in retaining generous tax exemptions, another way of capturing industrial policy (IDB, 2005).

Relations between the state and companies in Latin America are reflected in the trend in informal employment in the region.[5] There is evidence of a secular increase in this type of employment in the region in recent decades, which demonstrates the state's inability to create the necessary incentives for formal companies to assimilate the growing supply of workers, either under the old protectionist model of industrial policy or under the current model in any of its variants. According to Thorp (1998), in 1950 only 8.7 percent of urban manpower in Latin America was linked to informal employment. At that time, companies and formal employment were covered by protectionist policies, and demographic pressure stemming from urbanization had not materialized. Two decades later, this proportion had increased to 11.5 percent, threatening employment security in the region.

The World Commission on the Social Dimension of Globalization (2004) documents the rapid growth of informal employment in the region in the 1980s and 1990s. According to the commission, the percentage of self-employed workers in Latin America in the 1980s in activities other than agriculture was 29 percent, only three percentage points above the world average.[6] In the next decade, this percentage increased to 44 percent, twelve percentage points above the world average and very close to the average in Africa (48 percent, according to the information in Figure 4.3). Protected urban companies did not succeed in growing sufficiently to absorb the flow of migrants from rural to urban areas. Combined with the high costs associated with formal employment, this factor has turned informal and badly paid jobs into a persistent phenomenon.

According to figures from the Economic Commission for Latin America and the Caribbean (ECLAC, 2006b) in its latest report on the social panorama of the region, this trend has reversed itself slightly in some countries in this decade (especially Argentina,

---

[5] Carr and Chen (2004) synthesize the International Labour Organization's conceptual framework of informal employment.

[6] However, the criteria used to define informality in Thorp (1998) are not the same as those used to define self-employment according to more recent data.

Figure 4.3
Self-Employed Workers in Sectors Other Than Agriculture, 1980s and 1990s

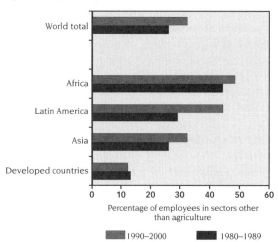

Percentage of employees in sectors other than agriculture

■ 1990–2000   ■ 1980–1989

Source: World Commission on the Social Dimension of Globalization (2004).

Chile, and Costa Rica) but has continued in others (Colombia, Nicaragua, Paraguay, and Venezuela being the most extreme cases). Even more worrisome is the fact that the income of people in this class of activities plummeted during the last decade in almost all countries of the region, with only Chile, Ecuador, El Salvador, and Panama excepted.[7] These problems are studied in more detail in Chapter 5.

GLOBALIZATION AND TRADE LIBERALIZATION POLICIES

In the 1990s, the increased participation of Latin American economies in international trade, finance, and technology flows and, to a lesser extent, international migration flows affected wages, employment, and social security conditions and exposed workers and their families to more opportunities, as well as to higher risks, than in the past. As happened with the phenomena of democratization and stabilization, globalization altered patterns of economic and social inclusion and exclusion for the benefit of some groups, but to the detriment of others.

Trade Liberalization and Its Effects on Labor Exclusion and Inclusion[8]

To benefit from the possibilities of growing international trade and obtain the blessing of investors and international creditors once again interested in Latin America after resolution of the region's debt crisis, in the mid-1980s Latin American governments began to put in place a set of reforms to open their economies to trade, finance, and investment.[9] The central element of this external liberalization was reduction of import barriers, which protected local production, especially in the industrial sectors. Between the mid-1980s and early 1990s, all of the region's countries began trade liberalization programs with reductions of at least fifteen points in the average tariff rate. Tariffs dropped from aver-

---

[7] This statement is based on a measure of average income of the urban population in low-productivity sectors: ECLAC (2006b), Table 28.

[8] This section is based on IDB (2003a, chap. 5).

[9] The Brady Plan, which was set up in 1989 to convert Latin American government debt with international banks, was the decisive factor in reviving the interest of investors and creditors. However, several countries had already adopted important opening and liberalization measures.

age levels of 48.9 percent in the years prior to the reform to 10.7 percent in 1999. Nontariff restrictions, which applied to 37.6 percent of imports prior to the reform, affected only 6.3 percent by the mid-1990s.[10] But the lower tariff and nontariff restrictions fueled imports, which grew as a proportion of GDP in most countries. For the region overall, import penetration grew from 22.6 percent in the 1983–1985 period to 36.2 percent in the 1998–2000 period. Export indicators also rose, although much less steeply, from 23.3 percent to 29.6 percent of GDP between the two periods.

Although in popular opinion, trade liberalization and overall unemployment are closely linked phenomena, this belief lacks empirical support. Unemployment rates in the region did not increase following the liberalization measures or as a result of the increased entry of imported products into economies. Likewise there is no basis for stating that total employment fell. However, this does not mean that liberalization did not have destructive effects on jobs in specific sectors, as in fact it did. Surprisingly, however, these destructive effects were relatively modest. Changes in the sectoral composition of employment were very small in comparison with the size of the measures and what all studies preceding the enactment of the liberalization measures had predicted.

Since reallocation of employment between sectors as a result of trade liberalization was very low, companies could be expected to adjust to liberalization in some other way. In part they did so by improving their efficiency and redirecting their production into more profitable activities. But most of the adjustment fell on workers through lower wages. In the case of Mexico, in companies affected by a forty-point tariff cut, real wages fell by an estimated 8–10 percent. For the overall manufacturing sector, tariff cuts at the end of the 1980s produced an estimated 3–4 percent fall in wages. Elimination of quantitative controls on imports may have had an even greater effect that is difficult to quantify (Revenga, 1997). In Colombia, where the average tariff dropped from 50 percent in 1984 to 13 percent in 1998, the effect on the average wage in the manufacturing industry was also 3–4 percent[11] (for the initially more protected industrial sectors, it was up to 7 percent).

It is surprising that the effects of trade liberalization on wages have been relatively severe in comparison with modest changes in employment and its composition. The most probable explanation for this phenomenon is that workers shared the rents (and inefficiencies) that protection gave to companies. Tariff reduction could be accommodated without great changes in employment by improving productivity and eliminating these rents. The disappearance of protection rents also weakened the power of unions, which lost influence in wage negotiations and in maintaining or expanding industrial employment. Not surprisingly, in most countries of the region, union participation rates fell in the 1990s to only 16.3 percent of the labor force in 1991–1995 from 20.1 percent a decade earlier or 25 percent in the second half of the 1970s.[12] However, there were other phenomena that contributed to the loss of union influence, especially reduction of employment in the public sector, expansion of temporary employment, and changes in legislation that governs the operation of unions.

---

[10] For eleven countries for which information is available. For a more detailed description see IDB (1997), Part II.
[11] The calculation reported by Attanasio, Goldberg, and Pavcnik (2004) is 4 percent but assumes elimination of the tariff.
[12] These are median figures for the countries for which data are available (see IDB, 2003a, chap. 7).

Traditional forms of hiring in the region have been partly displaced by new arrangements, such as outsourcing of services and temporary employment.[13] However, increased international trade has played at most a marginal role in this process, which on the demand side of labor has been driven by technological and organizational change, and on the supply side by the demand for greater flexibility, especially for women workers.[14] Evidence suggests that increased international trade has produced more informality only in countries with more rigid labor regulations.

Although competition from imported products has reduced wages in the affected sectors (and in some countries may have contributed to increasing informality), the emergence of new export sectors has created new labor opportunities in Latin America. Contrary to fears on this issue widely covered by the international press, studies conclude that workers in new agricultural export sectors or in maquiladora companies receive higher pay and have better working conditions than workers in any alternative available job. These conclusions are confirmed by the workers themselves in export zones of non-traditional crops in Guatemala or in the maquiladoras of Chihuahua and Ciudad Juárez in Mexico, to mention only two examples.[15]

Technological Change and Wage Gaps

While increased trade penetration has tended to depress workers' wages in the affected sectors, technological change, which has accelerated with globalization, has benefited Latin America's more-skilled workers. The widening wage gap between skilled and unskilled workers has been one of the phenomena that has generated the most reaction against globalization in the region.

Although the widening of wage gaps between workers according to education level has been an important phenomenon in Latin America, it has been less pronounced than is often claimed. A comparison of the wage income of workers who had completed tertiary studies with those who had completed secondary studies reveals an 18 percent increase (average for twelve countries in the region) in the income gap between the two groups during the 1990s: the ratio of the income of workers with tertiary education to that of those with secondary education increased in Latin America from 2.3 in the early 1990s to 2.8 in the early part of this decade.[16] If the comparison is between workers with completed tertiary studies and workers with completed primary studies, the increase in the gap is 7 percent. In contrast, if the calculation is between workers with completed secondary and completed primary education, the gaps narrowed slightly during the decade.

These trends are not common to all countries. For example, considering the gaps between incomes of workers with tertiary and secondary education, Argentina and Nicaragua show important increases (53 percent and 24 percent, respectively), whereas Brazil,

---

[13] For the case of Mexico, see Maloney (1999).

[14] The trend toward increased temporary and seasonal employment in agriculture is common to all of Latin America and dates from at least the 1980s. It is associated with expansion of agro-industry and seasonal export products, such as fruits and vegetables (Kay, 1995).

[15] A more complete summary is available in IDB (2003a, chap. 5).

[16] IDB Research Department calculation based on household surveys.

Honduras, and Panama show modest reductions. In several countries the trend toward expanding gaps at the start of the trade liberalization process has halted or reversed itself in recent years. In Mexico, the trend ended in 1994, when the North American Free Trade Agreement (NAFTA) entered into force, and in Colombia the gap worsened severely in the early part of the 1990s but reversed completely in later years.

Numerous studies have analyzed the causes of widening wage gaps in Latin America. Although several have found some relation with trade liberalization processes, most tend to conclude that the trend is due to technological changes associated with certain types of imports. A study that included Argentina, Brazil, Chile, Colombia, and Mexico found that wage gaps by manufacturing subsector had common patterns for technological reasons.[17] In synthesis, technological change seems to be a much more important cause of wage inequality than international trade.

The gender wage gap has followed a different path than gaps by education level (Table 4.1). Some studies show that the gap in remuneration for work between men and women with similar skill levels has narrowed or has remained stable for the last twenty years (see Tenjo Galarza, Ribero Medina, and Bernat Díaz, 2004, for the cases of Argentina, Brazil, Colombia, Honduras, and Uruguay; Ñopo, 2006, for the case of Chile). Even so, gender differences in wages persist (see Chapter 2).

FISCAL INCLUSION AND EXCLUSION

The previous sections of this chapter showed how democratization, stabilization, and globalization changed the patterns of inclusion and exclusion of social groups in Latin America. Democratization opened spaces for political participation by the working classes, indigenous groups, and women, but also strengthened the influence of interest groups with ability to organize at the national level or exert direct influence on political parties. Stabilization limited the access to cheap credit enjoyed by certain sectors and privileged groups, but also reduced the influence of the urban middle classes, whom price controls, artificial fixing of exchange rates, and increases in minimum wages of earlier periods had tried to benefit, albeit only in the short term. Trade, financial, and technological globalization helped erode the power of the urban middle classes, especially low-skilled workers, while strengthening the influence of workers with higher levels of education and owners of capital.

Democratization, stabilization, and globalization also changed the way a country's social and economic groups relate to the country's tax administration and public expenditures. This is no surprise, since fiscal policy is the way the state distributes resources to all sectors of society for collective purposes and for the needs and interests of specific groups. Consequently, participation by all the different social and economic groups in collection and allocation of fiscal revenue is a decisive factor in patterns of inclusion and exclusion.

---

[17] First, wage gaps widened *inside* subsectors and in the same subsectors in all countries. Second, the intensity of the phenomenon was related to the penetration of imports of inputs and capital goods in these subsectors. Third, the widening of wage gaps was much more sensitive to the technological content of imports than to their penetration (Sánchez-Páramo and Schady, 2003).

Table 4.1 Wage Gap between Men and Women (percentage)			
	1981	1989	1998
Argentina	43.5	36.5	34.7
Brazil	62.9	55.9	40.3
Colombia	38.7	28.7	14.7
Costa Rica	16.7	32.2	21.0
Honduras	n.d.	9.4	7.1
Uruguay	62.7	59.8	52.2

Source: Extracted from Tenjo Galarza, Ribero Medina, and Bernat Díaz (2004).
Note: n.d. = data not available.

The most important influence of democratization on fiscal systems should have been the adoption of strongly redistributive tax systems, as the median voter theory predicts. This theory predicts that if everyone voted, taxes and the size of governments would be greater in more unequal societies. Because of the income concentration effect, in Latin America there is in fact a tendency to impose high tax rates on individuals, with higher rates in countries with more inequality, also consistent with the median voter theory. There is also evidence that rates of income tax collection are higher in countries with greater inequality, even after the effects of differences in income per capita and voter turnout are isolated (Lora, 2006). However, collection rates in the region are very low by world standards and increased very little with democratization, possibly because of the influence of high-income groups on the design and application of tax rules. As is very well summarized by Richard Bird (2003: 41), a recognized expert on Latin American tax systems, the rich in Latin America have many ways to avoid paying direct taxes: "First, they can block progressive legislation; they can introduce incentives and exceptions to dilute its effects (always with the argument of 'national interest'); they can corrupt the tax administration or use their resources to tone down or delay its applications in legal ways; or they can escape with their funds from the jurisdiction." Also, as will be discussed later in this chapter, financial globalization has weakened the treasury's capacity to tax internationally mobile capital, and trade globalization has eroded taxes based on international trade. Governments have been forced to shift to higher indirect taxes, particularly value-added taxes (VATs), which is not an expected consequence of democratization.

Regarding public expenditure, democratization seems to have had a deeper effect, consistent with raising the share of social spending in total expenditure. At the world level, democratization processes have led, with a lag of some years, to an increase in social spending of 3 percent of GDP (Baqir, 2002). This phenomenon has also occurred in Latin America. Average public social spending in the region, as a percentage of GDP, grew around three percentage points between 1990 and 2003, from 9.6 percent to 12.8 percent, and real levels per capita increased substantially. In the early 1990s, the countries of the region allocated an average of US$314 per person (in constant 2000 dollars)[18] for items of public social spending. Thirteen years later, average spending per capita was 45 percent higher: US$457 per capita (ECLAC, 2006a).

---

[18] Education and health expenditures only. Social security public expenditure also increased, as will be discussed later in the chapter.

However, the influence of democratization on the distribution of the benefits of this social spending is less clear.[19] In Chile, where social spending is currently very progressive, democratization has been a decisive factor (see Box 4.2). However, in the rest of Latin America, there is no evidence that democratization or later political reforms have altered the distributive patterns of social spending, which tend to be approximately equal by income level.

With stabilization, the monetary sources of financing enjoyed by Latin American treasuries were closed, reducing the discretionary power of central banks (and through them central governments) to allocate resources, as shown earlier, but also imposing discipline on spending demands by legislatures. Adoption of fiscal responsibility laws in several countries,[20] which put caps on expenditure, the fiscal deficit, or both, also strengthened fiscal discipline.

When the sources of monetary financing disappeared, alternative ways to cover expenditure had to be found. Financial globalization, which accelerated with the Brady Plan in 1989 (conversion of long-term government debt instruments after the crisis of the 1980s), opened the possibility of external financing of fiscal deficits, at least temporarily. At the same time, financial globalization limited the possibilities of taxing capital income because of increased capital mobility and the need to compete for foreign direct investment. Consequently, the position of large national and international owners of capital was strengthened against other sectors in taxation decisions. For its part, trade globalization imposed very narrow limits on taxes on international trade, which in many countries were an important source of fiscal revenue. To compensate for these adverse trends and respond to growing pressure

> ## Box 4.2 The Chilean Fiscal Pact
>
> The return of democracy to Chile in 1990 brought with it an important reform of the tax system and targeting of public social spending. Unlike most tax reforms in Latin America, which are designed to increase receipts, the Chilean tax reform in the early 1990s was another mechanism for expanding social spending on the country's poorest population. In the end, it was one of the main campaign promises that brought the Concertación to power.
>
> After negotiations with the Concertación's opposition, it was agreed that income tax rates would be raised from 10 percent to 15 percent and the general VAT rate from 16 percent to 18 percent and that a commitment would be made to target new fiscal resources at the lowest income quintiles of the population. The main consequences of the implementation of these reforms are shown in Table 4.2 and Figure 4.4: Chile has the most progressive public social spending in Latin America and has a low level of tax expenditure, at least regarding indirect taxes.
>
> *Source:* Based on Lora (2006).

---

[19] Except in the case of conditional cash transfer programs such as Oportunidades in Mexico, as discussed later in the chapter.

[20] Argentina (1999), Brazil (2000), Peru (2000 and 2003), Panama (2002), Ecuador (2002), Colombia (2003), and Venezuela (2003). In Guatemala a fiscal pact was signed in 2000 that sets numerical targets but is not legally binding.

for spending generated by democratization and other factors,[21] governments had to turn to other sources of tax revenue, particularly VATs, and maintain or increase taxes on and payroll contributions by formal workers. In some countries with relatively mature social security systems, such as Colombia, workers' contributions to the system were raised considerably to cover the large deficits that resulted from the need to pay generous pensions to growing numbers of pensioners whose contributions had been insufficient or badly managed.[22]

Who Pays Taxes and Who Does Not?

The changes in the tax structures in Latin America as a result of the forces of democratization, stabilization, and globalization primarily involved composition rather than size. On average, tax receipts (not including social security contributions) totaled 16.3 percent of GDP in 2003, practically unchanged since the mid-1980s (15.4 percent) despite numerous reforms. The tax burden in Latin America is 6.8 percentage points of GDP lower than world standards. Brazil and Argentina, with tax burdens of 21 percent and 18 percent, respectively, are the two countries with the highest receipts; Guatemala, Panama, and Paraguay, with burdens of approximately 10 percent of GDP, have the lowest tax burdens. The main shift in composition has been in favor of VATs. Whereas receipts from direct taxes in the region have averaged around 4 percent of GDP in the last two decades (and are 3.5 points below the world level), VAT receipts rose from 2.9 percent of GDP at the end of the 1980s to 5 percent in 2003, offsetting the decline in taxes on international trade and numerous minor taxes. Total indirect taxes collected in Latin America (7.9 percent of GDP) do not differ from the world average.

As a consequence of these changes in composition, Latin America's lower and middle classes now experience the impact of the tax burden more directly. In the past, the effect of taxes (and other forms of protection) on imports strongly affected the purchasing power of these segments in relation to consumer goods, but not directly as in the case of VATs. For this reason, and because of the widely held opinion that the VAT is by nature a regressive tax, the middle and lower classes in the region have begun to have a politically important weight in the tax debate which they did not have in the past. In response, congresses have generally preferred to exclude the main items in popular consumption baskets from the VAT base or to tax them at lower rates. This is reflected in the high tax expenditure of indirect taxes in Colombia, Ecuador, Guatemala, and Mexico, where lost revenue resulting from VAT noncollection and specific tax exemptions exceeds 25 percent of potential tax collections (see Table 4.2). The resistance of the middle and lower classes to VATs has led to a constant search for other sources of tax revenue or to a cap on government spending. It may also have been an important factor in establishing spending programs targeted at the poor, for example, the conditional cash transfer programs,

---

[21] Demands on public spending tend to be higher in countries with higher levels of income per capita and to increase with the average age of the population. See IDB (1998a, chap. 8).
[22] Traditional (pay-as-you-go) social security systems are based on intergenerational transfers: current workers' contributions pay today's retirees' pensions. As the pay-as-you-go systems consolidated around Latin America, financial sustainability problems arose because of insufficient contributions during the early years of the systems.

		Direct taxes (income)			Indirect taxes (VAT and specific)		
		Receipts	Tax expenditure	Tax expenditure	Receipts	Tax expenditure	Tax expenditure
		Percentage of GDP	Percentage of GDP	Percentage of potential receipts	Percentage of GDP	Percentage of GDP	Percentage of potential receipts
	Year	(a)	(b)	(b / (a + b))	(a)	(b)	(b / (a + b))
Argentina	2005	4.3	0.7	14.7	7.7	1.9	19.4
Brazil	2004	5.4	1.0	15.0	9.6	0.4	4.4
Chile	2005	4.4	3.3	42.9	10.4	0.9	7.8
Colombia	1999	4.2	3.2	43.2	4.9	6.0	55.1
Ecuador	2000	3.0	2.3	43.4	6.1	2.6	29.9
Guatemala	2000	2.2	2.0	48.2	5.5	5.3	48.8
Mexico	2005	5.1	3.4	40.1	5.6	3.3	37.0
Peru	2003	3.8	0.9	18.5	7.3	1.7	18.4

Table 4.2 Tax Expenditures on Direct and Indirect Taxes

Sources: Cetrángolo and Gómez Sabaini (2006) and Lora (2007).

such as Oportunidades in Mexico and Bolsa Familia (Family Grant) in Brazil, that have been adopted in nine countries. What is perhaps even more important: the visibility of VATs may have created incentives for the lower and middle classes to increase their vigilance over the use of public funds and participate more actively in political life. As previously noted, in Latin America there are no pronounced biases in patterns of political participation by social class. There (as in the rest of the world), higher tax burdens tend to be associated with increased political participation.[23]

Those in the working classes with medium or high income from employment in the formal sector have also begun to perceive the fiscal and parafiscal burdens more directly. Through income withholding, wages are relatively easy to tax. This mechanism is applied to workers who earn above the taxable minimum, which on average in Latin America is 230 percent of income per capita. The formal working classes are also taxed with contributions to pension systems, which have increased in most countries. Based on averages from eleven countries, contributions to pension systems increased from 22.7 percent of

---

[23] After income level is controlled for, the correlation between tax receipts and voter turnout in a cross-section of seventeen Latin American countries is 0.547 (significant at the 5 percent level). This correlation is maintained when inequality (nonsignificant) and a fictitious variable for countries with compulsory voting (nonsignificant) are controlled for. With compulsory voting controlled for, the significance of voter turnout rises from 5 percent to 10 percent. (For developed economies, see Franzese, 2002.) This correlation reflects a relation of mutual causality (direct and indirect) between the two variables: societies with higher turnout are possibly societies whose citizens exercise more supervision over politicians' activities, which contributes to controlling corruption. When people have more confidence in their country's political system and consider public funds to be well used, they are more willing to pay taxes, which results in higher public expenditure and creates more incentives for electoral and political participation.

gross wages in the region before the reforms to 26.6 percent afterwards.[24] In addition to the parafiscal burden imposed by contributions to pension systems, in some countries other payroll taxes are imposed to fund transfers to training institutes and other social service programs. The case of Colombia, where the total parafiscal burden is more than 50 percent of wages, is exceptional among countries of the region (see Bernal and Cárdenas, 2003).

However, as discussed in Chapter 5, growing fiscal and parafiscal burdens on wages have contributed to the informalization of employment in the region. Informal workers are by definition excluded from fiscal policy with respect to tax and social security benefits. In fact, only 27 percent of the Latin American labor force is affiliated with social security systems, and only one-quarter of those over age 65 receive pensions. Since rates of social security membership are higher in the higher income groups, expenditure on pensions is the most regressive of all types of social spending. The most extreme case is again Colombia, where 80 percent of pensions are paid to the richest quintile of the population. The most equal pension spending among the countries of the region is in Costa Rica, which has an effective system of family-wide social security membership with broad coverage.[25]

The coverage patterns in Latin America show two different social inequality mechanisms that complement one another. The first one is social security benefits concentrated among the richest. This goes hand in hand with the exclusion of poor people from both contributions and benefits of the social security system. The second is generational segmentation of the population, in which older generations create tax pressures on younger ones and there is no guarantee that younger generations will receive the same social security benefits as the previous ones have.[26] Both exclusion processes are illustrated in the inconclusive fiscal comedy depicted in Box 4.3.

There has been little success in incorporating owners of capital into payment of taxes, as a result of globalization and the influence that companies and high-income individuals have on decision making and implementation of tax policy. The Economic Commission for Latin America and the Caribbean (ECLAC) estimates that foregone tax revenues (tax expenditures) due to exemptions from direct taxes represent more than 40 percent of potential receipts in Chile, Colombia, Ecuador, Guatemala, and Mexico (see Table 4.2).[27] The sectors that benefit most from these exemptions are usually those with high percentages of exporters, especially in the maquiladora sectors, and companies with foreign investment. However, a wide range of sectors enjoy exemptions, depending on the country.[28] Moreover, most studies conclude that tax breaks and exemptions play

---

[24] The eleven countries are Argentina, Bolivia, Chile, Colombia, Costa Rica, Dominican Republic, El Salvador, Mexico, Nicaragua, Peru, and Uruguay. Average based on authors' calculations using information from Gill, Packard, and Yermo (2005).

[25] The regressivity of expenditure on social security is not a universal pattern. In developed countries, participation rates are very flat by income level and fiscal transfers are progressive, especially where they are low in relation to the average income of the population (Australia, Canada, United States, Norway, and Switzerland). See Mueller (2003).

[26] For a more detailed analysis of social security systems in Latin America, see Mesa-Lago and Márquez (2007).

[27] Again, note that in some cases the calculations also include exemptions from payroll taxes.

[28] See the lists of sectors benefiting from tax breaks in IDB (2001a, chap. 17), Cetrángolo and Gómez Sabaini (2006), and Hernández et al. (2000). For a more detailed analysis of such breaks in Argentina, Brazil, and Chile, see Pessino and Fenochietto (2004).

a very modest role in corporate investment decisions and are not the best use of fiscal resources (see Cetrángolo and Gómez Sabaini, 2006; Hernández et al., 2000).

Who Benefits from Public Spending and Who Is Excluded?

It is not easy to determine who benefits from expenditure in areas such as security, environment, justice, or investment in infrastructure, because these services are nonexclusive public goods, in the sense that the benefit that some individuals receive does not exclude others from benefiting as well. In other cases, there may be exclusive benefits (for example, use of road infrastructure), however, there is no available information that relates spending to beneficiaries.

Most analyses of the impact of public expenditure concentrate on the social services of education, health, and social security and on some subsidies for utilities.[29] On public social spending, the most general conclusion that can be extracted is that it tends to be distributed more or less equally among income groups, which is to say that social spending is inadequately targeted to the lower classes. With the exception of Chile, where social spending is clearly progressive, total spending on education and health in Latin American countries reaches all large social groups equally (see Figure 4.4). In general, spending on primary education is progressive, but at other levels of education, expenditure tends to be concentrated on higher income groups because of the higher dropout rate in lower income groups. In health, distribution of spending differs greatly from one country to another: it is clearly progressive in Argentina, Chile, Costa Rica, El Salvador, and Honduras, approximately flat in Colombia and Uruguay, and strongly regressive in Bolivia. These distributive patterns were not very different a decade ago, which suggests that higher social spending has not been accompanied by increased participation in social services (IDB, 1998a).

Worse than the distribution of social spending on basic education or health in the region is that of spending on university education and subsidized utilities charges (IDB, 1998a, chap. 8), because consumption of these services is naturally concentrated in the middle and upper classes. But the fact that social spending and subsidies are not concentrated on the poor, or even that they benefit the middle and upper classes rather more than the lower classes (regressive distribution), does not necessarily mean that they aggravate disparities in income distribution. This happens only when the distribution of benefits is more concentrated than income distribution, as in the case of pension expenditure in some countries, for example, Colombia, where 80 percent of pensions benefit the richest quintile (see Figure 4.5).

Analyses of the impact of social spending assume that all benefits of such spending are received by users of social services. But this is not necessarily so. The beneficiaries of social spending, and public spending in general, are *also* teachers, doctors, nurses, and other public officials who receive wages, which are the most important component of social spending. Public sector payrolls are another case, like that of pensions in some coun-

---

[29] ECLAC (2006a, chap. 2) offers a recent compilation of the redistributive effects of social spending on the countries of Latin America. This publication compiles statistics and studies on distribution of spending on education, health, and social security by income quintile and country.

tries, in which expenditure tends to benefit the middle and upper classes substantially more, to the point of increasing income concentration in most Latin American countries.[30] This, of course, largely reflects the fact that public employees in the region have higher than average levels of education. However, for their levels of study, experience, and dedication to work, they are also better paid than their counterparts in the private sector. For example, Panizza (1999) found that in the mid-1990s, the average pay of public employees in eight Latin American countries[31] was 14 percent higher than that of their equivalents in the private sector. Jobs in public service in the region have other features that make them more attractive than other jobs, such as stability, attractive retirement conditions, and social benefits. Consequently, they offer an example of exclusion, because workers who are outside public service have very limited possibilities for access to these benefits. The few statistics available on jobs and pay suggest that public employment in the region may have become even more exclusive in recent decades. According to a study by the Bank's Dialogue on Transparency and Public Management, public employment in the region overall fell from 5.4 percent of the population in 1995 to slightly over 4 percent in 1999. However, the reductions in employment were not accompanied by a reduction in the value of the payroll: in most coun-

Figure 4.4

Distribution of Public Social Expenditure on Education and Health in Latin America, Various Years

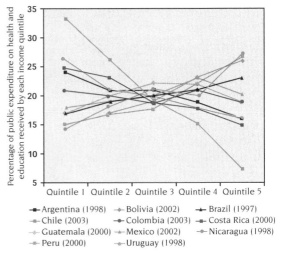

Source: ECLAC (2006a).

Figure 4.5

Distribution of Public Spending on Social Security (Pensions) in Latin America, Various Years

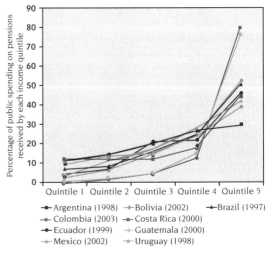

Source: ECLAC (2006a).

---

[30] More exactly, the quasi-Gini of spending on public employee pay in eleven of the region's countries averages 0.61, whereas the income distribution Gini in the same countries averages 0.51. See IDB (1998a, chap. 8).

[31] The eight countries are Colombia, Costa Rica, El Salvador, Honduras, Mexico, Panama, Paraguay, and Peru.

Box 4.3 Fiscal Exclusion: An Inconclusive Comedy in Five Acts

First Act. It is election day in a very unequal society. There is much popular rejoicing, although not all those who are on stage go to vote. At the end of the day, the party that proposed the heaviest taxes on the rich to finance higher social spending for the benefit of all has been elected.

Second Act. While the politicians are handing out beer to some campesinos in one corner of the stage, small groups of rich people are discussing how to arrange not to pay the new taxes: some decide that they will bribe tax officials; others that they will talk to the politicians to obtain an exemption because they are convinced that their companies are crucial for press freedom, generation of jobs, or exports; still others leave the stage, never to return.

Third Act. Public sector employees and workers in the largest companies realize what is happening and organize a demonstration to demand that the rich practice civic solidarity and the politicians keep their election promises. Scared, the politicians offer to set up a social security system with very low contributions in exchange for the promise of very generous pensions for all who want to join. The politicians explain to the demonstrators that until the day they retire, the money will be used to finance the promised general spending programs. The demonstrators are not at all convinced, but they leave the stage, some laughing, others threatening with sticks.

Fourth Act. Workers of all types are scattered around the stage. A team of tax collectors arrives on the right, demanding higher contributions from all who are close by. A few, mainly dressed as office workers, courteously give in to the demands, but others leave gradually by the left side of the stage.

Fifth Act. The group of workers who agreed to pay contributions has aged and are now accompanied by their grown-up children, who are dressed as office workers as their parents were before. Suddenly they begin to argue with the tax collectors and politicians who are at the back of the stage (their faces are not seen), demanding to be paid the pensions they were promised. The collectors try to explain that the only way to pay them would be to raise the taxes paid by themselves or their children, because almost all the other actors have disappeared from the scene without paying their taxes. The comedy is inconclusive, but those still on stage decide that a social pact would be the only reasonable way of bringing the others back on stage. Will they return? Will they reach an agreement? Will they find a way to put the agreement into practice?

---

tries expenditure on the public payroll actually increased after staff reduction measures (Echebarría and Cortázar, 2007).

In conclusion, fiscal policy in Latin America in the wake of the democratization, stabilization, and globalization processes has favored the inclusion of some groups, especially the lower classes, which have begun to participate in some of the benefits of spending and perceive tax burdens more directly. However, the richest families and owners of capital have maintained or strengthened their tax privileges, while the middle and upper working classes have increasingly split into an included group and another group that is excluded from both sides of the fiscal equation. These processes of fiscal exclusion and inclusion are a truly inconclusive social comedy (Box 4.3). How this comedy is resolved will depend on how Latin American societies solve their serious problems of fiscal exclusion.

Bad Jobs, Low Wages, and Exclusion

The last decade and a half has witnessed profound changes in Latin America's labor market. Growth in gross domestic product (GDP) per capita has been slower than in developed countries, deepening the divergence in income levels, and the labor force has continued growing at a relatively fast pace. Additionally, the changes brought about by democratization, economic stabilization, and globalization[1] have disrupted the traditional patterns of integration through public and formal employment without producing an alternative channel of social integration through the labor market. And even though unemployment surged to very large numbers in only five countries in the region during this time period, increasing informality and a slow rate of wage growth mean that most jobs being created are "bad" jobs that are precarious and low-paying.

A country's labor market plays a major role in social inclusion in that country. As labor represents the primary (if not only) source of income for the vast majority of the country's population, unemployment, bad jobs, or low wages mean material deprivation for workers and their families. Furthermore, employment in the formal sector is a condition for access to social insurance and social security, which link workers with the tax and social services systems, and the workplace provides a social space for participating in social and political organizations, including unions. Not having a job, or having only a precarious job, severs those links and makes the unemployed (or the precariously employed) and their families more vulnerable to the risks that the social security system aims to cover.

The trend toward increasing informality reduces the size of the group of workers who enjoy the protection of the local truncated version of the welfare state and generates new patterns of exclusion. Moreover, since their precarious jobs do not officially exist, these workers are vulnerable to exploitation and unsafe working conditions because they cannot present grievances or engage in union activities. The available evidence does not permit a determination of whether the problem is that employers prefer not to pay into public programs—or rather that workers themselves, pressed by budget constraints or other reasons, opt out of such programs. Regardless of the source, however, low participation is likely to result in poor access to medical care and low levels of coverage against old-age poverty, which, compounded with low wages, places workers in a difficult and vulnerable situation of exclusion.

Currently existing labor market institutions and regulations are often forces of exclusion. Social security taxes that are excessively high, inducing evasion and informality,

---

[1] For further discussion of these issues, please see Chapter 4.

and rules regarding hiring and firing that are too rigid and create incentives for formal employers to reduce their hiring are, among others, forces of exclusion in the labor market. But the increase in the share of low-wage jobs and the growth of informality create not a more adaptable, better-functioning labor market, but rather one that is hostile to productivity and income growth and increases the vulnerability and exclusion of a growing fraction of workers. Precarious jobs are also characterized by very low productivity and correspondingly low wages, often condemning workers and their families to poverty. Low wages and poverty are different phenomena, but they largely affect similar groups (two-thirds of low-wage workers live in poor households) and move along a common path (the evolution of poverty headcounts is largely determined by the performance of the labor market).

Although the issue of bad jobs has attracted a great deal of attention, most of the research in this area has concentrated on workers whose per capita family income falls below the poverty line. Such an approach, however, fails to distinguish between workers in low-wage jobs and workers in households with low participation rates (i.e., few members in the labor force). This chapter attempts to identify bad jobs through objective and measurable criteria that relate earnings to productivity, independent of family size, as well as to address the relationship between bad jobs and social exclusion.

The risk of holding a bad job is much more widespread today in Latin America and the Caribbean than at the beginning of the 1990s, as shown by the reduced difference in the incidence of low-wage jobs between the mainstream and those population groups traditionally considered vulnerable, such as women, youth, and low-skilled workers. Although the gulf between high- and low-wage jobs is expanding, the difference between the holders of good and bad jobs, in terms of human capital and related characteristics, is narrowing. Furthermore, workers in low-wage jobs are more likely than others to drop out of the labor force, and they have a higher risk of unemployment. Their ability to enjoy all the benefits of the society in which they live and to contribute to that society are thus seriously diminished.

Combating exclusion requires more than a description of the workers who suffer from it in the labor market. The recent increase in the number and incidence of bad jobs occurred while the region's economies were in a period of dramatic transformation. Conventional wisdom dictates that tight fiscal and monetary policies, along with privatization and trade liberalization, are the main culprits in the disappointing performance of the region's labor market. A careful consideration of the available evidence shows that the factors behind the increase in the incidence of bad jobs are more complex. Rising unemployment, mediocre levels of growth, and increasing demand among employers for workers with higher levels of education are the most important drivers of bad jobs, dwarfing the impact of other phenomena like changes in the structure of employment and increasing female participation.

WHAT IS A BAD JOB?

Discussion of the concept of "decent work," led by the International Labour Organization (ILO), has called into question the notion that a job—any job—is a solution to poverty. The ILO-sponsored World Commission on the Social Dimension of Globalization (ILO,

2004) stated that poverty in the developing world is associated not with lack of employment, but rather with the low productivity of existing jobs, and that such low productivity explains a slowing rate of poverty reduction in the 1990s.

There are two main approaches to defining bad jobs (see Márquez and Prada, 2007, and references therein). The first approach, job-based definitions, focuses on jobs with characteristics that lead to working poverty and sluggish wage growth. The second and more common approach, worker-based definitions, emphasizes the characteristics of workers (or potential workers) themselves, including gender, educational levels, and household poverty status.

It is important to remember that not all of the working poor hold low-wage jobs. For instance, a worker in a high-productivity, high-paying job might still be considered working poor if he or she has to support several other members of a household. Identifying low-productivity jobs thus requires measuring productivity independent of family size and structure. The concept of "bad jobs" used here assumes that wages generally reflect productivity; the hourly wage therefore serves as an indicator of productivity.[2] The threshold for defining "working poor" is the wage that would allow a worker in a family of average size and participation rates to earn a per capita family income above the moderate poverty standard of US$2 per day (Duryea and Pagés, 2003).[3]

As shown in Figure 5.1, although workers in low-wage jobs account for almost a quarter of the region's labor force, almost half of those workers do not live in poor households. Households in which workers have few dependents and/or in which most if not all household members work allow families to escape from or remain out of poverty in spite of having low-wage jobs. Nonetheless, almost two-thirds of the poor work in low-wage jobs that do not allow them to keep or lift their families out of poverty.

Figure 5.1

Poor Workers and Low-Wage Workers: Average, Latin America, 1998–2004

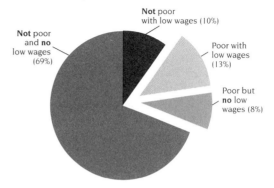

Source: Márquez and Prada (2007).
Note: Statistics represent percentage of the labor force between ages 15 and 64 that is employed and reflect the simple average for the period 1998–2004 for the following sixteen countries: Argentina, Bolivia, Brazil, Chile, Colombia, Costa Rica, Ecuador, El Salvador, Honduras, Mexico, Nicaragua, Panama, Paraguay, Peru, Uruguay, and Venezuela.

---

[2] See Mincer (1974) and Corcoran and Duncan (1979) for a more extensive discussion. While labor markets generally do not function free of imperfections such as discrimination and segmentation, empirical evidence generally supports a positive relationship between productivity and wages. For example, Lazear (1996) finds that when output per worker rises, half the productivity increase is passed on to workers in the form of higher wages.
[3] A thorough description of the methodology is presented in Márquez and Prada (2007).

Trends

Figure 5.2 displays the evolution of the incidence of low-wage employment in fifteen countries of the region. With the exception of Chile (since 1990), Costa Rica (since 1991), El Salvador (since 1996), Mexico (since 1996), and Brazil (since 1999), the share of workers in low-wage jobs increased throughout the region during the years covered in the figure. The rise was particularly notable in Argentina, which showed an increase from a negligible share in 1992 to 8 percent in 2003. The proportion of low-wage workers also increased substantially in Uruguay after 2000, in Colombia after 1994, in Paraguay after 2000, and in Venezuela after 1998, and particularly after 2001. Trends were less pronounced in Honduras, where the share declined until 1998 and increased afterwards; in Bolivia, where it increased until 2000 and stabilized until 2002; and in Nicaragua, where the three observations available suggest an increase from 1993 until 1998 and a decline from 1998 to 2001.

Figure 5.2 also illustrates that *there is a very high correlation between the incidence of low-wage employment and national poverty headcount estimates.* This correlation is equal to or above 0.9 in four countries and 0.7 or higher in eight out of ten countries for which national poverty data are available. An important implication of this finding is that in most countries, *the evolution of poverty headcounts is largely determined by the performance of the labor market, and in particular by the evolution of earnings.* Factors such as income transfers to poor households, changes in participation patterns, and changes in household formation are less important influences on poverty. An important exception is Brazil, where a decline in low-wage employment between 2002 and 2003 coincided with a large increase in poverty.

WHO HAS LOW-WAGE JOBS?

There is a broad consensus on the main characteristics of workers in low-wage jobs. Studies in the United States and in Europe find that workers in low-wage jobs are disproportionately female, young, and without a college education.[4] A similar situation prevails in Latin America.

Márquez and Prada (2007) analyzed the changes in the pattern of incidence of low-wage jobs for different population groups in Latin America, comparing the early 1990s and the period after 1997, including the first years of this century.[5] They found that female workers, in all countries and in both periods analyzed, were more likely to hold low-wage jobs compared to their male counterparts and were thus overrepresented among workers in low-wage jobs. Women, for example, accounted for nearly 45 percent of all workers in bad jobs, even though they constituted only 36 percent of all workers in the sixteen countries for which data are available for the early 1990s. Women remained overrepresented

---

[4] Examples for the United States include Bernstein and Hartmann (2000), Carnevale and Rose (2001), Mishel, Bernstein, and Schmitt (2001), Mitnik, Zeidenberg, and Dresser (2002), and Schochet and Rangarajan (2004). Duryea and Pagés (2003) and Duryea et al. (2006) review Latin American cases. Salverda et al. (2001), Marx and Salverda (2005), and Blázquez Cuesta and Salverda (2006) discuss European countries' experiences.

[5] Márquez and Prada's study is based on an unbalanced panel for sixteen of the region's countries for the period 1990–2004: Argentina, Bolivia, Brazil, Chile, Colombia, Costa Rica, Ecuador, El Salvador, Honduras, Mexico, Nicaragua, Panama, Paraguay, Peru, Uruguay, and Venezuela.

in the low-wage workforce in the late 1990s and the first years of this century, even when the increase in female participation in the labor force between the two time periods is taken into account.

Although there was a higher incidence of low-wage jobs among women in all countries in both periods, in the second period the gap between men and women shrank in ten of the sixteen countries for which data exist. The gender difference increased only in Mexico and El Salvador, remaining largely unchanged in Chile, Costa Rica, and Peru.

Across countries and periods, young workers (aged 15–24) were found to be more likely to hold low-wage jobs than either prime-age adults (aged 25–49) or, with a few exceptions, older workers (aged 50–64). Such a difference is typical and arises because workers' productivity and hence their wages increase over time as they accumulate human capital and experience (Borgarello et al., 2006; IDB, 2003a). In the early 1990s, young workers represented nearly one-third of the total employed in low-wage jobs, even though they accounted for only 22 percent of the labor force. Younger workers remained overrepresented among low-wage workers in the late 1990s and the first years of this century, though their share in both the low-productivity and total labor forces decreased. These changes reduced the difference in the incidence of low wages between youth and the rest of the population in most countries of the region, with the exceptions of Argentina and Chile.

Not surprisingly, in every country in both periods, the incidence of low-wage jobs was found to decrease as education levels increase. Nonetheless, the results show that the gap between skilled and unskilled workers is closing in most countries of the region.[6] This change, however, is generally not beneficial, as it is the result of an increase in the share of skilled workers in low-wage jobs rather than the share of unskilled workers in higher-paying jobs. Márquez and Prada (2007) found that after each group's participation in the labor force is controlled for, workers with lower educational levels are more likely to hold low-wage jobs than the rest of the labor force. However, they also report that the likelihood of having a low-wage job increased for workers of all educational levels between the two periods studied, with only isolated exceptions.

When area of residence is considered, Márquez and Prada (2007) found the expected concentration of low-wage jobs in rural areas compared with urban areas. This can be explained by the structural differences in the two labor markets and the relative importance of nonmonetary labor income in rural areas, a factor not considered in Márquez and Prada's (2007) analysis. The gap in incidence between rural and urban areas is closing in most countries, according to Márquez and Prada's findings, but widening in Chile, Honduras, and Bolivia. The evolution of this gap in some countries, such as Colombia and Nicaragua, is highly affected by migration from rural to urban areas.

---

[6] Unskilled workers are those with no education, those who have not completed primary education, and those who have completed primary but not secondary education; as a consequence, skilled workers are those who have completed secondary education and some tertiary. The mapping of specific grades into schooling levels varies across countries as well as across time within a particular country. The categorization of education groups used in this chapter applies the same definition across time for each country. For most countries, primary and secondary school are classified according to the "older" systems, since these are applicable to the cohorts analyzed. More details can be found in the appendix of IDB (2003a) and Sociometro's documentation at http://www.iadb.org/sociometro.

Figure 5.2
Evolution of the Incidence of Low-Wage Employment and Headcount Poverty

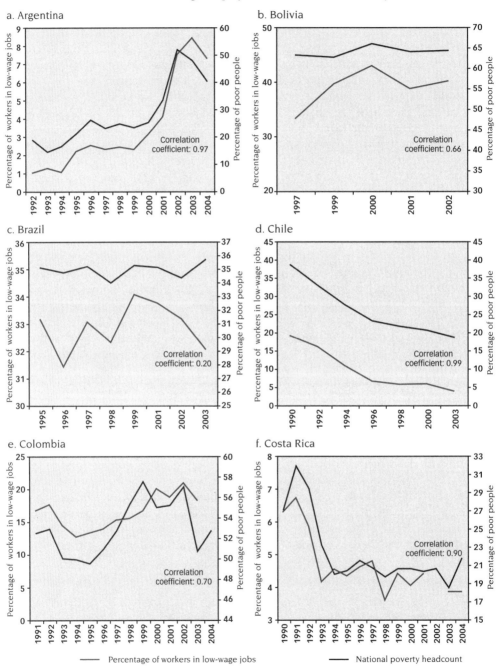

a. Argentina

b. Bolivia

c. Brazil

d. Chile

e. Colombia

f. Costa Rica

——— Percentage of workers in low-wage jobs

——— National poverty headcount

(continued)

Figure 5.2 (continued)
Evolution of the Incidence of Low-Wage Employment and Headcount Poverty

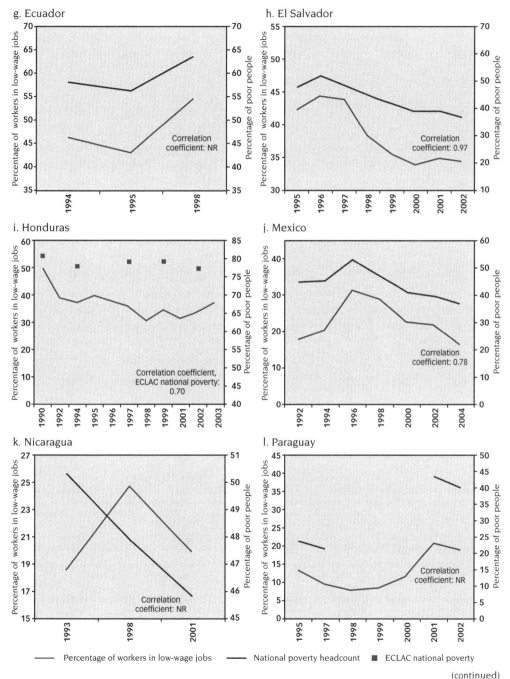

——— Percentage of workers in low-wage jobs   ——— National poverty headcount   ■ ECLAC national poverty

(continued)

Figure 5.2 (continued)
Evolution of the Incidence of Low-Wage Employment and Headcount Poverty

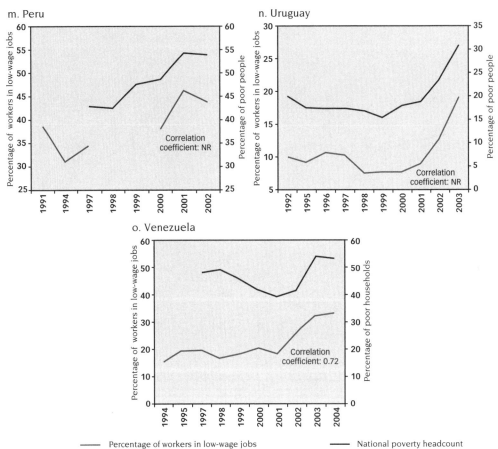

m. Peru

n. Uruguay

o. Venezuela

——— Percentage of workers in low-wage jobs ——— National poverty headcount

Sources for national poverty estimates: Argentina, Bolivia, Brazil, El Salvador, Nicaragua, Peru, and Uruguay: National Institutes of Statistics. *Ecuador, Honduras, and Mexico*: Economic Commission for Latin America and the Caribbean (ECLAC), *Social Panorama*, 2005. Additional sources (by country): *Bolivia*: Centro de Estudios Distributivos Laborales y Sociales (CEDLAS). *Chile*: Ministerio de Planificación y Cooperación (MIDEPLAN). *Colombia*: Departamento Nacional de Planeación (DNP). *Costa Rica*: Estado Nación. *Honduras*: Pan American Health Organization (PAHO). *Paraguay*: Urban data from Secretaría Técnica de Planificación del Desarrollo (STP-DGEEC). *Venezuela*: Fundación Escuela de Gerencia Social (FEGS).

Note: For all countries except Venezuela, national poverty estimates measure the percentage of people living in households with a standard of living beneath national poverty lines; for Venezuela, the estimates correspond to the percentage of poor (by national poverty standards) households. In the case of Honduras (panel i), ECLAC national poverty estimates, which measure the percentage of people living on less than the equivalent of US$1 per day, are used instead of national poverty data, for which only a small number of observations are available. Where years are missing from a particular panel, no data are available for that country for those years. NR = not reported.

In summary, workers in low-productivity jobs in Latin America are disproportionately female, young, rural, and without a college education—groups traditionally considered vulnerable.[7] Nonetheless, the difference in incidence of low-wage employment by gender, age, education, and geographic area is closing, because workers in other groups are becoming more vulnerable as well. Taken together, these two findings suggest that the incidence of low-productivity jobs is increasing and that low-productivity jobs are becoming a general phenomenon extending well beyond groups traditionally considered vulnerable (women, youth, unskilled workers).

CHARACTERISTICS OF LOW-WAGE JOBS

Individual earnings depend not only on workers' traits, but also on the characteristics of the firms that employ them. For example, Hachen (1992) and Haveman and Cohen (1994) find that firms with different characteristics vary their wage policies according to firm size, business strategies, production methods, and different sets of regulatory systems, among other characteristics.

Whether one is an employee, an employer, or a self-employed person influences one's chances of being in a low-wage job. Márquez and Prada (2007) find that in their sample of countries, the share of low-wage jobs held by formal employees and employers is smaller than these groups' share in total employment. Therefore, these groups have the lowest relative risk of being in a low-wage job.

The risk of having a low-wage job is higher for informal wage earners in Latin America, even though the evolution of this risk has been mixed, decreasing in some countries while increasing in others. The region's self-employed are more likely than other workers to have low-wage jobs, a tendency that increased between 1997 and 2004.

Salaried employees in low-wage jobs generally lack social security in the form of employment-based pension system affiliation or medical insurance. Between 1997 and 2004, 81 percent of workers holding low-productivity jobs did not participate in employment-based social security (Márquez and Prada, 2007). Again, even if some of these workers have chosen not to participate, their low wages compound their difficulties in planning for retirement and insuring themselves and their families against disability, illness, and death.

In most countries of the region, the share of low-wage jobs among informal wage earners increased in 1997–2004 relative to the early 1990s. This percentage increased in the later period even in Costa Rica and Chile, the countries with the lowest percentage of informal workers in low-wage jobs in the earlier period.

In those Latin American countries where the incidence of low-productivity jobs among all workers decreased between the two periods (Chile, Costa Rica, Mexico, and El Salvador), it also fell for workers without access to social security. In Brazil, Nicaragua, and Peru, the incidence of low-productivity jobs decreased from the earlier to the later period only for formal workers. The difference between the likelihood of being in a low-

---

[7] Research on other regions, including the United States and Europe, suggests that the characteristics of vulnerable groups such as low-wage workers, the working poor, and low-skilled workers are largely the same around the world.

Figure 5.3
Percentage of Low-Wage Jobs by Sector, National, 1998–2004

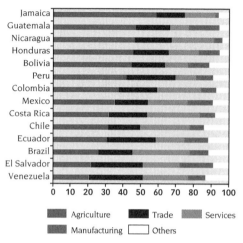

Source: Márquez and Prada (2007).
Note: "Agriculture" includes agriculture, hunting, mining, and fishing; "Trade" includes wholesale and retail trade, restaurants, and hotels; "Services" includes community, social, and personal services; "Others" includes construction, transport, storage, and communication, electricity, gas, water, financial services, real estate, and business services.

Figure 5.4
Percentage of Low-Wage Jobs by Sector, Urban, 1998–2004

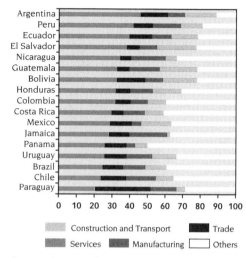

Source: Márquez and Prada (2007).
Note: "Services" includes community, social, and personal services; "Trade" includes wholesale and retail trade, restaurants, and hotels; "Construction and Transport" additionally includes storage; and "Others" includes agriculture, electricity, gas, water, financial services, real estate, and business services.

wage job for an informal and a formal wage earner increased between the two periods for every country except Venezuela, El Salvador, and Colombia (Márquez and Prada, 2007).

Low-wage jobs in Latin America are concentrated in a few industries. In the fourteen countries for which national data are available, low-wage jobs are concentrated principally in the agricultural sector (Figure 5.3), followed by retail trade and services (the last two in varying order across countries). The share of agriculture in low-wage jobs is larger than its share in total employment in all fourteen countries. Either services or retail trade holds a distant second place, depending on the country. As the link with agriculture suggests, low-wage jobs are likewise concentrated in rural areas, which are themselves disproportionately affected by social exclusion.

This panorama changes when the analysis is limited to urban areas (Figure 5.4), which makes it possible to consider more countries (because of greater data availability), as well as to control for the structure of employment in urban areas.[8] Since agriculture provides few jobs in urban areas, services and trade instead represent the majority of low-wage jobs there.

---

[8] Venezuela is the only country in Márquez and Prada's study for which urban data are unavailable.

That said, even though agriculture accounts for less than 15 percent of low-wage jobs in urban areas, in the urban areas of almost every country in Márquez and Prada's study, agricultural workers are still more likely than other urban workers to hold low-productivity jobs. Urban workers in retail trade have become more likely to hold low-wage jobs in every country studied but Mexico. In contrast, employees working in personal and community services are less prone to have a low-wage job than the average worker in the same country. Thus, the high concentration of low-wage jobs in services is driven by the increase in employment in the sector, rather than by a particular increase in the incidence of low-wage jobs in service activities.

Márquez and Prada (2007) also report that low-wage workers in Latin America work on average 4.4 more hours per week than others, though that gap varies considerably from country to country. Within these groups, approximately 10 percent of all employees and nearly 8 percent of workers in low-productivity jobs work less than thirty hours per week. Although in all countries, the majority of the labor force works more than forty-eight hours per week, workers in low-productivity jobs are less likely to hold a full-time job. This suggests that a significant and perhaps growing portion of the region's labor force holds two or more bad jobs rather than one good job.

In summary, in the countries of Latin America, low-wage jobs are mostly held by informal wage earners and the self-employed. Most of these jobs do not provide access to social security and the associated mechanisms of social insurance. The sector with the highest concentration of low-wage jobs in the region is agriculture, and the incidence of low-wage jobs in rural areas is much higher than in urban areas. In urban areas, though agriculture is still the sector with the highest incidence of low-wage jobs, most low-wage jobs are concentrated in personal services and trade.

THE DYNAMICS OF LOW-WAGE JOBS

The welfare consequences of holding a low-wage job vary according to the pattern of mobility in and out of bad jobs in the economy.[9] Workers in low-wage jobs tend to have a weaker attachment to their present job than their high-wage counterparts; however, transitions out of bad jobs generally do not lead to better jobs, but rather to unemployment or dropping out of the labor force.[10] As a consequence, workers in low-wage jobs have intermittent working lives, with periods of nonemployment between jobs.

As shown by data from Argentina, Mexico, and Venezuela, workers in high- and low-wage jobs differ in two particular ways in their transitions between employment and nonemployment and between employment/wage states within each occupational cat-

---

[9] For a more general and comparative description of the patterns of mobility in Latin American labor markets, see Duryea et al. (2006).

[10] In discussions of economic and labor issues, it is often useful (as here) to make a distinction between "unemployed" (which describes someone who currently lacks a job but is in the market for one) and "out of the labor force" (which means that one not only lacks a job, but is not seeking one). Throughout the chapter, "unemployed," "unemployment," and related terms should be taken to refer to this more limited, formal economic definition. The term "nonemployment" encompasses both of these states.

Figure 5.5
Persistence in High- and Low-Wage States by Country and Occupational Category, Early 1990s versus 2000s

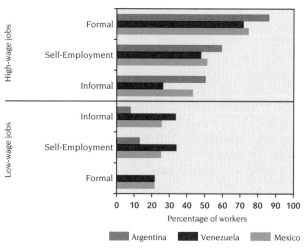

Source: Márquez and Prada (2007).
Note: The number of observations for Argentina in the "Low-wage jobs, Formal" category is too small to permit a valid estimate.

Figure 5.6
Mobility from Low- and High-Wage Jobs to Nonemployment, Early 1990s versus 2000s

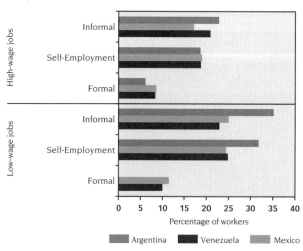

Source: Márquez and Prada (2007).
Note: The number of observations for Argentina in the "Low-wage jobs, Formal" category is too small to permit a valid estimate.

egory (formal and informal wage earner and self-employed) and wage level (high- and low-wage jobs).[11] First, the percentage of workers in low-wage jobs who move to other employment/wage states in each period is higher than the percentage of their high-wage counterparts who move to another state (Figure 5.5).

A second difference is that for a large fraction of workers in low-wage jobs, these movements are towards nonemployment status (unemployment or exiting from the labor force) (Figure 5.6). Workers in low-wage jobs show a much lower attachment to the labor force than their high-wage counterparts. In other words, workers in low-wage jobs (with the exception of those in formal salaried jobs) are more likely to move to nonemployment (exiting the labor force or unemployment) than workers in high-wage jobs. Furthermore, between the two nonemployment options, the more likely course for workers in low-wage jobs is dropping out of the labor force altogether rather than becoming unemployed. In contrast, workers in formal low-productivity jobs are much less likely to drop out of the labor force than informal workers, behavior more in line with their high-wage counter-

---

[11] See Duryea et al. (2006) for data description.

parts. Regarding the pattern of transitions between employment/productivity states, the data show that workers in low-wage jobs who do not drop out of the labor force tend to move between high- and low-wage employment within the same occupational status, as opposed to moving to another occupational status.

This pattern of transitions suggests that most low-wage informal employees and self-employed who leave low-wage jobs in the informal sector do not move to a high-productivity informal job but instead either drop out of the labor force or become unemployed. This confirms observations regarding the weaker labor force attachment of workers in low-productivity jobs.

The relationships between transitions and workers' characteristics are for the most part unsurprising. Although low-productivity workers' transitions are generally not affected in a substantial way by age—a possibly unexpected result—women's attachment to the labor force is overall lower than men's. Regardless of skill level, workers in low-productivity jobs display weaker labor force attachment than other workers (Márquez and Prada, 2007).

The picture that emerges from these transitions is troubling. Workers in low-productivity jobs, who are often already subject to other dimensions of social exclusion, have unstable work lives and often drop out of the workforce altogether. Although it can be argued that this pattern may be the result of individual preferences, it is likely that many workers are trapped in a life of bad jobs, poor employment opportunities, low and unstable earnings, and no social protection.

WHAT EXPLAINS THE EVOLUTION OF LOW-WAGE EMPLOYMENT?

The increase in low-wage work in Latin America has occurred during a period of wide economic fluctuations and profound structural transformations worldwide. Although the early 1990s were years of relatively high growth, subsequent financial crises (the Tequila crisis in Mexico, as well as crises in Russia, East Asia, Brazil, and Argentina) brought growth to a halt throughout the region. In almost all Latin American countries, economic performance in the late 1990s was at best mediocre, and the economies of some countries, such as Argentina, contracted greatly in the early years of the twenty-first century. Such deep economic fluctuations might explain an upward trend in low-wage employment. It is therefore important to assess whether such wide fluctuations in economic activity actually do account for the increase in low-wage work in Latin America between the early 1990s and the late 1990s/early years of this century.

In addition to being a time of economic turbulence, the 1990s were also years of rapid international trade liberalization. Most countries in the region reduced tariffs considerably, both for intermediate and final goods. The simultaneity of this process with the increase in low-wage and informal employment raises the question of whether increasing international trade is affecting the quality of jobs in the region. Another potential candidate for explaining the increase in low-wage work in the region is the well-documented decline in demand for unskilled labor in both developed and developing economies (see, for example, de Ferranti et al., 2004, and IDB, 2003a).

Two other important transformations may also account for the increase in low-wage work in Latin America. The first is the shrinking ranks of workers in manufacturing jobs and the growing ranks of workers in the service sector. As wages in rapidly expanding sectors, such as retail and wholesale trade or personal and community services, are quite low, the growth of these sectors could account for the region's growth in low-wage employment. The second transformation is the rapidly growing participation of women in the region's labor force. As female workers tend to receive lower wages relative to males, and an important fraction of low-wage employment is occupied by women, rapidly expanding female participation could also account for the region's increase in low-pay work.

The coincidence in time of a large number of factors that can, in principle, be associated with the rising incidence of low-wage work means that it is necessary to determine which of those factors, if any, have been more important than the others.

Economic Fluctuations

The rise in the share of low-wage employment that occurred in the middle and at the end of the 1990s in a number of Latin American countries coincided with a sharp deceleration of economic activity. This is particularly evident in Argentina and Uruguay during the financial crisis of 2001–2002, in Colombia during the period of growth deceleration after 1994, in Mexico during the Tequila crisis (1995), in Panama in 2000, and in Venezuela during 2001–2003 (Figure 5.7). Economic theory would predict an association between economic fluctuations and low-wage employment. Assuming that the supply of labor is fixed, or that it responds positively to higher wages, greater economic growth results in higher demand for low-wage workers and a rise in wages, which in turn can imply a reduction in low-wage employment. Note, however, that if unemployment or underemployment is high, a higher demand for labor may have little effect on wages, as firms can find extra workers without having to raise wages. The link between economic growth and growth in low-wage employment will also be less important if growth is not associated with a higher demand for the goods produced by low-wage workers.

Figure 5.7 shows that the correlation between the incidence of low-wage employment and economic growth is low in most countries. Not all the spikes in low-wage employment in the figure correspond to periods of deceleration in growth, nor does low-wage employment fall quickly when economic activity picks up.

Another indication that economic fluctuations cannot account for the bulk of the growth in low-wage employment emerges from a comparison of the incidence of the latter phenomenon across two years of similar economic performance. The results reported in Table 5.1 indicate that in most countries, the share of low-wage work increases even when data across years of similar economic growth are compared. Thus, the change in the proportion of low-wage employment is very similar whether one compares the average incidence in the period 1990–1997 against the average in the period 1998–2004 or the change in incidence across years of similar growth in each period. The only exception is Brazil, where the original data show a 2 percent increase between the two periods, whereas the cyclically comparable figures show a 1 percent decline.

These findings suggest that the increase in low-wage employment has causes that go beyond fluctuations in economic activity. Although the economic deceleration of the late 1990s was associated with an increase in the incidence of low-wage employment, the incidence of this phenomenon did not decline once economic growth picked up, provid-

Figure 5.7
Evolution of Low-Wage Employment and GDP Growth

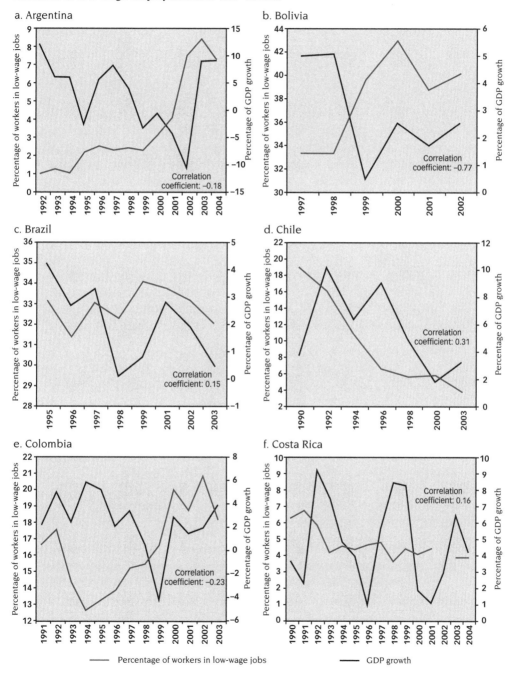

a. Argentina

b. Bolivia

c. Brazil

d. Chile

e. Colombia

f. Costa Rica

——— Percentage of workers in low-wage jobs   ——— GDP growth

Figure 5.7 (continued)
Evolution of Low-Wage Employment and GDP Growth

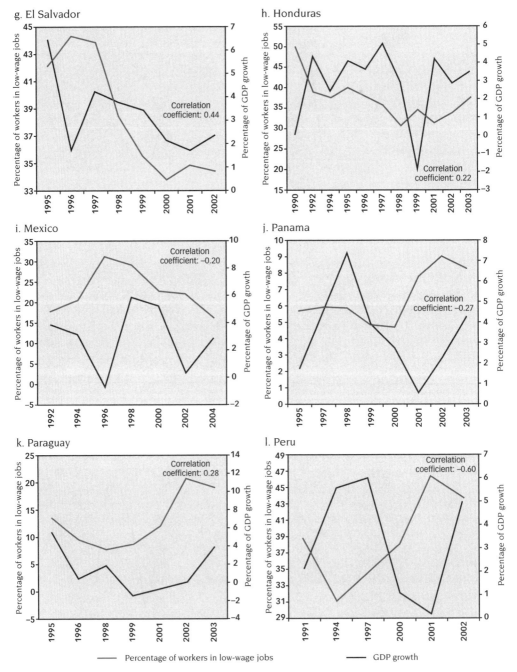

g. El Salvador

h. Honduras

i. Mexico

j. Panama

k. Paraguay

l. Peru

—— Percentage of workers in low-wage jobs　　　—— GDP growth

Figure 5.7 (continued)
Evolution of Low-Wage Employment and GDP Growth

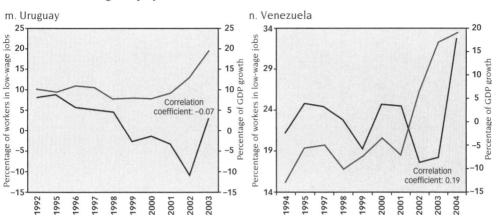

m. Uruguay   n. Venezuela

Correlation
coefficient: –0.07

Correlation
coefficient: 0.19

——— Percentage of workers in low-wage jobs   ——— GDP growth

Source: Pagés and Prada (2007).
Note: Figure displays real GDP growth between selected years (those years for which low-wage employment estimates are available). Where years are missing from a particular panel, no data are available for that country for those
years.

ing some clues to the seemingly structural nature of the increase. This is not to imply that
economic growth and economic fluctuations do not have *any* effect on low-wage work.
Pagés and Prada (2007) assess the average effect of economic growth and unemployment
on low-wage employment in Latin America.[12] According to their estimates, a 1 percent
reduction in GDP per worker leads to a 1.5 percentage point increase in the incidence of
low-wage employment.[13] Similarly, a 1 percentage point increase in the unemployment
rate is associated with a 3 percent increase in low-wage employment. To get a sense of the
economic relevance of the magnitudes of these percentages, it is useful to compute how
much of the (percentage) change in low-wage employment is accounted for by changes
in unemployment rates and changes in GDP per worker. The results of this exercise are
shown in Figure 5.8.[14] Although in a few countries, most notably Argentina and Colombia,
rising unemployment rates account for an important share of the increase in low-wage

[12] Pagés and Prada's study includes an unbalanced panel for fourteen of the region's countries for the period
1990–2000: Argentina, Bolivia, Brazil, Chile, Colombia, Ecuador, El Salvador, Honduras, Mexico, Panama, Peru,
Paraguay, Uruguay, and Venezuela. The data used for low-wage employment are those presented in Figure 5.7.
Data for unemployment are obtained from the Economic Commission for Latin America and the Caribbean; data
on GDP are from the Penn World Tables.
[13] These results are obtained by regressing the share of low-wage employment on a set of country fixed effects,
total unemployment rates, and GDP per worker. Very similar effects are found if, in addition to these variables,
time effects are also included as controls.
[14] Changes are computed for the first and the last year for which data on incidence of low-wage work, GDP per
worker, and unemployment rates are available. Although the dates change across countries, the data tend to start
in the early 1990s and finish in the year 2000.

Table 5.1 Percentage Change in the Incidence of Low-Wage Employment, Comparing Periods with Similar GDP Growth

Incidence of Low-Wage Employment — **Falling**

GDP Growth	Country	Percentage change in GDP growth rates 1990–97 vs.1998–2004	Percentage change in incidence of low-wage employment 1990–97 vs.1998–2004	Percentage change in incidence of low-wage employment Cyclically corrected	Selected years
Falling	Chile	−47	−61	−78	1990 vs. 2003
	Honduras	−39	−16	−2	1996 vs. 2003
	Mexico	−7	−3	−21	1994 vs. 2004
	El Salvador	−7	−19	−10	1996 vs. 2001
Rising	Costa Rica	9	−22	−39	1990 vs. 2004

Incidence of Low-Wage Employment — **Rising**

GDP Growth	Country	Percentage change in GDP growth rates 1990–97 vs.1998–2004	Percentage change in incidence of low-wage employment 1990–97 vs.1998–2004	Percentage change in incidence of low-wage employment Cyclically corrected	Selected years
Falling	Argentina	−95	195	221	1997 vs. 2004
	Brazil	−15	2	−1	1998 vs. 2003
	Colombia	−70	24	45	1993 vs. 2002
	Peru	−60	21	26	1997 vs. 2002
	Paraguay	−80	18	99	1996 vs. 2003
	Uruguay	−144	6	90	1995 vs. 2003
	Venezuela	−79	31	44	1999 vs. 2002
	Ecuador	−34	21	25	1995 vs. 1998
	Bolivia	−64	21	n.d.	n.d.
Rising	Panama	117	1	27	1995 vs. 2002

Source: Pagés and Prada (2007).
Note: n.d. = data not available.

Figure 5.8
Percentage Change in Share of Low-Wage Employment Accounted for by Changes in Unemployment Rates and in GDP per Worker, Early 1990s versus 2000s

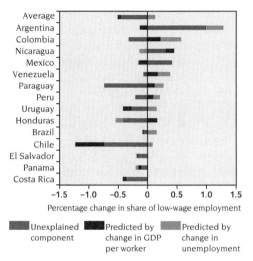

Percentage change in share of low-wage employment

| ■ Unexplained component | ■ Predicted by change in GDP per worker | ▨ Predicted by change in unemployment |

Source: Pagés and Prada (2007).

Figure 5.9
Relationship between Unemployment and Low-Wage Employment in Latin American Countries, 1999–2000

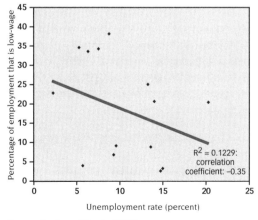

$R^2 = 0.1229$: correlation coefficient: −0.35

Source: Pagés and Prada (2007).

employment, in the rest of the region's countries, the effect of unemployment is small. Similarly, with the exception of Colombia and Chile, changes in GDP per worker account for either a negative or a small share of the increase in low-wage employment.

As in developed countries, there is a negative relationship between unemployment rates and the incidence of low-wage work within the sample of Latin American countries (Figure 5.9). Thus, although *in a given country* increases in unemployment are associated with higher incidences of low-wage work, countries with higher unemployment rates have lower incidences of low-wage employment compared to other countries. Most likely, countries with high unemployment are those whose institutional environment or labor policies reduce the incidence of low-wage work.

In sum, although economic fluctuations have an impact on low-wage employment, they cannot fully explain the large increases in the incidence of low-wage employment in the last decade in many countries of the region. The data also suggest a possible trade-off between lower unemployment and a higher incidence of low-wage jobs across countries.

Trade Liberalization

There is an ongoing debate over the effects of trade liberalization on wage levels, relative wages of skilled and unskilled labor, and worker conditions (see IDB, 2003a, and the references therein).

Traditional trade theory postulates that trade liberalization increases the relative price of unskilled labor in economies with a relative abundance of unskilled workers while producing the opposite effect in economies with abundant skilled labor. If that is the case, given that a large share of low-wage workers are unskilled, in Latin America and the Caribbean trade liberalization would be expected to be associated with a declining share of low-wage work.

These predictions, however, do not square with the empirical evidence. A rapidly expanding literature has documented an increase in the returns to education in the region during the 1990s.[15] Wages of workers with higher levels of education (tertiary) increased at a faster rate than those of workers with secondary education, despite the growing relative supply of workers with tertiary education. At the same time, and consistent with rising demand for skill, the wages of workers with secondary education remained constant relative to the wages of workers with primary education, even though the growth of the population with secondary education outpaced that of the population with only primary education. This increasing demand for education is driven not by the reallocation of employment across sectors—as would be the case if changes in the demand for skill were due to trade—but rather, by an increase in the demand for skilled labor within each sector (de Ferranti et al., 2004; Sánchez-Páramo and Schady, 2003; Attanasio, Goldberg, and Pavcnik, 2004).

A number of studies have proposed alternative channels to those provided by trade theory to explain these facts. One way to reconcile the facts with the theory is that in many Latin American and Caribbean countries, protection tended to be concentrated in sectors with a high relative use of unskilled labor. As protection declined with the progression of trade liberalization, wages in these sectors declined as well, increasing wage differentials between skilled and unskilled labor (Revenga, 1997; Hanson and Harrison, 1999; Attanasio, Goldberg, and Pavcnik, 2004). There is a growing consensus, however, that the influence of liberalization on the wage gap between skilled and unskilled workers has been modest and at most indirect, and that the rise in wage inequality can be better explained by other factors, such as the acceleration in technological change, which in turn leads to higher demand for workers with college education.

If increasing trade openness is associated with a rise in the proportion of low-wage work, this effect might be more visible in tradable sectors such as agriculture and manufacturing than in the service sectors. Table 5.2 presents evidence that this is not the case. The table shows the percentage change in the incidence of low-wage employment among unskilled workers in Latin America from the early 1990s to the early years of this century, distinguishing between a number of tradable (manufacturing, agriculture) and nontradable (construction and all service) sectors.[16] Low-wage work increased in manufacturing more than in other sectors in only two countries (Argentina and Ecuador). In the five countries in which the incidence of low-wage employment increased (Colombia, Ecuador, Paraguay, Peru, and Uruguay), the largest increase occurred in the service sectors, and in particular, in the construction and transportation sectors. Among the countries in which the incidence of low-wage work declined, only in El Salvador did the incidence fall less in manufacturing than in other sectors. In the rest, the incidence fell more in the tradable

---

[15] See, for instance, de Ferranti et al. (2004), IDB (2003a), and the references within.

[16] This analysis is restricted to unskilled labor in order to control for changes in the price of skill and their associated differential effects on low-wage employment across sectors with different skill intensities.

Table 5.2 Percentage Change in the Incidence of Low-Wage
Employment by Sector, Unskilled Labor, Early 1990s versus 2000s

| | Tradables | | Nontradables | | |
Country	Agriculture	Manufacturing	Construction and Transportation	Trade	Other Services
Argentina	11.4	317.2	227.5	200.7	205.2
Bolivia	13.8	19.7	56.7	15.7	1.0
Brazil	4.6	18.7	29.3	14.1	−0.6
Chile	−50.7	−65.6	−51.1	−62.0	−63.9
Colombia	26.8	43.0	76.7	37.3	10.4
Costa Rica	−15.2	−24.1	−15.3	−1.6	−17.7
Ecuador	14.9	36.6	24.1	20.1	15.2
Honduras	7.5	−33.3	−13.0	−17.8	−8.7
Mexico	5.0	−1.3	5.2	−0.2	16.5
Panama	82.9	−0.3	65.1	6.5	−12.5
Peru	12.4	0.6	14.9	31.1	11.3
Paraguay	−23.3	34.7	88.3	62.4	−2.5
El Salvador	−12.6	−0.1	−9.6	−8.8	−4.9
Uruguay	1.7	16.2	42.4	20.3	−13.9
Venezuela	29.7	58.2	58.6	50.6	15.5

Source: Pagés and Prada (2007).
Note: In this table unskilled labor refers to workers with up to secondary education.

than in the nontradable sectors (with the exception of Honduras, where the incidence increased substantially in the agricultural sector). Thus, Argentina and Ecuador were the only two countries where the incidence of low-wage work increased more in manufacturing than in the rest of the economy. This evidence, however, does not rule out the possibility that trade liberalization is affecting wages in *all* sectors; after all, changes in one sector can quickly spread to others. Pagés and Prada (2007) assess this issue by examining the relationship of low-wage employment to trade liberalization, using a measure of liberalization that summarizes changes in tariffs and tariff dispersion across countries of the region (Lora, 2001). They also control for technological change, as well as economic fluctuations and factors that affect female participation, in order to disentangle various causes of the rise in low-wage employment. They find that, with all these other factors controlled for, trade liberalization *reduces* the incidence of low-wage employment.[17]

There is therefore little evidence that trade liberalization has a *direct* adverse effect on low-wage employment. As will be discussed later in the chapter, however, trade liber-

---

[17] The magnitude of this effect is not small. It is found that a trade liberalization that resulted in a 10 percent increase in the trade liberalization measure (approximately equivalent to one standard deviation of this variable) would lead to a 10 percent decline in low-wage employment.

Figure 5.10
Percentage Change in Share of Workers in Low-Wage Jobs by Skill Level, 1990–1997 versus 1998–2004

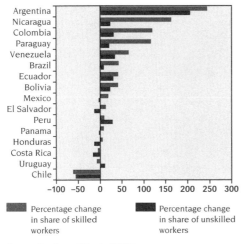

Argentina
Nicaragua
Colombia
Paraguay
Venezuela
Brazil
Ecuador
Bolivia
Mexico
El Salvador
Peru
Panama
Honduras
Costa Rica
Uruguay
Chile

-100 -50 0 50 100 150 200 250 300

■ Percentage change in share of skilled workers   ■ Percentage change in share of unskilled workers

Source: Pagés and Prada (2007).

alization may have an *indirect* adverse effect. This relates to the role of increased trade openness in facilitating imports of more modern capital and machinery, which in turn may facilitate the substitution of machines for low-wage workers, while increasing the demand for high-skilled workers who operate such technology. This effect would go in the direction of increasing the relative demand for skilled versus unskilled labor. The next section turns to the changing demand for skill and its effects on low-wage employment.

Skill-Biased Technological Change

As stated above, the consensus has been shifting toward another explanation for the increasing wage gap between skilled and unskilled labor. Most studies attribute this increasing gap to technological changes, such as the emergence of information technology, that favor the demand of highly skilled workers. However, even if trade cannot directly explain the observed patterns in skill demand, a number of studies have found an indirect association between trade and increasing demand for skill: industries that became more exposed to foreign competition as a result of trade liberalization in the region in the 1990s underwent a faster process of retooling and a higher increase in the demand for skilled labor. De Ferranti et al. (2003) explain these patterns by stating that increasing trade liberalization through the 1990s prompted firms to invest in new technology as competition in the goods market increased and, at the same time, declining tariffs made imports of foreign technology and capital goods more affordable. This, in turn, would have prompted a substitution of machines for low-skilled workers, and an increase in the demand for high-skilled workers who could operate more sophisticated technology.

If the shifting demand for skill caused the rise in low-wage employment in the last decade and a half, one would expect a greater increase in such employment among unskilled workers. Figure 5.10 shows, however, that the proportion of low-wage employment has increased at a higher rate among the skilled. This is particularly the case in Argentina, Nicaragua, Colombia, and Paraguay.

Another indication that the incidence of low-wage employment increased more rapidly among skilled workers is that the share of skilled employment increased faster among low-wage than among overall employment in the 1990s and early years of this century (Figure 5.11). It is unclear what was driving this phenomenon. Attanasio, Goldberg, and Pavcnik (2004) report an increase in the variance of earnings of skilled labor in

Colombia during the 1990s, and Pagés, Pierre, and Scarpetta (2007) report the same phenomenon for a wider group of countries from the early 1990s to the early years of the twenty-first century. Increasing demand for some professions requiring a college-level degree may be driving up the wages of some workers while driving down the wages of workers who hold a college-level degree but do not have the skills appropriate for these high-demand professions.

Another possible explanation may reside in the rapid increase in the number of universities in Latin America during the last fifteen years. If the degrees awarded by some institutions have little value in the market, an increasing number of university-educated workers may end up in low-paying jobs. This suggests that skill-biased technological change is, at best, only part of the story. Instead, the results presented here indicate that factors that require further exploration are causing an important rise in low-wage work among workers who traditionally are less vulnerable to this phenomenon.

Figure 5.11

Percentage Change in Share of Skilled Workers in Low-Wage versus Total Employment, 1990–1997 versus 1998–2004

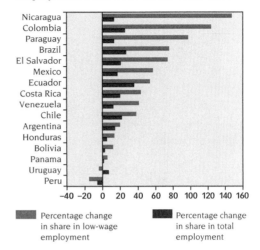

Nicaragua, Colombia, Paraguay, Brazil, El Salvador, Mexico, Ecuador, Costa Rica, Venezuela, Chile, Argentina, Honduras, Bolivia, Panama, Uruguay, Peru

–40 –20 0 20 40 60 80 100 120 140 160

Percentage change in share in low-wage employment

Percentage change in share in total employment

Source: Pagés and Prada (2007).

Nonetheless, and despite the recent increase, the incidence of low-wage work among skilled workers is much lower than among the unskilled. For example, at the end of the 1990s, the incidence of low wages among college-educated workers in Latin America was, depending on the country, between 5 percent and 25 percent of that among workers who had completed only primary education. Because of this disparity, the rise in low-wage employment among the skilled accounted, on average, for only 4 percent of the overall increase in low-wage employment in the region in the 1990s. The countries in which the incidence of low wages among the college-educated accounted for a higher share of the increase in low-wage work overall are Bolivia and Argentina, where it explained, respectively, 9 percent and 7 percent of the total increase.[18]

Pagés and Prada (2007) explore the importance of technological change and, in particular, the effect of openness in facilitating the spread of technological change to Latin America and thereby on the evolution of low-wage employment. With other possible de-

---

[18] This number is computed by decomposing the total increase into three components: (a) how much of the total increase is accounted for by the rising incidence of low-wage employment within each skill group, (b) how much is accounted for by the change in the shares of each skill group, and (c) how much is accounted for by a cross-term. Each of these components can be further decomposed within different education groups: primary, secondary, and college education. The statistics reported here are given by how much of the total is accounted for by the subcomponent in (a) that refers to college education. For more information on these decompositions, see Pagés and Prada (2007).

Figure 5.12
Percentage Change in Employment by Sector, Early 1990s versus 2000s

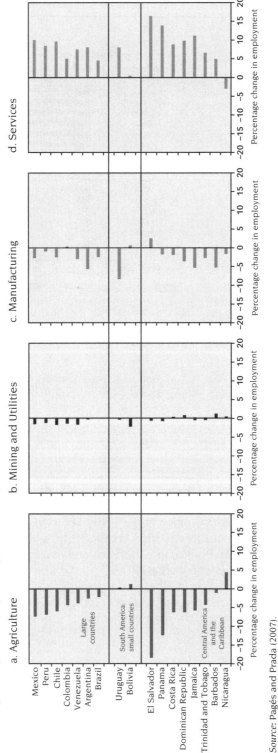

Source: Pagés and Prada (2007).

terminants of the evolution of low-wage work (economic fluctuations, trade liberalization, and supply shocks) controlled for, technological change is found to have a positive and statistically significant effect on low-wage employment.

In sum, trade has had two differentiated and opposite effects on low-wage employment in Latin America. On the one hand, a direct effect, possibly through an increased demand for unskilled labor, has led to a reduction in low-wage work. This is also reflected in the fact that, depending on the country considered, low-wage work increased less (or declined more) in the tradable than in the nontradable sector over the last fifteen years. On the other hand, trade may also have facilitated the importation of better technology, which in turn may have led to an increase in the demand for skilled labor and a decline in the relative demand for workers with lower levels of educational attainment. The second effect is likely to have been the dominant one in most countries.

The Rising Importance of the Service Sector

Since the early 1990s, most Latin American and Caribbean countries have experienced a decline in agriculture and manufacturing employment, while employment in the service sector has expanded considerably. The exceptions to this general trend are El Salvador, which saw a relative increase in employment in manufacturing between the early 1990s and the early years of this century; Bolivia, in which agricultural employment increased; and Nicaragua, in which agricultural employment increased and service sector employment declined (Figure 5.12).

To assess how much of the change in the incidence of low-wage employment is explained by this phenomenon, it is useful to decompose those changes into three components: how much of the overall change is accounted for by the rising incidence of low-wage employment within each sector of activity (the "within effect"); how much is owing to the shifting weight of the different sectors (the "shift effect"); and finally, how much is accounted for by a cross-term that assesses whether the sectors that expanded in terms of employment were also the sectors in which the incidence of low-wage employment increased (the "cross-effect"). The results of such a decomposition for countries in Latin America, presented in Figure 5.13, indicate that most of the increase in low-wage jobs in the region derives from increases in the share of low-wage jobs in each sector (the "within effect" in Figure 5.13).

Sectoral shifts (changes in the weight of each sector in total employment) are found to account for a negligible part of the rise in the incidence of low-wage employment but to account for some of the reduction in the countries in which the incidence has declined. Thus, with the exception of Peru and Bolivia—where these effects are somewhat more important—sectoral shifts account for a minor share of the total increase in low-wage work in Latin American countries. Yet they contribute to a larger share of the total change in countries that have experienced a decline in low-wage employment. This is particularly the case in El Salvador and Honduras, where sectoral shifts explain close to 50 percent of the decline. In fact, with few exceptions, sectoral shifts tend to reduce the incidence of low-wage work. This reduction is mostly driven by changes in the share of agricultural employment in total employment (Figure 5.14). Since wages in agriculture are lower than in other sectors, a reduction in the share of employment in this sector contributes to a decline in low-wage employment. This phenomenon accounts for about 10 percent of the decline in the share of low-wage employment in Costa Rica, Honduras, and Mexico and a higher percentage of the decline in El Salvador. An increase in the share of employment in agriculture also accounts for about ten percentage points of the increase in the incidence of low-wage work in Peru and Bolivia.

In comparison, changes in the share of other sectors in total employment account for a very small percentage of the total change in low-wage employment (Pagés and Prada, 2007). Thus, for example, although in all but two countries studied, an increasing share of retail and wholesale trade sectors in total employment is associated with an increase in the share of low-wage work, the changes are of very small magnitude. Results from Pagés and Prada (2007) also indicate that sector shifts are not statistically significant in explaining changes in low-wage employment.

Figure 5.13
Decomposition of Changes in Low-Wage Employment Incidence by Effect, 1990–1997 versus 1998–2004

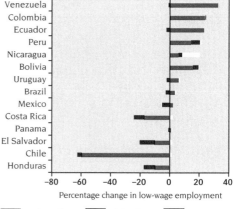

Source: Pagés and Prada (2007).
Note: Because of the magnitude of the Argentine data, they are not included in the figure. The data for Argentina are as follows: within effect = 214.90; shift effect = −4.28; cross-effect = 14.02.

Increasing Female Participation

Finally, supply shocks can also, at least in principle, account for the increasing share of low-wage employment in Latin America in recent years. While steady improvements in educational attainments in the region would have gone in the direction of reducing the share of employment in low-wage jobs, the substantial increase in female participation could have produced the opposite effect, as women tend to earn lower wages than men.

To investigate the quantitative importance of these composition effects, it is possible again to decompose the total increase in low-wage employment into a shift effect, which measures how much of the total increase is accounted for by increasing female participation; a within effect, which reflects whether low-wage employment increased for both males and females; and a cross-term effect, which measures whether female participation has increased in countries where low-wage employment has also increased.

Figure 5.15 presents the results of this decomposition. It is evident that the large rise in female participation in Latin America can account for only a very small fraction of the increasing share of low-wage employment. Moreover, the rising participation of women does not imply a faster increase in the proportion of low-wage employment for women as compared to men. On the contrary, Figure 5.16 shows that the share of low-wage employment increased more for men than for women in most countries of the region between 1990–1997 and 1998–2004. In fact, in at least three of the region's countries, the share of

Figure 5.14
Decomposition of Changes in Low-Wage Employment Incidence by Effect within the Agriculture Sector, 1990–1997 versus 1998–2004

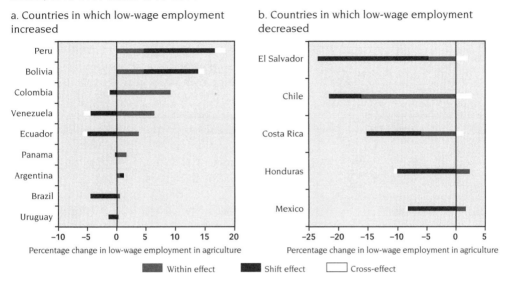

a. Countries in which low-wage employment increased

b. Countries in which low-wage employment decreased

Source: Pagés and Prada (2007).

low-wage employment increased for males while it decreased for females, suggesting poorer outcomes for male workers. Further evidence of these better outcomes for women is that the proportion of women in employment increased faster during the period in most of the region's countries than the proportion of women in low-wage jobs (Figure 5.17).

Still, increasing female participation may have depressed wages for both men and women. In that case, increasing female participation could have led to lower wages and a rising share of low-wage employment for women and for men. Pagés and Prada (2007) examine this issue and find that variables associated with increased female participation, such as lower fertility rates, lead to an increase in low-wage work. This effect, however, is very small. A decline in fertility of one standard deviation leads to an increase in low-wage work of 0.16 percent.

CONCLUSIONS

Politicians, employers, and workers in Latin America may share few complaints, but they are unanimous in their concern about the performance of labor markets in the region. The public's preoccupation with this issue is revealed on a daily basis in the press, and surveys such as Latinobarometer show that loss of employment and low wages are among the most pressing problems for the region's population.

For a growing share of that population, the labor market in the last decade and a half has not been part of a path of social integration, but rather a source of social exclusion. The labor market not only has acted as a resonance box in which discrimination and

Figure 5.15
Decomposition of Changes in Low-Wage Employment Incidence by Gender, 1990–1997 versus 1998–2004

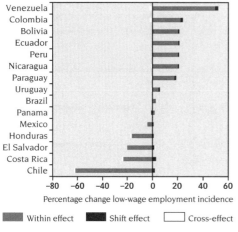

Percentage change low-wage employment incidence

▩ Within effect ▮ Shift effect ☐ Cross-effect

Source: Pagés and Prada (2007).

Figure 5.16
Percentage Change in the Share of Workers in Low-Wage Jobs by Gender, 1990–1997 versus 1998–2004

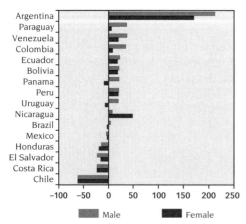

▩ Male ▮ Female

Source: Pagés and Prada (2007).

inequality in the acquisition of human capital is translated into earnings differentials, but also has excluded workers from employment and from well-paying jobs. The fact that social insurance and social protection are linked to formal employment has made the surge of unemployment and the explosion in the number of low-wage jobs the principal source of exclusion for the region's population, exclusion that is affecting groups usually considered protected by labor regulations (male, prime age, skilled workers).

The deficiencies of labor markets' performance are rooted in a multiplicity of factors that have affected the pattern and speed of growth in the region. Rising unemployment, mediocre economic growth, and increasing demand for education, prompted by increasing imports of capital goods and technology, all contributed to swelling the share of low-wage employment over the last decade and a half. In comparison, the effects of the changing structure of employment and the increasing participation of women in the labor force have been small, and in some instances, such as the declining share of agriculture in total employment, they have actually gone in the direction of reducing low-wage work.

The dynamics of low-wage work track the dynamics of poverty and exclusion. This has a number of implications for economic and social policy in the region. First, it implies that labor market developments, and in particular developments in the low-wage labor market, determine to a very large extent developments in poverty. Second, it also means that employment is not sufficient to escape poverty: many jobs do not pay enough to lift a standard-sized family out of poverty.

This implies that other policies will have to meet this need. Two groups of policies must be considered. The first group is concerned with increasing labor earnings. Better education policies for school-age children and access to adult education, for those past school age, are an important part of the package. Training policies, while providing some benefits in term of earnings, are in comparison much less effective and often end up helping only those with a comparatively better education. On the demand side, policies to promote the growth of higher-paying activities and rising minimum wages have some potential; however, such policies may also lead to unemployment, another form of exclusion in the labor market. The pertinence of their implementation has to be studied carefully in each case, and once in place they must be monitored carefully to ensure that the benefits outweigh the costs.

Figure 5.17

Percentage Change in Share of Female Workers in Low-Wage and in Total Employment, 1990–1997 versus 1998–2004

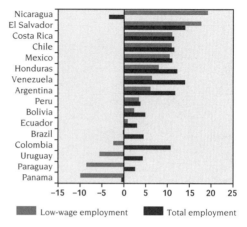

Source: Pagés and Prada (2007).

The second group of policies deals with government transfers and other public programs geared to increasing nonlabor earnings of poor families, whose visibility and importance is rapidly increasing in the region. These policies are important tools for alleviating the material deprivation that families suffer and can be very effective in raising their incomes and boosting their consumption of human-capital-building services (health and education in particular). However, government transfers act on the outcome (income) that families and workers receive from having a low-wage job or being unemployed. To the extent that the more complex dynamics that affect the pattern and speed of growth and generate the increase in the share of low-wage jobs in total employment remain unchanged, the more educated and healthier children of the beneficiaries of these transfers will end up working in the same low-wage jobs that excluded their parents in the first place (Levy, 2006).

Social Mobility
and Social Exclusion

S ocial mobility—or the lack thereof—occupies a unique place in the discussion of social exclusion. Whereas most measures of social exclusion depend on readily observed indices of well-being at discrete points in time, social mobility addition-ally involves largely intangible but undeniably powerful factors such as the memories, hopes, and expectations of individuals and families over time. Two societies with similar income distributions, for example, can have different welfare levels depending on the degree of social mobility; poverty and other manifestations of social exclusion are more bearable when individuals have a reasonable expectation of improvement in their own circumstances—or those of their children. On the basis of this understanding, the eco-nomic analysis of social mobility aims to track the evolution of income distributions over time, considering individuals over the course of a lifetime (intragenerational mobility) and families over generations (intergenerational social mobility).

These concerns are particularly important in Latin America and the Caribbean, which has, as shown in Figure 6.1, the greatest income inequality of any region in the world. Of course, the data in the figure represent only "snapshots" of conditions at one point in time. Over the longer term, income distributions may change much differently across countries because of economic growth; changes in human capital among different groups and in the population as a whole; changes in returns to assets, including human capital; and changes in labor market opportunities. All of these developments may systemati-cally benefit or harm certain groups of the population and thus prevent societies from ensuring equal opportunities for all.

Depending on the importance of inherited abilities—a much-debated issue—inter-generational social mobility in a country is closely related to the degree of equality of opportunities in that country. Higher intergenerational mobility is expected to decrease the influence of socioeconomic background on economic achievement in adulthood. As Friedman (1962) points out, income inequality is much more of a concern in a rigid system in which families stay in the same position in each period than in societies that have the same degree of inequality but also have greater mobility, equality of opportunity, and dynamic change.

The perceived fairness of social mobility can present major challenges to social co-hesion. If "winners and losers" or "haves and have-nots" owe their status to causes largely independent of ability and effort, economic growth is likely to be slowed as a result of inefficient allocation of human and other resources, and inequity in the distribution of income and other benefits is a contributing factor to political instability—and even vio-lence—among citizens who do not feel that they have a stake in existing social arrange-ments (see Chapter 10).

Holding total income and income distribution constant, relative social mobility can mitigate the effects of income inequality and poverty, as it implies that wealthier individuals change places with poorer individuals. As noted by Graham (2005a, 2005b) and Graham and Pettinato (2001), tolerance of inequality seems to be higher where there are perceived (even if not real) prospects for upward mobility. However, downward mobility is more likely to be a source of frustration and unrest than persistent poverty.

Figure 6.1

Income Inequality in Latin America and the Caribbean and Other World Regions

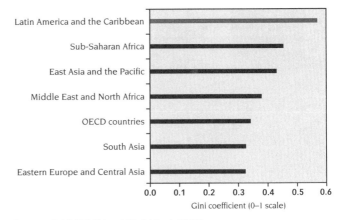

Source: ECLAC (2006b) and World Bank (2006).

This chapter analyzes social mobility in Latin America and the Caribbean and its impact on social exclusion. Of particular interest are the impact on social mobility of the expansion of education, urbanization, and the performance of labor markets. Although the chapter focuses primarily on intergenerational social mobility, intragenerational social mobility receives attention as well, as recent developments in labor markets and social policies have highlighted the dynamics of labor income.

MEASURING SOCIAL MOBILITY

Social mobility is usually defined as the way individuals or groups move upward or downward from one status or class position to another within the social hierarchy. Sociologists generally view social mobility in terms of movements between social classes or occupational groups. Although social class might provide a better overall measure of life chances, definitions of social class can lack precision and are prone to perceptual biases. Research in economics generally concentrates on earnings or income mobility, which represents a direct measure of resources, at least at a specific point in time, as do other quantitative measures such as educational attainment. It should be noted, however, that social mobility has no generally accepted definition other than a disruption in the link between initial conditions and individual outcomes. A more detailed discussion of these definitions is presented in Box 6.1.

Figure 6.2

Intergenerational Income Elasticities for a Sample of Developed and Latin American Countries

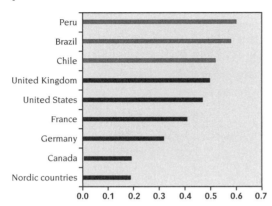

Sources: For developed countries, Corak (2006). For developing countries, Brazil: Ferreira and Veloso (2004); Chile: Núñez and Miranda (2007); Peru: Grawe (2001).

Figure 6.3

Estimates for Intergenerational Income Mobility Elasticities for Different Son Cohorts, Chile, 2004–2006

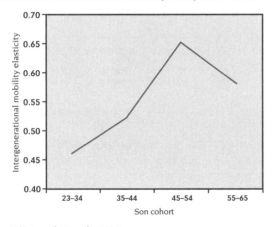

Source: Núñez and Miranda (2007).

WHAT IS THE LEVEL OF SOCIAL MOBILITY IN LATIN AMERICA AND THE CARIBBEAN?

Although data on intergenerational social mobility are widely available only for developed countries, research on the basis of available data in Brazil, Chile, and Peru suggests that social mobility in Latin America and the Caribbean is lower than in developed countries, including those with the lowest levels of mobility, the United States and the United Kingdom. Estimates for these three countries, as well as for developed countries, are presented in Figure 6.2. Intergenerational social mobility is usually measured by how much of the difference across permanent incomes in a parent generation persists across the incomes of their children in adulthood (more technically, how large is the intergenerational income elasticity between cohorts of children and parents). Additional evidence for Chile shows that, as a result either of increased mobility or of life cycle effects on earnings, mobility seems to be higher for younger cohorts (see Figure 6.3). Dunn (2003, 2004) finds a similar pattern for Brazil.

Caution must be exercised, however, in interpreting Figure 6.2 to gauge differences in social mobility across countries using intergenerational income elasticities. Countries differ significantly in the extent to which family economic status is related to children's labor market outcomes. From the child's perspective, however, the relationship between

Box 6.1   Understanding the Definition of Social Mobility

As defined by Behrman (1999), social mobility refers to movements on socioeconomic status indicators by specific entities (e.g., individuals, families, or population groups) between periods.

Timing

Changes in status take place either within an individual's life or across generations. *Intragenerational mobility* considers the lives or adulthoods of individuals within the same generation. For example, individuals' social status at a given point in their lives can be analyzed relative to their social status at an earlier point in their lives. The intervals chosen for these studies are generally months or years (five-year intervals are a particularly common choice). *Intergenerational mobility* considers families over more than one generation. The analysis focuses on dynasties, tracking social indicators of the parent and the child. A variety of periods and social indicators are used, depending on which aspect of mobility is of interest.

Indicators of Socioeconomic Status

Diverse variables are used to measure socioeconomic status, including continuous (income, earnings, and consumption), discrete (years of schooling), and categorical (occupation and marital status) ones. Some studies use a composite measure of socioeconomic level, which includes consumption of durable goods and educational attainment instead of income and wealth measures. The choice of the indicator is crucial for the type of mobility that is being measured. Income is the primary indicator of interest in this chapter.

Entities

The entities examined in social mobility research are generally individuals or families or subgroups of the former selected according to demographic or cultural characteristics such as gender, race, ethnicity, and religion. There is also interest in mobility of individuals, with personal/behavioral characteristics such as years of education, marital status, number of children, and labor force participation controlled for. There is a strong tie between entities, timing, and the choice of the socioeconomic status indicator.

Movements in the Mobility Context

The meaning of "movements" can create a great deal of confusion in the definition of

---

parents' and children's labor market outcomes provides a useful indicator of the persistence of social exclusion within a particular country.

An important caveat must be interjected at this point. Most research to date on intergenerational income mobility has focused on the relationship between fathers' and sons' incomes. This is because women's income can be biased, given issues of labor force participation as well as women's entrance into and exit from the labor market because of maternity and other life cycle issues that frequently require women to take on addi-

social mobility.[a] Movements can be total (absolute) or relative.

Total movements indicate changes in the income of all individuals with no change in the share of income that belongs to each individual or in individuals' relative position in the income distribution (Behrman, 1999).[b] In contrast, relative mobility implies changes in the position and share of individuals in the income distribution.[c]

Relative movements can be classified as one of two types: positional movements and share movements. A *positional* movement occurs when a person changes position in an overall income distribution. Positional movements are usually measured through changes in an individual's rank or percentile or in the decile or quintile of the income distribution to which he or she belongs. This notion is relative, since it is possible for an individual to experience relative income mobility even if there is no change in income.[d] A share movement occurs when an individual changes his or her share of total income. A *share* movement does not necessarily imply a change in position within the distribution. Both positional and share movements are examples of relative or exchange mobility.

Symmetric and directional movements are more concerned with total income than income share or income position. *Symmetric income movement* focuses on the magnitude of income changes but not on the direction, and *directional income movement* treats income gains and losses separately. It provides a measure of the number of people who had income gains and losses, focusing on quantifying total (or absolute) change. Since symmetric and directional movements are not the object of this report, they are not discussed further here.

Relative measures of mobility do not take into account changes in income level. Many researchers have argued that a society where all incomes are growing—that is, a society experiencing total mobility—is more dynamic and mobile even if there is no relative mobility (i.e., there is no change in rank orders) (Galiani, 2006).

---

[a] This section borrows extensively from Behrman (1999), Fields (2000), and Galiani (2006).
[b] This is not the mobility concept of interest here, and thus less attention will be devoted to total mobility.
[c] Total or absolute intergenerational mobility may reduce poverty without changing the relative position of each individual in the income distribution.
[d] The underlying assumption here is that relative movements require a predefined measurement of position, which can be deciles or quintiles or even a rank.

---

tional work in the home, such as taking care of an elderly parent or ill family member. As argued by Chadwick and Solon (2002: 335), the "neglect of daughters has stemmed partly from unconscious sexism and partly from a recognition that, in a society in which married women's labor-force participation rates are lower than men's, women's earnings may often be an unreliable indicator of their economic status."

Persistence at the Extremes

Levels of mobility in a society vary among income groups. Whereas higher levels of upward and downward social mobility exist in the middle ranges of income distributions, there is far less mobility among the richest and poorest groups. Lack of upward mobility among the poorest populations, which may be associated with poverty traps, is particularly prevalent among excluded populations (such as Afro-descendants in Brazil, as illustrated in

Table 6.1 Income Persistence in Bottom and Top Quintiles, by Race, Brazil

Population group	Bottom quintile	Top quintile
All	0.35	0.43
Afro-descendants	0.47	0.23
Whites	0.25	0.50

Source: Ferreira and Veloso (2004).
Note: Table presents the coefficients of the correlation between father and son incomes.

Table 6.1) and in poorer regions. Such social immobility can be associated with exclusion from basic services and markets, resulting from geographical isolation, segregation, or labor market discrimination. In addition, because investment in children depends upon family resources, the credit constraints of poorer families reinforce immobility.

Lack of downward mobility among the richest segment of the population is likewise clearly associated with certain traits, such as membership in a historically privileged racial or ethnic group (such as whites in Brazil) and residence in more-developed regions. The richest part of the population further enjoys greater access to better-paying jobs through greater access to higher education and "positive discrimination" in the form of various social networks. Social immobility at the high and low ends of the income distribution in Chile and Brazil, with comparable figures for other countries, is illustrated in Table 6.2.

Brazil displays a strong intergenerational persistence of wages at both ends of sons' conditional wage distribution. This implies that the wage mobility is low at both tails of the distribution. In the case of Brazil, the probability that the sons of fathers in the lowest quintile will remain in that quintile is 35 percent, whereas the probability that the sons of fathers in the richest quintile will remain in the richest quintile is 43 percent (Ferreira and Veloso, 2004). The lack of mobility at the tails of the income distribution may be a response to two sources of exclusion: the lack of opportunity for the children of the poor to acquire better skills and improve their employment prospects and the reproduction of socioeconomic privileges among the children of the "well-off." These figures also imply that there is more upward mobility from the bottom of the earnings distribution than downward mobility from the top: it is more likely that a poor person will become richer than that a rich person will become poorer.

Upper-tail immobility (inability to enter the upper classes) is usually linked to low levels of access to higher education opportunities or to segmentation in labor markets. Institutions such as credit markets, government loan guarantee programs, and public schooling are important in determining a society's degree of income mobility. Ferreira and Veloso (2004) present nonlinear estimates of the persistence of wages to provide a better idea of mobility across generations. Their results indicate that 62 percent of sons whose fathers' wages are below the median end up in the same wage group as their

Country	Study	Bottom quartile	Bottom quintile	Top quartile	Top quintile
Table 6.2 Comparative Evidence on Income Persistence in Bottom and Top Quintiles and Quartiles					
Developed countries					
Canada	Fortin and Lefebvre (1998)	n.d.	n.d.	0.32–0.33	n.d.
Sweden	Österberg (2000)	n.d.	n.d.	0.25	n.d.
United Kingdom	Blanden, Gregg, and Machin (2005)	0.37	n.d.	0.40	n.d.
United States	Peters (1992)	n.d.	n.d.	0.36–0.40	n.d.
	Grawe (2001)	0.40	n.d.	0.41	n.d.
Latin America and the Caribbean					
Brazil	Ferreira and Veloso (2004)	n.d.	0.35	0.55–0.56	0.43
Chile	Núñez and Miranda (2007)	0.39[a]–0.50	0.30[a]–0.37	0.54–0.55[a]	0.47–0.57[a]

Note: Table presents coefficients of correlation between father and son incomes. n.d.= no data
[a]Estimated from predicted income distribution.

fathers and that this fraction is much lower (53 percent) for sons whose fathers' wages are above the median. This is consistent with the borrowing constraints theory, since rich families are less likely to be financially constrained in investing in their children. Andrade et al. (2003) also find that borrowing constraints play a large role in determining the extent of intergenerational mobility in Brazil.

Additional Factors Related to Intergenerational Mobility

Other studies have identified further constraints on intergenerational mobility. Bourguignon, Ferreira, and Menéndez (2003) find that 20 percent of income inequality in Brazil (as measured by the Gini coefficient) is due to inequality of initial circumstances such as parental schooling, parents' occupation, and race. Núñez and Tartakowsky (2006) find a similar magnitude for income inequality in Chile.

Benavides (2002) focuses on the labor market opportunities of sons compared to their fathers in urban Peru and finds that, even though increases in migration and the expansion of formal education were supposed to increase mobility, these factors have largely been neutralized by a lack of change in economic and cultural relations. Although there is considerable dynamism between and among the medium-low and low social classes, there is no significant movement between high and low social classes.

Intragenerational Mobility

A range of issues must be considered in analyzing intragenerational mobility. Measurements of such mobility usually focus on earnings mobility, which is closely linked with the economic cycle, especially over short periods of time. The macroeconomic framework is thus crucial in determining earnings mobility, even after individual characteristics are controlled for. Any analysis must further take into account that high levels of intragenerational mobility are not necessarily desirable, as they imply high risk and variability in labor earnings. Likewise, very low levels of mobility may be related to poverty traps and are undesirable as well.

Several other factors must also be assessed. First, it must be assumed that adults will accumulate little or no human capital beyond what they currently have. Second, it must be borne in mind that individuals with the highest human and physical capital additionally have access to political and social connections as well as credit. Third, individuals and groups with low levels of education are vulnerable to poverty traps and are likely to remain at their (low) current social levels. Fourth, individuals aim to keep their consumption as smooth as possible, avoiding too much variance (or at least decline) in their lifetime income. Finally, in a globalized and technology-dependent world, there is an increase in demand for high-skilled workers, which can increase opportunities for some members of the population but intensify the exclusion of others (see Chapter 5).

Research on intragenerational mobility in the region finds no large-scale trend. Considering Argentina and Mexico from 1988 to 1996, Wodon (2001) finds no evidence of increased mobility overall in either country through time, although mobility in Mexico has increased among the young and the less educated. In recent work on Argentina, Mexico, and Venezuela, Fields et al. (2005) compare income mobility patterns during positive and negative growth spells and find no evidence to support the hypothesis that the groups that experience large earnings gains when the economy is growing are the same ones that experience losses during recessionary periods. Additionally, they attempt to determine whether individuals who start from a privileged position are those who experience the greatest gains in good times and the greatest losses in bad times. This appears to be the case in Mexico, but not in Argentina and Venezuela.

CURRENT PERCEPTIONS OF SOCIAL MOBILITY AND MERITOCRACY

Given that people respond to incentives, perceptions of social mobility and meritocracy are fundamental for the long-run prospects of economies and societies. Rational individuals will have little incentive to work hard and invest in human and physical capital if they do not believe that they have good chances of moving upward in society. Individuals who feel trapped in a situation with no prospect for improvement have fewer disincentives to engage in dysfunctional and antisocial behavior, since they have little or nothing to lose. At the same time, without investment in human capital and hard work, there are no chances for these individuals to move upward, which means that the poor will remain poor.

Figure 6.4 shows the relationship between social mobility and income inequality (measured with a Gini coefficient adjusted to be comparable among countries). As argued by Andersen (2000), there is no clear relationship between social mobility and inequality. However, Brazil, Colombia, Ecuador, and Guatemala are among the most "unfair" countries, with high inequality and low mobility.

Under these circumstances, it is hardly surprising that Latin Americans are generally pessimistic about their prospects for mobility and generally do not believe that their societies are meritocratic. An analysis of the Latinobarometer opinion survey by Gaviria (2005) presents some of the more telling statistics from this annual poll of seventeen countries in the region. As shown in Table 6.3, 74.1 percent of individuals surveyed in 2000 indicated that opportunities to overcome poverty are unequal, and 63.6 percent thought that poverty is not a consequence of lack of hard work. Conversely, 71.5 percent of the survey sample attributed success to personal connections.

Figure 6.5 presents perceptions of past and future mobility. According to the figure, Latin Americans believe that the past generation (i.e., their parents) was somewhat better off than the current generation. For perceptions of "past" mobility, the bars in the figure represent the difference between how one perceives oneself compared to one's parents. On the other hand, for "future" mobility, the bars show the difference between the social status of the next generation (one's child) compared to one's own social status. As the figure indicates, there are expectations among Latin Americans of upward social mobility for the future generation.

Figure 6.4
Social Mobility and Inequality in Latin America

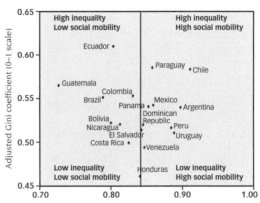

Social mobility index (based on teenagers, 13–19 years) (0–1 scale)

Source: Andersen (2000).
Note: Statistics for Argentina and Uruguay are based on urban samples only.

WHAT MAKES LATIN AMERICA AND THE CARIBBEAN LESS MOBILE? DETERMINANTS OF SOCIAL MOBILITY IN THE REGION

The level of intergenerational social mobility in a society is determined by a wide range of factors. Known influences include the following:

- *Variance of effort.* Some individuals work harder, for longer hours, or more effectively than others. Effort can be affected by many other factors, however, and measurements and perceptions of effort can be affected by observers' biases.
- *Degree of inherited ability.* Separating inherited ability from other factors poses an ongoing challenge, and both social science and biology continue to address the roles of "nature" and "nurture." Nonetheless, the role of inherited abilities cannot be disregarded in areas of endeavor such as music and sports, and real if less obvious inherited abilities may be expected to influence other activities as well.
- *Importance of family background.* The term "family background" encompasses a wide variety of factors such as parental education, parental income, and cultural background, factors that can be reinforced across generations by

Table 6.3 Perceptions of Social Mobility in Latin America and the Caribbean (percent)			
	2000	1998	1996
Opportunities to overcome poverty			
Same opportunities for all	25.9	n.d.	n.d.
Unequal opportunities	74.1	n.d.	n.d.
Causes of poverty			
Lack of hard work	36.5	n.d.	n.d.
Other	63.6	n.d.	n.d.
Success depends on personal connections			
Yes	71.5	71.3	76.4
No	28.5	28.7	23.6
Hard work leads to success			
Yes	46.2	45.1	44.4
No	53.8	54.9	55.6

Source: Latinobarometer data, processed by Gaviria (2005).
Note: Table presents percentages for each response among Latinobarometer respondents in the year specified. n.d. = no data.

assortative mating (i.e., marriage and parenthood among individuals of the same social class and/or income level). These factors can influence cognitive and noncognitive abilities, human capital accumulation, and employment opportunities. The means for transferring advantages and disadvantages across generations encompass such disparate factors as prenatal and infant nutrition, home environment and education, and access or lack of access to social networks.

- *Market failures (especially in financial markets) and credit constraints.* Families whose members cannot borrow to finance education, business start-ups and expansions, or housing remain "stuck" from one generation to the next in a suboptimal equilibrium of low earnings and investment.
- *Exclusion from the supply of basic services and access to markets.* Families subject to geographical isolation or various forms of discrimination are likely to have access to a low quantity and quality of services, including education and basic infrastructure, and enjoy only limited access to labor and other markets.
- *Segmentation in job creation in each occupational stratum.* Labor market segmentation can reduce mobility, as individuals belonging to excluded groups have less access to clusters of jobs characterized by higher job quality, earnings, benefits, and union coverage.
- *Lack of safety nets and compensatory programs.* Families who lack the protections of unemployment insurance and social security mechanisms must restrict their consumption and investment in response to shocks, including unemployment,

Figure 6.5
Perception of Social Mobility in Latin America

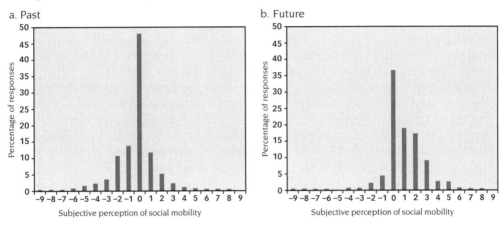

a. Past

b. Future

Subjective perception of social mobility

Subjective perception of social mobility

Source: Gaviria (2006).
Note: Subjective social mobility is the difference perceived by the respondent between the economic status of his or her generation and that of either the previous (past) or next (future), each expressed as a value on a scale from 1 (lowest) to 10 (highest). The values −9 through 9 result from subtracting the value assigned by the respondent to his or her own economic status from that assigned to his or her parents (in panel a), or from subtracting the value assigned to his or her children's economic status from that assigned to his or her own (in panel b).

illness, and natural disasters. The resulting missed opportunities for education, savings, and investment have ripple effects that can extend for generations.

It is almost impossible to estimate the influence of each of these factors, even in developed countries, in a rigorous way. Some factors, though, are particularly relevant to Latin America and the Caribbean: the role of education and the effects of the expansion of education coverage and education opportunities, urbanization and certain patterns of regional development, and the effects of recent labor market developments (macroeconomic stabilization, globalization, and technical change).

Education

Many Latin American countries have expanded educational coverage and access to formal education for all social levels. Nonetheless, quality matters as well, and the low quality of public education, together with the opportunity cost of going to school, results in high failure and dropout rates in the early years of secondary education.

Peru, for example, has undergone a massive expansion of its educational system. Benavides (2004) argues, however, that the country is experiencing only a weak version of meritocracy, with little benefit for social mobility; education, though directly linked with job placement, is not completely independent from social origins. Furthermore, as pointed out by Escobal, Saavedra, and Torero (1998), there are significant differences in access to education among social classes in Peru, especially in rural areas.

Although data remain scarce for Latin America and the Caribbean, some research-ers have attempted to study social mobility by using educational indicators. If family background is important in determining educational outcomes, one can argue that low social mobility results from the role of family background in providing opportunities for obtaining higher education. Even though educational mobility is only one of the channels through which earnings mobility is transmitted across generations, it is one of the main determinants of social mobility in meritocratic societies.

Not surprisingly, evidence from the region shows that children from high-income and more-educated parents are more likely to do better in life. One of the most widely used indicators of intergenerational educational mobility is estimates of schooling elasticity (the coefficient of the correlation between child and parent educational attainment, which measures the association between the educational achievement of cohorts of sons and fathers). As shown in Table 6.4, almost all available coefficients for Latin American and Caribbean countries are higher than those for developed countries, indicating that levels of mobility are lower in the region than in developed countries. The exception in the region is Chile (Table 6.5), where schooling elasticity has been decreasing, which implies more mobility for younger cohorts.

Other studies echo these results. Studying sixteen countries in the region, Dahan and Gaviria (2001) find that the correlation between parents' and children's education is 1.8 to 3 times higher in Latin America than in the United States. Andersen (2001) assesses social mobility via a measure of the importance of family background for the educational level of teenagers in eighteen countries of the region, using an indicator equal to one minus the coefficient of the correlation between family background and child schooling gap (higher values of the indicator imply less correlation). She finds that, as shown in Figure 6.6, Chile, Argentina, Uruguay, and Peru display higher social mobility, whereas Guatemala and Brazil are among the least mobile societies.

Behrman, Gaviria, and Székely (2001) also infer lower levels of social mobility in the region by finding low levels of educational mobility compared with those of the United States. They examine the intergenerational transmission of educational attainment in four Latin American countries and the United States. Their results indicate that the in-tergenerational transmission of educational attainment in Brazil, Colombia, Mexico, and Peru is higher than in the United States (see Figure 6.7). The results of Behrman, Gaviria, and Székely are corroborated by Gaviria (2005) using data from the Latinobarometer and the U.S. General Social Survey (see Figure 6.8). Behrman, Gaviria, and Székely also illus-trate gender differences in educational mobility in the region compared with the United States (see Figure 6.9). Their estimates for the intergenerational transmission of educa-tional attainment are higher for men in Brazil and Colombia, indicating that women are more mobile in these two countries. Men tend to be more mobile in the United States, Mexico, and Peru, though there is no great variance between the estimates for men and women in the United States and Brazil.

Trends in the distribution of intergenerational educational mobility for Mexico show that parents' education plays an important role in children's education, though some changes may be occurring. Binder and Woodruff (2002) argue that in urban Mexico, for example, the evidence on educational mobility is mixed. On one hand, the decrease in the intergenerational educational correlation in cohorts presented in Table 6.6 suggests

Table 6.4 Schooling Elasticity Estimates

Country	Elasticity
Developed countries	
Germany (Grawe, 2001)	0.43
United States (Grawe, 2001)	0.26
United States (Behrman, Gaviria, and Székely, 2001)	0.35
United Kingdom (Grawe, 2001)	0.19
Latin American countries	
Brazil (Behrman, Gaviria, and Székely, 2001)	0.70
Chile (Núñez and Miranda, 2007)	0.21
Colombia (Behrman, Gaviria, and Székely, 2001)	0.70
Mexico (Behrman, Gaviria, and Székely, 2001)	0.50
Peru (Grawe, 2001)	0.60
Peru (Behrman, Gaviria, and Székely, 2001)	0.50

an increase in intergenerational mobility over time; on the other hand, that rate of increase appears to slow or even reverse for the cohorts 23–29 years of age. An additional interesting pattern derives from a gender comparison for urban Mexico, as older women are revealed to have greater intergenerational mobility when compared to men.

Returns to education are very high in Latin America, which implies that differences in schooling eventually translate into differences in

Table 6.5 Schooling Elasticity by Cohort, Chile

Son cohort	Father–son schooling elasticity
23–34	0.15
35–44	0.15
45–54	0.24
55–65	0.41
Entire sample	0.21

Source: Núñez and Miranda (2007).

earnings. For example, for the case of Brazil, there is evidence that returns to education increase with levels of parental schooling (Lam and Schoeni, 1993). These factors are linked to family connections and better employment opportunities, which indicates that the intergenerational correlation for earnings can be even higher than that for levels of schooling. For Brazil and Colombia, Behrman, Gaviria, and Székely (2001) find very low educational mobility for children of parents with low levels of education (see Table 6.7).

Educational Quality and Cognitive Outcomes

Most studies on the relationship between education and intergenerational social mobility look at years of schooling completed. However, increasingly the evidence for the region shows important gaps in educational quality and cognitive outcomes between

Figure 6.6
Social Mobility Index
(Based on Teenagers, 13–19 Years)

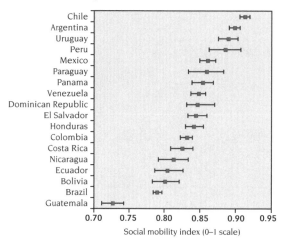

Source: Andersen (2001).
Note: Figure depicts point estimates and 95 percent confidence intervals. Statistics for Argentina and Uruguay are based on urban samples only.

Figure 6.7
Correlation between Parents' and Children's
Education Levels

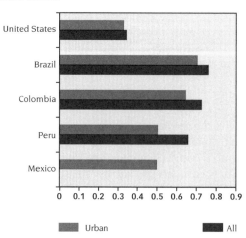

Source: Behrman, Gaviria, and Székely (2001).
Note: For Mexico, only urban data are available.

high- and low-income children. Researchers and policymakers are thus considering "equality of opportunities" in order to identify the causal processes determining the long-term labor market outcomes of children. Generational earnings mobility, understood in the context of equality of opportunities, thus offers an overall indicator of children's social inclusion. In practical terms, there is a need for measurements of the extent to which children have equal opportunities in life regardless of their social status or family background (see, for example, Corak, 2006, and Roemer, 2004). Since children start building the bases for human capital accumulation and development of cognitive abilities in early childhood, the effects of parental income on early childhood development, and in turn on human capital accumulation and productive capacity, must be taken into account.

Many studies have found that household economic resources, variously defined, are important determinants of children's health, which influences children's educational attainment. Rubalcava and Teruel (2004) find that maternal cognitive ability is an important factor in determining children's height—a proxy for overall health—and early childhood health is in turn eventually linked with schooling. Studying Mexican households, Mayer-Foulkes (2004) likewise finds that early childhood health and nutrition are strongly associated with the probability of continuing schooling later in life. Early childhood development also affects the productive capacity of adults through the effects of infant malnutrition and early infection on cognitive ability and various adult ailments.[1] Moreover, the medical literature suggests that deficits in early childhood are difficult if not impossible to offset later in life, particularly because of irreversible processes in brain formation.

Urbanization and Regional Development

Although recent research has not emphasized the importance of spatial issues (see, for example, Cass, Shove, and Urry, 2005), exclusion that results from a combination of urbanization, geographical isolation, inadequate transportation, and limited means of communication reinforces the existence of mobility traps in certain regions. The lower dynamism of rural and isolated poor areas, for instance, should imply relatively low levels of income mobility, and countries with higher percentages of rural population should similarly be expected to have lower levels of income mobility. Although the urbanization process and increased opportunities for migration from poorer areas may be expected to promote higher mobility, this expectation can be frustrated by development that is concentrated in certain regions and not accompanied by adequate migration opportunities into these regions from poorer areas.

---

[1] Diseases and conditions included in the review by Mayer-Foulkes (2004) include chronic bronchitis, acute appendicitis, asthma, Parkinson's disease, multiple sclerosis, chronic pulmonary disease, cardiovascular disease, coronary disease, and stroke.

Figure 6.8
Educational Mobility in Latin America and the United States

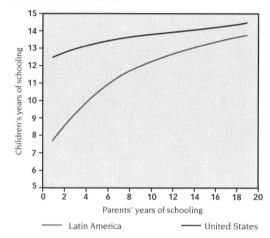

Source: Gaviria (2005), using data from Latinobarometer (2000) and National Opinion Research Center (various years).

Figure 6.9
Gender Differences in Intergenerational Transmission of Educational Attainment (Urban Populations)

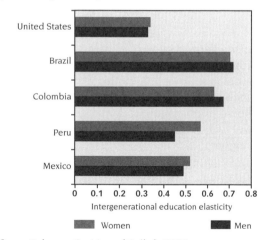

Source: Behrman, Gaviria, and Székely (2001).

	Child's characteristics	Father–child educational attainment correlations		Percentage exceeding parent's education level	
		Men	Women	Men	Women
Mexico, 1994 (urban areas)					
All cohorts	23–69 years of age	0.498	0.528	76	68
Cohort 1	50–69 years of age	0.569	0.588	64	49
Cohort 2	40–49 years of age	0.481	0.538	75	63
Cohort 3	30–39 years of age	0.425	0.491	80	73
Cohort 4a	23–29 years of age	0.491	0.493	79	78
Cohort 4b	Eventual schooling	0.497	0.489	83	80
Germany, 1984	19–26 years of age	0.237	0.016	n.d.	n.d.
Malaysia, 1988	8–50 years of age	0.194	0.226	n.d.	n.d.
Panama, 1983	18+ years, living with father	0.570	n.d.	n.d.	n.d.
	Father of above	0.680	n.d.	n.d.	n.d.
United States, 1984	20–30 years of age	0.418	0.402	n.d.	n.d.

Table 6.6 Measures of Intergenerational School Mobility: Mexico and Other Countries

Source: Binder and Woodruff (2002).
Note: Measures for Mexico use sample weights. Figures for cohort 4b are calculated using ascribed schooling attainments for those still in school as follows: twelve years of schooling are ascribed to students with fewer than twelve years of schooling, and eighteen years of schooling are ascribed to those with twelve or more years of schooling. n.d. = no data.

Problems of this nature have attended Brazil's "conservative modernization" pattern, characterized by the nonintegration of large segments of the population into modern sectors of the economy, society, and political system (see, for example, Gacitúa Marió and Woolcock, 2005a). The effects extend to regional development; one can identify distinct mobility patterns according to regional development and urbanization. These patterns seem to translate into lower social mobility in less-developed regions, as Ferreira and Veloso (2004) (see Table 6.8) find that income persistence varies substantially across regions.

Figure 6.10 depicts the positive relationship between social mobility and urbanization rates. This positive relationship may arise from the fact that for highly urbanized countries, it is easier to promote social mobility through access to education and labor market opportunities when children and workers are clustered in urban areas. Migrants to urban centers, especially those from isolated rural areas, tend to have broader economic and human capital opportunities than their parents, which should translate into upward social mobility. It is important to take into account, however, that urbanization is not a panacea, as it does not necessarily help all population groups. Using a social mobility index based on educational attainment levels of teenagers in eighteen countries, Andersen (2001) finds that, with the exception of those in Bolivia, urban teenagers

| Table 6.7 Intergenerational Education Transition Matrices (percent) | | | | |
Education of parents	Primary or less	Some secondary	Secondary	At least some higher
Colombia, 1997				
Primary or less	51.2	24.2	14.1	10.5
Some secondary	12.6	26.2	25.4	35.9
Secondary	9.1	17.3	25.4	48.2
At least some higher	2.2	6.5	14.2	77.1
Total	41.7	23.2	16.2	18.8
Brazil, 1996				
Primary or less	60.2	23.9	10.8	5.1
Some secondary	13.2	32.0	29.2	25.7
Secondary	5.5	19.0	32.7	42.9
At least some higher	3.5	11.9	19.9	64.7
Total	54.6	24.0	12.8	8.8

Source: Behrman, Gaviria, and Székely (2001).

Table 6.8 Intergenerational Income Elasticity in Brazil, by Region	
Region	Elasticity
National	0.58
Northeast	0.73
Southeast	0.54
South	0.62
Midwest	0.55

Source: Ferreira and Veloso (2004).

are not necessarily more mobile than their rural counterparts; that is, rural and urban teenagers are affected in approximately the same way by family background.

Labor Market Developments

The most important determinant of social mobility is the human capital that individuals bring to the labor market. However, labor market dynamics can also alter levels of social mobility, as returns to human capital vary with changes in the supply of and demand for certain groups of workers, either strengthening or weakening the effect of greater education opportunities on mobility. In addition, discrimination and labor market segmentation can lower social mobility, even in countries with ample access to education, by reducing the labor returns of educated but excluded groups.

Prospects for improved social mobility are further complicated by the fact that, with some exceptions, the region's labor markets have in recent decades suffered from stagnant wages, rising wage inequality—mostly associated with high returns to education— and increasing levels of unemployment. Possible explanations for these phenomena have been explored in the previous two chapters of this report. Researchers generally agree

Figure 6.10
Social Mobility and Urbanization Rates

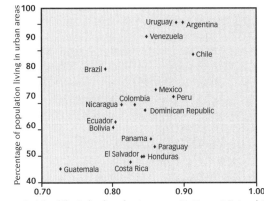

Source: Andersen (2000).
Note: Data for Argentina and Uruguay are based on urban samples only.

Figure 6.11
Household Income Inequality in Selected Latin American Countries, 1990–2005

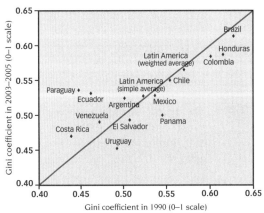

Source: ECLAC (2006b).

that the region's low wage growth stems primarily from an absence of growth in productivity, particularly among low-skilled workers.

Changes in labor markets have had a variety of effects on social mobility. As shown in Figure 6.11, national changes in the inequality of household income (i.e., the income of all members of a particular household) have displayed varying patterns, decreasing in some countries (Brazil, Colombia, El Salvador, Honduras, Panama, and Uruguay), increasing in others (Argentina, Ecuador, Costa Rica, Paraguay, and Venezuela), and remaining relatively constant in still others (such as Mexico and Chile). On the other hand, inequality in wages (i.e., the labor income of individual workers) has increased in the majority of countries in the region (Figure 6.12), decreasing only in Brazil and Colombia, and remaining unchanged in Argentina, Chile, Guatemala, and Honduras.[2] For purposes of simplicity, inequality in wages, rather than household income, is emphasized here.

Given that most of the region's population depends on labor income as its primary source of income, it is important to determine the conditions under which changes in income inequality, and more specifically in wage inequality, translate into changes in social mobility. Whether worsening inequality will correspond to lower social mobility clearly depends on the conditions underlying changes in labor mobility and how they affect families at different socioeconomic levels.

---

[2] Differences in the dynamics between wage inequality and total per capita household income inequality usually result from household demographics (assortative matching and fertility), female labor force participation, and transfers (government transfers and remittances).

Although data on these issues remain limited, some hypotheses can be advanced. With respect to returns to education, under low levels of intergenerational mobility in educational attainment, a widening gap of returns to skills should increase inequality and reduce social mobility as the advantages in labor market outcomes for some families increase over time. An increase in intergenerational educational mobility, on the other hand, should ameliorate the effects of widening gaps in returns to skill.

The available evidence suggests that the widening of gaps in returns to skills contributes to increased income inequality in some of the countries of the region that have experienced increases or no changes in wage inequality; in Mexico, for instance, the widening gap in returns to education explains 25 percent of the increase in income inequality between 1984 and 1994 (Legovini, Bouillón, and Lustig, 2005). In contrast, reduction in wage inequality in Brazil is associated with a decrease in both inequality of educational attainment in the labor force and the gap in returns to education (IPEA, 2006). As Figure 6.13 indicates, wage inequality decreased in Brazil between 1987 and 2004, and the ratio of skilled to unskilled workers' wages fell by 14.3 percent between 1987 and 1995 (Ferreira, Leite, and Wai-Poi, 2007); Gonzaga, Menezes Filho, and Terra (2006) found similar results when analyzing the skill premium in manufacturing.

Figure 6.12
Wage Inequality in Latin American Countries, 1990 and 2002

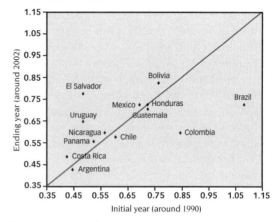

Source: ECLAC (2006b).
Note: Wage inequality is measured as the variance of the logarithm of hourly wages in urban areas.

Figure 6.13
Skill Wage Premium and Share of Skilled Workers in Total Employment, Brazil, 1987–2004

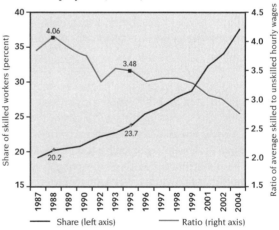

Source: Ferreira, Leite, and Wai-Poi (2007).
Note: Unskilled workers are defined as those who have ten or fewer years of schooling. Skilled workers are defined as those who have eleven or more years of schooling. No information is available for 1991, 1994, 2000, and 2003.

There are several explanations for the occurrence of these changes in Brazil. First, there was a reduction in the gap in wage returns by educational level, especially the gap between those with no education and those with primary education (IPEA, 2006), which may be attributed to the expansion of the country's primary education system. In addition, from 2001 onward, even returns to postsecondary education over no education started falling. Second, trade liberalization during the 1988–1995 period also contributed to the reduction in wage inequality in the country. Protection in Brazil had been particularly strong for skilled-worker-intensive industries and, unlike the experience in Mexico, Chile, and Colombia, trade liberalization in Brazil seems to have promoted wage gains at the bottom of the distribution. Liberalization efforts in the latter country have led to both productivity gains and wage gains for the poor and have promoted mobility, as well as reducing poverty and inequality (Ferreira, Leite, and Wai-Poi, 2007).

A more general explanation, for many countries in the region, is that increases in wage inequality have not translated directly into increases in household income inequality because of increased female labor force participation and lower fertility rates. Reductions in inequality arising from these factors thus do not necessarily translate into higher social mobility.

CONCLUSION

The measurement of social mobility in Latin America and the Caribbean is still in its infancy, but what is known so far presents a troubling scenario. Aside from limited progress in some countries and among some groups, most individuals in the region are unlikely to see significant improvements in their income or social position, or that of their children, regardless of effort or ability. Incentives to work, acquire skills, or refrain from socially undesirable behavior are seriously constrained when there is no clear path out of social exclusion.

Conversely, the much smaller portion of the population that enjoys income and opportunities comparable to those of the developed world's middle and upper classes displays little downward mobility, again regardless of (lack of) effort or ability. The consequences of this situation may not be apparent in the short term, but the long-term consequences cannot be ignored. With notable exceptions, privileged and more fully "included" citizens who have little chance of losing their means or status are unlikely to engage in innovation or risk taking that leads to economic growth and other forms of social dynamism. These privileges and advantages of fully included citizens may even lead to claims that members of more privileged groups, including public officials, are more concerned with maintaining their status than furthering the public good.

The region's low level of social mobility thus presents policymakers with an array of challenges. The first is to design policies and programs, and possibly to undertake legal reforms, that will equip individuals to participate in both the benefits and responsibilities of society. Improvements in educational quality and access, health care and nutrition, and access to credit represent only a few possible areas for improvement. Second, labor institutions, social security systems, and macroeconomic conditions must ensure that effort, talent, and socially desirable behavior are rewarded both immediately and across generations. Third, policymakers would be ill-advised to address insufficient social mobility with short-term redistributions of wealth that, though initially popular, may ultimately prove ineffective in improving the socioeconomic status of recipients in the long term. Policies must therefore emphasize equality of opportunities through the development of human and social capital rather than short-term attempts to equalize outcomes. Finally, policy-makers and politicians must find ways to convince the electorate and their colleagues that these policies are ultimately in their own interest and build support for their proposals accordingly. This may prove the hardest task of all.

CHAPTER 7

To What Extent Do Latin Americans Trust and Cooperate? Field Experiments on Social Exclusion in Six Latin American Countries

The puzzle of cooperation among humans remains central and relevant. In fact, in 2005 *Science* magazine listed "How did cooperative behavior evolve?" as one of the twenty-five most relevant scientific puzzles to be solved in the next quarter century. However incompletely understood, cooperation and collective action have represented pervasive and ubiquitous features of human experience across time, place, and income level. Cooperation—and the failure to cooperate—have affected societies in ways that range from the organization of hunters and gatherers and "tragedies of the commons" in the use of shared resources to automobile traffic control and responses to global warming. Moreover, many social interactions involving cooperation risk losses of efficiency as a result of externalities or problems with the provision of public goods, and some individuals "free-ride" on the contributions of others. When there is a lack of trust such free-riding intensifies, thus reducing opportunities to produce socially efficient outcomes and accentuating inequalities in the distribution of outcomes.

Free-riding and lack of coordination represent daily challenges in the lives of communities. For instance, when the state fails in the performance of its expected functions, communities attempt to solve collective action problems themselves, and in multiple ways. Households contribute labor to starting or maintaining local projects that benefit their neighborhoods, and neighborhoods contribute local funds that pay for security or playground maintenance. Child care, recreation parks, water provision, and street cleaning are all examples of projects for which groups contribute privately to public goods. Groups additionally organize to deal with problems other than those that arise from collective action, such as risk management involving credit, natural disasters, political violence, and crime. In these cases the formation of groups to deal with risk involves in itself a collective action problem, and payments for cooperation can be distributed across the group. Vulnerable groups in societies are more likely to face the challenges of collective action, either because they are left out of the regular channels that societies use to cooperate or because they face more vital risks in their daily lives and have a greater need to pool than members of other groups.

Free-riding and coordination problems have been studied by sociologists, psychologists, and more recently by economists. The last have engaged in highly controlled experiments involving relatively small groups of individuals whose members are typically given a particular sum of money and allowed to invest in a group exchange or keep the money. If participants invest in the group exchange, the returns on that investment will depend on what the group as a whole invests in. The experiment is designed so that the private return from keeping the money exceeds the private return from the group exchange; the social return of the group exchange, however, is higher than that of keeping the money. This experiment yields a dominant strategy in which an individual will contribute zero to the group exchange while hoping that the individuals will invest in the group exchange, even though that does not represent an optimal allocation (see Andreoni, 1988, and Marwell and Ames, 1979, among others). In other words, experiments try to replicate cooperation and related dilemmas as predicted by economic theory.

Economic experiments in this area have so far yielded two key results. First, economic theory overestimates the prevalence of free-riding. In fact, even though experiments find that outcomes are closer to the free-riding result (where nobody contributes) than to the socially optimal one (where everybody contributes), experiments show that individuals still contribute more than would be implied by pure self-interest (Rabin, 1993; Andreoni, 1995). This is particularly true in "one-shot," nonrepeated games, which contrasts with predictions based on a strong version of the free-riding hypothesis (Dawes and Thaler, 1988). A second and similar result is that violations of dominant strategies diminish with repetition and with game experience (e.g., Andreoni, 1988; Isaac and Walker, 1988; Kim and Walker, 1984). These findings have led researchers to explore possible explanations including "kindness," concern with reputation, and confusion on the part of individuals in regard to the rules of the game and the consequences of their decisions (Palfrey and Prisbrey, 1997).

This chapter attempts to build on existing research by studying the microfoundations and mechanisms that may affect the possibility of collective action and group formation by different social groups. Of particular note is the reporting of results from a field approach, using survey and experimental methods, that focuses on the behavioral aspects of the collective action problem while taking into account the social and economic contexts in which microinteractions happen. The research summarized here has involved the direct observation of individuals facing problems of trust, collective action, and uncertainty under different levels of social heterogeneity and exclusion. The experimental design of this project thus captures key dimensions of problems at the intersection of trust and exclusion and makes it possible to derive lessons on collective action and group-oriented behavior in societies.

COOPERATION AND SOCIAL EXCLUSION

Over time human societies have attempted to minimize losses resulting from problems of collective action by harnessing the conflict between individual and social outcomes through incentives, generally in the form of norms and laws.[1] Although the possibility of cooperation within a group is determined by multiple factors, one of the most controversial is group heterogeneity. Some argue that heterogeneity offers the additional incentives necessary for a small subgroup to be interested in providing a public good (Olson, 1965; Bergstrom, Blume, and Varian, 1986), yet others claim that heterogeneity creates difficulties in agreement and problem solving (Alesina and La Ferrara, 2000).

Since the benefits of economic and social progress are often unequally distributed, social heterogeneity is intrinsically linked to the problem of exclusion. Nonetheless, win-

---

[1] This section further discusses collective action, behavior, and social exclusion issues and may be read independently of the rest of the chapter.

ners and losers, haves and have-nots, and the included and the excluded can engage in mutually beneficial interactions if the collective action problem is solved. The importance of addressing this problem can hardly be overestimated, as few individuals have the option of living and working only with persons like themselves. Vulnerable individuals, for example, must interact with nonexcluded groups and individuals in environments including labor, housing, and informal and formal credit markets. Likewise, on other occasions heterogeneous groups share common spaces and must make decisions that affect their common interests, quite often with asymmetric stakes across subgroups. Riding public transportation, using public parks, participating in debate on a public issue, and voting all represent instances in which members of a society must make decisions that result in varying benefits and costs depending on the actions of other group members. Social scientists often refer to decisions of this type as a game, in order to facilitate the study of behavior in these situations.

Cooperating or forming groups to produce a group-beneficial outcome is usually costly in monetary or other terms. Sometimes a coordination game is involved in which each individual will benefit more if everyone else behaves in a socially optimal way, and the resulting payments thus drive individuals towards the best outcome without conflicts between individual and group interests. Other instances involve collective action games in which the optimal individual behavior would be not to cooperate, although everyone in the group would benefit if everyone cooperated. In either case, the group needs to find—and create—conditions under which individuals will choose to make decisions that benefit all members of a group even when those decisions are individually costly. These conditions are defined by several behavioral issues. Individuals may make decisions, for instance, according to a sense of group or subgroup affiliation, or social distance from or sympathy toward others in the group. Their personal evaluation of the benefits and costs of forming a group or cooperating in a collective action dilemma may be mediated by their expectations of the actions of others as well as their valuation of the distributional and efficiency consequences of their actions.

Formal and informal institutions play a major role in shaping individuals' decisions, as they provide key information for a person who is bearing the cost of group-oriented action. Individuals use information from the context in which a game operates in order to inform their decisions and therefore provide the best possible benefits for every player. It should be noted that those benefits may include an increase in payments to others, an increase in social welfare, or a decrease in inequality, because his or her preferences involve prosociality as part of his or her interests. In any case, the individual will collect information from his or her personal, group, and social contexts and transform the relative payments of the game when making his or her decision. Figure 7.1 illustrates how such a cognitive process may operate (Cárdenas and Ostrom, 2006), involving layers of information obtained from various contexts. The bottom left layer of information in the figure ("static game layer") involves the initial calculations about benefits and costs of a decision at a certain time t as a one-shot game, within the formal rules and action sets of the individual. Within our framework, individuals do not base their decisions to engage in collective action solely on this layer. They also consider the aspects of other elements, including dynamic aspects of the game in previous $(t-1)$ and future $(t+1)$ rounds ("dynamic game layer" in the figure) (e.g., whether the game will be repeated with the same

Figure 7.1
Layers of Information from Individual, Group, and Social Contexts That Transform a Game

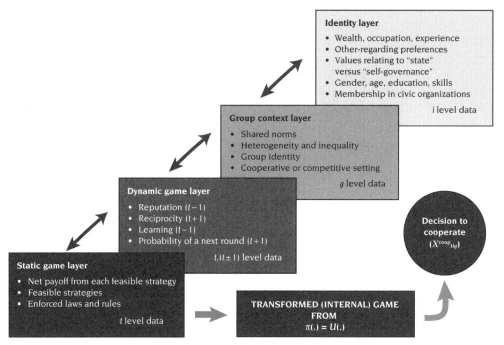

Source: Adapted from Cárdenas and Ostrom (2006).

players, and previous experience with the same players). Also, players will consider the composition of the group with whom they are playing ("group context layer") (e.g., an individual might be more willing to cooperate with certain players in his or her group than others, based on group membership, identity, or social distance). Finally, at the top right of Figure 7.1 ("identity layer"), the framework suggests that there might also be individual normative aspects or values that constrain the initial action set (e.g., certain values may eliminate antisocial or cheating behavior in games irrespective of their counterparts or the context). As will be shown in the results of our experiments, and as has been shown in previous behavioral literature, individuals seem to use these layers of information when deciding to trust others or to cooperate with others. The key proposition of this behavioral and institutional approach to the problem of collective action and group-oriented behavior is that individuals use information from their personal, group, and social contexts to transform the game situation and make the best decision according to their own personal and other-regarding preferences.

Solving the prisoner's dilemma, the tragedy of the commons, or any collective action dilemma requires individuals to trust their partners in the interaction. Trusting others under incomplete contracts, however, involves the possibility that the trusting action results in receipt of no benefits from the trustees and creates net losses for the trusting person. If the trustees reciprocate, though, the group increases its social net welfare.

Figure 7.2
Factors That Affect the Virtuous Circle of Cooperation (Reputation, Trust, and Reciprocity)

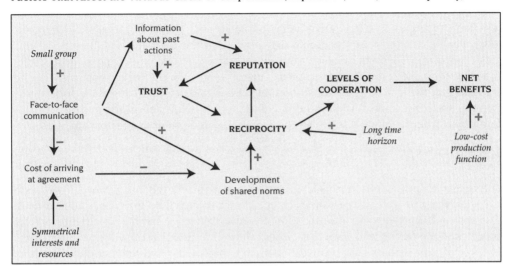

Source: Ostrom (1998).

If the game is repeated, players can engage in a virtuous circle of trust and reciprocity, building a reputation for being trusting and trustworthy and collecting information about the trust and trustworthiness of others in the group (Ostrom, 1998). If the game is played only once, players may still be willing to cooperate if institutions and personal characteristics provide sufficient positive information for players to involve themselves in group-oriented behavior.

The uncertainty of the intentions and actions of the other actors is a crucial part of the problem of collective action. Individuals may have information about past actions of specific individuals or more general patterns of past behavior by groups, as well as information on the social norms that usually guide the behavior of those interacting with them. As some uncertainty remains nevertheless, understanding the willingness to trust, cooperate, or engage in costly group-oriented behavior involves understanding individuals' risk preferences (Bohnet and Zeckhauser, 2004; Ashraf, Bohnet, and Piankov, 2006).

The behavioral literature on collective action suggests that a number of factors feed the virtuous circle of trust, reputation, and reciprocity (Figure 7.2). Several of these factors are associated with social exclusion and group inequality. The seminal work of Olson (1965) discusses how heterogeneity may affect cooperation and collective action, and social exclusion may affect the cycle of trust, reciprocity, and reputation in several ways. According to Ostrom's approach, exclusion may create not only different interests, but also different endowments and resources for those engaged in a group activity. Under these circumstances face-to-face communication may be more difficult or impossible if some individuals in the group are excluded, and in heterogeneous groups whose members know little about one another, there is likely to be only limited availability of information on the past actions of others. In-group and out-group effects thus make the development of shared norms across excluded and included groups particularly costly.

Equally relevant is the question of whether certain homogeneous groups are more or less likely to engage in cooperative behavior than others because of their socioeconomic level, wealth, or human capital. Some may argue that the poor are less likely to solve a collective action dilemma because their opportunity cost of cooperating is much higher than that for those less constrained by income or wealth. On the other hand, some would contend that the lack of assets or smooth income creates conditions for the poor to rely on their social networks and on others like them to provide key goods and services offered by neither the state nor private providers based on their market possibilities.

EXPERIMENTAL SETUP

The research undertaken for this chapter attempts to study the interaction between social exclusion and collective action in Latin America using a field experimental approach. The project began with the identification of a representative sample of individuals from six cities in the region who were then asked whether they would be willing to participate in a set of experiments that involved economic incentives. The full sample consists of more than 3,000 observations, or roughly 500 individuals per city from different backgrounds, socioeconomic levels, and age cohorts and both sexes in Bogotá, Buenos Aires, Caracas, Lima, Montevideo, and San José.

A team of researchers with experience in survey and field methods was selected to undertake the experiments and surveys in each city, and to guarantee homogeneity in the application of experimental protocols, those researchers in charge of each city participated in a training workshop at the launching of the project.[2] This workshop provided participants with a uniform approach to implementation and related fieldwork details such as sampling procedures, timing of actions (i.e., invitations, presurvey, experiments, postsurveys), elements to be included in experimental sessions, and the construction of questionnaires. Each survey team agreed to conduct twenty-five experimental sessions with an average of twenty participants each.[3]

With the sampling quotas defined, the first step of the fieldwork consisted of inviting individuals to experimental sessions. The sessions were arranged so that at least three sessions per city included only individuals from high-income strata and at least three other sessions included only individuals from low-income strata; the rest combined individuals from all strata. Around thirty individuals were invited for each session, under the assumption that approximately one-third would not show up for the session, with each experimental session allowed to go forward with roughly twenty participants.

Potential participants were invited several days before the scheduled sessions, and at the time of invitation, individuals were asked a set of basic demographic questions

---

[2] The training workshop was held in Bogotá at the beginning of 2007.
[3] The samples were selected in the cities using a stratified random sampling procedure. The strata were chosen on the basis of education, average family income of the districts or the territorial units that make up each city (in either quartiles or quintiles, depending on data availability), gender, and age (with four age groups: 17–27, 28–38, 39–59, and 60–72). The goal of the sampling procedure was to obtain empirical distributions of individuals within these combinations resembling those of the populations in the cities.

in order to enable the researchers to fulfill the sampling quotas described previously. Participants were additionally promised remuneration and provided with information on the expected monetary gains from their participation in the experiments. The day before each experimental session, the invited participants were reminded of the invitation with a phone call or home visit, and research staff worked with potential participants to arrange transportation if necessary. On the day of the sessions, the participants were welcomed by experimental teams, and at the appointed time, the sessions started. Following the experiments, participants in each session completed surveys designed to collect additional sociodemographic information and determine their attitudes, beliefs, and preferences regarding social exclusion, discrimination, minorities, and prosocial norms. To reduce the possibilities of idiosyncratic measurement error due to individuals' reading ability, the surveys were administered by the monitors of the experiments and supported by a group of pollsters specially trained for this purpose. After participants completed the surveys, they were paid, based on the results of one of the experiments (randomly selected by the monitors).

As one of the main goals of the study is to observe the effect of social heterogeneity on individuals' decisions, information on the socioeconomic composition of the groups in each particular session was made as salient and clear as possible. The participants met throughout the session in one room where they were able to see each other, although they were not allowed to communicate during the session. As the sessions progressed, participants received information about their peers, depending on the particular activity.

More than 3,000 people participated in 148 sessions in six cities, providing a unique data set that combines detailed data from their socioeconomic and demographic backgrounds with behavioral data from their decisions during the experiments. Each of the city teams conducted sessions of various group sizes, from ten to thirty-nine people, and each session followed the same protocol, with the same sequence of activities. This is the most comprehensive experimental data set to date in Latin America, given the number of countries included and the replicability of the designs in each city.

Table 7.1 provides basic demographic statistics of the sample, by city and overall, comparing it with a representative sample of individuals extracted from the national household surveys of the countries in the project (restricting the computation to the capital cities). The comparison reveals remarkable similarities between the experimental samples and those of the national household surveys; the only potential difference of note is that individuals in the experimental samples were slightly younger and more educated than the average individual in their respective cities.

Interactions among participants took place in a controlled setting where it was possible to observe how incentives, institutions, and norms may affect behavior, and the experiments were conducted in a manner that allowed measurement of how the degree of group heterogeneity affects individual decisions and group outcomes. The design follows the approach shown in Figure 7.3, which proposes a series of relationships among the key explanatory factors of collective action.[4] In this framework the working hypothesis is that

---

[4] The experiments in this project are adapted from previous work and experimental literature surveys including Berg, Dickhaut, and McCabe (1995), Binswanger (1980), Holt and Laury (2002), Barr (2003), Marwell and Ames (1979), Isaac and Walker (1988), Carpenter, Harrison, and List (2005), Harrison and List (2004), Cárdenas (2003), and Carpenter and Cárdenas (forthcoming).

Table 7.1   Demographic Characteristics of Participants in Experiments

Descriptive statistics	Bogotá	Buenos Aires	Caracas	Lima	Montevideo	San José	Six cities (weighted average)	
							Experimental sample	Household surveys
Average age	36	40	34	35	41	37	37	40
Percentage of female population	59	51	56	52	57	61	56	54
Percentage with public education	65	79	61	74	89	91	76	52
Percentage working in the public sector	10	16	20	21	28	22	20	11
Percentage with health care coverage or pensions	89	73	50	31	79	57	65	32
Parental relationship (percentage)								
Household head	39	43	24	31	46	37	37	38
Wife/husband	24	28	23	22	21	27	24	24
Son/daughter	27	26	40	38	25	23	30	27
Other	10	3	13	9	8	14	9	11
Marital status (percentage)								
Single	38	35	47	44	29	39	38	33
Formal or informal union	45	54	43	46	47	46	47	55
Divorced, widowed	16	12	10	9	24	15	15	13
Educational level (percentage)								
Secondary incomplete or less	35	15	10	16	52	59	31	48
Secondary complete	21	34	23	28	13	13	22	25
Tertiary complete or incomplete	44	51	67	55	36	28	47	27
Socioeconomic level (percentage)								
Low	42	33	21	41	19	28	31	
Middle	44	34	54	49	55	50	48	
High	14	33	25	10	25	22	21	
Sessions								
Number of participants	567	498	488	541	580	415	3,089[a]	
Number of sessions	28	25	25	25	28	17	148[a]	
Size of the group for the smallest session	12	14	14	14	14	10	10[b]	
Size of the group for the largest session	29	30	28	32	30	39	39[c]	
Average size per session	21	20	20	23	22	27	22	

Source: Cárdenas, Chong, and Ñopo (2007).
[a] These figures are not averages; they correspond to the total for the row.
[b] This figure is not an average; it represents the minimum for the row.
[c] This figure is not an average; it represents the maximum for the row.

Figure 7.3

Interaction of Mechanisms for Group-Oriented Actions: An Experimental Approach

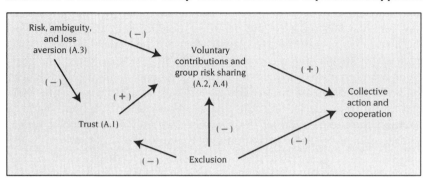

exclusion may affect trust and prosocial behaviors such as group formation and collective action in various ways, according to the relationships in Figures 7.1 and 7.2. Exclusion may negatively affect trust and voluntary contributions to a group project, as it reduces the availability of information about past actions and implies more asymmetric interests among players. Exclusion also reduces the sense of belonging to a group-oriented activity and therefore can affect voluntary contributions and group formation. In-group/out-group effects have additionally been reported (Marwell and Ames, 1979; Ostrom, 1998) as key factors in explaining collective action in groups.

The experiments provide key information about individual behavior and group outcomes regarding the possibilities for and limitations of collective action in groups, as well as clues regarding individuals' motivations and limitations in making decisions that may solve collective action problems. Ultimately, the results help to provide an understanding of how social heterogeneity and social exclusion affect possibilities for actions that create greater benefits to groups.

The experimental design was based on four activities (A.1–A.4) in which participants made individual decisions that had economic outcomes for themselves and for the others in their group.[5] Participants were informed before the first activity began that they would receive a payment based on the outcome of one of the activities (randomly selected by the experimenter). The four activities were undertaken in a session of two to three hours. The sequence of activities was as follows:

- **Experiment 1 (Trust Game):** In this game all participants in each session were randomly assigned to pairs, half of the participants assuming the role of player 1 and the other half player 2. The two groups of players were located in different rooms. Identities were never revealed, but each player was given information about demographic characteristics of the other player in his or her pair: age, gender, education, and an indication of socioeconomic level of the

---

[5] See Candelo and Polanía (2007) for details on the protocols used for the four activities.

neighborhood (high, medium, or low) where the player lived.[6] Both players received an endowment, and player 1 was then asked to decide how much of this endowment to send to player 2. The amount sent was then tripled on its way from player 1 to player 2. In the other room, player 2 was asked to decide the amount to be returned to player 1 for each possible offer from player 1. Each player knew in full the rules governing the operation of the game before being asked to make his or her allocation decisions. Immediately before making his or her decision, each of the players was asked to predict the decision that would be made by the other player. After both players had made their decision, the choice of player 1 was matched with the corresponding response for that amount by player 2, determining the outcome of the game.

This experimental game permits the measurement of the extent to which an individual trusts another person of similar or different socioeconomic characteristics, and whether the actions and characteristics of that individual affect the response of his or her partner in the game. In short, the game measures trust and reciprocity. Higher offers by the first individual are interpreted as signals of trust, and higher returns from the second individual are taken as signals of reciprocity. The game-theoretical prediction for this game is that player 1 will send an offer of zero, as there is no assurance that player 2 will return any amount. Replications of this game around the world have shown that people on average send half of the initial endowment to player 2, and that the returns from player 2 to player 1 generate a net positive return for player 1 of about 10–20 percent over what was originally sent.

- **Experiment 2 (Voluntary Contributions Mechanism):** In a second experiment, participants gathered in a single room and participated in a voluntary contributions mechanism (VCM) or public goods game. Each player was given a token that could be kept or invested in a group project. If a player kept the token, he or she earned an amount (e.g., $10). If the player invested the token in the group project (i.e., if he or she was a "cooperator"), his or her token and the rest of tokens in the group account each yielded a return of $1 to every participant in the group. A player who kept the token also received $1 times the number of tokens in the group account. Before they made their individual (private) decision whether to contribute to the group, the monitor announced orally and wrote on a board the gender, age, education, and socioeconomic composition (i.e., the number of individuals from high, medium, and low socioeconomic neighborhoods) of the group. Also, in order to capture expectations, the monitor requested that every participant write his or her prediction about the fraction of group members who would be cooperators.

---

[6] Characterization of neighborhood socioeconomic levels (districts or territorial units in which the cities were divided) was made on the basis of the average family income information that was gathered in the presampling stage.

The public goods or VCM experiment captures a similar dimension of trust, though in this case regarding a group instead of an individual, by measuring willingness to contribute a token to a public good and provide benefits to all group members. The decision to contribute to the group increases the benefits for all, but not contributing will always yield greater individual payments and thus provide an incentive to free-ride. Full cooperation yields greater payments to everyone than if full free-riding occurs, and the gains from cooperation increase with the number of players. A key element of the game is that no player knows in advance how many of the group members will contribute. The players know only general socioeconomic characteristics of the other players before making the decision.

- **Experiment 3 (Three Risk Games):** Each player individually made decisions in three games measuring individual attitudes in regard to risk, ambiguity, and losses.
  - The first game, measuring risk aversion, offered the participants a choice among six 50/50 lotteries with known probabilities and known outcomes that ranged from a sure low payment to an all-or-nothing higher payment (with the lotteries in between increasing gradually in expected value and in the spread of the low and high payment).
  - The second game, measuring ambiguity aversion, offered the same payments for the six lotteries mentioned. In contrast to the first game, however, individuals did not know the exact probabilities but were informed only that at least 30 percent of the chances were for the low payment and also at least 30 percent for the high payoff.
  - The third game, measuring loss aversion, used six lotteries with 50 percent probabilities for each outcome but included the possibility of negative payments in some cases.[7]

The individual risk games are based on three components of risk behavior. These three games allow a distinguishing of risk attitudes in terms of risk aversion, ambiguity aversion, and loss aversion. The first game measures risk aversion, based on known probabilities and known outcomes for six 50/50 lotteries. Choosing lotteries with lower payments can be interpreted as greater risk aversion. The second game measures risk ambiguity, and the third, loss aversion. The purpose of this activity is to generate measures of risk behavior in order to link them with trust and cooperative behavior.

- **Experiment 4 (Risk Pooling):** Each player was given the opportunity to choose whether to form a group (i.e., a "subgroup" of the group participating in the session) to share equally the gains from another risk aversion game or to play the risk aversion game individually. Once players decided whether to form the group or not, the total number of people forming the group was announced,

---

[7] To avoid negative payments the players were endowed with a fixed amount in this game regardless of gains or losses.

Figure 7.4
Participation in Groups and Organizations

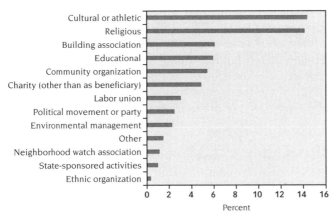

Source: Cárdenas, Chong, and Ñopo (2007).

and the players then made their decisions in their individual risk game.

This game measures individuals' willingness to join a group and to accept an even distribution of payments after choosing again a lottery like those available in the first of the individual risk games. As in the VCM game, the purpose of this game is to determine whether an individual will base his or her decision to join a group on the potential socioeconomic composition of the group (in this case, based on the socioeconomic composition of the group in the session). Again, players were not allowed to communicate with one another and were given only basic information about the composition of the session group (age, education, gender, and socioeconomic composition). It should be noted that in this game the most profitable group outcome would occur when all players joined the group and chose higher-risk lotteries (at 50 percent chance of the high payment, the expected value should yield greater payments to everyone in the group).

At the end of the last activity the monitor randomly selected one of the activities to be paid, and while one monitor calculated individual earnings and privately called upon each participant to distribute them, the remaining monitors interviewed each participant, filling out an individual survey with detailed information about socioeconomic characteristics and attitudes, beliefs, and preferences in regard to various dimensions of social exclusion.

BASIC SOCIOECONOMIC CHARACTERISTICS

Before turning to the experimental results, it is worthwhile to consider participants' answers to the questions on attitudes, beliefs, and preferences in regard to trust, collective action, and exclusion that they were asked after the completion of the experimental activities. The participants in the six cities of the project reported low levels of participation in organized groups (Figure 7.4). Cultural and athletic organizations accounted for the group participation of the largest number of participants, followed by religious groups; only about one out of seven individuals, however, reported participating in one of these types of organizations. Interestingly, state-sponsored and ethnic organizations had the lowest participant-reported participation rates among the choices.

Figure 7.5
Opinions about the Welfare State

a. Positive

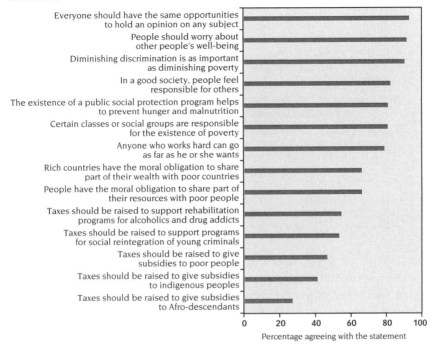

b. Negative

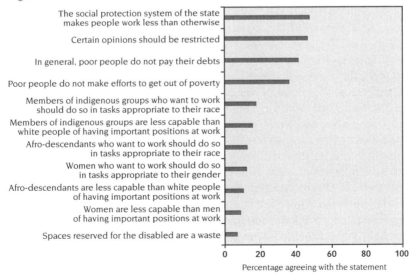

Source: Cárdenas, Chong, and Ñopo (2007).

Figure 7.6
Exclusion from Social and Economic Activities

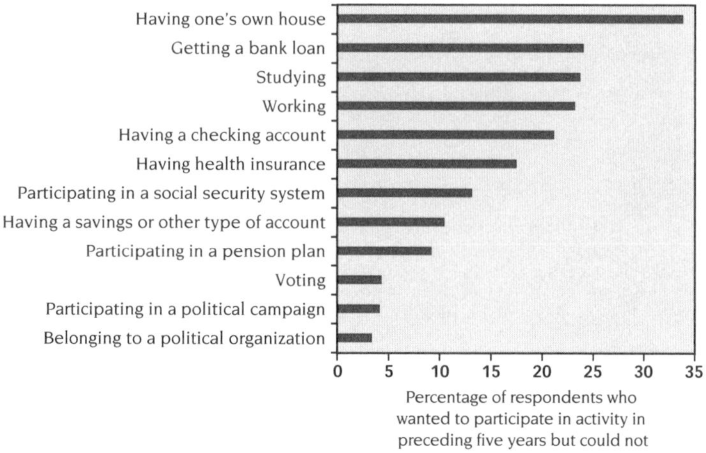

Source: Cárdenas, Chong, and Ñopo (2007).

After the question regarding group participation, participants were asked to agree or disagree with a series of statements regarding the scope and scale of the welfare state. Figures 7.5a and 7.5b show the results, separating positive from negative statements about the welfare state. In general, the positive statements that met with the most agreement involved equality of opportunities, lack of discrimination, and collective welfare. Statements proposing higher tax collection for redistributive purposes met with the least agreement among the positive statements.

Participants were additionally surveyed in regard to unmet financial or career desires (Figure 7.6). The most common unmet desire was buying a house, cited by one in three participants. Other important unmet desires were obtaining a bank loan, studying, and working, cited by one in every four participants.

Participants' perceptions of rights reveal areas of both frustration and satisfaction (Figures 7.7a and 7.7b). When participants were asked to identify areas in which they believed their rights had been violated, the top three choices from a list of twenty items were the opportunity to have a decent job, freedom of opinion, and justice and equal treatment under the law. The least cited areas were voting rights, freedom from torture, freedom of association, and the right to run for public office. As a matter of fact, almost 80 percent of participants reported having voted in their country's most recent presidential election. When participants were asked why they believed their rights had not been respected on at least one occasion in the preceding five years (Figure 7.8), the most frequently cited reasons were lack of connections, lack of money, and age. These results are consistent with those found in other opinion surveys of the region (e.g., Latinobarometer).

Regardless of their own situations, participants expressed a significant level of agreement on what groups in society are most vulnerable (Figure 7.9). Two-thirds of

Figure 7.7
Rights Reported as Not Respected

a. Political and civil rights

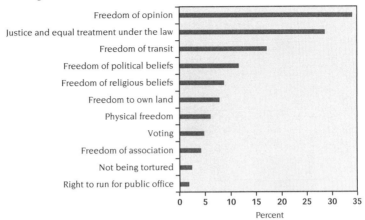

b. Social rights

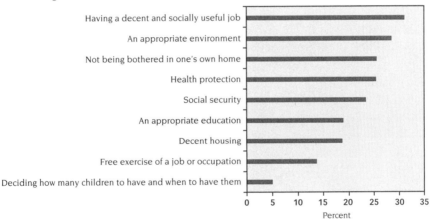

Source: Cárdenas, Chong, and Ñopo (2007).

those surveyed cited the elderly as the most vulnerable social group. Approximately one-third of respondents viewed children as the most vulnerable group.

Finally, the participant survey explored the notion of social distance and perceived causes of social conflict (Figure 7.10). Political differences, cited by almost half of respondents, represented the leading perceived cause of conflict. Approximately one-third of respondents cited differences in income and level of education as a cause of conflicts.

Figure 7.8
Explanations of Why Rights Were Limited or Not Respected

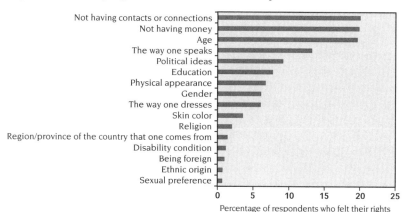

Source: Cárdenas, Chong, and Ñopo (2007).

Figure 7.9
Perceptions of Most Unprotected Groups

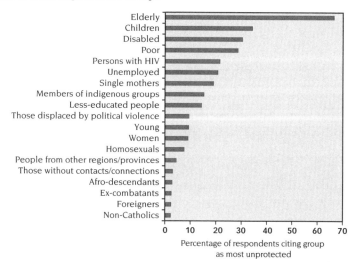

Source: Cárdenas, Chong, and Ñopo (2007).

Figure 7.10
Perceptions of Differences among People That Generate the Most Conflict

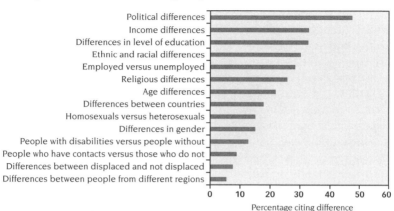

Source: Cárdenas, Chong, and Ñopo (2007).

LESSONS LEARNED FROM THE EXPERIMENTS

The following sections describe the most relevant and robust results that emerged from the group-level and individual data generated by the experiments described in this chapter.[8]

Finding 1: Latin Americans Are Willing to Trust and Cooperate

Consistent with previous observed experimental behavior, the game-theoretical prediction that people in the trust game would not send any amount as either player 1 or player 2 is rejected. Only 12 percent of the observed decisions made by the individuals who participated as player 1 involved sending player 2 nothing. The average offer was 44 percent of the initial endowment, and the median offer (made in 32 percent of the decisions) was 50 percent of the initial endowment. Although social efficiency is maximized when player 1 sends player 2 the entire endowment, letting player 2 decide the allocation of the tripled amount, this occurred in only 9 percent of the cases. An additional 15 percent of participants sent 75 percent of the initial endowment.

With respect to players 2, the experimental results also reject the prediction of self-ish behavior; the results confirm that reciprocity is the major driver of the behavior of players 2. Only 14 percent of players 2 decided to keep the entire amount in their hands after player 1's decision; half of these were those who offered a zero return to player 1 when player 1 had also offered them a zero amount. About 11 percent of players 2 did not return any amount to those players 1 who had sent them their entire endowment.

---

[8] The technical intricacies of the results summarized in this section are explored in more detail in Cárdenas, Chong, and Ñopo (2007).

Expectations of the other player's behavior largely explain the amounts sent by player 1 and the reciprocal responses of player 2. Additionally, individuals' behavior in other games works as a good predictor of behavior (i.e., more risk-loving individuals both made higher offers as players 1 and returned higher amounts as players 2). When demographic characteristics are analyzed, it is found that females sent slightly smaller amounts and also returned less than males, a result consistent with other findings in the economics literature. Education and socioeconomic status do not seem to explain variations in behavior of players 1, but players 2 of low socioeconomic status tended to return a smaller percentage of the amount received than did other players.

Figure 7.11

Trust, Education Gap, and Welfare Generation

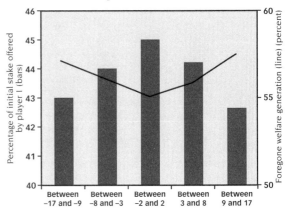

Source: Cárdenas, Chong, and Ñopo (2007).

It should further be noted that approximately one out of every four participants in the VCM game opted to contribute to the public good, which rejects the zero-contribution hypothesis in this game as well. Individuals did, in fact, cooperate, a finding consistent with other research. More interesting results emerge when the decision to contribute the token to the group account is explained as a function of game conditions, as well as of individual and group characteristics. First, behavior in this game was found to be consistent with behavior in other games. Decisions to cooperate in the trust game and in the risk-pooling game were significant predictors of the decision to cooperate in the VCM game. Similarly, expectations regarding trust and formation of groups largely explained cooperation in the public goods game. Socioeconomic characteristics do not seem to play important roles in the prediction of cooperation.

Finding 2: Even Though Latin Americans Trust and Cooperate, Social Distances Limit the Extent of Trust and Cooperation

A further important finding on the factors that drive trusting behavior on the part of trusting individuals in the first activity is that wider gaps in education between players 1 and players 2 were linked to reductions in the amounts sent from the former to the latter and in the percentages reciprocally returned. Figure 7.11 clearly illustrates the point, as the bars on both extremes (corresponding to large education gaps between players, either positive or negative) are shorter than those in the middle (corresponding to smaller education gaps). The result persists after individuals' characteristics (economic and demographic) are controlled for. Figure 7.11 also presents the average foregone social welfare associated with each group of education gaps, measured as the percentage of the total endowments that a pair of players failed to earn as a result of less than complete trust. As the figure suggests, such foregone welfare is greater among pairs of players with larger schooling gaps.

Similar results are obtained in the VCM and risk-pooling games. At the session level, another proxy variable for social heterogeneity, namely, the standard deviation of the years of education, shows negative correlations with the fraction of cooperators in a session, as illustrated in Figures 7.12 and 7.13.

Finding 3: Lack of Trust and Cooperation Has Direct Consequences for the Collective Welfare Generated

Although participants clearly displayed trust and cooperation in the experimental games, they did not do so to the maximum extent possible. Had participants performed at socially optimal levels, they would have increased their gains over actual results by 40 percent in the trust game, 71 percent in the VCM game, and 22 percent (in expected value) in the risk-pooling game. These percentages provide an idea of the magnitude of the social welfare that societies in the region fail to generate as a result of limitations on trust and willingness to cooperate.

These limitations on socially optimal behavior could arise from many sources. Social distance (or specifically, differences in education), as noted above, represents one of these sources. In fact, that variable alone reduces the size of the resulting social welfare "pie" by approximately 9 percent of total wealth in the trust game, 15 percent in the VCM game, and 3 percent (in expected value) in the risk-pooling game.

Figure 7.12
Heterogeneity of Session and Likelihood of Trust in Group

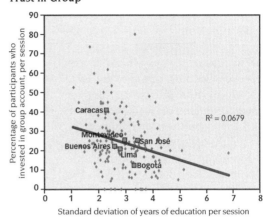

Source: Cárdenas, Chong, and Ñopo (2007).

Figure 7.13
Heterogeneity of Session and Likelihood of Pooling Risk

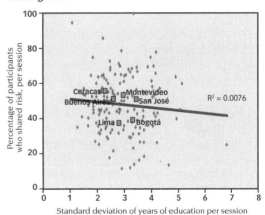

Source: Cárdenas, Chong, and Ñopo (2007).

Finding 4: "Tit-for-Tat" Motivates Latin Americans to Trust and Cooperate

In the trust game, players 1 expecting reciprocation made greater offers to players 2, and players 2 who expected greater offers were also willing to return greater amounts to players 1. In fact, players 2 were willing to allocate a return 2.5 times the size of 100 percent offers of initial endowments on the part of players 1. That return rate decreased with the amount sent by players 1.

Finding 5: Expectations Are Largely Met

Figure 7.14
Expectations of Cooperation versus Actual Cooperation

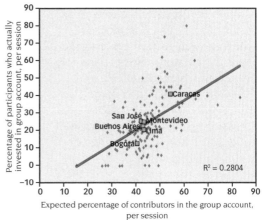

Source: Cárdenas, Chong, and Ñopo (2007).

Expectations about prosocial or group-oriented behavior have predictive power in explaining results. In both the trust and the VCM games, the participants were asked to predict the behavior of their peers in their sessions, based on demographic information about the groups' composition. Only 10 percent of participants in the role of player 2 predicted that players 1 were going to send 0 percent of the initial endowment. Slightly more than 38 percent predicted they would be sent 50 percent, and 13 percent of players 2 predicted that player 1 would send them 100 percent of the initial endowment. The forecasts by players 2 proved remarkably accurate. On the other hand, participants in the VCM game predicted, on average, that 44 percent of players would contribute to the group account, and only 7 percent of participants predicted that no one would cooperate in the game. Participants were able to provide a rather accurate prediction of the actual rate of cooperation in the VCM game in their sessions and acted based on a reciprocal strategy. When players expected more people to cooperate in the game, they were more likely themselves to cooperate. Overall, the predicted fraction of cooperators could map the actual fraction of people contributing to the public good, as shown in Figure 7.14.

Finding 6: Socialization, Trust, and Cooperation Are Remarkably Linked for Latin Americans

During the last activity, the risk-pooling game, an average of 48 percent of players decided to join the income-pooling group, with participation rates in individual sessions ranging from 11 percent to 100 percent. More interestingly, the fraction of those willing to join the income-pooling group was highly correlated with the fraction of contributors to the group account in the VCM game, as shown in Figure 7.15. Although these games are designed to measure different dimensions of group-oriented behavior, both might be driven by similar motivations such as in-group or sense of belonging effects. On average, groups who showed greater levels of contribution also showed greater levels of group formation.

An examination of trusting behavior by players 1 in the trust game shows that those who contributed to the group account in the VCM game sent on average 50 percent of their endowment in the trust game, while those who did not contribute sent only 48 percent. Likewise, those who joined the income-pooling group in the risk-pooling game sent offers in the trust game that were about 8 percent higher than the offers by those not joining the group. A similar pattern is confirmed for players 2 in the trust game. Those contributing in the VCM game returned about 8 percent more to their player 1 partners in the trust game, and those who joined the income-pooling group in the risk-pooling game returned almost 6 percent more to their player 1 partners.

Figure 7.15

Link between Decision to Cooperate in Voluntary Contributions Mechanism (VCM) and Risk-Pooling Games

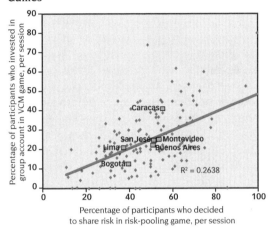

Source: Cárdenas, Chong, and Ñopo (2007).

The results also suggest interesting differences in regard to the average behavior per city. Participants in Bogotá and Lima showed lower cooperative behavior compared to their counterparts in the other cities of the project. On the other hand, players in Caracas seemed to be, on average, more cooperative than players in the other cities, as shown in Figures 7.12 to 7.15.

CONCLUSIONS

The results from the series of experiments reported here provide new evidence on how group-oriented behavior can emerge among members of groups and what factors may help or constrain choices that benefit individuals and groups. Like those of previous research, the present results show that trust, cooperation, and group formation are highly correlated. Experimental groups with clearly favorable conditions for trusting others were also those whose members were willing to contribute to a public good or to form a group to share income from an uncertain lottery. Finally, expectations regarding the behavior of others were found to be powerful predictors of actual behavior.

The findings on expectations are of crucial importance, for various reasons. First, if people can predict with some accuracy the behavior of those in the same room, based only on a short observation of those in the room and listening to very basic data about the demographics of the group, this means that individuals do pay attention and condition their group-oriented behavior to the immediate context and not only to individual traits of the group members. Secondly, expectations are key informants of economic decisions, and as such they can also misguide people towards behavior that is not group-beneficial, thus leading groups into traps or undesired equilibria.

Education, used here as a proxy measure of socioeconomic status, helps to explain the trusting and cooperative behavior of Latin Americans for several reasons. First, education in itself was found to be associated with higher levels of risk aversion among participants, as well as higher levels of trust and trustworthiness. (It did not, however, increase participants' likelihood of contributing in the VCM game.) On the other hand, groups with higher degrees of heterogeneity in education showed reduced cooperation and group formation. In the trust game, pairs in which players displayed greater differences in education (education gaps) were characterized by lower amounts sent from player 1 to player 2. Thus, educational attainment on the part of some individuals is not an unmitigated benefit for groups. On the one hand, education can help to develop the cognitive skills required to overcome the limitations of risk aversion and thus can in turn enhance trust. On the other hand, education confers status, and differences in educational level can increase group heterogeneity, social distance, and out-group effects, while diminishing a sense of belonging; these factors can in turn hinder collective action. Consequently, if gaps in education within a group become a source of social distance, they can create barriers to trust and cooperation.

These differences in education, which were found to be linked to the cooperative and trusting behavior of Latin Americans, were in turn linked to possibilities for social welfare generation. Pairs of players with wider education gaps (in the trust game) and groups of players with higher heterogeneity in education (in the VCM and risk-pooling games) generated social outcomes that were smaller than those of their peers with smaller education discrepancies.

From a policy perspective, the findings in this chapter are quite compelling. As extensive research in economics and related disciplines shows (e.g., Putnam, 1994; Fukuyama, 1995), cooperative behavior and group formation leading to social capital buildup and trust are beneficial to societies' economic growth (Knack and Keefer, 1997). In this context, policymakers should not lose sight of the fact that inclusive policies will yield not only short-run benefits, but also long-term, more durable results. If anything, the key lesson of this chapter for policymakers is that inclusion policies are investment policies.

PART II

Beyond Material Deprivation

PART II Beyond Material Deprivation

M aterial deprivation is one of the crucial outcomes of exclusion, but it is just one aspect of the deprivations suffered by the excluded. As a dynamic process, social exclusion affects all dimensions of social life in ways that limit the ability of the excluded to function and, therefore, to acquire and use capabilities that are valuable in a market economy. Not only do the excluding features of societies affect the behavior of the excluded and curtail their access to and use of material resources, but they also restrict access to the formal and informal institutions that provide services and opportunities to included groups.

This is not a recent discovery. Poverty studies use a poverty line that refers to an income level below which families cannot fully participate in society as a consequence of lack of resources, and the concept of multiple deprivations has been used at least since Townsend's seminal 1979 study of poverty in Britain. However, as Burchardt, Le Grand, and Piachaud (2002) point out, even if it is clear that the excluded suffer deprivations for causes other than low incomes, most research in the area fails to reflect these other elements.

Facing the challenge of social exclusion and advancing inclusive policies requires a deeper understanding of these other dimensions of exclusion. Addressing all these dimensions, however, goes well beyond the scope of what this report and its authors can reasonably attempt. Rather than try to address comprehensively all of the dimensions, this section focuses a spotlight on the role played by certain policies and institutions in producing or combating social exclusion.

The following chapters focus on five specific issues that, to some extent, have been considered key culprits in the "in or out" debate about social exclusion in policy circles. In particular, they focus on privatizations, social movements, crime and violence, access to financial services, and lack of documentation, and show how the dynamics in each case follow specific paths that are not necessarily consistent with conventional wisdom.

For instance, looking at policies such as privatizations, measures aimed at increasing access to financial services, and provision of documentation through the lens of social exclusion shows that there is often a failure to understand how the different dimensions of exclusion interact and change the impact of policies for excluded groups. Privatizations might have an exclusionary impact for the laid-off employees of privatized public enterprises, but also might have surprising inclusive impacts through the expansion of service coverage of the new private firms. Disbursing social transfers through debit cards can, under certain conditions, not only increase the income of recipient families, but also increase the ability of these families to open and use savings accounts. More sophisticated targeting methods might have a surprising exclusionary impact in situations in which excluded groups of the population do not have access to civil registration.

Political and electoral systems that exclude disadvantaged groups of the population reduce those groups' ability to influence government actions through "normal" political channels and open the door to the emergence of contentious politics and social movements. Geographical segregation increases the exposure of disadvantaged groups to crime and violence, both because the rich retreat into gated communities with private security and because the disadvantaged lack the social, economic, and political resources needed to access the preventive and corrective forces of the judicial system and the police.

It is hoped that these examples will help other researchers and the policy community deepen the understanding of the societal traits that shape social exclusion, its determinants, and its dynamics.

Privatization and Social Exclusion in Latin America

After the widespread crises of the 1980s, most Latin American countries embraced institutional and economic reforms intended to reduce fiscal deficits and inflation, liberalize economies, and modernize the state apparatus (Lora, 2007). These reforms inevitably changed the relationship between citizens and the state. Before the reforms the state was seen as a great and even paternalistic social benefactor, serving as both a large-scale employer and a provider of a vast array of goods and services through active participation in markets. This view has changed substantially in recent decades.

While the economic and institutional effects of reform in Latin America have been extensively analyzed, only recently has research focused on how reform has affected the way in which citizens relate to the state. Effects on particular groups and their social and economic inclusion are only now beginning to be considered. This chapter addresses these effects by assessing how one of the most important reforms, the privatization of state-owned enterprises (SOEs), has measurably changed both perceptions and realities of social exclusion.

Latin Americans have generally disapproved of privatizations since the initial stages of structural reforms in the early 1990s. Nevertheless, opinion poll approval ratings for privatization have substantially increased in recent years as the benefits of specific privatizations have become more apparent. A growing majority of the Latin American population is able to enjoy the benefits of privatized enterprises, especially in improved access to and quality of basic services, which in turn improves access to a wide array of economic and social activities. Recent progress notwithstanding, approximately two out of every three Latin Americans take a negative view of privatizations. In the last round of polling by Latinobarometer (2006), covering seventeen countries, only 30 percent of Latin Americans said that they were "satisfied or very satisfied" with the results of the privatization of public services, "considering price and quality."

What shapes Latin Americans' opinions of privatization? Gaviria (2006) has shown that support for privatization is closely linked with wealth and the perception of social mobility. The richest quintile of the region's households are on average 8 percent more likely to approve of privatizations than the poorest quintile. Also, regardless of income level, households whose members perceive that they have experienced or may yet experience social mobility are much more likely than others to approve of privatizations.

More subjective explanations for popular discontent—and perceptions that privatization has exacerbated social exclusion—suggest that this discontent stems from a widespread belief that privatizations have given private investors, who are seen as members of the economic elite, control over assets considered important for the country involved

(Birdsall and Nellis, 2002). These feelings became especially apparent during the privatization of telecommunications in Mexico and Peru.

Popular approval of privatizations is further diminished by the absence of a political consensus on which activities should be under government control. According to a 1998 survey conducted by the *Wall Street Journal Americas* in fourteen Latin American countries, on average 31 percent of those interviewed thought that airlines should be under government control, with 26 percent supporting government management of television stations and 61 percent believing that water services should be provided by the government.

It should also be noted that public perceptions of who benefits from privatizations, at least in the short term, have some basis in fact. Those who approved of privatizations in the *Wall Street Journal Americas* poll were also those who identified themselves as belonging to the political right, being in the higher deciles of the income distribution, and actively participating in as well as being the first beneficiaries of economic improvements in their countries. Though some may benefit more than others in the short run, there is no definitive answer to questions such as whether privatizations ultimately exclude groups that are already worse off in favor of wealthier interests.

Most research on the effects of privatizations has evaluated the efficiency or productivity gains of private over public management. These gains, however, hold little immediate interest for the public at large, which is probably much more aware of direct welfare effects. This chapter therefore attempts to assess widespread claims that privatizations increase social exclusion and inequality. In particular, the chapter analyzes whether the effects of privatization per se can explain why it has found relatively little favor in the region.

PRIVATIZATION AND EXCLUSION IN THE SHORT RUN

It is generally agreed that privatizations in Latin America have brought significant gains in productivity and efficiency.[1] This is notable because Latin America was a pioneer in promoting private participation in infrastructure projects; between 1990 and 2003, about half of the total US$768 billion private sector investment in developing countries was directed to the region. The role of various sectors in the privatization process can roughly be gauged by their respective shares of total privatization revenue. In Latin America, 75 percent of that revenue has been derived from the public service and infrastructure sectors, with 11 percent coming from the financial sector, and the rest from the fuel and manufacturing sectors.

Nonetheless, the extent of privatization in Latin America has varied across industries, and in no country of the region have all SOEs been privatized. Most Latin American countries have privatized their telecommunications, electricity, and, to a lesser extent, water and sanitation services. In contrast, privatization of railway companies, airlines, airports, and expressways has been less widespread. Privatization of the financial and industrial sectors has not been substantial, because private participation in these sectors was already extensive. Most countries have maintained the presence of at least one offi-

---

[1] See Brown, Earle, and Telegdy (2005) for an example.

cial bank and retained government control over companies related to natural resources such as oil, natural gas, and copper. Even Chile, one of the countries that has most aggressively embraced the privatization of state-owned enterprises, has maintained official control of companies in key sectors such as copper, oil, banking, the postal system, railways, and ports.

Within the overall trend toward privatization, its extent has differed greatly across countries. As shown in Figure 8.1, for example, some countries with large state sectors such as Costa Rica, Ecuador, and Uruguay privatized only a few companies in the last decade of the twentieth century, whereas other countries, including Argentina, Bolivia, Panama, and Peru, sold off state companies with total values of more than 10 percent of gross

Figure 8.1

Privatization Revenues in Latin America and the Caribbean, 1990–2000

(Percentage of GDP, 1999 dollars)

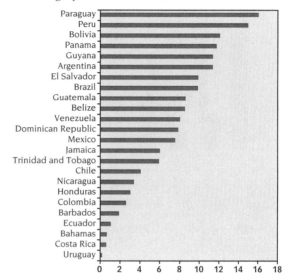

Source: Chong and López-de-Silanes (2005b).

domestic product (GDP). Uruguay was the only country that did not privatize companies in its electricity, oil, and telecommunications sectors over this period, perhaps because proposed privatizations were explicitly subject to a popular referendum, a mechanism used in no other country in the region. At the other extreme, Argentina underwent a privatization process that affected practically all infrastructure sectors as well other sectors in which the state was involved; notable exceptions involve some provincial health companies as well as some national and provincial banks.

In Latin America, state companies have been transferred to the private sector primarily to achieve greater efficiency.[2] Before privatization, Latin American SOEs had largely displayed failings common to firms managed according to political criteria: decisions were made in regard to employment, investment, location, or innovation that proved detrimental to profitability and efficiency, thus producing fiscal deficits and undermining institutional frameworks. Evaluating the microeconomic effects of privatization in five Latin American countries, Chong and López-de-Silanes (2005a, 2005b) found that privatization considerably improved companies' profitability and efficiency. Typically, after privatization, companies increased their net-income-to-sales ratio by fourteen percentage points, mainly through improved efficiency, as unit costs dropped by an average of 16 percent. Figure 8.2 summarizes the study's main findings related to profitability.

---

[2] Although the revenues that governments derived from privatizations undoubtedly represented another significant motivation, primarily fiscal issues lie beyond the scope of this report.

Figure 8.2
Profitability Changes after Privatization in
Latin America

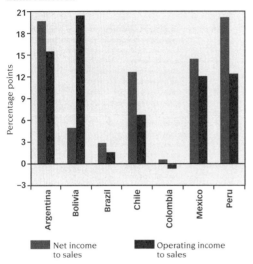

Net income to sales   Operating income to sales

Source: Chong and López-de-Silanes (2005b).
Note: The components of the variables are defined as follows: net income is equal to operating income minus interest expenses and net taxes paid, as well as the cost of any extraordinary items; operating income is equal to sales minus operating expenses, minus cost of sales, and minus depreciation; and sales are equal to the total value of products and services sold, nationally and internationally, minus sales returns and discounts.

Other indicators yield similar results. For example, the sales-to-assets ratio increased on average 26 percent in Latin American companies that were privatized, and the sales per employee indicator rose notably as well. In Chile and Mexico, the two most outstanding cases, sales per employee doubled in privatized companies, and in certain companies the increases were several times larger. These results might at first glance seem to stem from simply lowering costs and reducing the workforce. In fact, however, in the wake of privatization, company production substantially increased even as the average sales-to-assets ratio and sales per employee improved. Mexico and Colombia registered the greatest average production gains (of 68 percent and 59 percent, respectively). Brazil, which trailed the other countries in the study, increased production by a nonetheless impressive 17 percent.

Increasing productivity in these formerly state-owned enterprises, however, is generally perceived to have come at the cost of labor force reductions and social benefit cuts. In particular, it is commonly held that most workers dismissed from public enterprises in Latin America have been forced to enter the informal sector, thereby losing a stable source of income and access to social benefits. This view is not without a basis in fact: since public companies have often been used to create employment for political reasons, short-run job reduction has generally been necessary to make these companies viable as part of the privatization process.

The magnitude of job losses due to privatization in six Latin American countries is shown in Figure 8.3. Whereas industry-adjusted job losses in Chile averaged only about 5 percent, in Peru and Argentina the industry-adjusted average of job reduction in privatized SOEs was in excess of 37 percent. However, the effect of privatizations on unemployment in Colombia seems to have been relatively modest, at least in the electricity sector, where most privatizations took place (Chong and López-de-Silanes, 2005b).

These short-term findings, however, do not tell the whole story of privatization and employment. In the medium term, many firms ended up rehiring workers who had initially been fired during the privatization processes—once it became clear that the "wrong" workers had been dismissed. As shown in Figure 8.4, privatizations in Latin America have offered a prime example of this so-called adverse selection problem.

Since some workers who were let go did in fact end up in the informal sector (Chong, López-de-Silanes, and Torero, 2007), it is clear that social exclusion as a result of privatization layoffs did occur, but this problem was in some cases mitigated by the rehiring of the laid-off workers.

Whether the efficiency gains from Latin American privatization have been driven by productivity-enhancing investment, or by reductions in jobs and social benefits, remains unclear. Although in some large countries large numbers of workers have been dismissed as a result of privatization, in other countries privatized firms have actually created a significant number of new jobs in the medium term. Still, net job loss or creation is not the only factor to consider. More relevant is how particular cases, with particular changes in the relationship between citizens and the larger institutional and economic framework, have led to greater integration or greater social exclusion.

DYNAMICS OF PRIVATIZATION, EMPLOYMENT, AND EXCLUSION

Critics of privatization maintain that employment reductions are both the primary means of driving up productivity and the major cause of the exclusion of low-skilled and elderly workers from the formal labor market. Although the limited evidence available suggests that labor cost reductions do contribute to profitability gains after privatization, these savings do not explain the bulk of increased profitability (La Porta and López-de-Silanes, 1999). Moreover, job reductions are not the only means of increasing labor productivity, and even when they do occur, they may be accompanied by other cost-cutting measures such as lower wages and benefits.

Figure 8.3
Percentage Changes in Employment after Privatization in Latin America

a. Mean values

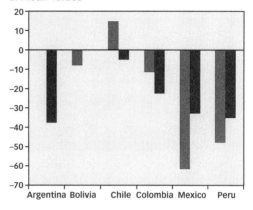

b. Median values

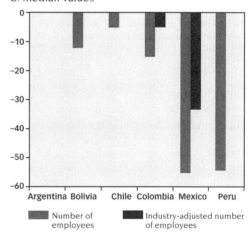

Number of employees
Industry-adjusted number of employees

Source: Chong and López-de-Silanes (2005b).
Note: The number of employees corresponds to the total number of workers (paid and unpaid) who depend directly on the company. The industry-adjusted number of employees is computed by augmenting the preprivatization number by the difference between the cumulative growth rate of the number of employees of the firm and the cumulative growth rate of the number of employees of the control group in the postprivatization period relative to the average number of employees before privatization. For Argentina, the mean number of employees is not available; for Chile and Peru, the median industry-adjusted information is not available; for Bolivia, the industry-adjusted information is not available.

Figure 8.4
Re-employment after Privatization, by Region

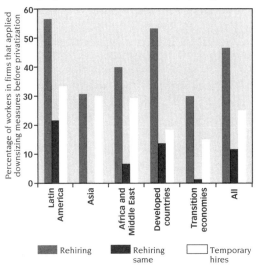

Percentage of workers in firms that applied downsizing measures before privatization

Rehiring Rehiring same Temporary hires

Source: Chong and López-de-Silanes (2005a).
Note: Original list based on 1,500 firms. Sample reflects the 225 firms that applied downsizing measures before privatization.

Productivity, though, cannot be viewed in isolation. Taking into account other labor indicators, Chong and León (2007) find mixed evidence on the benefits of privatization. Managers in privatized firms earn significantly higher wages than their counterparts in either state-owned firms or firms that have always been private, whereas the wages of lower-skilled workers in privatized firms do not differ significantly from those of similar workers in private or state-owned firms. On the other hand, working conditions appear to have significantly deteriorated in the transition from public to private ownership. In addition to labor deregulation throughout the region, there has been a clear trend toward reduction in non-wage labor costs, especially social benefits. In other words, privatized and private firms seem to be favoring temporary workers over those with permanent contracts and employing more low-skilled workers. Under these circumstances, workers' ability to organize has been diminished, and privatized firms display significantly lower unionization rates than state-owned enterprises.

In some instances, though, productivity gains from privatization have led to higher wages and increases in other forms of remuneration. In Mexico, wages in a broad sample of privatized companies increased an average of 76 percent from 1983 to 1994, well above those in the rest of the economy. Even more surprising, wages increased substantially more for blue-collar workers than for office staff (122 percent compared with 77 percent in the 1983–1994 period). Workers in many privatized companies have additionally benefited from ownership participation programs introduced to increase worker interest in privatization. In Colombia, average wages in privatized manufacturing firms increased by 25 percent after privatization. As in other countries, however, it appears that other labor conditions have deteriorated and the influence of labor unions has been eroded.

A further concern is what has happened to those workers who were laid off during the restructuring process, either before or after privatization. This segment of the population, usually drawn from the groups that are most vulnerable to economic shocks of any kind, arguably faces the greatest risk of social exclusion due to privatization. In fact, one of the leading concerns surrounding privatization has been that laid-off workers may be unable to obtain a similar job in the private sector because of age, low skills, or the accumulation of human capital that is not transferable to other industries. Although data limitations have made it nearly impossible to seriously address this issue on a large scale in most countries, Chong, López-de-Silanes, and Torero (2007) have analyzed the conditions of laid-off workers in Peru both before and 10 years after privatization. Even though these laid-off workers were given a compensation package, the study found that the average worker suffered a significant initial hit after being fired, which validates concerns regarding the impact of privatization on inequality and social exclusion. On the other hand, the study also found that workers' wages and benefits eventually recovered to the same level as those of private sector workers in their industry.

Perhaps more surprising is that "stayers" in Peru command higher wages and benefits than comparable workers who had been laid off because of privatization or who had always been in the private sector. Workers in Peru's former SOEs have apparently been able to extract more than other workers as a result of firm market power, union power, or favorable terms of a collective contract that remains in force. This result also helps to explain why the compensation of workers who have lost their jobs because of privatization reverts to the mean of the corresponding private sector industry.

As noted above, social exclusion does not operate only through specific markets such as the labor market. It can be assessed as well through outcomes related to the welfare of the excluded population. Such an approach reveals that the typical worker in Latin America who is laid off as the result of privatization consumes his or her compensation package within the first two years, usually through investment in a home or through the creation of a small business. Unfortunately, however, the average new business fails by the end of that period, and the worker moves on to activities related to his or her previous employment. These results contrast with the belief that workers lose in the long term after privatization and that workers who lose their jobs are condemned to unemployment or poverty.[3] In general, workers laid off as a result of privatization experience a significant setback at first, then quickly recover until their wages and benefits converge with those of similar workers in the private sector.

DISTRIBUTIVE AND SOCIAL EFFECTS

The most important social and distributive effects of privatizations in Latin America may involve citizens in their roles as consumers rather than workers. In the postprivatization era, some firms in the region have been seen as exerting monopolistic power, affecting both supply and prices. Whether these perceptions have a factual basis is debatable, but they have undoubtedly influenced how the region's population views privatization.

The privatization of public resources provides an important example, as its effects on poverty and inequality are a combination of two factors. First, prices usually increase significantly in the wake of privatization, which can prove particularly difficult for low-income groups. On the other hand, privatization of services often leads to expanded coverage, greatly benefiting groups that are on average even poorer. In addition, symbolic

---

[3] Other relevant studies that focus on wages and employment are Tansel (1999), which uses retrospective data for Turkey; Galiani and Sturzenegger (2005), which focuses on one firm in Argentina; Haskel and Szymanski (1992), which examines the United Kingdom; Brown, Earle, and Vakhitov (2006), which studies Ukraine; and Chong and López-de-Silanes (2005a), which shows that adverse selection plagues privatization retrenchment programs, casting doubts on privatization's negative impact on employment.

issues as well as material outcomes are relevant, as access to public services may generate a sense of inclusion and provision of basic rights to historically excluded populations.

Recent research on the effects of privatization on income and inequality has reached revealing conclusions. A comparative study by McKenzie and Mookherjee (2003) found that electricity and water privatizations had positive effects for all income groups in Argentina.[4] In Bolivia, however, telephone privatization was found mainly to have benefited the middle class, among whom the expansion of coverage was most evident. It should nonetheless be noted that the approach pursued by these authors offers only a partial overview of the benefits of privatization, because it does not consider effects other than income.

Several recent studies, including work sponsored by the IDB, offer very convincing evidence that privatization yields benefits in addition to those just described. Several studies have found important benefits from privatization in terms of health, time management, and beneficiaries' employment opportunities in Argentina, where privatizations have met with widespread opposition. Galiani, González-Rozada, and Schargrodsky (2007), for instance, found that the expansion of waterworks to marginal shantytowns around Buenos Aires by a privatized firm led to a significant reduction in the number and severity of children's episodes of diarrhea. Households additionally realized significant savings of both money and time because they no longer had to look for water. Even households that had illegal connections before privatization experienced improvements in health, as the water available through those connections was of very poor quality. Those who previously had no connections saved time, as they no longer had to bring water from faraway dwellings. These results parallel those from previous work (Galiani, Gertler, and Schargrodsky, 2005) showing that the privatization of water services in Argentina was followed by a 5–7 percent reduction in child mortality, with the greatest effects in the poorest areas.

In another category of services, González-Eiras and Rossi (2007) have addressed the effects of the expansion of privatized electricity networks on health outcomes in Latin America. Access to electricity and continuity of service have important indirect effects, as refrigeration problems can lead to food spoilage and public health problems such as food poisoning and malnutrition, particularly among children. The authors found that in Argentine provinces where electricity distribution was privatized, the frequency of low birth weights decreased relative to provinces that maintained public networks, with similar results for child mortality.

Somewhat more mixed results have emerged from research by Barrera-Osorio and Olivera (2007) on water service in Colombia. Privatization of Colombia's water services has shown positive effects overall, according to these authors, especially in urban areas, where both coverage and water quality have increased. In addition, poorer areas have experienced an increase in the frequency of water service, at the expense of decreasing frequency in richer areas, and the weight-to-height index—a proxy for health status—has increased for children in privatized municipalities. At the same time, major increases in water service prices may have outweighed the benefits yielded by other improvements.

In Peru, however, as in Argentina, IDB-sponsored research has found privatization to be largely beneficial, particularly for campesinos and poor rural workers. Torero, Naka-

---

[4] In electricity, for example, the benefits for the poorest 30 percent of the population represented 2–3 percent of their income.

sone, and Alcázar (2006) found that the continuity and reliability of privatized electrical service in Peru allowed users to spend less time on agricultural work and more on non-agricultural or leisure activities, with positive effects on income and welfare. Similarly, Chong, Galdo, and Torero (2005) found that privatizing Peru's telephone service delivered important benefits to the rural poor. In randomly selected villages where the government required the private company, Telefónica del Perú, that replaced the SOE to install public telephone booths, residents experienced improvements in income; particularly notable increases occurred in nonagricultural income, which is crucial for stabilizing the income of the rural poor. Although this benefit resulted from government requirements rather than the goodwill of the company, it is also true that the public company could not or did not want to provide public telephone booth service in the past, which suggests that government can target the benefits of privatization to favor less privileged social groups. In this case, privatization has clearly served to reduce social exclusion.

The expansion of service that has accompanied privatizations not only affords the less well-off the immediate opportunity to use the services provided, but also offers the possibly more important benefit of a sense of inclusion in society. Increased access to such services further allows Latin Americans to enjoy a higher quality of life and provides them with the opportunity to generate more stable sources of income.

CONCLUSION

Privatizations can be socially inclusive, but delivering their benefits to the poor requires government regulation of privatized companies. Although the benefits of privatization per se may be debatable, it is clear that a carefully designed transition, sound management, and adequate oversight of the process are necessary, and that social costs and benefits must be taken into account as well. It is especially important to consider the psychological and ideological factors that influence perceptions of whether privatization has inclusive benefits. Research in behavioral economics, particularly the field of prospect theory pioneered by Kahneman and Tversky (1979), has identified three such psychological factors that are particularly notable. The first is the tension between individual experience and aggregate statistics: exclusion as a result of negative personal outcomes such as job loss weighs much more heavily than small and widely dispersed gains.

A second and related psychological factor is that, in social exclusion as in other areas, individuals give much greater weight to losses than gains in respect to their initial situation. Finally, perception is biased toward short-term outcomes. Individuals are thus more likely to notice sudden changes than gradual changes such as increases in the coverage or quality of certain services.

Even if widespread perceptions of privatization's effects do not necessarily match officially recorded and "objective" measures of progress, policymakers ignore those perceptions at their own peril. Politicians and officials cannot simply dismiss objections to privatization as mistaken or vaguely assure voters that their conditions will eventually improve. In Latin America, where public confidence in the competency and honesty of government is low, a different approach is needed to convince much of the electorate that privatization can and does reduce rather than increase social exclusion.

Exclusion and Politics

THE DEMOCRATIC SYSTEM AS A POINT OF EXCLUSION

Beginning in the late 1970s, a wave of democratization swept through Latin America and the Caribbean; by the early 1990s all of the countries with presidential systems were electing their leaders through competitive elections. Given that democracy entailed formal political equality for all citizens and an end to repression, democratization was expected to markedly increase the political influence of previously disadvantaged groups and enable rapid advances against social and economic exclusion. Democracy has provided such groups with new opportunities to organize and make demands while at the same time increasing the incentives of political parties and leaders to respond to their claims. But despite the formal equality of political rights granted in the countries' constitutions, for various reasons the democratic system still limits the formal channels of influence of some citizens, who in practical terms have little voice.

For the first time in some countries, the new democratic systems extended the vote to all adult citizens.[1] But the lack of proper documentation for citizenship, such as national ID cards and birth certificates, prevents some citizens from exercising fundamental rights, including voting, as well as from accessing some basic services (see Chapter 12). Even for those with documentation, the difficulty of accessing polling places, particularly in remote areas, may limit some citizens' inclusion in electoral processes. In part because of problems of access, on average about 36 percent of the region's eligible population abstained from voting in the most recent presidential elections. Though this level of abstention was greater than that for Central and Eastern Europe and Western Europe (28 percent and 29 percent, respectively), it was considerably lower than that of the United States, Canada, and Africa (Payne, Zovatto G., and Mateo Díaz, 2007). Abstention was a more serious problem in a few countries, reaching nearly 60 percent in Colombia and surpassing 50 percent in Guatemala and Paraguay.

The democratic system also remains a point of exclusion for some groups of citizens because they are less likely to be nominated and elected to positions of power in the legislature, the executive, or subnational governments. For example, despite advances during the 1990s, in 2002 women held just 15 percent of lower house seats, 12 percent of senate seats, and 13 percent of ministerial positions in the region (Htun, 2005). Indigenous peoples are also underrepresented in elected positions: Peru, 8.0 percent of

---

[1] Previously, literacy requirements had effectively excluded many poor people and members of indigenous groups from taking part in elections in Chile (before 1970), Ecuador (before 1979), Peru (before 1980), and Brazil (before 1985) (Yashar, 2005: 37).

legislature versus 47 percent (of population); Ecuador, 3.3 percent versus 43 percent; Guatemala, 12.4 percent versus 66 percent; and Bolivia, 25.2 percent versus 71 percent (Bull, 2006; IDB, 2006c).[2]

Political exclusion can also occur because citizens have varying amounts of resources with which to exercise political influence. Given the high costs of electoral campaigns, money is a cherished resource of political parties and individual candidates. Wealthy persons' financial contributions and close connections with other socioeconomically important groups tend to afford them influence in politics, whereas the poor, if unorganized, have little to bargain with but their votes. More educated and wealthy citizens also tend to be more informed about politics and to participate in it more intensively, thus providing them with greater influence in policy decisions.

The political system also acts as a point of exclusion in more subtle ways. In some countries, rights to organize and free speech, as well as basic civil rights, such as due process and property rights are not adequately protected, particularly in remote areas which justice and other public institutions do not reach. Other rights of citizenship, including equality under the law and protection against discrimination, are often insufficiently provided to the poor, the uneducated, women, indigenous peoples, and other groups.

In addition, some citizens' voice in the new democratic systems is limited in practice by deficiencies of representative institutions, especially political parties. Party systems in many countries are weakly institutionalized, and elected officials are widely viewed as failing to address pressing societal needs and to represent their communities between elections. Since parties typically do not distinguish themselves clearly in terms of alternative policy approaches or ideologies, politics is driven less by issues than by the distribution of targeted benefits and favors, such as public works, jobs, and contracts. When votes are exchanged for specific benefits instead of to support political organizations representing different programmatic alternatives, elections lose much of their potential value for citizens as mechanisms to influence policy decisions in their favor. Given their lack of resources, excluded groups tend to be more susceptible to being co-opted in this manner.

Organized groups take clear and unified stances on public issues and are more likely to receive attention from elected officials. However, the collective action of individuals with common interests is difficult to sustain because individuals have a strong incentive to free-ride on the efforts of others. It turns out that small groups, such as the wealthy or textile manufacturers, tend to be more successful at organizing than large groups such as consumers, peasants, and the poor (Olson, 1965; Bates, 1981). With small groups, a larger share of the benefits of collective action accrues to each individual, making the expenditure of time and money more worthwhile. For this reason, the interests of well-organized minorities often win out over those of the majority, since the majority cannot organize at the same level.

Given the high level of income inequality typical in Latin America, many excluded groups, such as the poor, informal sector workers, and peasants, are quite large and lack-

---

[2] Indigenous peoples in Bolivia obtained a considerably larger share of representation in the constituent assembly elected in 2006.

ing in resources; therefore, they find it difficult to become and stay organized. To some extent, there is a disconnect between the potential electoral clout of such groups and their ongoing political clout in regard to influencing the content of policies. This, along with the weak institutionalization of party systems, helps account for the prevalence of populist strategies for winning and exercising power in which politicians are elected on the basis of their personal connection with voters and vague promises to improve the conditions of the masses. But given the lack of organization of such groups, these politicians, when elected, frequently either break their promises and pursue a different policy course or adopt populist economic policies in which short-term gains in economic output and salaries are eventually reversed in the context of inflationary crises.

Organization around common interests is a key vehicle for advancing excluded groups towards greater degrees of social and political integration. However, such advancement is not automatic or easy, which partly explains why socially and economically disadvantaged groups with limited voice in the political system often remain in that condition for a long time, even in a democratic system. Even when they become organized, there is no guarantee that their influence will persist over time, that their demands will be fulfilled, or that they will gain ongoing representation in the political system (see Chapter 4).

THE RISE OF SOCIAL MOVEMENTS

The deficiencies of democratic systems in Latin America in providing adequate representation and participation to marginalized groups have contributed to the emergence of social protest movements. The frustration of some sectors of the population with the democratic system was compounded by the region's debt crisis, economic stabilization measures and market-oriented reforms, which entailed profound changes in the patterns of inclusion and exclusion (see Chapter 4). Democratic systems were perceived to have made little progress in satisfying unmet social needs or in creating transparent, efficient, and corruption-free governments. Thus, while democracy expanded opportunities to organize and protest, it failed to fulfill its promise to enhance social, economic, and political inclusion.

It was in this broad context that the battleground of politics shifted in several countries, at least temporarily, from the ballot box, political parties, and the congress to the streets (or the fields). Groups resolved to directly challenge the government and make claims, instead of asserting their interests mainly through institutional channels. In a number of countries, such movements have succeeded in placing issues on the policy agenda, promoting legal and constitutional reforms, overturning unpopular government policies, preventing policies seen as adverse to their interests from being adopted, and even forcing the removal of popularly elected presidents.

What factors explain why once-quiescent social groups were able to overcome considerable obstacles to their collective action and emerge as substantial protest movements, effectively challenging the status quo and making existing power holders pay attention to their demands? The emergence of social movements has been examined by a vast literature in sociology and political science (see, for example, Tilly, 2004; McAdam, 1982, 1994; Morris and McClurg Mueller, 1992; Giugni, 1998; Elster, 1985; Yashar,

2005; Scott, 1990; Tarrow, 1998). Three broad theoretical approaches can be delineated. One approach focuses on the impact of socioeconomic deprivations and changes in social and political opportunity structures in motivating and permitting collective social action. A second emphasizes the role of group-level processes, values, and belief systems in shaping collective interpretations and identities. From this perspective, groups' identities (e.g., as workers, women, indigenous peoples) are not determined purely by their inherent characteristics or their social condition, but by themselves in interaction with their surroundings (Yashar, 2005). A third approach focuses on the costs and benefits for individuals of joining protest actions and how these are shaped by individuals' preferences and the incentives provided by social movement organizations and their leaders. The experience of a few of the region's more prominent social movements highlights their political significance and the role of different causal factors in their mobilization.

Brazil's Landless Rural Workers' Movement (Movimento dos Trabalhadores Rurais Sem Terra, or MST) emerged as a nationwide force in the early 1980s on the basis of land occupations concentrated at first in the southern state of Rio Grande do Sul. By occupying land deemed not productive, the MST has pressured federal and state governments to expropriate and redistribute privately held land. This has resulted in the settlement of about 350,000 families onto their own land. More than just a protest movement, the MST has built an entire organizational network through which it offers education, housing, medical centers, and financial credit.

The emergence of the movement can ultimately be traced to a salient structural characteristic in Brazil: a high level of inequality in the distribution of land. Other structural changes in the decades prior to the early 1980s, such as the development of mechanized agriculture, which brought casual day laborers to the countryside, the decline in industrial output, which deterred young people from migrating to urban areas, and the liberalization of the political regime contributed to the rise of the movement. The movement also owed its success to its ability to acquire resources (including money for schools and other services for members on occupied land) and the ability, partly because of the nature of the cause, to apply selective rewards to participants—namely, a share of the cooperatively owned land (Bull, 2006). But the MST's collective action was also inspired and made possible by the example of other social movements organizing against the country's military dictatorship; ideological influences, such as liberation theology; and the support of other organized groups, including the church. The steady expansion and increasing influence of the movement owes much to the interaction among and between the landless and their leading religious supporters, which led the participants to reinterpret the costs and benefits of taking action, focusing more on the collective values of solidarity and the broader goals of the movement over purely individual material objectives (Carter, 2003).

Similar to the MST, the unemployed workers (*piqueteros*) movement in Argentina formed in relation to an obvious structural condition: the surge in urban unemployment to above 15 percent over the period 1985–2002. By the late 1990s, the *piqueteros* had organized numerous protests in Argentina's main cities, including massive roadblocks. As a result of the protests, the government granted social assistance in the form of temporary jobs, special subsidies, and food assistance.

The formation of the movement was clearly related to economic factors, including the sharp increase in unemployment, the inflexibility of the labor market, and rising levels of poverty. Argentina's deep economic crisis in 2001–2002 provided the impetus for consolidating the *piqueteros* as a social movement. In addition, reductions in state social assistance, the weakening of informal neighborhood support networks, and the decline of unions removed some of the buffers against the emergence of social protests (Bull, 2006). Two key events in the mid-1990s—mass layoffs of industrial workers and the privatization of the state petroleum company (Yacimientos Petrolíferos Fiscales)—were also precipitating factors in the formation of the movement.

Several other countries in the region also experienced rising unemployment rates and economic crises yet did not experience the emergence of a well-organized social movement of unemployed people. Key to the *piqueteros'* initial success in effectively challenging the Argentine government were the adoption of roadblocks as the method of struggle and the widespread appeal of their criticism of the exclusionary nature of both the country's political regime and its economic model. The state's response of providing social subsidies (*planes sociales*), which the *piqueteros* could administer themselves, strengthened their organizational structures and provided incentives and strategic tools for motivating participation in the *piquetero* movement (Svampa and Pereyra, 2003; Wolff, 2007).

Finally, in several Latin American countries, indigenous peoples have assembled important national social movements that have influenced debates on constitutional reform and demanded changes in economic and other policies. They have also taken part in broader social mobilizations that have forced presidents from office. Given the historical efforts of Latin American politicians and governments to replace ethnic identities with class-based identities and to assimilate ethnic cultures, mobilization of indigenous peoples has caught many by surprise (Yashar, 2006). Powerful organizations have emerged in Ecuador and Bolivia, initially with the objective of defending local autonomy. These movements have called for a number of reforms, including legal recognition, representation, autonomy, and multicultural education, and have entered politics by forming national political parties in some cases, fielding candidates and winning political office at all levels of government (Van Cott, 2005).

The emergence of these movements is certainly related to the long history of exploitation and exclusion of indigenous peoples in these countries. But while indigenous peoples had taken part in social mobilizations in the past, the mobilizations beginning in the 1980s have been the first in which ethnicity-based claims, including the demand for recognition of special rights as native peoples, have been at the forefront along with social and economic claims. Thus, the current wave of organization among indigenous peoples relates not just to ongoing characteristics of the social and economic structure, but to a politicization of ethnic identities over the past two to three decades (Yashar, 2005, 2006). According to one account, this politicization of identities has occurred at least in part because of changes in the state's institutional relationship with the countryside and indigenous peoples in particular. In the mid-twentieth century, the state sought political support and control over the masses through corporatist, class-based forms of interest representation in which people who joined state-sponsored peasant organizations gained access to redistributed land, social programs (including health care), subsidies, and credit. In this context, indigenous peoples' identity as peasants was privileged, and they were granted previously denied freedoms and access to the state. Because of the freedoms granted from previous forms of labor control and because of the weak reach of the state, in practice indigenous peoples, especially in the Amazon, but also in the highlands, obtained a fair degree of autonomy to put in place indigenous community practices (Yashar, 2005, 2006).

Given economic constraints and resistance to the rising power of class federations, by the 1980s states began to reassert control over peasant federations, liberalize agricultural markets, reduce rural social programs, and open up communal lands for sale on the market, all of which tended to threaten the autonomy and viability of indigenous communities. These changes in the institutional context contributed to the politicization of ethnic differences and the development of indigenous movements. At the same time, democratization and decentralization provided indigenous groups with the political space to organize, protest, and increase their participation in politics.

WHAT DIFFERENCE CAN SOCIAL MOVEMENTS MAKE?

What changes have social movements achieved that the political system could not?

The political system is where power transactions or exchanges take place—politics being understood as the exercise of power. Social movements, as agents of social change (della Porta and Diani, 1999), have one major recourse for influencing these transactions: protest. The politics of social movements is "contentious" in the sense that the movements' claims usually conflict with someone else's interests (Tilly, 2004: 3, citing McAdam, Tarrow, and Tilly, 2001). "Contentious politics" is a form of collective action used by groups that have no regular access to institutions, whose claims are unaccepted or not yet part of the political agenda, and who express their interests in forms that challenge the established order (Tarrow, 1998: 3).

To respond to protest, the state produces social policy or it polices protest: the state either represses the movement, negotiates with it, or uses both strategies at the same time (della Porta and Diani, 1999: 240). Social policy is both the cause of protest and the response to it. In that sense, protest and policy mutually affect one another (Meyer, 2003). Social movements, in turn, can use different entry keys to access the political system and change processes and their outcomes.

Recognition

Ethnically divided countries or those with minority cultures need to deal with the issue of whether or not to recognize diversity. The recognition of difference implies a change in the meaning of citizenship and identity. The definition of "liberal culturalism" sets a broadly accepted frame for these states, where the effective protection of individual rights should be accompanied by group-specific rights and policies that recognize different identities and respond to the needs of ethnic cultural groups (Kymlicka, 1995).

Organized pressure from indigenous movements has resulted, through constitutional reforms in numerous countries, in considerable advances in the legal recognition of the rights of indigenous peoples collectively and of individuals within indigenous groups. Processes for obtaining recognition, although symbolic, mobilize the population behind the reforms, demonstrating the electoral potential of the ethnic minority and easing access to the ballot. This process, which primarily serves to remove institutional constraints, is in itself a factor behind building a viable party (Van Cott, 2005), which in turn paves the way for obtaining formal inclusion in representative institutions.

Changes in the Policymaking Process

One way of changing policymaking processes is by gaining formal and sustained access to political power through representation in the institutions where transactions take place. Presence in formal institutions brings a significant change in the positions occupied by different actors: they start to participate on more equal terms. Together with the formation of political parties, one road to effective integration in decision making has been the design and implementation of mechanisms and reforms such as quotas and reserved seats for representative institutions.

Not only have social movements sometimes gained access to formal institutions, but they have also influenced the decision-making process at its different stages (agenda setting, lawmaking, implementation, monitoring, and accountability) by informally influencing the exercise of power. They have exerted this influence through contacts with elected representatives at all decision-making levels, members of the government, public administration officials, and the media, or even through inclusion in policymaking through participation in committees, ad hoc commissions, consultative bodies, advisory boards, and the like. A number of agencies have also been created throughout the region to deal with discrimination against certain groups.

Changes in Public Policy

Agenda Setting

Social movements have influenced the different stages of policymaking first by attracting public attention to new issues, increasing the saliency of existing issues and including these issues in the political agenda, and second by participating in the design, implementation, and monitoring of public policies. Being an agenda setter means raising awareness of certain problems, changing public opinion, and convincing decision makers of the need to introduce new regulations. Not only have social movements contributed to changes in existing policies, but they have opened up and created new areas for policymaking (women, indigenous peoples, environment, etc.). The formation and success of movement-based parties, such as indigenous parties, have changed the agendas of other parties (i.e., nonindigenous parties) and have also led such parties to change the profile of their candidates by including more indigenous candidates.

Policy Design, Implementation, and Outcomes

Alterations in legal provisions do not immediately translate into real changes in people's lives. Moving from approved legislation to effective implementation and concrete gains in terms of equality takes political will and financial and technical resources. Given that contemporary social movements in the region did not start to mobilize in a meaningful way until the end of the twentieth century, it is possible to find evidence of partial gains but probably too early to talk about sustained policy changes. That said, and leaving aside recognition provisions enshrined in countries' constitutions, there has also been noticeable progress in approving laws that address racial and ethnic discrimination, collective land entitlements, customary law, the creation of special antidiscrimination agencies and institutions, the inclusion of new census categories to quantify the size of different groups, the formation of new political parties, affirmative action policies to provide formal representation in governmental institutions, and the establishment of consultation mechanisms at different decision-making levels.

Social movements have also influenced the later emergence of other types of movements (Meyer and Whittier, 1997) and have sometimes paved the way for subsequent policy changes (Meyer, 2003). However, implementation of new policies has often advanced at a slower pace than their introduction into the political agenda and their conversion into enacted legislation because of financial and technical limitations, combined with a shortage of mechanisms for accountability between the state and the groups.

Value Change in Public Opinion

Social movements have altered agendas, and in doing so, they have also shaped public opinion on particular issues. But causality also goes the other way: social movements very often need a critical mass of public support to achieve their goals. Gaining public resonance on a particular issue means convincing the population of the importance of the issue for the group and for society as a whole. Changing public opinion starts with gaining progressive recognition that discrimination exists and therefore that inequalities result not just from traditional socioeconomic differences, but also from race, gender, or ethnic and cultural origins.

Sustained Inclusion

It is not easy to assess when and how a particular group has gained sustained inclusion within society. If a social movement is able to change the political system in all of the areas discussed above (i.e., recognition, representation, inclusion through consultation procedures, ability to set the agenda and being part of the design and implementation of public policies, making substantial progress in terms of the fairness of policy outcomes, and changing public opinion), one can argue that its inclusion in the system will be sustainable.

For "in-between" scenarios, William Gamson (1975, cited in della Porta and Diani, 1999: 228) establishes a typology that includes "co-optation," in which a movement obtains recognition without public policy changes, and "pre-emption," in which there are policy changes but no acceptance. According to some of the findings in the empirical literature, exclusively ethnic-based or culturally based movements should be more likely to be co-opted, whereas exclusively issue-based or socially based movements should be more prone to pre-emption.

DETERMINANTS OF SUCCESS AMONG SOCIAL MOVEMENTS

What characteristics of social movements and the political system have been instrumental for the achievements discussed in the previous sections? Why are certain movements able to achieve certain objectives whereas others are not? Under what conditions is mobilization likely to achieve some advances in terms of inclusion? What are the necessary and sufficient conditions that lead to a successful integration?

Type of Movement

Depending on the context, certain features of a movement can be more relevant than others in determining the outcomes it achieves. The likelihood of a movement's success has to do first with the quality of leadership and its capacity to mobilize and hold members together. Leaders may have different qualities ranging from the political entrepreneur or political broker to the charismatic and visionary leader. To a much larger extent than would be desirable, an organization's survival very often depends on the leadership's capacity to control the movement, to cope with internal divisions, to reformulate claims, and to make the necessary transitions between different phases of the movement.

A group's organizational capacity depends on its size, composition, and resources. The smaller and more homogeneous a movement, the greater its chances of organizing quickly. The more resources available, the greater its negotiation and trading capacity and, therefore, its influence. If the group does not have resources or the capacity to influence policy by conventional means (i.e., parties, representation in political institutions), it will tend to use protest as a way to gain access to influence. Even if in theory smaller groups should be better able to organize, in this case, "the larger, more volatile, more public, and more diverse" the movement, the more difficult for government to seek "minimally, domestic peace" (Meyer, 2003: 1).

Clearly related to the origins and composition of the movement is the type of identity that ties the members of the group together. Identity, in turn, is key to understanding group members' goals and possibilities for achieving them. Some (e.g., Hooker, 2005) have argued that group identity defined in cultural or ethnic terms is a stronger determinant of social movement success than a group's population size or organizational capacity. However, the downside of basing claims on cultural difference is that it may influence the nature of responses given by the political system, privileging policies of recognition over policies against discrimination.

Social movements can also be distinguished in terms of the strategies and repertoires that they use. Repertoires are the types of political action deployed, such as coalitions, associations, public meetings and gatherings, demonstrations, petitions, pamphlets, and statements to the media (see Tilly, 2004: 3). The legitimacy of protest is strongly dependent on these forms of mobilization. Sometimes, certain repertoires, like violence, or the persistent use of a single strategy can delegitimize protest, if the strategy implies high costs for the rest of the population.

Type of Goals

A distinction can be made between "macro claims" (i.e., macropolitical objectives that position the group in terms of broad political objectives) and "micro claims" (i.e., micropolitical objectives, which are the specific material gains the group hopes to make). To attract support, the movement should have clear targets that are easy to communicate, appealing, and compelling to the public. The general and personal implications for people of a particular issue raised by a movement will determine its capacity to amplify public support, in terms either of perceived urgency or of the prospects of payoffs.

Sometimes protest movements do not grow out of socially organized groups; rather, they emerge around short-term targets. Such movements can be extremely efficient because they can introduce an issue into the public agenda at a low cost for individuals, but at a high societal cost, given that sometimes the types of protest used can affect an economic sector, citizens' security, or public infrastructure (Mauro Machuca, 2006).

Certain objectives have a greater capacity to gain other groups' support. The extent to which an issue can draw support from other groups depends on its scope and exportability, as well as its territorial contingency (i.e., whether it is a local or national/transnational issue). In some cases, issues can be so powerful that they can gather support from influential players outside of the movement.

The framing of a goal may also influence its likelihood of success. Very often, macro claims are negatively framed as the rejection of something, whereas micro claims are presented in positive terms, as something essentially good and to be achieved. It is precisely when the claim can be turned into positive propositions for action that its likelihood of survival increases, as well as its ability to be translated into public policy.

Political Space

Political space is defined as the possibility for a social movement to form or influence a political party. Social movements and the state operate in a "political opportunity structure" (Tarrow, 1998; Tilly, 1978). Groups will not engage in protest if they can reach a target using conventional politics. If the existing party system offers space for the entry of new actors—as members of existing parties or through new political forces—and a fair aggregation of interests, the group will not engage in the cost of mobilizing.

Policy Space

The capacity of movements to pursue certain claims is also dependent on whether context allows for an opening up of the policy space to a new issue. The readiness of the system to open itself up to a new issue is related to the degree of permeability of the elite class, which in turn will be influenced by the perceived level of pressure from different actors such as the social movement itself, public opinion, other stakeholders, and the international community.

Once an issue finds a place on the political agenda, there is a decisive moment for it to translate into a policy reform. The players involved in decision making are aware that new policies very often result from a change in the balance of power, but that they can, in turn, affect the balance of power. There is, therefore, a risk that attention paid to an issue will be diverted to another issue as time goes by and power alignments change. Neither the policy space nor coalitions last forever.

Transaction Points

The political system is the place where power transactions take place. The amount and type of these transactions will be shaped by the institutions that make up the political system, which set the structure of opportunities and constraints. In that sense, some political settings are more conducive than others to spawning social movements. Under certain conditions, democracy promotes social movements, just as social movements promote democratization (Tilly, 2004). It appears that protest is more likely in systems with a mix of open and closed factors (e.g., political regimes that are transitioning from authoritarianism to democratic rule), with shifting alignments (i.e., low electoral stability), or with divided elites (i.e., that might become influential allies and bring resources to emerging movements) (Tarrow, 1998: 76–80). Accordingly, the intensity of social mobilizations that have swept Latin America and the Caribbean during recent decades can be interpreted as a natural consequence of these factors.

Democracy, together with other trends in institutional reform, has progressively relaxed the constraints and created a more permissive institutional environment in the region. For instance, decentralization has opened up space for participation at lower cost, because social movements can start organizing in a meaningful way in areas where they have a large number of potential members. Proportionality of electoral systems, openness of party systems, and the decline of traditional parties have also facilitated the entry of new competitors. Other institutional settings have also favored social mobilization: new electoral districts in areas with large indigenous populations, reserved seats for indigenous candidates, the possibility for movements and not just parties to participate in elections, and greater ease in registering parties and entering the ballot.

Opportunities for successful mobilization also depend on the capacity of the political system to adjust to external challenges. In some cases, the system delegitimizes protest by giving partial responses; adjusting political representation, including the movement in formal and informal democratic procedures and in the discussion of certain issues directly concerning its interests, and producing relatively low-cost policies are all partial answers. In that sense, the system can momentarily open certain transaction points to maintain the overall status quo in terms of power shares.

CONCLUSION

Social movements are not the cause of the erosion of democracy but rather the consequence of structural dysfunctions that lead to expressions of discontent. Claims from ethnic and culturally based movements have challenged the nature of the state and the understandings of citizenship. Beyond that, ethnic and cultural boundaries tend to overlap with socioeconomic classes. In that sense, protest has revolved not only around the fact that individuals belonging to these groups lack the same opportunities as the average citizen (i.e., *individual rights*), but also around the fact that the group's distinctive culture and needs are not recognized (i.e., *collective rights*).

As long as structural problems in terms of substantial inequalities in access to socio-economic and political resources remain unresolved, there will be more or less serious episodes of contention and political crisis that will put political systems in the region under pressure.

For that same reason, social movements are usually more part of the solution than part of the problem. The emergence and intensity of social movements can be interpreted as a positive sign of the evolution of democracy in the region, where a progressive opening and removal of barriers has led to mobilization.

Social mobilization has the potential to increase the voice of the excluded. Engagement in politics can enhance the understanding of realities and possibilities for change and can bring about some change. In some cases, mobilization can bring about lasting changes in the political system (in the allocation of power over decisions) and lead to changes in policies reflecting greater inclusion. In other cases, smaller changes may result that change agendas, alter mentalities, and in the long term may open up opportunities for more lasting and meaningful changes in the political system and public policies. In the short and medium term, it is true, social mobilization can aggravate social conflict and complicate democratic governance. But this may be a necessary price to pay, although it must be managed with care, without repression, with accommodation, and with consensus-building efforts.

Social Exclusion and Violence

**There used to be clear rules: no one
would steal in the shantytown.
If and when they stole, they would
do it outside the shantytown. Now,
they rob you in the shantytown
and everywhere.**

—"Las cuatro chapas del desamparo"

The past few decades in Latin America and the Caribbean have witnessed a series of economic, social, and political transitions that have changed the patterns of inclusion and exclusion. Movements within the region, including migration from rural areas, related rapid urbanization, institutional change, and the slow growth of formal employment, reinforce the population's historical reliance on informal mechanisms and transactions for survival. The judicial and law enforcement systems have only weakly adapted to the new challenges and continue to leave large segments of society without adequate access to justice and economic and physical security.

As Figure 10.1 shows, regional rates of homicide in some Latin American and Caribbean countries reach levels typically seen only in those areas ravaged by war. Yet the battles that are generating this carnage are taking place not in war zones, but within socially excluded communities in Latin America, fought not by soldiers and guerrillas, but by a minority that uses violence to fulfill its needs. Within such communities, residents cannot depend on those institutions designed to protect them, and violence becomes an instrument to achieve certain outcomes, such as justice, security, and economic gain through means that disrupt the life of the community. Where justice is acquired through revenge, security through violent assertion of authority, and economic gain through robbing, mugging, and intimidation, the vast majority of law-abiding residents are left without options. In such communities, people have come to recognize the person next door not as a neighbor, the policeman not as a protector, the community leader not as a consensus builder, but each as a potential threat. Many studies, ranging from anthropological fieldwork in the marginalized areas of shantytowns, favelas, barrios, and villas (Caldeira, 2000; Márquez, 1999; Goldstein, 2003) to advanced geospatial studies that record incidences of violence (Beato, 2002; Consejo de Seguridad, 2006), report that homicide rates are much higher in these neighborhoods than in middle- and upper-class neighborhoods.

Figure 10.1
Homicide Rates, Western Hemisphere, 1995–2002

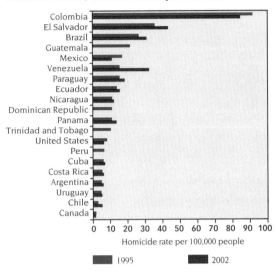

Homicide rate per 100,000 people

■ 1995   ■ 2002

Source: Author's compilation using data from Pan American Health Organization, and Cohen and Rubio (2007).
Note: No data available for Dominican Republic, Guatemala, Trinidad and Tobago, and Peru for 2002.

Social exclusion is a contributing factor to violent outcomes, regardless of whether violence takes place in a developed Western European country or in a burgeoning Central American state. Those who resort to violent acts most often lack access to legitimate economic opportunities and the personal or social contacts required to obtain many of the services and resources available to mainstream society. When conventional methods of obtaining and working for increased social status, higher income, and wider influence are limited, as they often are in marginalized areas, some feel compelled to resort to what the mainstream considers illegitimate means, including violent acts (Reiss and Roth, 1993). Residents of socially excluded communities are well aware of the lack of options available to them and the consequences of lacking the money to pay off corrupt police and judges, the influence to avoid extortion, or the confidence to resist gang recruitment. For those with few or no prospects for economic advancement, profitable opportunities to be gained through illicit and violent means serve as a deadly magnet. As state institutions fail to provide security and justice, others—such as violent community leaders, gangs, or corrupt police—may step in to mete out alternative forms of justice and revenge.

Issues of security, authority, justice, identity, and economics are tangible in the violent acts used to secure them in socially excluded areas, beyond the influence of state institutions and mainstream paradigms of conflict resolution. The consequences are severe and further sap scarce resources from Latin American and Caribbean countries that are treading a rough road towards economic development and modernization of democratic institutions. Violence eats away at the delicate social fabric that holds communities together through difficult economic, social, and political periods and shatters the trust, security, and solidarity that take years to build. This chapter discusses how social exclusion and violence interact in a vicious circle that leaves the socially excluded in a very hostile social environment where the borders between legal and illegal, legitimate and illegitimate are often fuzzy and uncertain. In this environment violence is used by a minority to acquire justice, security, authority, and economic gain. The use of violence by this minority, however, affects the lives of the majority of excluded people who do not resort to violence.

Table 10.1 Classification of Violence by Motive, Type, and Actors in Latin America and the Caribbean

Motivation	Type of violence	Victimizers	Victims
Interpersonal or social: domination, revenge, control, debts, disagreements, unknown intimidation	Domestic or interfamilial: physical, sexual, verbal, psychological deprivations, neglect	Male partners, fathers, relatives, friends, acquaintances	Female partners, children, seniors, relatives
Economic: crimes with little or no structure	Fights, injuries, homicides	Gangs, acquaintances, unknowns	Friends, acquaintances, unknowns
	Homicides, rapes, robberies	Common delinquents, gang members	General population, members of gangs or groups
Economic and power: organized crime	Homicides, injuries, assaults	Drug traffickers, organized gangs	Leaders, judges, journalists, citizens, gang members
Politics	Homicides, massacres, kidnappings, injuries	Guerrillas, paramilitary troops, government forces	Peasants, rural residents, counterguerrilla forces, soldiers, police

Source: Concha-Eastman (2002).

VIOLENCE DEFINED

Violence is generally described as "an intentional use of force or power with a predetermined end by which one or more persons produce physical, mental (psychological), or sexual injury, limit freedom of movement, or cause the death of another person or persons (including him or herself)" (Concha-Eastman, 2002: 44). For the purposes of relating violence to social exclusion, the focus is on violence fueled by the need for power and economic opportunities. Interpersonal and domestic violence also has indirect and direct external effects that perpetuate violence throughout a community. As shown in Table 10.1, violence in Latin America and the Caribbean is most often perpetrated by family members, gangs, common delinquents, assailants unknown to the victim, or acquaintances. Other perpetrators may include corrupt policemen and extrajudicial forces. Their victims—family members, street children, acquaintances, the general population, rival gang members, or at higher levels, government or civil society leaders—are victims of abuse, homicide, injuries, assaults, and robberies (Concha-Eastman, 2002).

A prolific amount of research is available on violence, some of which has focused specifically on Latin America (e.g., Concha-Eastman, 2002; Dowdney, 2005; Morrison, Buvinić, and Shifter, 2003; Reiss and Roth, 1993; Fajnzylber, Lederman, and Loayza, 1998; Londoño, Gaviria, and Guerrero, 2000; Moser and McIlwaine, 2000, 2001; Rotker, 2002; Riaño-Alcalá, 2006; Moser, Winton, and Moser, 2003). Those who study violent outcomes generally agree that a large number of factors contribute to the problem. Various structural and cultural characteristics present in a community may interact with both individual and social factors to produce a set of behavioral outcomes, both among individuals and throughout the community. Crowded housing conditions, high levels of migration in and out of a community, increasing numbers of single-parent households, and economic decline may all significantly affect the amount of violence in a community by contributing to the breakdown of social capital (Morrison, Buvinić, and Shifter, 2003; Reiss and Roth, 1993). Availability of guns, media portrayals of violence, the aftermath of civil war, and changing cultural norms all play a part in inducing violence in a community (Morrison, Buvinić, and Shifter, 2003). Age, socioeconomic level, employment status, drug or alcohol abuse, early exposure to aggressive stimuli or violence, and experience as a victim of or witness to physical or psychological abuse can also predispose individuals towards violent acts (Morrison, Buvinić, and Shifter, 2003).

Economic conditions factor into the incidence of crime and delinquency in a community, including the average income, the income distribution of the society in which the community is embedded, and the level of education (Fajnzylber, Lederman, and Loayza, 1998). Gender also has a significant effect on an individual's propensity to use violence, as males may be predisposed to more violence for a number of physiological, cultural, or situational reasons, such as higher rates of alcohol and drug use and economic pressure to provide for their families.

In socially excluded communities, including some indigenous communities, fieldwork has shown that these areas suffer more from violence than those at higher socioeconomic levels (Caldeira, 2000; Heinemann and Verner, 2006, citing Borjas, 1995; Katzman, 1999, quoted in Buvinić, Morrison, and Orlando, 2002). A study in the Brazilian city of Belo Horizonte showed that socially excluded areas such as slums, where "several social welfare and life quality indicators . . . were considerably inferior [in comparison] to other [areas] of the city," had higher numbers of homicides (Beato, 2002: 3). Such areas had higher percentages of employment in the informal sector, higher child mortality and illiteracy rates, and poorly developed urban infrastructure. Peixoto, Moro, and Viegas Andrade (2004) also found that homicides in Belo Horizonte are concentrated in less-developed areas such as favelas and are correlated with ecological factors such as social and physical disorder. Homicide rates are negatively associated with the level of infrastructure development and positively associated with longer police response time. Agencies that record death statistics in São Paulo reported in 1995 that those areas with the highest rates of murder (between 75 and 96 murders per 100,000 inhabitants) were some of the poorest in the region, while those with the lowest rates were located in richer areas (Caldeira and Holston, 1999). Surveys of Bogotá, Mexico City, and Santiago, Chile, show that the poorest and most marginalized areas of these cities report the highest homicide rates (Consejo de Seguridad, 2006; Fundación Mexicana para la Salud and Centro de Economía y Salud, 1998; Silva Lira, 2000).

THE ROLES OF VIOLENCE: JUSTICE, SECURITY, AUTHORITY, AND ECONOMIC GAIN

In socially excluded communities in Latin America, violence emerges with diverse causes and distinct aims. This section addresses the aims of violence, including for what and how it is used in these communities. An important note should be made here: while violence is pervasive in many marginalized areas and has a serious impact on the lives of most residents, the majority of people living in these areas do not resort to and use violence. The media, politicians, and residents of the middle and upper classes often sensationalize reports of violence and label communities as dangerous (in what Moser and McIlwaine [2000: 68, 2001: 106] call "area stigma"), leaving the impression that most, if not all, residents in these areas resort to constant aggressive behavior. This is far from the case. Most residents, including young males, try to avoid and ignore violence for fear of the consequences of becoming involved and escalating the dangers present to them. Nonetheless, many residents succumb to the feeling that they have no power to stop violence.

For those residents of these communities who do resort to violence, several factors contribute to their decision to do so. In the absence of a strong, legitimate, and equitable state presence and of opportunities available to mainstream society, communities must locally construct alternative means of satisfying their needs and ensuring a sense of order. When crime increases or employment opportunities decline, the population of such communities suffers from a lack of physical and economic security. When this is combined with the pressures of globalization, consumerism, and inequality, community residents may view alternative forms of authority, work, and control as the means to assuage insecurity and may resort to taking matters into their own hands (Caldeira, 2000). In some cases, residents of marginalized communities have been able to work together to ensure public safety and the provision of public services, as in the widely noted case of Villa El Salvador in Lima (Woolcock, 2005).[1] In other circumstances, however, those who take control do so with intentions or means not in the community's best interest.

Members of socially excluded communities who employ violence do so in order to achieve one or more of the following aims: asserting authority and visibility, acquiring cultural identity, enforcing security, meting out vigilante justice, or achieving economic goals. In areas where social capital has eroded and insecurity is prevalent, some people build literal and figurative walls between themselves and their communities, utilize private forms of security, support vigilante groups, or turn a blind eye to private and illegal acts of extrajudicial vengeance (Caldeira, 2000). Others may abandon conventional standards of working in formalized labor sectors, as the opportunities available to socially excluded people are substandard, stagnant in the sense of offering no prospect for use as a stepping-stone to better opportunities, or nonexistent. Within this context, some individuals may view the use of violence as a superior method of meeting certain tangible needs.

---

[1] Community members in Villa El Salvador were able to mobilize to promote the provision of public services in their community, which was otherwise marginalized and lacking in key public goods.

The Informal Privatization of Justice

A key aim of violence in socially ex-cluded communities is the provision of justice, most often through some form of violent punishment. The lack of a fair and functional judicial system, including adequate legal representation, unbiased rulings, due process of law, and preserva-tion of human rights, may force citizens to abandon justice through normative institutional means and instead take the law into their own hands or to depend on others to resolve conflicts for them (Con-cha-Eastman, 2002). For many socially excluded members of society, courts, judges, juries, and a fair trial are beyond the means of their connections and be-yond their expectations.

Figure 10.2
Public Confidence in the Judicial System

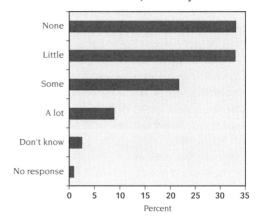

Source: Latinobarometer (2005).
Note: Figure reflects responses to the question "How much confidence do you have in the judicial system?"

Even among the Latin American population as a whole, there is little confidence in the judicial system. Figure 10.2 shows the results of a 2005 Latinobarometer question that found that two-thirds of those surveyed expressed little or no confidence in the judicial system in their country, while only 22 percent reported having "some" confidence in the judiciary. Only 9 percent of respondents reported having "a lot" of trust in their country's judicial system. Given that this survey included people in the middle and upper classes, who generally have adequate access to judicial institutions, it may be reasonably hypoth-esized that the percentage of the population reporting confidence in the judicial system would be even lower in socially excluded communities.

When judicial systems fail to adequately serve certain segments of the population, citizens may be inclined to formulate their own standards of justice and devise their own methods for meting it out. An international study conducted by Children in Orga-nized Armed Violence found that in those areas characterized by a weak state presence, armed groups tended to oversee and judge disputes within their communities, even among those residents unaffiliated with their groups (Dowdney, 2005). In her fieldwork in the favelas of Rio de Janeiro, Goldstein (2003) describes the use of revenge, homicide, and brutal punishment by various actors—gangs, bandits, police, and individuals—as a substitute for an absent or nonfunctioning judicial system. When the state fails to pro-vide security and services in the favelas, gangs may intervene as a mediating force and provide a form of justice to which community members are willing to turn a blind eye (Goldstein, 2003). While these gang members engage in illegal activities, they also fill in for the justice system, and this dual role often induces neighboring citizens to tolerate and excuse their actions.

Fieldwork in socially excluded and impoverished communities in Colombia also reveals the use of vigilante measures and violence as a means of achieving justice. Reporting the results of a series of interviews with young men, Moser and McIlwaine (2000) note their frequent utilization of force and violence, often referred to as the "law of the strongest" and the "law of knives." A different study by the same authors revealed that in many cases of violence and force, residents felt that taking the law into individual or group hands was the only means available to them, given the lack of available alternatives, their mistrust of state institutions, and rampant corruption (Moser and McIlwaine, 2000). Statistics collected by authorities in Bogotá throughout 2005 consistently reveal that the most common reason behind homicides is revenge, covering both murder due to honor and that related to debt (SUIVD, 2006).

The use of extrajudicial means of conflict resolution may have adverse consequences for the community as well as those actors who resolve conflict through violence. High death rates of young males in socially excluded areas may be explained by cycles of revenge among rival gangs or the escalation of interpersonal conflicts among those who do not see the justice system as having an active role (Goldstein, 2003). Community residents who want to avoid violence and resolve conflicts through institutional means may be afraid to do so, as it could put their own safety in jeopardy. One young woman in an Argentine neighborhood expressed her concern about reporting drug dealers on the street to the police for fear that she would suffer retaliation. She explained in an interview that she was "scared to talk to the police because [she] could be killed" and that recording criminal acts with a camera "would be [her] death or the death of [her family]." Given this fear, she instead chose silence.[2]

The lack of institutionalized forms of justice allows various actors to step in and provide justice for a select few in their own interests and for their own gain. Those who may be opposed to these actors or have little or no access to a legitimate judicial system are left with few options. The failure on the part of the state to adequately provide justice not only affects those who deserve legal rights and judicial action, but also forces community residents to submit to the adverse informal institutions created and maintained by vigilante actors.

Security

Beyond the aims of imparting informal forms of justice, violence is also used in socially excluded communities as a means of acquiring security. The absence of state-provided security and the high degree of mistrust of the police subsequently forces communities to resort to alternative sources of protection. Violence is employed for resistance against competing actors and interests, including corrupt policemen, extrajudicial forces, rival gangs, and common vandalism in the community. In some favelas of Rio de Janeiro, drug lords and gangs involved in organized crime provide community members with security and other services, such as money to pay for food, medicine, or child care, creating incentives for residents to refrain from reporting their actions to the authorities.

---

[2] "Yo tengo miedo de hablar con la policía porque puedo ser boleta de toque, porque yo veo a los patrulleros, pensé en una filmadora, pero eso sería mi muerte o la de mi familia, por eso no denuncio porque incluso yo misma veo a los patrulleros que vienen por el barrio." Interview with Jovita, Barrio Santa Elena, by Ana Lourdes Suárez y Carlos, Fundación SES, October 13, 2006. Author's translation.

Figure 10.3
Public Confidence in the Police

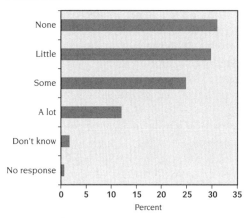

Source: Latinobarometer (2005).
Note: Figure reflects responses to the question "How much confidence do you have in the police?"

Since the state is unable to provide these services—and those state entities responsible for providing such services act as a "corrupt," "repressive," or mistrusted force—the services are valuable to residents who otherwise would not have them (Moser, Winton, and Moser, 2003: 73). Widespread mistrust of institutions such as the police is common throughout the region. The Latinobarometer annual survey of public opinion consistently reveals little or no public confidence in the police. Figure 10.3 shows that in 2005, 61 percent of Latinobarometer respondents have "little" or no confidence in the police. Moser and McIlwaine (2000) note that the police are the least-trusted institution in many Colombian barrios, where many of their interviewees believed the police to be unreliable and likely to exacerbate conflict. Fieldwork in Caracas, Venezuela, exposed similar perceptions of the need to acquire security—especially to defend the community from the police forces. One Venezuelan youth who had spent considerable time living on the streets of Caracas explained that while he believed the police used to be less violent, "Now they catch you on the streets and in front of everybody they throw tear gas at your face. They also beat and kick you . . . as if you were a dog" (quoted in Márquez, 1999: 213).

Lack of faith in and frustration with the police is also evident in a number of interviews conducted in 2006 in various neighborhoods in Argentina. Interviewed residents often responded that the police rarely or only weakly responded to threats facing their community. One 17-year-old male complained that "The police don't come or they come and do nothing. There is so much crime. . . . I want the police to come and do something."[3] Lack of faith in the police discourages many victims of crime from turning to them for help. The 2000 Latinobarometer asked interviewees to whom they turn after a criminal or violent incident; as Figure 10.4 shows, less than half (44.6 percent) indicated they turn to the police, while 40.5 percent said that they do not report their victimization to anyone.

Given such lack of confidence in the police and the absence of institutions that adequately ensure security and peace within Latin American and Caribbean countries—and more so in socially excluded communities—it is no wonder that there is friction within these areas as others step in. When the police are viewed as no better than the criminals they are supposed to protect against, citizens feel they have no options but to remain silent or take matters into their own hands.

---

[3] "No anda la policía o no hace nada. Hay mucha delincuencia, se viven drogrando y los mismos vecinos te roban. . . . [Quiero] que pase la policía y que haga algo. Porque pasan, pero no hacen nada." Interview with Jonatan, Barrio Primavera, by Graciela Ramirez, Fundación SES, October 29, 2006. Author's translation.

Figure 10.4
"After You Have Been a Victim of Crime, Whom Do You Turn To?"

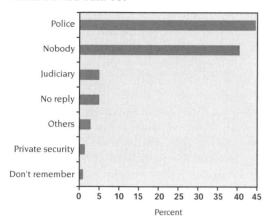

Percent

Source: Authors' compilation using Latinobarometer (2000).
Note: Figure reflects responses to question other than "not applicable."

Authority through Visibility

Violence may also be used to assert authority in situations where it is lacking and to demand the visibility of socially excluded individuals. In areas where state institutions are absent and police are corrupt or perceived as having little authority, members of the community and various social groups may step in with the intention of exerting power, influence, and control. Caldeira (2000: 91) reported, based on her fieldwork in Rio's favelas, that "Crime is a matter of authority. The people . . . think that the increase in crime is a sign of weak authority, be it of the school, family, mother, church, government, police, or justice system."

The need to vent frustration and to acquire a feeling of authority and visibility through attention—albeit negative attention—may also induce certain individuals to resort to violence. After a former street child from Rio de Janeiro took passengers on a public bus hostage for a number of hours, an incident that eventually ended in his violent death (CNN, 2000; Padilha, 2002), sociologist and former Brazilian Minister of Public Security Eduardo Soares commented:

> A boy with a gun can make us feel . . . fear. . . . He can recover his visibility and affirm his social and human existence. . . . It's a pact: the boy exchanges his future, his life, his soul, for . . . the small glory of being acknowledged [and] valued. (quoted in Padilha, 2002)

Those who either assert their power in the absence of legitimate institutions or who feel the need to externally force themselves upon society to assuage their feelings of invisibility use violence in order to establish their authority, power, and influence. Riaño-Alcalá (2006) notes that violence among youth in Colombia is directly related to social exclusion and the invisibility of those who come from poor areas. Such youth have little connection with society and are excluded from those mainstream areas and public spaces where social interaction generally occurs. Instead, these invisible youth begin to engage in "territorial practices of civil protection and policing" (160–61), which is, for them, a form of expressing their citizenship and establishing a connection to the community. The aim of violence, as employed by youth, is to assert and reinforce their connection to the community, thus becoming visible. In this context, violence is used by excluded youth as a means of communication with and participation in a community that otherwise ignores them.

When segments of society are ignored, subject to prejudice, and unable to either benefit from or contribute to society, the need for existence and recognition in the face of stigmatization can have adverse consequences (Padilha, 2002). Socially excluded individuals lack visibility, recognition, and authority within society in the way that they are treated and are able to treat others. For the minority that uses violence, it may be seen as a method of re-establishing control and authority in the face of social exclusion.

Economics

Beyond the needs to ensure security, mete out justice, and assert authority, the consequences of social exclusion may induce some to use violence for economic gain. In communities where residents have trouble meeting their needs through formal and mainstream mechanisms, the lure of gangs, drug trafficking, or acts of individual violence such as robbery may be stronger. Latin America has one of the highest levels of economic inequality in the world (Székely and Hilgert, 1999). The inability to acquire needed or wanted goods and the awareness that hard work will rarely amount to significant improvements in one's quality of life may prove a selling point for some that violence through criminal acts presents a more profitable outcome. The proliferation of organized crime and the increasing connections[4] between it and neighborhood *pandillas*[4] or *naciones*[5] is a significant contributor to the spread of criminal and violent activities; in many countries with organized armed groups, crime is the leading form of economic gain, followed by drug dealing (Dowdney, 2005). Violent acts, including armed robberies and kidnappings, are common methods for economic profit among these groups (Dowdney, 2005). The importance of territory as a space in which to conduct illicit activities and to secure a profit often leads to violent disputes between rival gangs (Dowdney, 2005).

The economic situation of many in marginalized areas may often be unstable, desperate, and exploited, and their economic opportunities are often limited and informal. Without skills or the means to acquire them, many are forced into unemployment or street vending. In interviews in 2005, many young men in Rio de Janeiro who joined gangs described their experiences working on the city's streets as a "degrading" experience. To them, "selling candy on the streets or on a bus, or selling water at intersections . . . [was] seen as desperation, not as jobs that provided a solid sense of identity and respect. In this context, invitations from gang-involved friends or colleagues became attractive. For some young men, gang involvement was the only stable employment they ever had, or the first or only opportunity to enter the 'work' market" (Barker, 2005: 73; see also Dowdney, 2005). In Rio de Janeiro's favelas, many young males interviewed felt "despondent about their prospects for low-paying wage labor" and indicated that while gangs "rule through violence, fear, and terror, they often provide the only economic stimulus available to poor communities" (Goldstein, 2003: 169).

---

[4] *Pandilla* (or *mara*) is a common name for a gang in Honduras and El Salvador; the first of these is also common in Mexico.
[5] *Naciones* are gangs common in Ecuador.

CONCLUDING REMARKS

The lack of security, access to justice, and economic opportunities in marginalized communities has contributed to the proliferation of violence in Latin America and the Caribbean in recent years. In order to combat social exclusion and the consequent challenges of violence, policymakers must find a balance between the need for control (including the state's monopoly on force, the preservation of citizen rights and security, and the maintenance of law and order) and the need to refrain from exacerbating violence by threatening human rights and alienating segments of the population.

In the short term, policymakers in the region must respond to violence through an increased law enforcement presence in affected communities and the monitoring of high-risk repeat offenders.[6] In the longer run, policymakers must create programs that will resolve the underlying issues fostering social exclusion and violent outcomes. Such policies should target weaknesses in judicial, law enforcement, and educational systems and labor markets to provide access for socially excluded individuals, discourage the use of violent methods to satisfy certain needs, and protect members of marginalized communities who are affected by others' use of violence. With respect to police-community relations and law enforcement, programs such as the Youth and the Police project in Belo Horizonte, which set up workshops and seminars involving police and youth groups, have been shown in some preliminary evaluations to improve relations between communities and the local police (Ramos, 2006). Police forces should also be trained to show more respect to arrested offenders and youth. In parallel to improvements in law enforcement techniques and relations, communities should be encouraged to set up policing programs coupled with community town hall meetings to set priorities (Moser, Winton, and Moser, 2005). Placing responsibility and power in the hands of community residents may increase security and reduce feelings of vulnerability in those neighborhoods affected by violence.

It is additionally imperative to address the weaknesses and disorganization of judicial systems in the region and ensure due process of law and fair treatment to individuals without connections or money. Improving the capacity and availability of public defenders and increasing the availability of legal representation is essential. Crackdowns on corruption within judicial systems will limit the ability of those with money to buy their way out of trouble. The state of prisons and rehabilitation programs must be improved—rehabilitation programs that train former offenders in vocational skills have proven effective, as have those that provide risk-focused treatments to allow these people to successfully reintegrate into society (Moser, Winton, and Moser, 2005).

Policies to combat social exclusion and to integrate all members of society are difficult to target and to implement. However, given the exclusion and violence prevalent throughout Latin America and the Caribbean, policymakers must strive to ensure that institutions and policies work to include these vulnerable segments of the population and protect them from the devastating effects of violence.

---

[6] Moser, Winton, and Moser (2005) offer a detailed description of various programs that have been shown to be effective, ineffective, or promising.

CHAPTER 11

Exclusion and Financial Services

Financial exclusion refers to the processes that impede the access of different population groups to the financial system. The key financial services that can be provided by formal and semiformal institutions include deposit accounts, credit accounts, transaction services, and private insurance products.[1] Although a wide variety of institutions and products are available in Latin America and the Caribbean, large shares of the population continue to conduct personal and business transactions through informal channels, using cash for their transactions.[2]

The benefits of financial inclusion are many. Access to savings products can help families smooth consumption and avoid the limitations inherent in depending on cash flow alone.[3] Maintaining cash in a wallet or under a mattress often presents challenges because of intrahousehold allocation conflicts, self-commitment difficulties, inflation, or high exposure to theft. Access to transaction services such as debit cards, ATM cards, and checking accounts can produce large savings in time and opportunities for better control of funds. These services facilitate drawing funds or making payments. The electronic management of funds through computers, cellular telephones, and other devices can have large returns for entrepreneurs, who can also access relevant business information in a timely manner. Access to credit is critical for increasing the productivity of home businesses, farms, and small and medium-sized enterprises. Entrepreneurs and farmers may also invest in higher-return projects when they can purchase insurance against idiosyncratic or aggregate risks.

It is well recognized that the poor face higher risks for job loss, health crises, and even climatic and natural disasters. While economic theory suggests that more vulnerable populations should have higher rates of precautionary savings, empirical studies have found just the opposite: analysis of household survey data suggests that only 15 percent of poor households in Latin America and the Caribbean have savings accounts, whereas the rate is twice as high for nonpoor households (Tejerina and Westley, 2007).[4] Although the poor may attempt to save by investing in their homes or saving "in kind," these informal methods are not sufficiently liquid, and these assets can lose value during times of covariate (economy-wide) shocks, precisely at the time of greatest need (Sadoulet, 2006).

---

[1] Semiformal institutions include microfinance institutions, cooperatives, and popular credit and savings institutions that are typically subject to little or no regulation compared to commercial banks (Sadoulet, 2006). These semiformal institutions often follow standards of operation that have been established apart from formal regulation authorities.

[2] Informal channels include family members, friends, and local loan sharks.

[3] Consumption smoothing is a central objective of life cycle and other microeconomic theories (Deaton, 1992).

[4] The estimates are weighted by the population of the sample of twelve countries.

Table 11.1 Percentage of Households with Credit or Savings (Formal, Semiformal, or Informal)

	Year	Total		Poor		Nonpoor		Urban		Rural	
		Credit	Savings	Credit	Savings	Credit	Savings	Credit	Savings	Credit	Savings
Bolivia	2000	12.9	9.9	10.0	4.0	17.4	18.0	17.0	13.4	5.7	3.9
Dominican Republic	2001	21.0	25.1	16.9	9.8	22.7	31.7	21.8	30.2	19.5	16.0
Ecuador	1998	11.3	22.7	8.2	7.9	12.7	29.9	12.3	29.3	9.7	12.6
El Salvador	2002	2.6	n.d.	2.0	n.d.	2.9	n.d.	2.8	n.d.	2.3	n.d.
Guatemala	2000	11.1	17.2	9.6	2.7	12.4	29.4	12.0	30.6	10.4	6.9
Haiti	2001	n.d.	11.7	n.d.	3.7	n.d.	23.9	n.d.	25.0	n.d.	4.3
Jamaica	1997	10.5	68.2	9.6	48.9	10.7	72.7	10.9	73.1	10.1	62.7
Mexico	2002	23.5	29.6	21.2	23.6	28.3	42.2	24.6	33.5	19.9	16.0
Nicaragua	1998	17.4	7.4	9.7	1.8	22.3	10.9	21.7	11.0	11.8	2.7
Panama	2003	34.7	38.6	28.6	12.7	36.8	47.7	38.1	46.4	28.4	24.6
Paraguay	2001	4.2	5.1	4.0	1.9	4.2	6.3	5.0	7.6	3.0	1.9
Peru	2001	12.4	4.5	8.5	0.9	15.8	7.6	14.9	5.8	6.8	1.6
Average (weighted)		18.9	23.2	16.2	15.0	22.6	33.9	20.9	28.3	14.1	11.8

Source: Tejerina and Westley (2007).
Note: n.d. = data not available.

Table 11.1 shows the percentage of households reporting credit or savings through any source (formal, semiformal, or informal), and Table 11.2 shows the percentage only for those with credit or savings through formal or semiformal institutions, based on a review by Tejerina and Westley (2007).[5] According to their classification, the "formal and semiformal institutions" category includes regulated financial institutions, such as banks, as well as unregulated financial institutions, which in most cases refers to different types of credit unions and nongovernmental organizations. The "informal" category includes all sources of credit that are not considered financial institutions, such as rotary savings and credit associations (ROSCAs), moneylenders, and relatives. Tejerina and Westley's information is based on national household surveys which inquire about savings accounts and loans obtained in the preceding year.

Even if the least restrictive definition is used as in Table 11.1, less than one-quarter of households declare holding savings or credit, according to the weighted average. Dropping the informal providers as in Table 11.2 reduces the levels of the "banked" populations, particularly in the case of the households reporting that they have obtained a loan in the preceding year.

Much variation is observed across countries and socioeconomic groups. Of the twelve countries included in Tejerina and Westley's (2007) study, Jamaica, Panama, and the Dominican Republic have the highest coverage of savings accounts, but only in Jamaica do more than 50 percent of households have an account. In Peru, Paraguay, Nicaragua, and Bolivia, by contrast, fewer than 10 percent of households report having savings accounts. However, the gap between the poor and the nonpoor within each country is striking, as are the gaps between rural and urban households. Across the twelve countries, 28.3 percent of the nonpoor report holding savings, whereas only 10.0 percent of the poor report having them. In their extensive analysis of survey data, Tejerina and Westley find that the gaps in savings between the poor and the nonpoor are larger than the gaps in use of credit. The urban-rural gap in the use of financial services is also important. Use of formal or semiformal credit in rural areas is 3.8 percent compared to 7.4 percent in urban areas, and use of formal or informal savings is 8.4 percent in rural areas compared to 22.2 percent in urban areas.

Most empirical work in this area struggles with the problem of assessing *access* to financial products rather than *usage* of the products, a very different concept. This is particularly challenging in regard to measuring access to formal credit, since individuals may have the ability to secure credit but may not have considered the possibility of doing so or may have considered it but decided against pursuing it. Various techniques have been developed to measure access to credit, including direct elicitation, a series of objective and hypothetical questions based on self-reported status, and key informant methodology. The pivotal challenge, however, remains. Empirical estimates suggest that access to financial markets remains a challenge for large sectors of Latin America and the Caribbean, most notably poor rural households. For large shares of the population, financial transactions take place with only minimal involvement of formal and semiformal financial institutions, with individuals relying on extremely informal arrangements rather than deposit and credit accounts.

---

[5] The typical question in the household survey was "Do you have a savings account of some type?"

Table 11.2 Percentage of Households with Savings or Loans from Formal or Semiformal Institutions

	Data Shown	Total		Poor		Nonpoor		Urban		Rural	
		Credit	Savings	Credit	Savings	Credit	Savings	Credit	Savings	Credit	Savings
Bolivia	2000	7.0	9.9	5.3	4.5	9.7	18.0	9.3	13.4	3.2	3.9
Dominican Republic	2001	10.9	25.1	5.8	9.8	13.1	31.7	12.5	30.2	7.9	16.0
Ecuador	1998	9.8	22.7	4.9	7.9	12.2	29.9	12.0	29.3	6.4	12.6
El Salvador	2002	1.3	n.d.	0.5	n.d.	1.7	n.d.	1.6	n.d.	0.7	n.d.
Guatemala	2000	6.4	16.8	4.2	2.5	8.3	28.9	7.7	30.0	5.4	6.7
Haiti	2001	n.d.	11.7	n.d.	3.7	n.d.	23.9	n.d.	25.0	n.d.	4.3
Jamaica	1997	3.8	59.4	1.0	40.2	4.5	63.9	4.8	62.2	2.7	56.3
Mexico	2002	6.2	20.6	5.3	14.8	8.2	32.9	7.1	24.1	3.3	8.4
Nicaragua	1998	10.4	5.6	5.0	0.9	13.8	8.6	13.8	8.9	5.9	1.3
Panama	2003	17.5	35.2	8.4	9.9	20.7	44.0	21.0	42.5	11.3	22.1
Paraguay	2001	3.4	3.7	1.7	0.7	3.1	4.8	3.7	6.0	1.5	0.7
Peru	2001	3.5	4.5	1.5	0.9	5.1	7.6	4.4	5.8	1.4	1.6
Average (weighted)		6.3	18.0	4.5	10.0	8.3	28.3	7.4	22.2	3.8	8.4

Source: Tejerina and Westley (2007).
Note: n.d. = data not available.

A variety of factors, from both the supply and demand sides, explain these low participation rates. High minimum balances, monthly fees, and transaction fees deter the participation of low-income clientele in semiformal and formal institutions. The annualized estimated cost of maintaining a deposit account in Brazil and Mexico in 2004 was estimated at US$50 and US$400, respectively, based on a modest set of transactions (Ketley, Davis, and Truen, 2005). A lack of trust in financial institutions is typically a main reason provided by respondents who do not have a bank account. The pervasive fear that savings will be confiscated by authorities on either a permanent or temporary basis was unfortunately given credence during economic crises in Brazil and Argentina. The concern that inflation may erode balances is also a common concern. Strict requirements regarding documentation are also an important barrier to participation. Banks commonly require proof of address in the form of utility bills and proof of steady employment in the form of a series of wage receipts. A formal address and a steady or formal job are common eligibility requirements for opening deposit accounts in the region, according to research by Ketley, Davis, and Truen (2005). The extralegal nature of unplanned communities, established without municipal plans, can contribute to financial exclusion, since dwellings in these communities often lack official addresses as well as formal connections to utility services.[6] Workers in the informal sector and in particular industries are less likely to be able to provide proof of steady salary and employment sufficient to open a deposit account at an institution that requires such proof. Based on a survey of the five largest formal banks in fifty-eight countries, Beck, Demirgüç-Kunt, and Martínez Pería (2006) report that the requirements of a formal sector job and a physical address effectively exclude the majority of the population from opening accounts in developing countries. Ketley, Davis, and Truen (2005) find that the requirements for opening a deposit account in Mexico and Brazil are more exclusionary than those in Kenya or South Africa, primarily because of the required proof of salary income.

Financial literacy and cultural preferences also play an important role, leading less-advantaged individuals to prefer alternative savings instruments such as investing in their home ("saving in bricks") or through informal savings clubs (ROSCAs). Although these alternatives provide some opportunities for consumption smoothing, they do not provide the full benefits of financial inclusion.

The lack of interest in opening a bank account is a serious deterrent to expanding financial participation. Household survey data in Brazil indicate that one-third of households that do not have bank accounts do not want one (Kumar, 2005).

In terms of supply factors, the higher administrative costs associated with screening and monitoring clients who may lack traditional inputs such as credit histories or collateral lead to higher fees for services. ATMs may not be placed at the same concentration in high-crime areas, potentially disadvantaging low-income populations.

The legal and regulatory environment in a country provides important incentives for lenders. In most countries in the region, it is not legal to use inventories (movable products) as collateral, only real estate or new automobiles (Fleisig, Safavian, and de la Peña, 2006). Countries without a secure transactions environment in which repossession

---

[6] See Galiani, González-Rozada, and Schargrodsky (2007) for a description of an innovative program that addresses these extralegal issues with respect to extending water services in Argentina.

of collateral can be conducted in a timely fashion provide poor incentives for loans to be broadly extended. The lack of developed credit registries further restricts offers of credit to a select set of clients with outstanding records in regard to business transactions (Galindo and Miller, 2001). Moreover, information on bank account features, charges, and costs of borrowing money may not be widely disseminated in accessible language. The degree of discretionary authority loan officers have in approving or denying loans to applicants provides an opportunity for discrimination and favoritism to enter decision making. Audit studies in which demographic characteristics vary across applicants with matched eligibility characteristics provide the best way of measuring these costs of exclusion (Yinger, 1986; Neumark, 1996), but these are only beginning to be conducted in the region and would be difficult to conduct in tightly knit communities where it would be unlikely for strangers to apply for credit.

DIRECT AND INDIRECT INTERVENTIONS TO EXPAND PARTICIPATION IN FINANCIAL SERVICES

Concern about welfare consequences resulting from exclusion from the banking sector has led some governments to promote the extension of banking services, particularly to the rural poor (Besley, 1995). In 2001, Mexico launched a $150 million program to expand banking institutions in rural areas (Taber, 2004). The National Savings and Financial Services Bank (Banco del Ahorro Nacional y Servicios Financieros, or BANSEFI) has two main objectives: (a) to mobilize savings deposits, particularly in areas previously unserved by banks, and (b) to help popular savings and credit institutions meet licensing requirements through technical assistance and a one-time subsidy for upgrading.[7] Banking fees are intentionally kept at a minimum, with no transaction fees charged and only a minimal service fee (about US$5) charged to open an account (Taber, 2004). The BANSEFI program has successfully extended banking services to the unbanked population, with the number of savings accounts in Mexico increasing from 850,000 in 2001 to 3.3 million five years later. By May 2006, there were 523 BANSEFI branches, one-half located in areas unserved by commercial banks (Gavito Mohar, 2006). A full 70 percent of BANSEFI's customers are women, with average savings balances of US$150.[8]

The explosion of microfinance institutions in the region is often described as a response to the high transaction costs of banking with formal institutions. While these institutions have been extremely successful in extending access to credit to small businesses and the moderately poor, success in reaching the most marginalized populations has been more mixed (Hashemi and Rosenberg, 2006; Copestake et al., 2005; Hulme and Mosley, 1996). A private sector institution in Bolivia, the Promotion and Development of Microfinance (PRODEM), uses technology to overcome many of the most challenging barriers to financial access. The institution has sixty-five branch offices located in rural communities lacking reliable communications infrastructure. PRODEM offers deposit

---

[7] BANSEFI is a successor to the National Savings Institution (Patronato de Ahorro Nacional, or PAHNAL), a previous government program focused on promoting saving accounts in rural areas.

[8] This gender composition and low average balance are in part a reflection of the fact that more than one million government subsidies under the cash transfer program Oportunidades are intentionally provided to women through these accounts.

and credit accounts to rural communities through a specialized network of ATMs. The ATMs extend to "unconnected" communities using electronic smart cards in which are embedded the account information and biometrics of the client. The rural branches can communicate digitally with the central office and can rely on hard electronic media when telecommunications services are limited. Along with geographic barriers, PRODEM addresses cultural barriers and low levels of financial literacy through its specialized technology. According to PRODEM estimates, 27 percent of its customers are illiterate and therefore unable to read standard instructions for financial transactions (Bazoberry, reported in Hernández and Mugica, 2003). To overcome this obstacle, a series of interactive transactions has been modified to be voice-activated in Bolivia's three main languages (Spanish, Quechua, and Aymara), using a simple series of color-coded touch screen transactions. A fingerprint identification system eliminates the need for clients to self-identify regularly using a long account number, which may be merely a hindrance for some customers and for others a cultural affront. PRODEM does not charge a fee for each smart card transaction, instead collecting a modest annual fee (about US$7).[9] By 2006, 255,966 customers had savings accounts and 77,476 customers had active loans (Microfinance Information Exchange, 2006). Although the smart card is activated by fingerprint identification, it is important to note that opening an account requires a valid national identity card.[10]

Land-titling programs, inspired by the seminal work of Hernando de Soto (2000), have proliferated in the region, with the promotion of access to credit as a primary objective. The theory behind these programs is that once families can provide collateral to a bank in the form of the title to their property, the bank will be willing to extend them credit. Impact evaluations of various land-titling programs have shown mixed results with respect to the effect of titling on leveraging credit. Research by Galiani and Schargrodsky (2005) in Argentina found that even when they received title to land (in a quasi-experimental situation), most residents did not satisfy other requirements for obtaining loans, such as formal employment status and personal documentation. Having a title to land was not, therefore, a sufficient condition for increasing access to credit. Evaluations of land-titling programs in Peru and Uruguay have yielded similar results. Boucher, Barham, and Carter (2007) found that the land-titling program in Peru has reduced the share of households that describe themselves as quantity-rationed (defined as lacking collateral). However, they also found that the inability to reduce exposure to risks remained the primary constraint to rationing credit in Peru, with the increase in risk-rationed households muting the effect of titling. In his evaluation of land-titling programs in Uruguay, Gandelman (2007) also found that property ownership did not increase access to the formal banking system or less formal financial institutions. Of households who had requested credit in the preceding year, 93 percent were required to show personal identification and 74 percent were required to show documentation of their wages, whereas only 4 percent were asked to present home ownership documents. The emerging literature thus

---

[9] See Sadoulet (2006) and Hernández and Mugica (2003) for more information.
[10] "Banks and Microfinance Institutions Sponsor Promotions and Incentives to Increase Clients," *La Razón* (La Paz, Bolivia), October 11, 2005.

suggests that personal identification is an important binding constraint for accessing credit, whereas the possession of a property title is required less often.

Other interventions in the region have important implications for expanding financial access to excluded populations, even if increasing such access is not the primary objective of the programs. Many social programs in the region, including conditional cash transfer programs, have shifted to electronic payment of benefits rather than distributing cash to beneficiaries (Duryea and Schargrodsky, 2006). The previous system of distributing cash through administrative offices typically resulted in long lines, and allegations of kickbacks to administrative officers and political bosses were not uncommon.

Although providing subsidies through electronic intermediaries is becoming increasingly common in Latin America and the Caribbean, the services offered and the flexibility provided by the different programs ranges widely. In many countries, including Argentina and Brazil, beneficiaries can only withdraw money from the beneficiary account; they cannot deposit additional funds. The Oportunidades program in Mexico, in contrast, allows beneficiaries to deposit other funds in the beneficiary accounts, and a new option is available to apply for loans (Ayala Consulting, 2006). Although distributing program benefits through banks may encourage some subsidy program participants to open deposit accounts, a more comprehensive intervention such as that in Mexico provides more services to beneficiaries and includes more users in the financial system. As of May 2006, 1.2 million savings accounts had been opened for Oportunidades beneficiaries.

How do beneficiaries view these new payment systems? In an evaluation of the shift to debit cards for the transfer of benefits in a welfare program in Argentina, Duryea and Schargrodsky (2007) found that beneficiaries report high levels of satisfaction with the new system, with 87 percent rating the new debit card system as more efficient.[11] The high levels of satisfaction are highly correlated with savings of time. Moreover, the time saved in retrieving benefits is associated with an increase in hours of work. Beneficiaries also reported fewer problems meeting medical expenses after receiving the debit cards, suggesting that the electronic system provided an instrument to smooth consumption. Although only a small proportion of beneficiaries (4 percent) reported that they had been paying kickbacks on their benefits, this fell to 0.03 percent when the payments were made electronically to the accounts. The survey results also suggest that each household individual gains independence in the use of his or her own money under the system of payment by ATM. The percentage of households surveyed that declare that the household head and his or her spouse decide the use of their own money independently from one another increased from 6 to 12 percent. The results of the evaluation in Argentina regarding time use and autonomy have particularly important implications for women, who tend to bear the time-intensive burdens imposed by the obligations of cash transfer programs.

The design of the electronic transfer card itself can promote social inclusion. In the case of the Jefes and Jefas program in Argentina, as well as the follow-up program Plan Familias, the debit cards were designed to have exactly the same appearance as bank

---

[11] The study was based on a difference-in-difference design, since some households changed their payment method and others remained constant, depending on their area of residence.

cards held by high-income individuals, so as not to stigmatize beneficiaries as welfare recipients. The debit cards complemented a tax rebate policy implemented by the Argentine government aimed at drawing more expenditure into the formal economy. Under this policy, the country's value-added tax is reduced by 15 percentage points, from 21 percent to 6 percent, for program participants for purchases made using the debit cards issued by the program. The tax savings is returned to the debit or credit account.

Although the quality and variety of products sold at formal establishments in Argentina is higher on average than that of products available through informal shops, low-income families typically face high effective prices at these establishments, because they do not have a bank card and therefore cannot take advantage of the associated rebate.[12] Evaluation of the modification in the program revealed that beneficiary families shifted their purchases to more formal establishments, making 10 percent more of their monthly expenditures in these establishments after receiving the debit card.[13] Beneficiaries clearly take advantage of the additional opportunity to shop in places typically frequented by higher-income clientele. Thus the country's new approach to distributing benefits in welfare programs has assisted the government's efforts to shift expenditures to the more formal economy, potentially increasing the tax base for social policy.

Permitting the deposit of funds from other soures into individual electronic accounts originally designed for a single social program requires a particular administrative framework for the accounts, but this flexibility can be important for promoting savings. After the second monthly payment under the Oportunidades program, 94 percent of beneficiaries hold accounts with positive balances. After the fifth cash payment, 5 percent of beneficiaries make deposits into the account from other sources of income (Gavito Mohar, 2006).

An inclusive financial sector allows poor and marginalized populations to access a broad range of financial services, such as credit, savings, mortgages, and insurance. Financial inclusion can be promoted through larger-scale reforms of the financial sector, including legal reforms that broaden the definition of collateral to movable inventories and strengthen a secure transactions environment as well as support for credit registries. However, inclusion can also be accomplished through well-designed interventions that lie outside the immediate realm of the financial sector. Extending identity documents at both the personal and residential levels has important implications for access to financial services. Social programs that distribute benefits in the form of electronic payments can be structured to promote beneficiaries' inclusion and expansion into different financial products. New technologies applied to completing transactions, such as cellular telephones, have shown tremendous potential for reducing physical barriers to access. Microfinance institutions have demonstrated that doing business with the nonrich can be profitable; the next challenge is to expand this success to the remaining unbanked. Improving financial access should help families reduce their vulnerabilities to shocks and smooth consumption as well as enable them to respond to better investments.

---

[12] The unit cost of products sold may also be lower at formal stores, potentially offsetting the tax that is presumably avoided by shopping in informal shops.

[13] This again involves a difference-in-difference estimation strategy, with the beneficiaries who received the card increasing their purchases 10 percent more than those who did not change status.

Modern Forms of Program Delivery and Exclusion

In agricultural and premodern societies, access to political and economic spheres depended on informal social networks, and formal laws often assigned different rights and responsibilities to individuals according to their ethnicity, race, and gender. Civil registration documents played an important role for the inheritance of property among eligible populations, but not in everyday life for the majority of individuals. Modern life, however, increasingly requires an individual to have official proof of identity to fully exercise essential functions at transaction points such as opening a bank account, voting in elections, obtaining microcredit or more formal credit, holding title to land, or holding a formal sector job. The millions of individuals in the region who lack valid personal identification are effectively shut out from economically productive activities available to their fellow citizens.

Moreover, in Latin America modern forms for delivering social programs have often clashed with traditionally marginalized populations lacking identity documents. Although the extent of underdocumentation in Latin America and the Caribbean may be relatively lower than that observed in other areas of the world, including Africa and South Asia (as measured by children's civil registration status), the Latin American and Caribbean region has moved rapidly to modernize targeting systems and adopt new methods of distributing program benefits. Unfortunately, however, those efforts have often had the unintended consequence of excluding the most vulnerable from social assistance programs.

SIZE OF THE UNDOCUMENTED POPULATION

A birth certificate represents an individual's first contract with the state, a formal recognition of his or her name and identity with an implicit demand for future services. Among children younger than five in Latin America, approximately 15 percent lack a registered birth certificate (UNICEF, 2005). National estimates of the underregistration of births range from 7 percent in Peru to 23 percent in Bolivia and 26 percent in the Dominican Republic (Duryea, Olgiati, and Stone, 2006). Although comparable estimates of the lack of documentation among adults have not been produced regionally, reflecting in part the lack of a uniform and recognized methodology for accurate measurement, some information is available regarding a few specific countries in the region (Duryea, Olgiati, and Stone, 2007). In Peru, the National Civil Registry (Registro Nacional de Identificación y Estado Civil, or RENIEC) estimated that 1.5 million adults in that country did not have a national identity card (Documento Nacional de Identidad, or DNI) in 2005 (RENIEC, 2005). The National Commission on Modernizing the State in Ecuador estimated that 15 percent of that country's total population is not registered (CONATEL, 2006). Estimates from recent censuses in Bolivia and Paraguay place the number of adults without national identification cards at 750,000 and 127,000, respectively (Duryea, Olgiati, and Stone, 2007).[1]

Traditionally excluded groups tend to have higher rates of underdocumentation, although there are some important exceptions. Throughout the region underregistration of births is higher in rural areas than in urban areas. Children from low socioeconomic backgrounds are less likely to be registered by age 5, and in many countries certain ethnic and racial groups have higher rates of underregistration. In the north and northeast regions of Brazil, for example, characterized by lower levels of education and income and a high concentration of Afro-Brazilians, birth underregistration is three times higher than in the wealthier south (IBGE, 2006). Although the birth registration of children does not vary significantly by gender in the region (Duryea, Olgiati, and Stone, 2006),[2] in some countries rural adult women are less likely to possess national identity documents than rural men. For example, in rural areas of Peru, 17 percent of women older than eighteen lack any identity document (DNI or passport) versus 9 percent of their rural male counterparts (INEI, 2006). In Paraguay rural women are also approximately twice as likely to lack a national identity document as their male counterparts (DGEEC, 2004).

Exclusion from social and economic programs can additionally occur on a discretionary basis when program administrators disregard rules or even laws guaranteeing universal access; lack of compliance with some laws suggests that these behaviors may not be interpreted as discretionary but the acceptable practice. Qualitative research suggests that school directors in the region commonly use the lack of birth certificates to ration scarce places in schools and to restrict scholarship funds to less-marginalized children (Ordóñez and Bracamonte, 2005). While practices vary across countries, the pattern for Nicaragua has been observed regionally. Children there are permitted to attend school provisionally but are not permitted to receive the diploma for finishing the primary level, nor are they permitted to enroll in the secondary level, without presenting a birth certificate. In Honduras children may enter first grade but will not be promoted to second grade unless a birth certificate is presented (Ordóñez and Bracamonte, 2005). According to 2001 household survey data for Brazil, 8 percent of children age 7–9 were reported not to be attending school because of a lack of documentation (Duryea, Olgiati, and Stone, 2006). While discretionary action on the part of individual agents may exclude individuals from participating in social programs in the region, it is also important to explore the more structured processes that have exclusionary impacts.

TARGETING

In a context of scarce resources and concerns about fraud and leakage in social programs, including the capturing of program benefits by better-off groups, technocrats in Latin America have embraced methodological advances in the delivery of social assistance.

---

[1] Not all countries have a national identity document, but all countries have official identity documents such as birth certificates, voter registration cards, taxpayer identification cards, and passports.
[2] No significant gender difference is found for registration rates of children under age 5 among the countries studied.

Figure 12.1
Steps in the Design and Implementation of Social Programs
Where Underdocumentation Can Lead to Exclusion

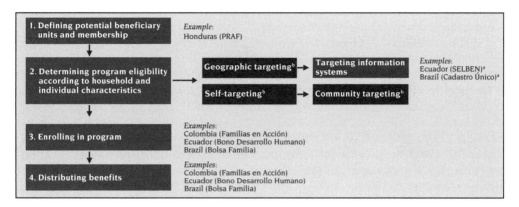

Source: Duryea, Glassman, and Stone (2007).

[a] Requirement dropped after revision of targeting system.
[b] Indicates this approach is not typically associated with exclusion based on documentation at this step.

The desire for greater accountability requires procedures to verify eligibility for program benefits and monitor the transfer of funds. Rather than providing nonindividualized benefits on a geographical basis, program administrators utilize specific information on individual families and individuals to determine program eligibility and benefit levels. This trend in program design has also been seen in developed countries seeking more efficient use of resources. Much emphasis has been placed on the development of screening procedures to reduce "errors of inclusion," that is, the leakage of benefits to nontargeted individuals. However, a trade-off may occur in the push to reduce errors of inclusion, with errors involving the exclusion of targeted individuals magnifying as additional filters are added to programs.

Social programs can therefore unintentionally intensify the social exclusion of the undocumented by treating official identification documents as strict requirements for program participation. Initial exclusion can have a particularly severe impact when there are only limited opportunities to enter the program at a later time under a revised set of conditions because new openings will not arise or because reassessment opportunities occur only infrequently. Many information systems used for program targeting, for instance, update their household rosters only every two to three years—a major delay from an individual family's perspective. In some countries, such as Colombia and Ecuador, families can request to be reassessed on demand, but few households are aware of this right.

It is particularly interesting to consider how conditional cash transfer programs interface with documentation issues, because these programs have been at the forefront of adopting new targeting and benefit distribution technologies in the region. Figure 12.1 illustrates the different stages in program design and implementation in which the lack of identity documents can lead to exclusion. Programs with relatively strict documentation requirements have effectively excluded undocumented populations through screening or verification procedures.[3] Other conditional cash transfer programs, however, have taken a more flexible approach to eligibility requirements, incorporating the acquisition of identity documents into program objectives.

It is worthwhile to consider a few programs. As is the case for many conditional cash transfer programs, the Bono Desarrollo Humano (BDH) program in Ecuador uses an information system to target beneficiary households. The SELBEN (Sistema de Identificación y Elección de Beneficiarios), also in Ecuador, includes information from a short survey on dwelling characteristics as well as the human capital and earnings potential of family members. The national identification number of all household members is included in the SELBEN database, as well as the birth certificate number of all children up to age 16. Families who score in the lowest two quintiles according to a statistical estimation proxying poverty status are eligible to participate in a series of targeted programs. However, families cannot be entered into the SELBEN if the head of the family or her spouse does not have a national identity document, effectively excluding them from all social programs that use the SELBEN for targeting, including Ecuador's conditional cash transfer program (Cely, 2005). Although there have been exceptions to this regulation, with some families not meeting the documentation requirements initially being entered into the SELBEN on an idiosyncratic basis, they do not pass later checks of the targeting database and are dropped from it (Cely, 2005).[4] A 2003 evaluation of the SELBEN found that the lack of documentation was an obstacle to inclusion in the SELBEN, especially for families in rural areas and older persons (Habitus, 2003, as cited in Cely, 2005).[5] The targeting system is only the first filter for inclusion; the conditional cash transfer program itself, the BDH, requires documentation from the head of the family as defined by the program. The targeting system designed by Brazil in 2002, the Cadastro Único, also records the different identity documents of family members in addition to characteristics of dwellings and personal characteristics (de la Brière and Lindert, 2005). Initially, official documentation of the defined family head was a required piece of information for inclusion in the registry (stage 2 exclusion in Figure 12.1) (de la Brière and Lindert, 2005).[6] Program administrators, however, quickly recognized the exclusionary impact of this condition and revised the eligibility requirements (Castañeda and Lindert, 2005). The information system for Cadastro Único continues to collect the information needed to facilitate the cross-referencing of individuals across different programs, but inclusion in the targeting database is not predicated on identity documents.

---

[3] This section on conditional cash transfer programs and documentation is excerpted from Duryea, Glassman, and Stone (2007).

[4] The program is more lenient with respect to the documentation of minors. The binding constraints refer to the documentation of the head of the family, as defined by the program, or her spouse.

[5] The requirement for documentation to enter the SELBEN was dropped in a subsequent reform; however, the requirement for documentation to enter BDH was retained. Calculations provided by the SELBEN showed that 115,994 households that satisfied the eligibility requirement in terms of the proxy test for poverty status were deemed not eligible to participate in BDH because the mother in the family lacked a national identity document (DNI) (IDB, 2006d).

[6] Information for the Cadastro Único is collected by municipalities. In a 2003 audit, 63 percent of municipalities reported that they made entry into the database conditional on documentation (de la Brière and Lindert, 2005).

However, as in the case of the conditional cash transfer program in Ecuador, the defined head of the family is required, in order to enroll in Brazil's conditional cash transfer program, Bolsa Familia, to provide an official form of identification, such as a social security card, taxpayer identification card, or voter card. Engel Aduan (2006) reports the lack of documentation among designated family heads has resulted in a rejection rate of 10 percent from the program. Traditionally excluded groups have been found to be particularly vulnerable to omission from the targeting system for the program. A recent government study found that 16 percent of residents of Quilombo communities, isolated areas inhabited by descendants of escaped Afro-Brazilian slaves, lacked any form of an official identity document and will be excluded from program benefits even after a planned extension of the targeting system to their communities (Cézar Nunes, 2007). Targeted documentation campaigns are planned to address this challenge.

Conditional cash transfer programs in Mexico and Central America can be characterized as taking a more neutral approach to official documentation, with administrators preferring to use other ways of selecting and enrolling beneficiaries in recognition of the high rates of underregistration among indigenous and poor populations. Oportunidades (previously Progresa, Mexico), Red de Protección Social (Nicaragua), and PRAF (Programa de Asignación Familiar, Honduras) do not require official documentation at the targeting and program enrollment phases. Oportunidades, for example, accepts local forms of identification that include photographs (Acosta Urquidi and Burstein, 2006). However, some programs have found that too much flexibility with respect to identity encourages misreporting. In response to some families' listing ghost or neighbor children to receive higher benefits, PRAF began verifying the birth certificates of all children described as family members of a potential beneficiary household.

Some countries attempt to limit potential clashes between eligibility rules and underdocumentation by undertaking civil registration campaigns in communities immediately before a program is launched. In Colombia, for example, communities with high rates of underregistration that are scheduled to be included in the conditional cash transfer program Familias en Acción are first provided, through a targeted campaign, with information about civil registration before the program is launched locally. The information system SISBEN (Sistema de Selección de Beneficiarios para Programas Sociales—System for Selection of Beneficiaries for Social Programs) collects information on documentation status, but entry into the conditional cash transfer program is open to those with missing documentation. However, families do not receive the subsidy available through the program until the mother meets the documentation requirements for herself; missing documentation for children is not penalized for the first six months after enrollment in the program. Ordóñez and Bracamonte (2005) report that many families experience delays in receiving benefits as a result of problems with their documentation, although less than 5 percent remain permanently excluded from receiving benefits. Although Colombia's approach of allowing enrollment but denying payment is somewhat more lenient than denying program eligibility, once the preprogram documentation campaign has run its course, no formal resources are available from the cash transfer program to subsequently assist families in obtaining their documents. To reduce potential exclusion from Bolsa Familia, Brazil has also begun to focus registration campaigns on poor communities.

Some social programs have incorporated documentation as a program target rather than a prerequisite. The most proactive stances are taken by Chile (Chile Solidario), Argentina (Plan Familias), and Peru (Juntos), where identity documents have become objectives for participating families with members lacking identity cards or birth certificates. In Chile Solidario, families are not subject to behavioral conditions but rather set objectives in seven areas, including identification, with the help of social workers. In 2004, 14 percent of beneficiary families set a goal of obtaining identification for at least one family member (Galasso, 2007). In the first year of its Programa Puente, Chile Solidario issued over 26,000 DNIs to poor families who were undocumented at the start of the program (Provoste Campillay, 2004). In the design phase of Plan Familias, pilot surveys in two Argentine municipalities indicated that 15–17 percent of intended beneficiaries lacked national identity cards, and the program subsequently developed procedures to assist families in acquiring identity documents. In the first year of the Juntos program in Peru, 85 percent of the 15,000 cases of mothers and children lacking identification were resolved.

Social programs that have adopted identification of beneficiaries as an objective have learned that it is not sufficient to make demands upon clients or civil registration systems without providing supporting resources. Many families with long-standing identity issues find themselves in a legal quagmire they are unable to navigate without skilled assistance. The provision of notaries, social workers, and lawyers is often necessary to help families navigate complex codes.

BANKING

The shift to distributing welfare subsidies through financial institutions represents a further modernizing trend that may have magnified exclusion.[7] Banking institutions in Latin America and the Caribbean generally require official documentation for face-to-face transactions or opening individual accounts. Most transfer programs, such as Familias en Acción in Colombia, require the main beneficiary to possess a national identity card because the bank where she collects her benefits requires this when verifying payments; when programs decide to provide benefits via electronic means, very few continue to offer recipients the option of collecting benefits in cash from the administrative office, a necessary condition for those who lack the documents required by banks (Agencia Presidencial para la Acción Social y la Cooperación Internacional, 2005). Oportunidades in Mexico is an important exception. Although most beneficiaries have embraced the financial accounts associated with Oportunidades, a small but solid proportion of the program's clients continue to collect in cash.

There may be many potential benefits to shifting the payment systems of social programs from cash to electronic payments through financial systems. For example, in Argentina and Ecuador the government varies the date of payments for the cash transfer programs based on the last digit of the recipient's DNI, reducing possibilities for crime.

---

[7] Because distributing cash is dangerous for program administrators and can be linked to accusations of corruption, transfer programs increasingly are shifting to distributing subsidies through financial institutions.

These benefits, however, may come at the price of not including the most vulnerable families in the programs.

REFORMS TO EXTEND COVERAGE

Achieving universal coverage of identity documents is particularly challenging in environments in which the percentage of hospital births is low, previous generations lack documentation, and trust in public institutions is low. The intergenerational transmission of "invisibility" presents one of the most difficult challenges to overcome, because another layer of complexity is added when parents lack documentation. Even children of undocumented parents who are born in hospitals with official witnesses present must pass through an additional bureaucratic layer, since an undocumented mother must present two witnesses of her own birth to establish maternal identity, and the witnesses themselves must possess valid identity documents. Social norms pose additional problems, as some mothers would prefer not to register their children at all rather than officially declare them fatherless. Successful campaigns to extend documentation must address cultural issues as well as legal obstacles faced by many families.

Many countries have eliminated fees for registration within a specific time period after birth, typically the first month, but direct costs pose only part of the problem. For those in rural and remote areas, journeying to the civil registry office can involve considerable indirect costs in regard to time and travel. Some countries have developed mobile units, including boats, to reach particularly remote areas. Regular visits by these units, rather than irregular campaigns, are necessary for sustained progress in reducing underregistration and maintaining up-to-date documentation for adults.

Until recently, entries into the civil registry in the region continued to be made manually in bound books that were not necessarily catalogued in any centralized system, and it was difficult to capture this information on photocopies or microfilm for use elsewhere. The challenges to modernizing civil registration in Latin America and the Caribbean are striking; in Mexico, for example, until quite recently the decentralized civil registries of the country's thirty-two states had more than 100 different formats and procedures for registering births. With a few exceptions such as Chile and Mexico, few countries in the region have overhauled their civil registries with efficient procedures and integrated computer technology. Most countries remain far from their goals in this area, and deep institutional reform is essential to meet those goals. Efforts to improve coverage have so far largely concentrated on short-run campaigns that have failed to produce lasting results. Nonetheless, more than a few countries are moving steadily in the direction of providing unique identification numbers at birth that follow individuals across different documents and programs, complete with biometrics. Until countries universalize identification, the rules that govern social programs must carefully address the issue of underdocumentation.

PART III

Advancing Inclusion

Inclusion and Public Policy

Social exclusion in Latin America and the Caribbean continues to evolve in ways that are still poorly understood. This report has examined how newer, more modern forces are interacting with centuries-old forms of exclusion based on race, ethnicity, gender, and other group traits, inducing a more complex form of exclusion that is evident in much of the region today.

The excluded are poor and have chronically unstable work lives. Low wages and exclusion from social insurance mechanisms make the excluded more vulnerable in all dimensions of their social life. Neighborhoods rife with crime, lack of access to basic social and public services, discrimination, political disenfranchisement—all compound to limit the ability of the excluded to obtain outcomes valuable in a market economy. A large fraction of the excluded population belongs to groups that have been historically excluded based on their race, ethnicity, gender, and other group traits: exclusion in the region is as brown-skinned as poverty is. But looking at exclusion exclusively through the lenses of ethnicity, gender, and race can obscure the impact of modern forces of exclusion which affect an even wider and more diverse group within the population.

An especially important locus of these modern forces of exclusion is the labor market. The increase in the number of low-wage jobs is a bad omen for productivity and growth, and for many the labor market has become a source of exclusion rather than a path towards social integration (see Chapter 5). A growing body of literature on the impact of the investment climate on employment generation (Aterido, Hallward-Driemeyer, and Pagés, 2007, and references therein) suggests that economic growth and an improving business climate are crucial for attacking bad jobs as a source of exclusion. At the very least, one could argue that a faster-growing economy is better positioned to finance the transfer of resources towards (traditionally and modernly) excluded groups with much less political cost than a stagnant economy.

That said, the multidimensional nature of social exclusion in areas such as labor markets should alert us to the ineffectiveness of silver bullets, like economic growth, in attacking it. Exclusion needs to be deconstructed in its many interrelated dimensions via a range of actions at different societal levels by different social actors.

What role can public policy play in *overcoming* exclusion derived from such distinct forces and *advancing* inclusion to ensure more equal access to services and opportunities for all citizens? Like the literature on exclusion itself, the literature on public policy and inclusion is highly limited and relatively narrow, with little systematic evidence on what works best. There are no dynamic theories of how exclusion works, no body of research and analysis about how to construct "inclusive" public policies, no fixed set of applied policies and programs tested and ready to come off the shelf. Few, if any, policy initiatives use the term "inclusion" as the principal policy objective.

Yet the region is not starting from zero. There exists a set of policy instruments, institutions, and laws that are designed to promote more inclusive outcomes for specific groups or improve the performance of groups in key areas. In many instances protest movements have been successful in defining groups by the process that generates their exclusion (*piqueteros* and the unemployed in Argentina, for example), or in re-creating the social and political identity of traditionally excluded groups (such as the *movimiento indigenista* in Ecuador) (see Chapter 9 for a discussion of this issue). Some results have been tested over time; the effectiveness of other interventions is still to be determined. Beyond single program interventions, less is known about the whole—that is, which of these instruments, policies, or laws is most critical or what key instruments work together to promote inclusion and how they do so. What is the broader framework within which distinct policies and programs operate? Can we learn something more fundamental about how public policy in regard to inclusion operates, or is it all country and sector specific?

Given such a limited knowledge platform and the perils inherent in overgeneralizing for very distinct national policy and exclusion contexts, this chapter offers very modest objectives. It seeks to contribute to an understanding of the workings of public policy and inclusion by first analyzing—via a set of fundamental questions—the nature of inclusion being sought (e.g., is it static or is it dynamic?). After surveying the nature of inclusion, it then argues that it is more accurate to look at inclusive public policy as a public policy process rather than as a public policy end point (i.e., a single objective achieved at one point in time). It concludes by briefly reviewing how such an understanding may help in a rethinking of how nations view and construct an approach to combating exclusion. Chapter 14 follows the framework laid out in this chapter to provide more specific Latin American and Caribbean experience with the public policy building blocks of inclusion.

Given the current constraints of evidence, experience, and knowledge, the chapter seeks to make an analytic contribution to the thinking, or more likely rethinking, of public policy in regard to inclusion using the inputs of previous chapters. Such analytic objectives do have concrete policy implications, as they can inform and strengthen the content of strategies, policies, and action plans that need to follow in order for inclusion to be achieved in any particular national context. To begin to construct such an analytic framework, though, one must return to the original question posed in this volume—what is social inclusion to achieve?—and ask what this means for "inclusive" public policy.

ADVANCING INCLUSION VIA PUBLIC POLICY: TOWARDS SOME FUNDAMENTALS

To What End? Setting the Parameters for Inclusion and Public Policy

What does an inclusive society look like? What would public policies designed to achieve inclusion be seeking? Very broadly, an inclusive society would be a society with low rates of inequality based on group characteristics and high rates of social mobility among classes (Chapter 6). In this inclusive society, opportunities and services would be available equally based on the rights of citizens, and advancement would be based on merit and effort. Political representation would be increasingly representative and resources apportioned on a nondiscriminatory basis (Chapter 9). An inclusive society would not necessarily be devoid of poverty and social ills, but the color of a person's skin and the wealth of a person's parents would not be key determinants of who is poor, how well he or she is educated, or whether he or she receives proper medical care (Chapter 2).

An inclusive society is not just about inclusive outcomes, however. Inclusion affects not only the results of public policy, but also the way those results are achieved. Inclusion aims to achieve equality in access and opportunities for excluded groups by bringing excluded groups into the social, economic, political, institutional, and community structures that make decisions about access and opportunities. In most cases, this represents a significant transformation regarding the way resources are apportioned, political institutions are designed, and opportunities are accessed (Chapters 4, 5, 9, and 12). Inclusion is thus central to democracy, for greater inclusion advances the quality of representation (Chapter 9). When inclusion is viewed in this way, a society cannot be economically inclusive without being politically and socially inclusive as well. An inclusive society would not likely have equality in education without also fostering greater political participation and local participation in schools. Many argue as well that inclusion and the fundamentals for addressing the region's inequality can realistically be achieved only via a social compact (Birdsall and Menezes, 2004).

Can any nation in the world today be said to have arrived at inclusion for all groups? Can inclusion be achieved in one public policy field and not another? For example, despite significant progress, have women achieved equality of opportunity in any nation? Among the developing regions of the world, Latin America and the Caribbean is the one that has made the most significant progress in women's education, labor force participation, and political participation. Yet at the same time, the region has some of the highest rates of occupational segregation for females in domestic and clerical work, has not achieved standards of equal pay for equal work, and has large majorities of women employed in informal work, particularly indigenous women. The example of gender illustrates that inclusion is not a single arrival point, but a continuum of different "degrees" of inclusion in distinct fields (e.g., labor markets, political participation, social interactions) that may be at different stages of advancement over relatively long historical periods (Chapters 1 and 2). Even within a specific public policy field—say, education—there can be distinct degrees of inclusion (Chapter 2). For example, inclusion of members of indigenous groups may be more advanced in one subfield (primary education) than another (university-level education), and although inclusion has increased markedly for women at the university level, indigenous women have sustained the smallest gains among women in this area.

Is inclusion pursued for all groups simultaneously and in the same way? Looking back in time historically offers another insight into what might now be understood more as a spectrum of inclusion, not a single end point (Chapter 1). Movements or advocacy for inclusion can be led by a single group (e.g., women, although many women may belong to a number of excluded groups) or by the combined forces of a number of excluded groups. For example, although the U.S. civil rights movement of the 1960s was principally led by African Americans, a key policy result, the 1964 Civil Rights Act, barred discrimination on the basis of a wide range of group traits (race, religion, gender, ethnic origin). In the U.S. case, the women's movement began at the turn of the last century with a push for the right to vote, and the civil rights movement for African Americans made strong and rapid advances in the 1960s based on a wider set of voting, civil, economic, and social rights. Although the women's movement gained steam earlier, gender was "added" at the last minute to pending congressional civil rights legislation by some who hoped it would doom the whole advance. The U.S. experience demonstrates what is observed world-wide: that the inclusion process can have distinct historical trajectories and different priorities for different groups, as well as unplanned, historical accidents.

Viewing inclusion more as a spectrum of inclusions in distinct fields (e.g., cultural, employment, education, as reviewed in Chapters 1 and 2) allows for a better understanding that groups may have different priorities in that inclusion at different points in time (e.g., indigenous peoples seeking land rights and cultural autonomy; persons with disabilities seeking physical access to government buildings and workplaces). This is not to deny the important commonalities among groups and the importance of groups working together towards equality of opportunities. At its core, groups are seeking access to their rights, those provided to all citizens regardless of their skin color or ethnic origin. To continue with the example of the U.S. civil rights and women's movements, at different points in time these two movements collaborated with one another and advanced key policies that benefited all excluded groups.

Will a nation arrive at inclusion and never regress? Even those nations considered highly advanced towards inclusion cannot be considered in a static state. Developed countries that have gone through periods of nation building in which they expanded suffrage and economic inclusion can regress and fracture. New socioeconomic pressures or pressures exerted by the arrival of new migrant groups may result in the reassertion of old or new patterns of discrimination. European countries such as France and Germany, hosting an influx of immigrants from Muslim countries in the context of slowed economic growth, face challenges of inclusion on different terms than considered for earlier groups. The prior chapters have laid out how Latin America and the Caribbean can evolve into more complex forms of exclusion even before making significant advances against the traditional sources of exclusion, such as those based on race and ethnicity.

VIEWING INCLUSION AS A PUBLIC POLICY PROCESS

This multidimensional, multigroup understanding of inclusion as sought progressively over time offers a distinct perspective on what inclusive public policy is and what it is not. Inclusive public policy is *not* a single policy or policy end point. It is not a goal whose achievement means that none of the mechanisms designed to promote inclusion are needed any longer. As set forth in the questions above and in Chapter 1, inclusive public policy should be seen as a dynamic policy *process* aimed at actively promoting social, economic, and cultural equality, addressing past and present discrimination of excluded populations, and achieving diversity on a continuously improving basis. "Process," in this instance, means that advances in one area are needed to make advances in the other; for example, social and economic inclusion cannot be achieved without political inclusion as well. This stems both from the interrelated nature of exclusion (e.g., exclusion in one field is linked or gives rise to multiple other exclusions), and from the very nature of societies, which are constantly changing and introducing new schisms or even new excluded groups. Although this may seem straightforward, and some might argue that development itself is a process, an understanding of it is not reflected in the way public policies are designed to advance inclusion.

When inclusion processes begin to take shape, they do so in an environment in which exclusion is likely still operating in many sectors. This means that new programs, policies, and campaigns are initiated while existing programs and policies may continue to produce exclusionary

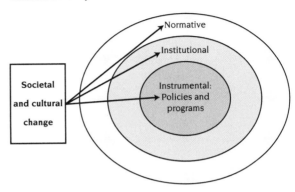

Figure 13.1
Inclusion Policy: Three Levels

outcomes, or conversely that policies and programs intended to be inclusionary may have unintended effects that must be adjusted midcourse.

The dynamics resulting from the simultaneous forces of inclusion and exclusion in a society cause the public policy process to move not in a straight line forward, but forward in some areas, not much at all in others, and backward in yet others. On a purely observational level, this mirrors what is commonly perceived by excluded groups; they may advance in some fields but not others, or at least in distinct time frames. As noted in the initial questions posed in the previous section, inclusion rarely, if ever, seems to come to a finite end point; rather, new outcomes (both inclusive and exclusive) continue to feed back into a public policy process of further refinement and advances in structure. As previously observed, developed countries thought long to be on the road to inclusion can veer backwards with the exclusion of new groups.

Understanding inclusion as a process means that the impact of a single policy or program cannot be considered in a vacuum. If exclusion is embedded in a range of institutions, processes, and social interactions, then its undoing is a multilayered, dynamic process in which advances in regard to one form of exclusion may be spurred by advances in another field (e.g., political representation). In understanding inclusion as a long-term process, gone is the notion that there is a single program or initiative that in itself will achieve inclusion. There is no silver policy bullet. Inclusion is a long-term, ever-dynamic process.

Three Levels: Normative, Institutional, and Instrumental

If inclusion is a process, of what does it consist? Although there are distinct historical, cultural, and social differences among countries, this chapter proposes that public policy operates within three interrelated levels to address inclusion (see Figure 13.1) and that public policy on these three levels interacts with societal and cultural changes, resulting in a much larger societal process (illustrated in Figure 13.2). These three levels—or frameworks—are the normative, institutional, and instrumental.

The normative framework refers to the fundamental laws and constitutional provisions of a nation that govern the fair treatment and rights of citizens in a nondiscriminatory manner. This is the "macro" framework from which institutions and later policies and programs for inclusion derive and operate. Inclusion calls for a constitutional and legal framework that recognizes collective (group-based) rights as well as individual rights.

The institutional framework refers to the set of institutions that develop and execute laws, programs, and policies. For public policy to succeed in advancing inclusion, the institutions that design and administer laws, policies, and programs must also operate inclusively.

Finally, the specific instruments—policies and programs—designed to achieve proinclusionary outcomes constitute the instrumental framework. In an ideal situation these inclusionary outcomes would feed back into the normative and institutional frameworks, whose changes would in turn result in new programs and policies that deepened the inclusionary outcomes. Chapter 14 discusses in greater depth distinct Latin American and Caribbean experience within each of these three frameworks.

Once an inclusion process has begun in some form, all three levels—normative, institutional, and instrumental—appear to be represented, albeit with very distinct levels of intensity. There is simply no known example in which a nation has sought to address inclusion or some form of group-based stigma and discrimination and effected only a program change, without institutional and legal changes as well. Inclusion even in its incipient stage involves all three policy levels in some form. This stems most fundamentally from the multidimensional nature of exclusion—from a nation's constitution, to inside its institutions, to within the programs and policies of its government.

On any of these three levels, public policy does not function in an isolated fashion. Rather, public policy operates in distinct national contexts in which society at large both influences policy and is influenced by it. Nina Pacari Vega (2004) writes that inclusion is twofold, encompassing both governments and societies at large. How society at times propels change, takes to the streets, or incorporates gains (or losses) from government policies shapes very distinct inclusion processes at the national level. What do we know about how social inclusion happens or can be made to happen via the interactions of society and public policy? Although we can find different actors linked to inclusion examined in the political science literature—that is, the role of social movements, political parties, and elites (Chapter 9)—few studies have been conducted with the explicit intention of mapping how social inclusion does (or does not) happen.[1]

Such a mapping might begin to unlock a more systematic understanding of the interactions among the three policy levels and how public policy links to the wider context of societal and cultural change—change that is both an input ("driver") and output ("result") of the inclusion process. The record of gender inclusion in Latin America and the Caribbean clearly tells the story that changes within society—in the role of women, respect for their rights, their economic contributions—have been fundamental to the public policy changes that have been driven by or responded to changing societal notions about women (Buvinić and Roza, 2004).

---

[1] Aggleton, Parker, and Maluwa (2004) lay out a framework related to overcoming stigma and discrimination rooted in HIV/AIDS.

Figure 13.2
Inclusive Public Policy: A Dynamic Process

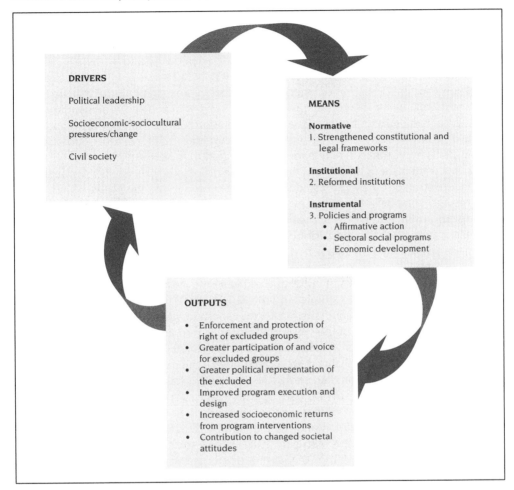

Deconstructing the key elements of an inclusive public policy process, one can view distinct factors or drivers that play a critical role in inducing the changes in policy "means"—within the normative, institutional, and instrumental frameworks—necessary for public policy to lead to more inclusive outcomes. Figure 13.2 illustrates these relationships in their rudimentary form. Societal drivers stimulate the distinctive changes at the normative, institutional, and instrumental levels that contribute, in the best-case scenario, to more inclusive outcomes in specific fields or sectors. These inclusive public policy outcomes in turn feed back into motivating and stimulating additional normative, institutional, and instrumental changes that stimulate additional outcomes. Indeed, as noted in the initial questions posed in this chapter, inclusion does not reach a finite end point. Countries have been known to regress in regard to incorporating new groups into their societies even after other groups have been included successfully.

Drivers

Who or what is able to stimulate the chain of social, political, and economic changes needed to advance towards inclusion? Although other factors can be noted, the principal "drivers" of such a process identified in the literature are political leadership (as manifested in "political will") to implement needed social, political, and economic changes; civil society (more highly organized and active civil organizations lead to both pressure and support for public policy changes); and socioeconomic and cultural change. When functioning well, dynamic inclusion processes include organized and representative civil society organizations with both national and international links, representative and more proactive political leadership and institutions, and wider cultural and social change, which propels acceptance of and leadership in regard to inclusion.

At the center of many analyses of the key forces propelling inclusion is the role played and leadership exerted by representatives of excluded groups themselves. Civic organizations and alliances of organizations are as essential to the lifeblood of democratic development (well studied) as to inclusion (less studied). The advancement of women's rights in Latin America and the Caribbean has been the result of coordinated advocacy by women's organizations, principally in the 1980s and 1990s. Indigenous organizations have become essential sources for articulating social demands and for political organization, as evidenced in the advances of indigenous movements in the Andean nations in recent years and the election of Evo Morales in Bolivia. Nina Pacari Vega (2004), Ecuador's first indigenous minister of foreign affairs, writes that social inclusion should be viewed from two perspectives: inclusion of the views of indigenous peoples in the national economic and political debate, and the social inclusion that indigenous authorities should exercise for their local societies by voicing their communities' opinions and participating in local decision making. As Aggleton, Parker, and Maluwa (2004) found in studying civic organizations for persons with HIV/AIDS, participation within such organizations is essential to overcoming societal stigmas impeding self-identification with the disease. Advocacy flows from the self-identification and mutual support provided by participation within such civil organizations. Judith Morrison (2006) points to the example of Organización de Desarrollo Etnico Comunitario (ODECO), a Honduran nongovernmental organization comprised of indigenous and Afro-descendant groups that has increased these groups' access to the president and high-level decision makers and has translated this greater access into greater influence in national policymaking. Ecuador offers a case in which years of organization by indigenous peoples followed by the organization of Afro-descendant groups has played a central role in that nation's path towards social inclusion (see Box 14.4).

The political system has also had to adapt to the changing pattern of inclusion and exclusion by responding to, or at least dealing with, the demands of groups whose political identity does not arise from race or ethnicity, but rather from their lack of access to resources and employment. Social movements such as the Landless Rural Workers' Movement (Movimento dos Trabalhadores Rurais Sem Terra, or MST) in Brazil or the *piqueteros* in Argentina interact with the political system in two important ways (see Chapter 9). First, with their practice of contentious politics they are able to nudge the political system towards taking action to distribute resources to their members. Second, the MST and the *piqueteros* themselves have been used by the government to channel resources (such as land titles or cash transfers) towards their members.

The policy advocacy role of civil organizations in Latin America and the Caribbean in particular has benefited greatly from international contacts and international networks; thus an advanced version of Figure 13.2 would include international dynamics as well. AfroamericaXXI and Mundo Afro function via partner organizations of Afro-descendants throughout Latin America and the Caribbean that build regional identity and support wider regional rights processes, such as the follow-up to the 2001 United Nations Conference to Combat Racism, Racial Discrimination, Xenophobia and Related Intolerance in Durban, South Africa, and the Regional UN Santiago Conference of Latin American and Caribbean representatives in 2000 that developed Latin American input and commitments to the Durban Conference. Romero Rodríguez, the founder of Mundo Afro, explains the international dynamic in the Afro-descendant community following the Santiago Conference:

> Santiago forced Afro-descendents of the Americas to place their development within a regional perspective and to articulate the demands along with their sister communities. This created a new drive, in which these communities began to look at themselves in relation to the African Diaspora in the world. . . . Afro-descendents must generate proposals and present their perspective on development agendas in order to make the human rights debate more profound [in order to] prompt action and changes in attitudes on involvement by governments and their institutions. (quoted in Morrison, 2006: 222)

Political leadership can play a role as either a driver of or a brake to the inclusion dynamic. Authoritarian governments, in particular, may base their power and identity on highly institutionalized exclusion enforced through exclusionary laws and extralegally through violence. The South African political leadership, highly sheltered via institutionalized racism after 1948, severely repressed the active civic organization of black South Africans. Only after decades of civic organization and civil disobedience, and growing international isolation and sanctions, did the elite finally give way to the dismantlement of apartheid in 1990. Although such an agency was much sought after by Afro-Brazilians, it was the leadership of President Luiz Inácio Lula da Silva that eventually proved to be the catalyst in the creation of the Special Secretariat for the Promotion of Public Policies for Racial Equality (Secretaria Especial de Políticas de Promoção da Igualdade Racial, or SEPPIR), the national agency on race (see Box 14.2).

All three of the drivers discussed are simultaneously providing input into a nation's inclusion process when it is in its fuller phase. In Latin America and the Caribbean today inclusion processes, or movements for the rights of key excluded populations, are front and center in the political life of several nations; in others an inclusion debate is barely perceptible. Possible explanations for these differences in timing and prominence include the following, many of which relate to the quality and nature of the societal "drivers": political stability/political leadership, strength and presence of civil society organizations, strength and intensity of past repression/exclusion, and the dynamics of new forces of exclusion, such as violence and marginal work. Chile's most recent innovations in social policy via Chile Solidario, investments in indigenous development, and policy attention to persons with disabilities can be partially attributed to the country's political history and recent electoral (party) stability, which has avoided chronic political swings that politicize and undermine the effectiveness of government institutions and programs.

The Inclusion/Exclusion Dynamic: Making History

How does the interrelationship of civil and political society work in practice towards inclusion? While systematic study of inclusion in specific national contexts is scant, one can observe an identifiable interrelated process at work in periods of heightened histori-cal social and political movements. In countries outside of the region, one can detect historical periods in which more intense reforms and programs were inaugurated in con-centrated time frames, constituting important historical moments of change. Depending on the country, these higher-profile historical periods represent the confluence of so-cioeconomic pressures, institutional political change, and the growing visibility of social movements. Examples of such periods include postapartheid South Africa; the United States in the 1960s, with the civil rights movement, and in the early twentieth century, with the women's suffrage movement; and Malaysia in the 1980s, with the country's New Economic Policy. In these cases, one can clearly see the importance of the confluence of activated civil organizations drawing on political will or leadership (governmental) and propelled by socioeconomic changes that bring inclusion to the forefront as a national priority in key moments in a nation's history. Within Latin America and the Caribbean, seeds of historical change may also be in process with the election of Bolivia's first indig-enous president in 2006 and the election of Lula in Brazil, who has put a new spotlight on the inclusion of Afro-Brazilians.

TOWARDS ADVANCING INCLUSIVE PUBLIC POLICY

As stated at the chapter's outset, how public policy *does*, or more importantly, *can* work to advance inclusion is a vastly open field. Systematic review of policies and their impacts, and more importantly of the interactions among different policies (e.g., what changes trigger what other changes), is scant. Even affirmative action, the public policy most associated with addressing exclusion, has been subject to little systematic research in respect to Latin America and the Caribbean. Given the multidimensional nature of exclusion, it is widely agreed that to be effective, affirmative action must be part of a complementary "set" of proinclusion policies; yet the content and nature of this set of complementary policies is rarely spelled out or more importantly introduced along with a new affirmative action effort.

The review of exclusion and Latin American and Caribbean experience presented in this report points to some key conclusions to guide future public policy:

- The inclusion process is dynamic and interrelated; changes in one area (e.g., education, Chapter 2) are necessary, but are not sufficient, to bring about changes in another (e.g., labor markets, Chapter 5).

- Inclusion is not achieved at a single point in time, but is more realistically viewed as a spectrum of advances in a wide range of sectors at different points in time.
- Countries do not "arrive" at inclusion and remain fixed there. Countries can regress in some forms of exclusion and advance in others; individuals may experience discrimination based on their group affiliation in some areas and not others (Chapter 1).
- New groups and new forms of exclusion (e.g., exclusion as a result of violence, Chapter 10) likely need to be considered and addressed over time, as they arise, with the groups integrated and the new forms of exclusion remedied; this places the incorporation of rights frameworks at the center of institutionalizing inclusive societies (Chapter 1).
- Inclusion should change outcomes, but most importantly it should change *how* outcomes are achieved and how *opportunities* are made available in a society. Thus, central to inclusive public policy is changing the nature of participation and decision making, as well as the nature of political representation in democratic societies.
- Excluded groups can have different priorities in advancing towards inclusion, and the historical sequencing of these advances can differ from group to group.

The formulation and implementation of inclusive policies is a very complex process in which changes in norms, institutions, and policy are driven by the interplay of different social actors in a particular historical setting. This means that no "one size fits all" kind of prescription will be of much help to policymakers interested in advancing inclusion. History and the analysis of historical experiences of the process of inclusion are a better guide to the extent that they help us understand how different actors in different countries have interacted within different normative, institutional, and policy frameworks to achieve (or fail to achieve) a more inclusive society. This is the purpose of the next chapter.

The Inclusion Process in Motion in Latin America and the Caribbean

The picture of exclusion in Latin America and the Caribbean presented in this report is complex and ever changing, one in which traditional sources of discrimination are interacting with new, more complex forms of exclusion associated with democratization, macro stabilization, and globalization. The last twenty-five years have seen advances and setbacks for different groups regarding different exclusionary factors in a historic inclusion/exclusion cycle that has changed both the targets of exclusion and the mechanisms through which they are excluded.

In many countries in the region, the public policy case is still being made for the fundamental importance of greater inclusion in unlocking the pervasive inequality, poverty, and injustice plaguing the region. The "outsiders" are no longer marginal, but comprise large majorities of distinct populations. Public policy knowledge and experience on attacking exclusion is sorely limited, particularly in regard to the kinds of exclusion found in Latin America and the Caribbean. Yet elements of public policies and programs that can begin to address this inclusion/exclusion cycle are in evidence throughout the region. The objective of current policy initiatives is not inclusion explicitly and entirely but an inclusive outcome, such as redressing past discrimination (e.g., an affirmative action program) or improving educational performance, relevance, or access for excluded groups (e.g., bilingual education). Thus, the limited policy lessons available so far are drawn from policies and initiatives not necessarily termed inclusionary, but intended to have an inclusionary impact. The chapters in Part II of this report present a few examples of what is known about the inclusionary impact of certain types of program interventions, albeit a number that unintentionally replicate or create new exclusionary outcomes.

This chapter provides a more in-depth look at some of the legal changes, institutions, policies, and programs within the public policy framework for inclusion presented in Chapter 13. The intention is not to provide specific countries with specific policy recommendations, but rather to use a very sparse set of policy experiences to illustrate the conundrums—and the possibilities—of inclusion processes. The intent here is analytical, not operational. Inclusion initiatives are the product of strategies and action plans of nations and institutions, not analytic reports. Most importantly, policy recommendations in this area must be the product of civic participation and democratic processes that lie at the core of any set of national initiatives for inclusion. The review here is intended to be illustrative rather than exhaustive, helping support a larger framework for understanding the fundamental elements of inclusive public policy, drawing, as possible, on regional experience. The objective is to help, by examining national experience "in early practice," to set a framework within which individual countries might gain insight into their own public policy processes and guide rethinking, research, and new policy initiatives.

INCLUSION AT THREE LEVELS

As laid out in Chapter 13, what can be observed not only in Latin America and the Caribbean but also in many developed and developing countries is an inclusion "process" through which public policy operates on three distinct but highly interrelated levels: the normative level, the institutional level, and the level at which policies themselves are implemented. There is no historical example of an inclusion process that acted exclusively on one of these levels without affecting the others, but country experiences vary according to the intensity of change within each of these three levels as well as in the nature of the changes being pursued. This section is intended to give a fuller description of the initial stages of inclusion "in motion" at the three levels, drawing, as possible, on examples from countries in Latin America and the Caribbean. A set of boxes accompanies this review, detailing specific national experiences.

Level 1: The Normative Framework and Regional Experience

The normative framework refers to the fundamental laws and constitutional provisions of a nation that govern the fair treatment and rights of citizens in a nondiscriminatory manner. Inclusion calls for a constitutional and legal framework that recognizes collective (group-based) rights as well as individual rights. Slowly and historically the most egregious examples of exclusionary normative frameworks are being removed worldwide (e.g., apartheid in South Africa, slavery, and segregation—although the caste system still persists in some Asian countries). With a premium on individual rights, however, the importance of the incorporation of collective-based rights has been less recognized. Individual rights frameworks often fail to recognize that individual rights can be violated if group-based discrimination is left unchecked. Collective rights incorporate both protections against group-based discrimination and affirmative policies to seek to redress the subordination of the excluded group. In this context, affirmative policies and positive discrimination become fair instruments (rather than unjust or discriminatory to those who are not recipients of the benefits) to combat structural inequality that affects excluded groups (Saba, 2004). These collective rights include access to land, cultural and territorial rights, and equal access to and fair treatment by the judicial system.

The normative instruments to enshrine collective rights are both international and national laws. There are at least twenty-nine international conventions and declarations related to discrimination, the majority of which have been ratified by Latin American and Caribbean nations. Included are United Nations (UN) conventions on basic universal human rights and the rights of excluded groups such as women and racial/ethnic populations, as well as conventions of the International Labour Organization (ILO) governing labor rights and workplace discrimination. These conventions, once ratified by national legislatures, take precedence over national law. Declarations, unlike conventions, do not require ratification by national legislatures.

A number of Latin American and Caribbean nations have advanced in respect to national legislation that recognizes key populations as excluded groups within a sovereign nation, explicitly protecting and sanctioning cultural, ethnic, and racial diversity. One example is the Colombian constitution, which defines the nation as a multicultural nation; another is Colombia's Law 80, which protects collective land rights (see Box 14.1). Other countries have enacted national laws against discrimination based on race (Brazil, Ecuador), ethnicity (Peru), or gender (Chile and many others).

In part because of Latin America and the Caribbean's history of authoritarian regimes, the inter-American legal system has largely devoted its resources to countering the violation of basic civil and political rights (via torture, illegal imprisonment, "disappearances," and murder). Violations of social, economic, and cultural rights based on group affiliation have taken second place in the work of the Inter-American Commission on Human Rights and the Inter-American Court on Human Rights (Rossi, 2003). In recent years, the commission has begun to hear cases involving gender discrimination or discrimination against migrants, but a strong normative international framework for the region is still in its early stages. Apart from individual petitions to the international courts, the principal vehicle for advancing the protection and enforcement of collective rights on an international or regional basis is required reporting to international agencies (e.g., the above-mentioned Inter-American Commission and Court on Human Rights) as well as new obligations and reporting in connection with international meetings. The most important of these forums for inclusion within the region have been the United Nations Conference to Combat Racism, Racial Discrimination, Xenophobia and Related Intolerance (held in Durban, South Africa, in 2001) and the Fourth United Nations Conference on Women (Beijing, China, 1995).

As the international framework evolves, this places continued importance on the evolution of strong national normative frameworks. On a national basis, enforcement is the single most essential factor in ensuring that rights on paper become inclusion in practice. A number of nations in the region are moving to create a specific institution with the mandate to enforce and advance constitutional protections. In 2003, for instance, Mexico approved a comprehensive antidiscrimination law and created, to assist enforcement, the National Council to Prevent Discrimination (Consejo Nacional para Prevenir la Discriminación, or CONAPRED). The law bars discrimination on the basis of gender, ethnicity, disability, sexual preference, and religious affiliation.

A normative framework that is appropriate for advancing inclusion must respond to particular national histories and dynamics. Donald Oliver (2006) writes that in the case of Canada, with its founding by two nations, Britain and France, and native indigenous population, the advancement of multiculturalism (e.g., the country's 1988 Multicultural Act) did not prove as successful as pursuing normative changes to protect individual rights (e.g., the Canadian Charter of Rights and Freedoms, the Canadian Human Rights Act, and the Employment Equity Act).

Enabling excluded groups to assert land and property rights is linked to advances not only in regard to the normative framework, but in specific programs and policies as well. The lack of birth registration documents for many women in Peru, for example, limits their ability to gain title to their land (Vega, 2006). Addressing the lack of birth certificates for large portions of the region's population (Chapter 12) will unlock access for excluded segments of the population to a range of citizenship rights enshrined in law, including the rights to vote, to own land, and to attend school.

Normative frameworks are key to accessing another income-generating asset of excluded populations: their own human capital. The majority of Latin American and Carib-

Box 14.1 Colombia: Advancing Inclusion, Starting with the Constitution

Normative. The drafting of a new constitution in 1991 was a milestone for social inclusion in Colombia not only in the legal recognition of diversity and multiculturalism, but also in the political inclusiveness of the process of constitutional change. The constitutional revisions recognized Colombia as a multicultural nation and set quotas reserving two seats in the Senate for members of indigenous groups and two seats in the House of Representatives for Afro-descendants. Under the new constitution, indigenous groups were granted autonomous (legal and sociopolitical) territories, within *resguardos,*[a] and Afro-Colombians were given collective ownership of large pieces of land on the country's Pacific coast. Most of these provisions are regulated by Law 70/93, which called for development plans for Afro-Colombians as a key input for the National Development Plan.

Institutional. The normative recognition of multiculturalism and multiethnicity that stemmed from the new constitution was accompanied by institutional changes. The Ministry of Interior houses the new Division of Ethnicities (Dirección de Etnias), in charge of designing and implementing the constitutionally guaranteed development plans for redressing the exclusion suffered by different ethnicities and races, as well as advising relevant agencies on mainstreaming inclusion in national policies and programs. Key ministries such as Education,

Health, Housing, and Environment created small offices to promote excluded groups' rights and to coordinate the implementation of specific programs such as that governing the establishment of quotas for entrance to public universities for members of indigenous groups. These offices promoted program and policy changes such as a special module for incorporating Afro-Colombian history and culture into Colombian public school curricula, sustainable development initiatives in the Pacific and Atlantic coastal areas, and special rankings for people with disabilities in the allocation of housing. They are often the first, however, to suffer fiscal restrictions in times of financial tightening.

Instrumental: Policy/Programs. One of the first investment programs benefiting Afro-Colombians was a sustainable development program for the Pacific Coast—Plan Pacífico—approved in 1994 with IDB financing. Poverty rates for Afro-descendants living on the country's Pacific coast are more than double the national average: 85 percent live in poverty, compared to a national average of 32 percent. Institutional assessment and implementation of the Pacific coast plan, however, has been weak, resulting in dispersion of resources and uncompleted basic infrastructure projects. The government of Colombia partially cancelled the loan with the intent of designing a second stage, building on lessons learned. Drawing on the experience with the Pacific coast, in 2003 the National Council on Social and Economic Policy (Consejo Nacional de Política Económica y Social, or CONPES) issued the first national affirmative action policy aimed at redressing social exclusion of Afro-Colombians (CONPES 3310). This policy encompassed all of Colombia and addressed the humanitarian crisis created by displacement of Afro-descendants.

CONPES 3310 is far from being implemented, but it is a pivotal step towards recognizing Afro-Colombian exclusion and developing specific measures to remedy it, such as a state policy for the country's Pacific region (home to a large number of Afro-Colombians), the mainstreaming of social inclusion, better targeting of benefits, and improved collection of socioeconomic data on Afro-descendants. Compliance with Decision T-025 of the Constitutional Court (2004), obligating the state to do everything possible to re-establish the rights of the country's war-displaced population and enable them to live productive lives, could also benefit Afro-Colombians. The new sanctions under this decision are so strong that failing to comply with the mandate could result in imprisonment of public officials.

Participation. Whereas indigenous groups have been able to consolidate a political movement ensuring participation in the reserved (quota) seats of the national congress, Afro-descendants face continued challenges in building internal consensus for a coherent political participation. Not all of the country's black citizens identify themselves as Afro-Colombians; some do not want to self-identity for fear of discrimination; and those living in the northern part of the country complain about the overattention to the Pacific coast. The establishment of the Consultiva de Alto Nivel, a citizen consultative group for public policy regarding Afro-Colombians, is a start, but much more needs to be done to attack the many roots of political exclusion for Colombian Afro-descendants. The fact that groups of Afro-descendants may not necessarily feel represented by those named to represent them, and their concerns about the fairness of the process of selecting representatives, create important organizational challenges for the political organization of Afro-descendants in Colombia.[b]

---

[a] There are more than 560 *resguardos* in Colombia, home to more than 800,000 members of the country's indigenous groups.

[b] Discussions held with the Afro-Colombian Working Group, hosted by the IDB's Colombia country office, Cali, Colombia, December 14–15, 2005.

bean nations (fourteen out of twenty-six) have ratified all eight ILO conventions related to the four core labor standards: the prohibition against child labor (Conventions 138 and 182); the prohibition against forced (slave) labor (Conventions 29 and 105); the right of free association and collective bargaining (Conventions 87 and 98); and freedom from discrimination (Conventions 100 and 101).[1] Among the other twelve countries, the pattern of nonratification does not appear to be particularly correlated with the most pervasive violations of core labor standards among countries (Daude, Mazza, and Morrison, 2003), but rather is found to be correlated with institutional weaknesses and legislative delays. The protection of labor rights depends critically on proactive national enforcement and resources.

All told, the national and international normative framework is a fundamental building block of inclusive public policy that not only ensures basic protections for civil groups but also unlocks access and protections for income-generating assets critical to overcoming exclusion. Advancing normative frameworks makes a larger contribution as well; these frameworks contribute more fundamentally to societal recognition of discrimination against excluded populations, and as such can serve as a stimulus to advance institutional and instrumental change. In the dynamic three-level process that results, the normative framework cannot serve its macro role in protecting and ensuring the basic rights of citizens without commensurate advancement and enforcement of both the institutional and instrumental frameworks.

Level 2: Inclusion and Institutions

In order for public policy to succeed in advancing inclusion, the institutions that design and administer laws, policies, and programs must also operate inclusively. Existing institutions reflect endemic bias and often replicate exclusion, even after the elimination of overtly discriminatory rules (e.g., segregation, apartheid, legal prohibitions on female participation). To advance inclusion, institutions must be fairly representative, have explicit mechanisms for participation of excluded groups or their representatives, and run relatively efficiently and effectively (not, for example, on a clientelistic basis for elite interests). Exclusionary characteristics are often embedded in weak or corrupt institutions, argues Thorp (2007). In societies in which levels of social exclusion are known to be high, institutional reform and redesign are paramount to dislodging exclusion embedded in the operation of key public services (e.g., police, courts): who is hired and how, and how resources are apportioned. The two key elements of the institutional framework reviewed here are public institutions—at the national, local, and state levels—and civil institutions, which channel and articulate the interests and needs of excluded groups.[2]

---

[1] The freedom from discrimination conventions call for a national policy to eliminate discrimination in employment, training, and working conditions on the grounds of race, color, sex, religion, political opinion, or national or social origin and to promote equality of opportunity and treatment.

[2] The operation of private sector institutions also affects the inclusion cycle but is treated in this chapter explicitly as it relates to public policy, which includes policies and programs to support greater inclusion in the private sector and in private sector employment.

Government Institutions

A source of many of the mechanisms through which exclusion is transmitted or replicated in the region can be traced to the operation of public and private institutions. These include myriad forms of institutional exclusion such as health facilities that treat Afro-descendants and members of indigenous groups in a discriminatory fashion, government resources steered disproportionately to favor the elite, government hiring that does not encourage diversity or representativeness, and programs that never reach into the communities of the intended beneficiaries, all leading to a reassertion of exclusion with each new political administration.

Efforts to advance inclusion through institutional change can be seen in a number of countries in the region, with work in the areas of institutions promoting gender equality and indigenous peoples' rights offering a longer trajectory of experience. In the case of gender, institutional reform and diversity were sought both through improving representation in national legislatures and public institutions (via quotas) and through institutional change: creating new institutions, reforming existing ones, and moving to "mainstream diversity" and inclusion. Efforts to make government institutions more inclusive can be viewed as taking place through two distinct tools: political representation and quotas and institutional change.

Political Representation and Executive Branch Quotas

The region has comparatively greater experience with quotas to increase the political representation of excluded groups, predominantly women (see Chapter 4), than with any other form of quota. Beginning with Argentina in 1991, half of the countries in Latin America established quotas to ensure female legislative representation, with most setting a quota of 30 percent representation—well below the overall representation of females in the voting population (typically more than 50 percent). Argentina, Colombia, Costa Rica, and Ecuador are considered to have more progressive laws; Colombia in particular applies the 30 percent quota law to female representation in high-ranking executive branch posts as well (Ross, 2007). Colombia is among the few countries that set aside seats in the legislature (i.e., reserved seats, not percentage quotas) for Afro-descendants and members of indigenous groups. In an effort to advance executive branch parity, the Chilean government of Michele Bachelet has named women to half of the cabinet-level positions in the administration and to half of the subcabinet, regional, and administrative positions (Ross, 2007). In a review of gender quotas in Latin America, Mala Htun (2004) concludes that, on average, quota laws have boosted women's legislative presence by 9 percent in the region; closed-list proportional representation electoral systems with placement mandates and large electoral districts work best in this regard (Htun, 2004).

Increasing participation and representativeness does not, however, produce more inclusive outcomes single-handedly. Research on the performance of women in legislatures both in the United States and in Latin America demonstrates that women legislators are typically more active on issues of women's, children's, and family rights, but that on broader issues, party affiliation is a better predictor of legislators' voting behavior (Htun, 2004). Most importantly, as women's numbers rise and they link to networks of other women legislators, they are able to have a greater impact on policy. A study comparing twelve U.S. state legislatures found that those with women's caucuses had a higher legislative output on feminist issues than those without such caucuses, regardless of the actual number of female legislators (Thomas and Welch, 2001).

Experience to date demonstrates that representation and executive branch quotas must be seen as one of the tools of inclusion that must work with other instruments to bring about more inclusive outcomes. In the case of quotas, enforcement via effective sanctions and multiparty alliances appears to be particularly significant. Marcela Rios, lead investigator with Santiago's Latin American Faculty of Social Science (Facultad Latinoamericana de Ciencias Sociales, or FLACSO), advocates that quota laws be accompanied by constitutional changes to reform electoral laws (i.e., institutional changes linked with normative changes), since some electoral systems are better designed than others to increase representation of women.

Institutional Change: Creating, Reforming, and Mainstreaming

To advance institutional change and management reform, two principal options have been pursued in the region to date. One common option is the creation of specialized agencies, ministries, or councils to oversee public efforts to advance the rights and interests of excluded groups. A second option is to create new institutional channels and devote new resources to "mainstreaming" consideration of excluded groups or key excluded groups within existing institutions. With both options—mainstreaming and specialized agencies—institutional and management changes are sought to increase access and quality of government services to excluded groups (e.g., location of offices, mobile facilities) and to improve outcomes by addressing how institutions relate to and work with such groups.

Regarding the first option, the region has now had more than two decades of experience in the creation of specialized government ministries, not all of it favorable. The key concern is whether sufficient resources and political clout are provided to these agencies to effect change or whether mandate without power or resources leads to a further marginalization of excluded groups via such agencies. A number of ministries and bureaus for indigenous peoples were set up with the re-establishment of democracy in the region during the 1980s, but many of these agencies have yet to be modernized to become more representative of the distinct indigenous peoples in the various countries they serve. Additionally, all Latin American and Caribbean nations now have a ministry or some type of department dedicated to women's inclusion and empowerment, eight with ministerial ranking (Brazil, Chile, Costa Rica, Guatemala, Honduras, Panama, Paraguay, and Peru).[3] Most have been established through legislation, executive order, or ministerial decree (IDB, 1998b). Another sixteen countries have set up parliamentary commissions devoted to women's issues, and five countries (Argentina, Bolivia, Colombia, Nicaragua, and Peru) have women's ombudspersons or staff in the ombudsperson's office in charge of gender issues (Buvinić and Roza, 2004).

---

[3] In the case of Peru, the ministry is for both gender and social development.

Brazil provides the most prominent example of a new ministry created to lead and coordinate race issues for the country's majority Afro-descendant population. The Special Secretariat for the Promotion of Public Policies for Racial Equality (Secretaria Especial de Políticas de Promoção da Igualdade Racial, or SEPPIR) was created in 2003 and is charged with coordinating government interventions to combat racism and advance socioeconomic conditions for the country's large Afro-descendant population (see Box 14.2). In Uruguay, the city of Montevideo has created a special ministry on Afro-descendants to examine the specific policy needs of the Afro-Uruguayan population (Morrison, 2006).

Much of the literature on the performance of national machineries, agencies, and offices draws attention to their continuing marginality or precariousness in terms of budget, institutional capacity, or government influence (INSTRAW, 2005; DAW, 2004). It has been harder to track the role of such institutions in terms of their contributions to the wider public policy process and stimulus to new policies, programs, and instruments. Buvinić and Mazza (2005) note that at least some of the significant advances for women in the region must be partly attributable to new institutional dynamics set in motion via these institutions. This record includes the ratification of national conventions to combat violence against women as well as equal opportunity legislation (ECLAC, 2004). Two elements that seem to be central to the effective functioning of offices dedicated to gender are a very high level of support or patronage from the executive branch of government (which translates into budget support) and strong alliances with women's organizations in civil society. These alliances include not only national networks, but also international and regional women's alliances that serve as a forum for sharing national policy experiences and building financial support and political visibility for the women's movement.

Mexico is one of the few countries that has created an "umbrella" agency or commission (CONAPRED, 2003) to address equal opportunity for a broad range of groups. Research is scant on the advantages/disadvantages and effectiveness of such umbrella agencies versus single-group advocacy agencies. Clearly, national context and the nature and size of distinct groups are essential to determining the right institutional configuration, one that both advances the rights of particular excluded groups and prevents the fractionalization or marginalization of those rights as accorded only via group-specific intervention. The idea of an umbrella agency has the appeal of potentially increasing the efficiency and effectiveness of government functioning via a larger political constituency, a larger support base grounded in citizenship rights, and synergies among groups. With such an umbrella agency, however, groups may be concerned that they are losing a direct government channel or may have greater difficulty advancing some group-specific inclusion priorities.

A second principal institutional strategy for inclusion, mainstreaming the interests and concerns of excluded groups within existing government ministries and programs, can be complementary to creating a specialized agency to handle these interests and concerns, but in theory, effective mainstreaming should obviate, over time, the need for such a separate agency. The methods for mainstreaming vary substantially with the policy task at hand. Reaching and serving excluded groups and adequately addressing the many sources of exclusion requires changing the way that institutions operate, where they are located, and the way their programs are designed and executed. This includes changing management decision making and inducing greater transparency and competi-

Box 14.2 Brazil: Promoting Inclusion for the Region's Largest Afro-descendant Population

Brazil's history of exploration, colonization, and transatlantic slave trade marks it, like many other countries in the Americas, as a country with a long record of exclusion and discrimination in regard to those in its population who are descended from slaves.

The country's myth of racial democracy has slowly come undone over the past two decades. In a report for the United Nations Committee for the Elimination of Racial Discrimination (CERD) in 2003, Brazil acknowledged that "For many decades, the myth of a nationality characterized by the harmonious and perfect fusion of three races responsible for the construction of a 'racial democracy' in the country, was propagated." The report concluded that "for long periods of time, the Brazilian State and society . . . revealed themselves incapable of implementing effective mechanisms to incorporate Afrodescendant, indigenous peoples and members of other discriminated groups into the larger society" (CERD, 2003: 5).

This recognition was achieved through the actions of an active civil society for Afro-descendants, indigenous peoples, and other excluded groups. The sparks that set fire to the discussion surrounding this issue could be first credited to the United Nations Conference to Combat Racism, Racial Discrimination, Xenophobia and Related Intolerance (held in Durban, South Africa, in 2001), which led to a wider debate within Brazilian state and civil society regarding affirmative action and stimulated the establishment of quotas for Afro-descendants and other excluded groups in public sector hiring and education. Although it is still too early for evaluation and impact, affirmative action policies and programs remain hotly contested and debated in Brazil.

Government appointments in the Lula presidency have reflected this policy shift. Four Afro-descendants have been appointed cabinet ministers, including Matilde Ribeiro as minister of racial equality and Joaquim Barbosa as the first Afro-Brazilian supreme court justice.

AFFIRMATIVE ACTION IN HIGHER EDUCATION: SPOTLIGHT ON INSTRUMENTAL CHANGE

Although Afro-descendants make up over 45 percent of the Brazilian population, as of 2003 they accounted for less than 2 percent of the college and university population. The state of Rio de Janeiro was the first to introduce legislation, implemented in the State University of Rio system, calling for quotas for Afro-descendant students and students from the country's public school system, as well as a quota for students with

tiveness in government hiring and contracting. One method of inducing mainstreaming changes involves the creation of offices, advisors, or panels within each government agency that ensure the consideration of excluded groups throughout institutional operations and provide mechanisms for oversight. Another method is revising the rules and

disabilities. The first class was admitted under this law in 2003.

Other federal and state universities have since implemented affirmative action policies, although not on a uniform basis. These include universities in the state of Mato Grosso, the Federal University of Brasilia, the State and Federal Universities of Bahia, and the Federal University of Paraná (Global Rights, 2005). In January 2005, a national law providing tax breaks to private universities if they reserve a minimum of 20 percent of their seats for the poor was enacted. "We're paying a debt built up over 500 years," explained President da Silva at the law's enactment (quoted in Lloyd, 2004).

Affirmative action in higher education is still relatively new in Brazil and has created substantial controversy and court challenges, which both impede advances in the program and hinder evaluation of early experiences. Recent data from the State University of Bahia reveal that students entering under the quota system in 2003 earned grades only slightly lower (0.2 percent) on average than all other students, with Portuguese language majors under the quota system earning slightly higher grades (0.4 percent). Most importantly, the most significant barrier found for students who entered under the quota system was the ability to finance their stay in school.

SEPPIR: CREATING A NEW INSTITUTION TO ADDRESS RACE

A key initiative of President da Silva's first term was creating the nation's first coordinating ministry on race. The Special Secretariat for the Promotion of Public Policies for Racial Equality (SEPPIR) was created in 2003 and marks a step forward for the Brazilian government and a new approach to the promotion of inclusion and equality via ministerial coordination.

The secretariat has the same status as other Brazilian government secretariats, and it is leading efforts with several government bodies, including the Ministries of Education, Foreign Affairs, Agriculture, and Justice, to raise awareness on inequality and exclusion, promote targeted policies (such as affirmative action and quotas), and develop projects to improve the socioeconomic conditions of Afro-Brazilians. SEPPIR expresses its commitment to coordinating policies to protect individual rights as well as the rights of racial and ethnic groups, especially Brazil's Afro-descendant population. As a ministry with convening and coordinating powers but no direct management of programs or significant resources, however, SEPPIR faces significant challenges in financing, technical capacity of staff, and institutional arrangements.

procedures for government contracting and hiring. At an even finer level, the next section, dealing with actual instruments and programs, describes a number of methods used for increasing the access of excluded populations to programs and the impact of programs on those populations as a complement to institutional reforms.

A less-used option in the region, but one that is more common in OECD countries, is explicit quotas or mechanisms to increase the participation of firms run by excluded groups (often termed "minority-owned businesses") in government procurements of goods and services. These mechanisms are designed to promote economic inclusion by diversifying the range of providers typically receiving business via government procurement, often seeking to increase the competitiveness of systems of contracting and the transparency of mechanisms for awarding contracts. Brazil is one of the few countries in the region with quota provisions governing government contracting that set aside a certain (albeit small) amount of government contracting business for members of excluded groups.

Civil Society

Organizations representing excluded groups, which may include nongovernmental organizations (NGOs), grassroots organizations, and community groups, are central to a functioning public policy process to advance inclusion. Such organizations not only provide organized input and support to ensure inclusion via public institutions and programs, but also serve as forums for advancing self- and group identity, which is essential to overcoming exclusion. Institutional change in the direction of inclusion in any of the forms discussed—"mainstreaming," new institutions, or management reforms—involves the direct involvement and support of civil society organizations.

Civil society organizations and alliances of such organizations play a critical institutional role as the principal interlocutors between public institutions and excluded groups. They also have a hand in executing projects and programs themselves and translating their experience with these projects into advocacy for more effective policies and institutions. The Lula government has designated local Afro-Brazilian NGOs as the main executor of government services in local Quilombo communities (see Chapter 12), including managing programs related to hunger relief and the national conditional cash transfer program, Bolsa Familia. Civil organizations in various countries have found mutual advancement through collective organizations that permit a wider negotiating platform with and impact on the public sector. The Organización de Desarrollo Étnico Comunitario (ODECO) in Honduras represents both indigenous and Afro-descendant populations, owing to the country's Garifuna population of mixed indigenous/African origin. ODECO's representative base has enabled it to serve a great advocacy and program function for the nation's large poor and excluded populations. Organizations representing excluded groups have each benefited from links with similar organizations in developed countries providing financial, technical, and advocacy support.

Civil society organizations play an even more fundamental role in the societal transformation required to advance towards inclusion. The experience of exclusion, particularly when rooted in centuries of oppression, can trigger resistance and alienation if not transformed through the formation of common social identities based in common experience (Hall, 1990). In their study on HIV/AIDS-related stigma and discrimination in Latin America and the Caribbean, Peter Aggleton, Richard Parker, and Miriam Maluwa (2004) found that the creation of community organizations of people with HIV/AIDS was essential to combating the effects of stigma and discrimination. Through civic participation, such groups were able to create varied "project identities" that opened up new channels for overcoming exclusion through group identity, collaboration, and civic action.

Level 3: The Instrumental Level—Some Programs and Policies from Latin America and the Caribbean

Perhaps the areas most identified with public policy to promote inclusion are the specific programs and policies designed to address past discrimination or ensure greater equality for excluded populations. These programs and policies must be seen, however, within the wider public policy context, which includes a normative and institutional framework that contributes to more successful, better-designed, and better-executed policies (see Figure 13.2).

Programs and policies are carried out by national, state, and local institutions and serve to (a) identify excluded populations as the basis for better policies and programs, (b) redress past discrimination and remove exclusionary barriers, and (c) proactively advance improved socioeconomic conditions of excluded populations. To advance towards inclusion, inclusive policies and programs cannot be seen as small, isolated interventions that take place while the large gamut of public policy continues to produce highly exclusive outcomes. For example, a small program to improve the results of excluded populations in regard to entrance into university education, although helpful, can have only a limited impact if the bulk of public education spending and emphasis provides low-quality elementary and secondary education to those same excluded populations, with the result that most members do not even complete secondary school. Following this line, the instrumental policy process must be seen as dual directional: reforming and "undoing" major policies and programs with highly exclusionary outcomes together with implementing new proactive measures designed to achieve greater inclusion. Both redesign and new construction require attention to both universal and targeted programs, not one or the other.

Universal programs by their very definition are designed to benefit the entire citizenry (e.g., universal primary and secondary education, universal health programs). In nations with long histories of exclusion, exclusion is embedded in the normal conduct of "universal" programs and policies, which may have begun with the intention of universality but ended up benefiting only elites in practice. Social security and labor benefits are one example of a program of universal design—aimed at supporting all formal sector workers—that through the years has come to benefit the shrinking percentage of elite formal sector workers with long-term contracts (see Chapter 4). Labor regulations to ensure social security benefits, protection from arbitrary dismissal, severance pay, and other benefits formed the basis of the "rights" accorded to Latin American and Caribbean citizens following World Wars I and then II (Gordon, 2004). Over time, benefits for all evolved into "privileges for a few" in Latin America and the Caribbean through three key forces: exclusionary, corporatist hiring and business practices; the growth of informal employment; and globalization (Gordon, 2004). Thorp (2007) argues that the patterns of embedded exclusion in Latin American and Caribbean society have evolved through the combined forces of economic/production models, political structures and social policies that led to the disempowerment of large groups.

Exclusion embedded in programs and policies can be found not only in these macro, historical tendencies that affect universal programs, but also in the day-to-day administration of targeted programs. Claudia Jacinto, Cristina García, and Alejandra Solla (2007) studied youth neighborhood programs in Argentina, whose target population is marginal poor youth. They found that the design of these programs often did not take into account the very complex realities of community life in marginal neighborhoods and youth expectations. As a result, the programs often induced new cleavages or subexclusions within these communities, splitting them into groups of program participants versus nonparticipants or elevating community program organizers to a higher status than participants. Programs for marginal youth, argues Wendel Abramo (2004), often treat youth as a singular subject and fail to address their needs for autonomy and participation in order to yield inclusive outcomes.

Where does one begin, then? If exclusion is multidimensional and occurs simultaneously across sectors (e.g., education, labor markets, health), what instrumental-level changes should be advanced? How does one simultaneously attack existing program and policy exclusion and advance new inclusive instruments? Again, public policy literature offers few guideposts to date, and national experience is varied.

The distinct program and policy types discussed in the following subsections—affirmative action/antidiscrimination measures, sectoral policies (e.g., education, health, labor markets), conditional cash transfer programs, and economic development/empowerment—highlight the interrelated (potential) impacts of proinclusion interventions. Underlying a functioning instrumental framework for inclusion are the basic data on excluded groups, collected both nationally (principally via censuses and household surveys) and on a program-by-program basis through civil registration and basic identity documents (e.g., birth registration and national identity cards). Previous chapters have demonstrated that in both censuses and civil registration, Latin American and Caribbean countries suffer from major deficits: poor data collection on excluded populations and higher underregistration and lack of identity documents for excluded groups (see Chapter 12). Regional efforts supported by the IDB, such as Todos Contamos I and II and direct support for national censuses, along with data collection and civil registries are fundamental elements for advancing a common platform for launching better-targeted and more effective public policies.

Affirmative Action/Antidiscrimination Measures

Worldwide, affirmative action is perhaps the policy most associated with redressing past discrimination. Affirmative action should be more accurately seen as one implement in the instrumental toolbox for inclusion; its effectiveness relies heavily on enforcement and implementation as well as the larger context of complementary policies and programs. Unfortunately, discussions of affirmative action are often mired in debates over "special preferences" and fail to consider the role of such preferences as one tool in a wider inclusion process.

Although the region's experience with affirmative action to date is limited, affirmative-action-type policies and programs can be found in a number of sectors (Buvinić, 2004; IAD, 2004; AfroamericaXXI, 2006). They appear most widely in political representation quotas (see "Level 2: Inclusion and Institutions") according to gender, race, and ethnicity, with gender garnering the widest coverage. There are limited quotas of this type in such fields as public housing, employment, and education. In its points-based beneficiary selection system, Chile provides ten extra preference points to persons with disabilities who apply for public subsidies or housing programs; Brazil has quotas for Afro-descendants and members of indigenous groups for public sector hiring and for university entrance (see Box 14.2). A compendium of affirmative action and legal instruments for Afro-descendant populations in the region compiled by AfroamericaXXI lists ten countries as having such tools.

Affirmative action instruments are used more broadly in other parts of the world and extend to such fields as private sector employment, corporate ownership, and university funding in which the region has little experience. Malaysia has perhaps the most comprehensive affirmative action program, introduced as an integral part of its New Economic Policy. Quotas in the Malaysian program correspond to three distinct ethnic/national groups and cover corporate ownership, education, and employment. Despite dire warnings by the World Bank of the negative effects of such a comprehensive approach to affirmative action, Malaysia's program has succeeded, without social unrest, in democratizing and opening up corporate ownership and addressing significant income inequalities among groups. In the United States, affirmative action instruments are moving from an emphasis on government procurement preferences for minority-owned businesses towards promoting greater diversity among larger companies and in government procurement contracts. This shift is being pursued both to open up new markets to minority-owned firms and to improve the market access of many companies to minority customers (Boston, 2006).

Outside the formal definition of quota systems or affirmative action programs are initiatives that support the implementation and enforcement of antidiscrimination policies or laws. In most cases, excluded populations have limited resources to seek enforcement of their rights on either an individual or group basis. Judicial or law enforcement reforms and programs play a key role in this area. The state and federal governments in the United States, for example, support legal aid clinics for the poor that include legal representation for cases involving discrimination, as well as specific proactive enforcement programs, for example, to ensure equal opportunity in credit lending or housing. As with other policies and programs, enforcement and implementation in affirmative action are particularly important to success. Barbara Bergman (1996) argues that the limited impact of affirmative action policy in the United States can be explained largely as a result of inadequate enforcement by U.S. agencies.

Often overlooked in the role of affirmative action is its indirect contribution to breaking the cycle of public denial surrounding the impact of past discrimination and to social and cultural change that can augment other policy initiatives. An admissions director at a Brazilian state university explains, "The biggest advantage of this quota system is that it has broken this myth of a nonracial society. Brazilians have by and large always believed there are no white Brazilians or black Brazilians. But the debate over quotas has forced everyone to confront the fact that racism, discrimination and social exclusion are alive and well here" (quoted in Jeter, 2003). As stated earlier, although affirmative action is one of the policies most associated with inclusion, it is also mired in controversy and debate in many countries (see Box 14.2). Its critics fear that it utilizes discriminatory methods to undo past discrimination, creating new sources of tensions based on race and ethnicity. As evidence of its continuing controversy in the United States, the U.S. Supreme Court recently issued a partially divided opinion striking down school desegregation plans intended to foster primary and secondary school diversity ordered by the courts (Barnes, 2007).

Sectoral Policies and Programs: Education, Health, Labor Markets

A key to undoing the replication and perpetuation of exclusion via existing institutions and achieving targeted advances for excluded groups lies within sectoral social policies. These include policies and policy implications in education, labor markets, health, and nutrition (see Boxes 14.3 on reproductive health, 14.5 on HIV/AIDS, and 14.6 on justice), as well as social protection/cash transfer schemes. An adequate collection of data and statistics on race, ethnicity, disabilities, and other characteristics of exclusion is needed as a baseline to better identify how programs and policies are affecting excluded groups disproportionately, in order to better refine and redesign sectoral programs. Earlier chapters have demonstrated, for example, that despite educational advances for women overall, indigenous women are among the most poorly educated; Afro-descendant and indigenous men and women earn a disproportionate share of low wages and are more highly represented in the informal sector (Chapter 5). Policy responses aimed at addressing these substantial disparities require great attention to the multiple roots of the disparities and the multiple factors that affect them.

Inducing greater inclusion in education demands, for example, not only attention to equitable access and participation for racial, ethnic, and other excluded groups at all levels of education, but also particular attention to physical access for persons with disabilities, multicultural and bilingual education, and a reduction of disparities in school quality among neighborhoods linked to race or ethnicity (Verdisco, Calderón, and Marshall, 2004). In targeting social exclusion via education, Marshall and Calderón (2006) highlight the need for policies designed, first, to improve schooling for poor people by increasing access and lowering costs, and second, to raise the demand for schooling by increasing its expected returns. For persons with disabilities, the key barriers to expanding inclusive education include stigma and discrimination, invisibility, lack of accessible transportation, perceived cost, and gender discrimination (boys with disabilities are more likely to be sent to school than girls) (Massiah, 2004). Experience in the region with more inclusive education methods includes providing bilingual education (e.g., Bolivia, Ecuador, Honduras); expanding physical access and introducing innovative pedagogy to include people with disabilities in regular classrooms (e.g., Mexico's "inclusion in higher education" program); introducing and adapting the curriculum to stress multicultural heritage and the contributions of Afro-descendants and indigenous peoples to national culture and history (e.g., Colombia); and linking education and school attendance with programs to eradicate the worst forms of child labor (e.g., the Dominican Republic, where indigenous, migrant, and Afro-descendant children are disproportionately represented among child laborers). A shift in data collection and analysis must accompany advances in inclusion achieved via education. Developed nations much more frequently measure how specific groups (e.g., females, Afro-descendants) perform under their social or economic programs in order to ascertain whether the programs are creating greater disparities among various sectors of society and to aid in program redesign or complementary interventions.

Reproductive health (see Box 14.3) offers a particularly compelling area for attention in which the region is far behind even other developing regions, and there are significant differences in infant mortality for excluded groups (e.g., Chapter 2 notes higher rates of infant mortality for indigenous over nonindigenous populations living in the same area).

Many of the region's labor market policies and programs have yet to be explored for their contribution to greater social inclusion (Chapter 5). What is striking across the region are the barriers encountered by excluded groups in the labor market, despite the advances made in education among these groups. In a study of whites, *pretos* (Afro-descendants), and *pardos* (those of mixed race) in Brazil, labor market returns from education were found to vary significantly with parents' position in the earnings distribution scale and the gradient of skin color (Arias, Yamada, and Tejerina, 2002). The study's authors found that the earnings gap actually *increased* for Afro-descendants relative to whites the more education they received (with all other differences in education, parents' income, etc., controlled for), whereas at the lower end of the scale, the earnings gap relative to whites was smaller, and *pretos* and *pardos* had more similar earnings.

In spite of their educational advancement, women have not enjoyed commensurate gains in labor market earnings, despite increasing rates of labor force participation (see Chapter 5). Occupational segregation for women—clustering of women in low-paid sectors of domestic work, teaching, and office work—is pervasive in Latin America and the Caribbean. Despite important economic shifts in occupational structure and macroeconomic circumstances from 1989 to 1997, occupational segregation by gender in key countries was not found to decrease as would be expected (Deutsch et al., 2004). This suggests that cultural and social factors of exclusion persist in counterintuitive ways in response to economic changes that would normally induce shifts. As detailed in earlier chapters, the rapidly growing informal labor market has itself become a key factor in the current dynamics of exclusion in the region. Excluded groups continue to be overrepresented in informal work, lacking key benefits, protection, and access to productivity-enhancing training. Women represent more than one-half of the informal sector, and their average earnings are lower than those of men in the informal sector (Barrientos, 2004).

The most promising results in the region in the labor market field come from a series of evaluations of youth training programs in the region (e.g., in Argentina, Chile, Peru) that demonstrate that women, as a proxy for excluded groups, realize greater returns to training and placement services than men. The placing of women in traineeships in firms under the auspices of these programs is likely enabling women to leapfrog over the hiring discrimination they encounter and the disadvantages they face in having more limited contacts.

The first study of the gender effects of labor intermediation services, conducted on Mexico's National Employment Service in Mexico City (Flores Lima, 2007), found positive effects for men over a control group that did not participate in the service, but no significant impact for women. This study, and an upcoming study of Chile's labor intermediation service, help show the way toward actions needed to ensure that job placement services

Box 14.3 Inequality and Exclusion in Reproductive Health

An important factor in exclusion that limits many women's opportunities in life is their uneven access to information and quality services in reproductive health. Total fertility has declined to an average of 2.4 live births per woman of reproductive age in Latin America and the Caribbean, but remains over 4.0 in some of the poorer countries and among many of the poor. Teenage fertility in the region is high and socially uneven, as shown in the figure to the right, and progress in reducing maternal mortality has been slow. Income and education gaps, as well as attitudes rooted in cultural factors and gender norms, are to blame, as are health care systems that do not adequately reach the excluded and poor.

Maternal mortality (which is correlated with total fertility rates as well as income and the quality of prenatal and perinatal care) has remained essentially unchanged over the last fifteen years at an average of 190 per 100,000 births. It is particularly high among indigenous and other disadvantaged groups, for whom cultural and language barriers and other considerations, including reports of substandard care and mistreatment, can act as disincentives to seeking hospital deliveries and care.

Most reproductive-health-related problems in the region could be solved by broadening the coverage and quality of health services, prenatal care, and birth attendance, along with their affordability and pertinence; applying multisector ap-

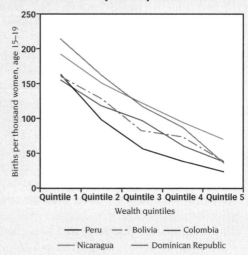

Adolescent Fertility Rate by Wealth Quintiles

Births per thousand women, age 15–19

Wealth quintiles

— Peru   — - Bolivia   — Colombia
— Nicaragua   — Dominican Republic

Source: World Bank, "Socioeconomic Differences in Health, Nutrition, and Population" (available at http://poverty2.forumone.com/library/topic/3438/4346/). Based on Demographic and Health Survey 2001–2005 data.

proaches, including education, social well-being policies, and the involvement of communities, families, and both women and men in reproductive health; and promoting measures to raise awareness of and access to contraception and safe practices. Public health measures such as the vaccination against human papilloma virus (HPV), which is responsible for virtually all cases of cervical cancer, should be encouraged in the region, following the lead of a growing number of adopters elsewhere in the world.

appropriately serve as vehicles for improving the quality of jobs found by excluded groups rather than reinforcing existing occupational segregation and exclusion.

Conditional Cash Transfer Programs

Conditional cash transfer programs, now in place in more than twenty countries in the region, take into account key aspects of gender empowerment and decision making in their delivery of cash subsidies and health benefits via mothers. Another objective—to break the intergenerational transmission of poverty from parents to children—mirrors a similar goal of eradicating intergenerational transmission of exclusion. Conditional cash transfer programs also take into account implicitly the interrelated forms of exclusion, in terms of access to health services and the multiple roots of children's failure to attend school. Ethnic and racial participation and performance in such programs, however, has yet to be studied, and the data collected on the outcomes achieved by such programs are not disaggregated along these lines. Thus, it is simply not known whether such programs serve to overcome (or reinforce) exclusion, and in what ways. A social inclusion spotlight on such programs might provide potential opportunities to improve program outcomes and performance via an examination of whether there are disparate outcomes for distinct groups constraining these programs from having a more significant impact in key countries. Most important in terms of impact would be the exclusion dimension of what comes next, that is, how successful conditional cash transfer programs are at leading to a lasting exit from poverty. Santiago Levy (2006) argues that this is precisely the weakness in such programs, for children may be healthier or better educated after a conditional cash transfer intervention, but may then be recirculated into exclusionary labor markets and neighborhoods where those gains cannot be realized as a long-term exit from poverty.

Economic Development/Advancement

A different range of policies and programs come under the rubric of promoting economic development and empowerment of excluded populations. These include programs to promote economic development in geographic areas with high concentrations of targeted ethnic or racial populations; provide excluded populations with greater access to credit and business development services and greater support in their utilization; support land reform and property rights; and provide access to quality infrastructure, transport, and markets.

Targeting regional development provides an opportunity to address in a more integrated fashion distinct roots of exclusion: limited job opportunities and business development, marginalized neighborhoods, and lack of access to vital social services. The interrelated impacts of specific forms of exclusion are often most visible in isolated rural regions or urban neighborhoods where there are high concentrations of targeted racial and ethnic populations. The IDB currently supports a series of regional development projects, including one in Bocas del Toro, Chile, and another in Darien, Panama, which explicitly seek to incorporate participation and decision making by local ethnic and racial populations and regional development based on cultural and ethnic identity. In the Chilean case, the participation methods have introduced an inclusion focus into the project

"Development with Identity," which draws on the strengths, assets, and aspirations of the Mapuche peoples and is supported by a substantial investment (US$150 million) from the national government.

Margarita Sánchez (2004) recommends that economic development programs oriented to Afro-descendant communities in particular take into consideration participatory development methods that rebuild the social capital and leadership diminished by multiple forms of exclusion. Among the lessons from Afro-descendant community development that Sánchez includes are the importance of (a) simultaneous strengthening of nongovernmental organizations and networks, (b) incorporation of training tools for community participants targeted to overcoming historical barriers (e.g., self-esteem, gender roles, identity), and (c) linkage with wider social and economic development projects and programs.

There is a widespread perception that the economic advancement of excluded groups is hindered by their more limited access to credit to build income (businesses) and assets (home, property ownership). Lenders can discriminate against members of excluded groups via a variety of methods: applying stricter credit standards, charging higher interest rates, and requiring more collateral on loans to borrowers from these groups than from favored borrowers (Elliehausen and Lawrence, 1990, cited in Torero et al., 2004). In the United States, for example, systematic evidence of blatant discrimination against African Americans who sought to purchase homes in predominantly white neighborhoods led to major reforms in lending practices and disclosures. Recent research into direct discrimination in credit markets in Latin America and the Caribbean, however, is limited.

Many believe that the lack of credit availability for excluded groups in Latin America and the Caribbean may operate through more indirect channels than the blatant discrimination found in the industrialized countries (Chapter 3). Instead, exclusion and discrimination in the region are manifested in the preconditions imposed on applicants from excluded groups to qualify for formal credit, as well as the generally high average rates charged to members of such groups for the credit extended. In their literature review and study, Máximo Torero and his colleagues (2004) found in the case of Peru that the whiter the household, the greater its access to credit, but the marginal effect was quite small. They speculate that a range of indirect factors may be at play in the region, including factors correlated with race and ethnicity (e.g., income instability) and more limited access to needed private assets and public goods. In the case of many Latin American and Caribbean countries, it may well be that a host of factors, such as lack of verifiable collateral, land title, or basic identification, impede even basic loan qualification for members of excluded groups.

Creating new opportunities for firms owned by representatives of excluded or minority groups requires the breaking of clientelistic economic relationships between firms based on past relationships rather than competitiveness. As Thomas Boston (2006) argues, the economic disadvantages faced by minority-owned businesses are rooted historically in unequal treatment in all spheres of life: economic, social, political, and legal. Boston describes a new, promising area for promoting minority-owned firms in the United States: supplier diversity programs with major U.S. companies. To break old patterns, companies are urged to diversify their supplier base and encourage their vendors to do so as well. The most notable U.S. organization encouraging supplier diversity, Boston notes, is the National Minority Supplier Development Council, which has been instrumental in increasing the purchases of goods and services from African-American-owned businesses in the United States from $86 million in 1972 to more than $80 billion in 2003.

Another excluded group for which economic and social empowerment has yielded results is persons with disabilities, in particular, through efforts in some countries to make cities and services (e.g., schools) more accessible to these persons. The experience of Curitiba, Brazil, has shown that systems that are inaccessible to those with disabilities are far more costly than accessible ones (Massiah, 2004). In the area of accessible transport, key lessons include universal design principles, equal access to public transport, and special services for people with special needs (Wright, 2001, cited in Massiah, 2004).

ADVANCING INCLUSION IN LATIN AMERICA AND THE CARIBBEAN: WHAT NEXT?

Shaping Effective National Inclusion Processes

Observation of all three levels of policy "means" in inclusion processes in Latin America and the Caribbean shows that the intensity and urgency to advance has varied markedly from country to country. For example, Colombia's national process has emphasized normative changes (see Box 14.1), whereas in Chile, new investments and instruments for indigenous peoples, for example, have been the strongest focus. There is simply no known example in which a nation sought to address inclusion or some form of group-based stigma and discrimination with only a program change, that is, without institutional and normative changes as well. The case of Ecuador (Box 14.4) demonstrates changes at all three levels, as well as the inclusion of distinct changes to address the needs of populations such as those living with disabilities and those with HIV/AIDS. If one views inclusion as a multidimensional, multigroup process, this places emphasis on developing distinct country models and processes that rely on interaction with civil society groups within a given nation, as well as the sequencing of normative, institutional, and policy changes to address the most substantial national needs and weaknesses first.

The IDB's Social Inclusion Trust Fund has placed particular emphasis on supporting, understanding, and analyzing social inclusion as it advances in particular "leader" countries (IDB, 2006a). Support is targeted not to single policy interventions, but to key stimulus actions that can have a larger, reverberating impact on a range of inclusion outputs along the inclusion policy spectrum. The distinct weights assigned to normative, institutional, and instrumental changes reflect distinct country differences and needs. In Jamaica, for example, addressing HIV/AIDS-related discrimination is particularly pressing as a focus for national social inclusion (see Box 14.5).

Of the three levels of policy means more broadly, the role of normative constitutional changes is likely to be the least transformative in current times, save cases such as South Africa (Richards-Kennedy, 2006), as constitutions and legal frameworks in many countries have been modernized in the transitions to democracy in the late twentieth

Box 14.4 Social Inclusion in Ecuador

Ecuador is a diverse, multiethnic nation with sizeable populations of Afro-descendants and indigenous peoples, as well as organized civil society groups for persons with disability and persons living with HIV/AIDS. Civil society movements and the national government have played critical driving roles in advancing an agenda to promote social inclusion.

Ecuador has undertaken actions to promote social inclusion through normative, institutional, and policy mechanisms. These actions represent the initial framework of a national process to advance inclusion. Much remains to be done to develop medium- and long-term public policies directed towards excluded groups, to ensure the financing and effective functioning of civil institutions, and to provide increased political focus on financing and expanding targeted initiatives for these groups.

KEY NORMATIVE CHANGES

- In 1992 approximately four million hectares of land were granted to indigenous Ecuadorans—one of the largest land rights concessions in Latin American history—and their territories were designated as inalienable.
- The Constituent Assembly of 1997 approved the collective rights of indigenous peoples and Afro-descendants in Ecuador (outlined in Articles 83, 84, 85) and recognized Ecuador as a multicultural and multiethnic state.

- In 1998, Ecuador ratified International Labour Organization Convention 169 and approved the Law of Indigenous Peoples and Nationalities (vetoed in 2003 by then-President Noboa). That same year, indigenous peoples created the Council on Development of Nationalities and Towns of Ecuador (CODENPE) to pressure for implementation of the 1997 constitution's mandate of community participation in government planning, actions, and decision making.
- On May 9, 2006, Ecuador's National Congress passed the Law of Collective Rights for Afro-Ecuadoran Communities, creating the National Council on Afro-Ecuadoran Development (Consejo Nacional de Desarrollo Afroecuatoriano, or CONDAE) to design policies and strategies for the development of Afro-Ecuadoran communities. The transition issues created by the implementation of the law have generated serious conflicts that are still being resolved.

KEY INSTITUTIONAL CHANGES

- In 1988, Ecuador officially recognized intercultural bilingual education as a system within the Ministry of Education. A dedicated national department was established, along with departments in sixteen provinces, bilingual schools and colleges, and teacher training programs.

- In 1986, the first congress of the National Council of the Coordination of Indigenous Nationalities (Consejo Nacional de Coordinación de Nacionalidades Indígenas, or CONACNIE) established the Confederation of Indigenous Nationalities of Ecuador (Confederación de Nacionalidades Indígenas del Ecuador, or CONAIE). The objectives of CONAIE are to bring together the indigenous peoples and nationalities of Ecuador; to fight against colonialism and oppression from authorities; and to fight for territorial and land rights, educational rights (intercultural/bilingual), cultural identity, and the dignity of indigenous peoples.

- In 1996, CONAIE played a major role in the formation of Pachakutik (Pluri-National Pachakutik United Movement—New Country), an electoral coalition of indigenous and nonindigenous social movements. Since its creation, the movement has elected representatives to various posts at the local and national levels. In 2000, for example, 5 high-level administrative officials, 31 mayors and 173 municipal and provincial council representatives were elected.

KEY POLICIES AND PROGRAMS (INSTRUMENTAL)

- From 1998 to 2002, the first phase of the Development Project of the Indigenous and Black Communities of Ecuador (Proyecto de Desarrollo de los Pueblos Indígenas y Negros de Ecuador, or PRODEPINE) invested a total of US$50 million in programs to address the needs of these communities and help improve their livelihoods.

- In May 2002, an executive decree approved the creation of the Indigenous Fund for Development, which was allocated US$10 million for its operations. Responsibility for the Fund was assigned to CODENPE.

- The first national database for generating specific information on indigenous issues was launched in 2002 (managed by a technical secretariat in the Ministry of Social Welfare, in collaboration with indigenous organizations).

- In 2004, a system of indicators called SISPAE (Sistema de Indicadores Sociales del Pueblo Afroecuatoriano) was created. It is part of SIISE (Sistema Integrado de Indicadores Sociales del Ecuador) and housed within a technical secretariat in the Ministry of Social Welfare. Its mission is to facilitate the collection of quantitative socioeconomic information on Afro-Ecuadorans.

Box 14.5 Jamaica and HIV/AIDS

It is estimated that approximately 1–1.5 percent of the adult population of Jamaica is living with HIV/AIDS. In Jamaica, HIV transmission is predominantly through heterosexual contact, with the highest prevalence of HIV infection reported in tourism resort areas (2.6–3.0 percent). Within that group, an alarming 43 percent of reported AIDS cases are female, and the rate of death among them is approximately 42 percent. Adolescent females have a higher rate of contracting the virus than adolescent males (2.5 times as high), and heterosexual women are predominantly affected by the epidemic. The epidemic has a particularly strong impact on families in which single mothers and grandmothers are heads of households.

Because of its association with behaviors that may be considered socially unacceptable by many people, HIV infection is widely stigmatized. People living with the virus are frequently subject to discrimination and human rights abuses: many have been thrown out of jobs and homes and rejected by family and friends, and some have even been killed.

Stigma and discrimination constitute one of the greatest barriers to dealing effectively with the epidemic. Those groups most exposed to contagion have limited or inadequate access to services that provide basic care, education, and nutrition. Although there are a number of programs and policies in effect aimed at assisting members of vulnerable groups living with HIV/AIDS, the country remains challenged by cultural and behavioral attitudes that have changed little to date.

DEVELOPING A RESPONSE: NORMATIVE, INSTITUTIONAL, AND INSTRUMENTAL

Jamaica has benefited from a high level of commitment on the part of the Ministry of Health to addressing issues related to HIV/AIDS and expanded support from civil society. Six ministries (the Ministries of Local Government and Community Development; Labour and Social Security; Tourism; Education, Youth and Culture; Health; and National Security) are involved in the implementation of a national policy on HIV/AIDS. Other stakeholders include the National AIDS Committee, the Jamaica Council of Churches, Jamaican and international AIDS-related nongovernmental organizations, and the Parish AIDS Committees Center for HIV/AIDS Research, Education and Services.

The Jamaican attorney general has also reviewed existing laws and made recommendations regarding the development of new legislation to address issues raised by the AIDS epidemic in Jamaica. These recommendations urge all agencies to

- balance the rights of individuals against those of society;
- issue clear and specific guidelines with respect to confidentiality, notification, discrimination, and laboratory testing;
- protect students infected with HIV/AIDS (or who have a family member infected with the virus) from being excluded or dismissed from institutions of learning on account of their HIV/AIDS status or that of their relative.

century. What is more pressing in Latin America and the Caribbean is the refinement and advancement of legal protections and the transformation of rights on paper into rights in practice via enforcement and proactive implementation. Although the scope of normative legal and constitutional changes needed in the region may be limited, there is some evidence that normative changes can play an important catalytic role in stimulating follow-on institutional changes and new policies and programs designed to give life to constitutional commitments.

A priority for normative change in inclusion in many countries of Latin America and the Caribbean remains land and property rights and access to capital (Chapter 4). Much of the region's economic exclusion stems from unequal access to income-generating assets. A new generation of land-titling and land reform programs in the region benefit women, indigenous peoples, and Afro-descendants and recognize collective and community land ownership. These groups suffered for centuries under normative frameworks that did not recognize or would not grant them titles to their land (Chapter 2).

Focusing on Key Institutional and Policy Changes

In all inclusion processes, institutional and instrumental changes are seen most frequently occurring in conjunction with one another. Again, this stems logically from the embedded nature of exclusion. One cannot institute effective new programs and policies with the same personnel and institutional processes that have previously actively bypassed excluded populations or have no credibility or record with excluded populations.

Of the three levels of policy change, few would disagree that the most widely needed impulse for change in Latin America and the Caribbean is in the area of reforming elite-based or elite-benefiting institutions and implementing a new generation of public policies that serve the poor and excluded in more effective and comprehensive ways. Research reviewed in Chapter 3 showed the differing weights of group and class (e.g., income) identity in exclusionary outcomes.

Although the great variability by country within Latin America and the Caribbean in the nature of exclusion and the specific groups affected must be recognized, key areas of institutional policy change can be and have been more broadly identified region-wide, given common histories of elite-driven politics and economies. European inclusion policies (Atkinson, 2004) have targeted labor markets as a key focus; José Antonio Ocampo (2004) argues that the focus in the Latin American and Caribbean context should be on both education and labor markets. Within education, Chapter 2 argues for the urgent need to reduce inequalities in primary education and improve school quality.

One policy guidepost (Marshall and Calderón, 2006) in the area of eradicating exclusion is to focus on key "entry points" where greater inclusion might have greater follow-on impacts on other areas of exclusion. Income-generating entry points are considered the most fundamental in this regard: education, labor markets, land and property ownership, and business development. Although not income-generating per se, justice presents a particular urgency because of its pivotal role in the ability to access other rights and is frequently a focus of civil rights movements in developed countries (see Box 14.6).

Box 14.6 Strengthening Inclusion via the Judicial System: A Key for Latin America and the Caribbean?

In the inclusion toolbox of developed countries, labor markets and economic opportunity have often played a more prominent role than judicial reform, violence prevention, and law enforcement. At the most basic level, this reflects the longer development and different level of functioning of judicial systems in developed nations. Justice is no less critical to inclusion in developed countries, however; indeed, in Europe today, one of the flagship programs of social cohesion is incorporating access to justice (Sanahuja, 2007). But in developed countries, it has been possible to promote inclusion by utilizing the court system more actively to address specific denials of rights. In contrast, in the rare instances that judicial channels are pursued by excluded groups in Latin America and the Caribbean, they find that they can more readily obtain justice by seeking redress via the inter-American court system rather than their national judiciaries.

In Latin America and the Caribbean, the judicial system is more likely to be seen as reproducing or even accentuating economic and social inequalities (Cappelletti and Garth, 1996) than as a vibrant source for advancing group-based rights. As Chapter 10 lays out, judicial and law enforcement systems in the region have weakly adapted to new challenges and growing violence and continue to leave segments of society without adequate access to justice and economic and physical security. In this context, violence becomes an instrument for achieving certain outcomes, such as justice, security, and economic gain, and a new force of exclusion (see Chapter 10).

Fernando Carrillo-Flórez (2007) argues that after fifteen years of (albeit limited) judicial system reform, justice is still not a priority in the region in the fight against exclusion and social fragmentation. He asserts that the lack of effective judicial protection is the "Achilles' heel" of inclusion in Latin America and the Caribbean. In particular, he insists that access to justice and fair treatment within the courts has not been made a policy priority, nor has it been designed to be an integral part of strengthening judicial systems. An effective public judicial service is one of the public policy areas with greatest political content, he notes, as it involves

A critical next step in the region is both to identity the strategic key entry points and to make the lessons learned from past policies in regard to inclusion more systematic and more useful in shaping future policies. This will require a much more systematic review of both the efficiency and equity aspects of public policies in regard to key entry points. A series of IDB strategies, policy documents, and studies seek to undertake such a review in regard to key public policy areas and offer a substantial reference.[4] The previous chap-

---

[4] See www.iadb.org for policies, studies, and strategies, including those regarding citizen participation, gender, indigenous peoples, social inclusion, labor markets, health, and education.

a collection of variables that strike directly at the heart of the principles of equality and nondiscrimination. He points to the region's Defensorías del Pueblo, systems of public defenders, as young institutions, fragile in the majority of cases and very vulnerable to political intervention. Because of the lack of public legal representation, the rates of preventive detention in Latin America are extremely high, over 70 percent on average, compared to 30 percent in Spain and France.

Among the initiatives for access to justice that Carrillo-Flórez (2007) recommends are

- giving priority, in the region's judicial reform agenda, to public legal assistance for members of excluded or low-income groups, and to access to justice;
- modernization of legal procedures to reduce the cost of access to the courts and other barriers, including simplification of laws and procedures;
- new forms of teaching and training in the law that incorporate the social functions that judges and lawyers must perform in

reversing decades of injustice towards excluded groups;
- advancing not only penal justice, but also civil, family, labor, and housing justice—areas that are traditionally marginalized in judicial reform programs (DeShazo and Vargas, 2006);
- programs to promote basic civil and legal education;
- initiatives to instill in law professionals a sense that providing pro bono legal services is a civic responsibility;
- community-based programs and initiatives to empower excluded populations, such as community justice agents;
- more systematic planning, management, and monitoring of public policies regarding justice;
- incorporation of a network of institutions for better coordination of the different policy components;
- incorporating special legal jurisdictions for indigenous and ethnic communities, the need for which is recognized in legislation in a number of countries in the region.

ters have presented policy perspectives in each of these areas, most specifically in the areas of labor markets (Chapter 5), financial services (Chapter 12), education (Chapters 2, 3, and 13), and business development (Chapters 8, 9, and 11). Specific policy recommendations applicable to individual countries, as stated at the outset of this chapter, are not the purview of this analytical work. Rather, they must be the product of the very national and multilateral strategy and consensus processes that inclusion dictates.

Although the range of program and policy interventions needed at the instrumental level seems daunting, the perspective of national experience and of the larger public policy process offers some relief. In the region today, the priorities and target instruments vary substantially based on national experience and are still considered to be in their very early stages. Coverage, even in the areas of key entry points, is limited. To date, there are still relatively few programs and policies with much longevity in the region, and few programs collect data disaggregated according to group identification, with the exception of data on gender. In comparison, developed countries have a full complement of programs and policies spanning each of the above areas—affirmative action/antidiscrimination, sectoral policies, and economic development—with a much wider range of programs and policies in each of the areas.

The diversification of policies and programs along the many dimensions of exclusion is more representative of developed countries than of Latin America and the Caribbean, where norms, institutions, and policies and programs can be seen as not yet encompassing the wide political, economic, and social dimensions of the problem of exclusion. For example, affirmative action or quota-based systems are relatively prevalent in many countries in a wider range of areas, but in Latin America and the Caribbean the measures involved are predominantly political party quotas, principally those for gender. International experience indicates in very broad terms that as the inclusion process evolves over time, inclusion policy can move to greater diversity and specificity of instruments (policies and programs) even if there is not always full societal consensus, particularly as strengthened civil society and more representative government provide the means to open up new channels for policy intervention.

Returning to the Foundation

To advance ultimately towards inclusion, though, demands a return to its foundation. There is no single identifiable cause nor a single definable solution to the multiple layers of political, economic, and social marginalization that have produced high rates of social exclusion in Latin America and the Caribbean. Progress towards inclusion in the region requires significant efforts both to better define and comprehend the forces that create *exclusion* and to better understand as well the public policy process needed to significantly advance *inclusion*.

For Latin America and the Caribbean, the most basic step forward in public policy to combat exclusion begins with the recognition of some fundamental truths:

1. Exclusion is too complex, multidimensional, and changing for single, isolated policies to be effective in combating it.
2. Public policy to advance inclusion must be viewed, designed, and evaluated as part of a comprehensive set of diverse interventions within a policy process that integrates the role of civil society and societal change.
3. When designing interventions, public officials must think horizontally and vertically about needed changes and reforms on three levels—laws, institutions, and instruments—as each depends on the others.
4. A key to developing sustainable national inclusion processes in Latin America and the Caribbean lies in the evolution of democratic systems in the region towards greater representativity and participation, the heart of developing more inclusive public policies.

5. The systematic evaluation of existing policies and programs for their impact on inclusion, the identification of key opportunities not available to excluded populations, and basic data collection must begin now if countries are to have the ability in subsequent years to enact a new generation of evidence-based policies and programs that contribute to vibrant national inclusion processes.

Unearthing and addressing the dynamics of exclusion and inclusion via public policy will play a central role in the region's future. That future, many argue, must place fundamental citizens' rights—political, social, human, economic, social, and cultural—at the core of achieving inclusion (Abramovitch, 2004). Without greater advances in inclusion based on fundamental citizen rights, Latin America and the Caribbean will continue to suffer from its legacy of exclusion and remain the most unequal region in the world.

References

Abramovich, Victor. 2004. An Approximation to a Rights Approach to Development Strategies and Policies in Latin America. Paper presented at the seminar, Rights and Development in Latin America: A Working Seminar, December 9–10, Santiago, Chile.

Acosta Urquidi, Mariclaire, and John Burstein. 2006. ¿Qué puede haber dentro de un nombre? Estudios de caso sobre identidad y registro en América Latina y el Caribe. Paper presented at the IDB seminar, Derecho desde el Comienzo: Registro, Identidad y Desarrollo en América Latina y el Caribe, February 2, Washington, DC.

Acuña, Cecilia, and Mónica Bolis. 2005. Stigmatization and Access to Health Care in Latin America: Challenges and Perspectives. Paper presented at the 29th Congress of the International Academy of Law and Mental Health, July 4–8, Paris.

AfroamericaXXI. 2006. *Compendio normativo de acciones afirmativas para comunidades afrolatinoamericanas.* Washington, DC: AfroamericaXXI.

Agencia Presidencial para la Acción Social y la Cooperación Internacional. 2005. Aprendizaje colectivo: Programa Familias en Acción. Colombia.

Aggleton, Peter, Richard Parker, and Miriam Maluwa. 2004. Stigma, Discrimination and HIV/AIDS in Latin America. In Mayra Buvinić and Jacqueline Mazza, with Ruthanne Deutsch, eds., *Social Inclusion and Economic Development in Latin America.* Washington, DC: IDB.

Alesina, Alberto, and Eliana La Ferrara. 2000. Participation in Heterogenous Communities. *Quarterly Journal of Economics* 115(3) August: 847–904.

Altonji, Joseph G., and Rebecca M. Blank. 1999. Race and Gender in the Labor Market. In Orley C. Ashenfelter and David Card, eds., *Handbook of Labor Economics.* Volume 3C. Amsterdam: North-Holland.

Álvarez, Eduardo. 2000. *Pathways to Accessibility: Disability and the Physical Environment in Latin America and the Caribbean.* SDS Working Paper. Inter-American Development Bank, Washington, DC.

Andersen, Lykke E. 2000. Social Mobility in Latin America. Instituto de Investigaciones Socioeconómicas, Universidad Católica Boliviana, La Paz.

———. 2001. *Social Mobility in Latin America: Links with Adolescent Schooling.* Research Network Working Paper no. R-433. Inter-American Development Bank, Washington, DC.

Andrade, Eduardo, Fernando Veloso, Regina Madalozzo, and Sergio G. Ferreira. 2003. Do Borrowing Constraints Decrease Intergenerational Mobility? Evidence from Brazil. Getulio Vargas Foundation, Rio de Janeiro. Unpublished.

Andreoni, James. 1988. Why Free Ride? Strategies and Learning in Public Goods Experiments. *Journal of Public Economics* 37(3) December: 291–304.

————. 1995. Cooperation in Public-Goods Experiments: Kindness or Confusion? *American Economic Review* 85(4) September: 891–904.

Angeles, Hugo, and Martha Rojas. 2000. Migración femenina internacional en la frontera sur de México. *Papeles de Población* [Universidad Autónoma del Estado de México] 23 (January–March): 127–51.

Angell, Alan, Pamela Lowden, and Rosemary Thorp. 2001. *Decentralizing Development: The Political Economy of Institutional Change in Colombia and Chile*. New York: Oxford University Press.

Arends, Mary. 1992. Female Labor Force Participation and Earnings in Guatemala. In George Psacharopoulos and Zafiris Tzannatos, eds., *Case Studies on Women's Employment and Pay in Latin America*. Washington, DC: World Bank.

Arias, Omar, Gustavo Yamada, and Luis Tejerina. 2002. *Education, Family Background and Racial Earnings Inequality in Brazil*. SDS Working Paper. Inter-American Development Bank, Washington, DC.

Ashraf, Nava, Iris Bohnet, and Nikita Piankov. 2006. Decomposing Trust and Trustworthiness. *Experimental Economics* 9(3) September: 193–208.

Aterido, R., M. Hallward-Driemeyer, and C. Pagés. 2007. The Impact of Regulation, Access to Finance and Corruption across Firms. Inter-American Development Bank and World Bank, Washington, DC. Unpublished.

Atkinson, Tony. 2004. The European Union Experience with Social Inclusion Policy. In Mayra Buvinić and Jacqueline Mazza, with Ruthanne Deutsch, eds., *Social Inclusion and Economic Development in Latin America*. Washington, DC: IDB.

Attanasio, Orazio, Pinelopi K. Goldberg, and Nina Pavcnik. 2004. Trade Reforms and Wage Inequality in Colombia. *Journal of Development Economics* 74(2): 331–66.

Ayala Consulting. 2006. Country Program Profiles—Mexico. Report prepared for the World Bank for the Third International Conference on Conditional Cash Transfers, June 26–30, Istanbul. Available at http://info.worldbank.org/etools/ICCT06/DOCS/TemplateCCT_EN.pdf.

Babcock, Linda, and Sara Laschever. 2003. *Women Don't Ask: Negotiation and the Gender Divide*. Princeton, NJ: Princeton University Press.

Baqir, Reza. 2002. *Social Sector Spending in a Panel of Countries*. IMF Working Paper no. 02/35. International Monetary Fund, Washington, DC.

Barker, Gary T. 2005. *Dying to Be Men: Youth, Masculinity and Social Exclusion*. Abingdon, England: Routledge.

Barnes, Robert. 2007. Divided Court Limits Use of Race by School Districts. *Washington Post*, June 29.

Barr, Abigail. 2003. *Risk Pooling, Commitment, and Information: An Experimental Test of Two Fundamental Assumptions*. CSAE Working Paper no. 187. Centre for the Study of African Economies, Oxford, England.

Barrera-Osorio, Felipe, and Mauricio Olivera. 2007. *Does Society Win or Lose as a Result of Privatization? Provision of Public Services and Welfare of the Poor: The Case of Water Sector Privatization in Colombia*. Research Network Working Paper no. R-525. Inter-American Development Bank, Washington, DC.

Barrientos, Armando. 2004. Women, Informal Employment and Social Protection in Latin America. In Claudia Piras, ed., *Women at Work: Challenges for Latin America*. Washington, DC: Inter-American Development Bank.

Barrón, Manuel. 2005. Cuánto cuesta ser provinciano a un empleado de Lima Metropolitana: una aproximación mediante Propensity Score Matching. *Observatorio de la Economía Latinoamericana* no. 47.

———. 2006. *Exclusion and Discrimination as Sources of Inter-Ethnic Inequality in Peru*. PUCP Working Paper no. 253. Pontificia Universidad Católica del Perú, Lima.

Bates, Robert H. 1981. *Markets and States in Tropical Africa: The Political Basis of Agricultural Policies*. Berkeley, CA: University of California Press.

Beato, Claudio. 2002. Crime and Social Policies in Latin America: Problems and Solutions. Woodrow Wilson Center Update on the Americas. Available at http://www.wilson center.org/topics/pubs/CitizenSecurity7.pdf.

Beck, Thorsten, Asli Demirgüç-Kunt, and María Soledad Martínez Pería. 2006. *Banking Services for Everyone? Barriers to Bank Access and Use around the World*. Policy Research Working Paper no. 4079. World Bank, Washington, DC.

Beckett, Megan, and Anne R. Pebley. 2002. *Ethnicity, Language, and Economic Well-Being in Rural Guatemala*. Working Paper Series 02–05. Labor and Population Program, RAND, Santa Monica, CA.

Behrman, Jere R. 1999. Social Mobility: Concepts and Measurement. In Nancy Birdsall and Carol Graham, eds., *New Markets, New Opportunities? Economic and Social Mobility in a Changing World*. Washington, DC: Carnegie Endowment for International Peace and Brookings Institution Press.

Behrman, Jere R., Alejandro Gaviria, and Miguel Székely. 2001. *Intergenerational Mobility in Latin America*. Research Department Working Paper no. 452. Inter-American Development Bank, Washington, DC.

Behrman, Jere R., Alejandro Gaviria, and Miguel Székely, eds. 2003. *Who's In and Who's Out: Social Exclusion in Latin America*. Washington, DC: IDB.

Bello, Álvaro, and Marta Rangel. 2002. Equity and Exclusion in Latin America and the Caribbean: The Case of Indigenous and Afro-Descendant Peoples. *CEPAL Review* no. 76 (April): 35–53.

Benavides, Martín. 2002. Cuando los extremos no se encuentran: un análisis de la movilidad social e igualdad de oportunidades en el Perú contemporáneo. *Boletín del Instituto Francés de Estudios Andinos* 31(3): 473–94.

———. 2004. Educación y estructura social en el Perú: un estudio acerca del acceso a la educación superior y la movilidad intergeneracional en una muestra de trabajadores urbanos. In Patricia Arregui, Martín Benavides, Santiago Cueto, Jaime Saavedra, and Barbara Hunt, eds., *¿Es posible mejorar la educación peruana? Evidencias y posibilidades*. Lima: GRADE.

———. 2006. Nota técnica sobre indígenas y afro peruanos. Inter-American Development Bank, Washington, DC, and Grupo de Análisis para el Desarrollo (GRADE), Lima. Unpublished.

Benavides, Martín, Máximo Torero, and Néstor Valdivia. 2006. Pobreza, discriminación social e identidad: el caso de la población afrodescendiente en el Perú. World Bank, Washington, DC, and Grupo de Análisis para el Desarrollo (GRADE), Lima. Unpublished.

Benavides, Martín, and Martín Valdivia. 2004. Metas del Milenio y la brecha étnica en el Perú. Grupo de Análisis para el Desarrollo (GRADE), Lima. Unpublished.

Berg, Joyce, John Dickhaut, and Kevin McCabe. 1995. Trust, Reciprocity, and Social History. *Games and Economic Behavior* 10(1) July: 122–42.

Bergman, Barbara R. 1996. *In Defense of Affirmative Action*. New York: Basic Books.

Bergstrom, Theodore, Lawrence Blume, and Hal Varian. 1986. On the Private Provision of Public Goods. *Journal of Public Economics* 29(1) February: 25–49.

Bernal, Raquel, and Mauricio Cárdenas. 2003. *Determinants of Labor Demand in Colombia: 1976–1996*. NBER Working Paper no. 10077. National Bureau of Economic Research, Cambridge, MA.

———. 2005. *Race and Ethnic Inequality in Health and Health Care in Colombia*. Working Papers Series no. 29. Fundación para la Educación Superior y el Desarrollo (FEDESARROLLO), Bogotá.

Bernstein, Jared, and Heidi Hartmann. 2000. Defining and Characterizing the Low-Wage Labor Market. In Kelleen Kaye and Demetra Smith Nightingale, eds., *The Low-Wage Labor Market: Challenges and Opportunities for Economic Self-Sufficiency*. Washington, DC: U.S. Department of Health and Human Services and Urban Institute.

Bertrand, Marianne, and Sendhil Mullainathan. 2001. Do People Mean What They Say? Implications for Subjective Survey Data. *American Economic Review* 91(2): 67–72.

———. 2004. Are Emily and Greg More Employable than Lakisha and Jamal? A Field Experiment on Labor Market Discrimination. *American Economic Review* 94(4): 991–1013.

Besley, Timothy. 1995. Savings, Credit and Insurance. In Jere Behrman and T. N. Srinivasan, eds., *Handbook of Development Economics*. Volume 3. Amsterdam: North-Holland.

Binder, Melissa, and Christopher Woodruff. 2002. Inequality and Intergenerational Mobility in Schooling: The Case of Mexico. *Economic Development and Cultural Change* 50(2) January: 249–67.

Binswanger, Hans P. 1980. Attitudes toward Risk: Experimental Measurement in Rural India. *American Journal of Agricultural Economics* 62(3) August: 395–407.

Bird, Richard M. 2003. *Taxation in Latin America: Reflections on Sustainability and the Balance between Equity and Efficiency*. ITP Paper no. 0306. International Tax Program, Institute for International Business, Joseph L. Rotman School of Management, University of Toronto, Toronto.

Birdsall, Nancy, and Rachel Menezes. 2004. Toward a New Social Contract in Latin America. *Policy Brief* [Center for Global Development and Inter-American Dialogue] 3(2) January: 1–8.

Birdsall, Nancy, and John Nellis. 2002. *Winners and Losers: Assessing the Distributional Impact of Privatization*. Working Paper no. 6. Center for Global Development, Washington, DC.

Blanden, Jo, Paul Gregg, and Stephen Machin. 2005. Intergenerational Mobility in Europe and North America. Report. Centre for Economic Performance, London School of Economics, London. Available at http://cep.lse.ac.uk/about/news/Intergenerational Mobility.pdf.

Blázquez Cuesta, Maite, and Wiemer Salverda. 2006. *Low Pay Incidence and Mobility in the Netherlands—Exploring the Role of Personal, Job and Employer Characteristics*. Working Paper no. 04/06. Amsterdam Institute for Advanced Labour Studies, University of Amsterdam, Amsterdam.

Blomberg, S. Brock, Jeffry Frieden, and Ernesto Stein. 2005. Sustaining Fixed Rates: The Political Economy of Currency Pegs in Latin America. *Journal of Applied Economics* 8(2) November: 203–25.

Bohnet, Iris, and Richard Zeckhauser. 2004. Trust, Risk and Betrayal. *Journal of Economic Behavior & Organization* 55(4) December: 467–84.

Borgarello, Andrea, Suzanne Duryea, Analía Olgiati, and Stefano Scarpetta. 2006. Informal Jobs for Youth: Stepping Stones or Traps? Unpublished.

Borja-Vega, Christian, and Trine Lunde. 2007. Economic Opportunities for Indigenous People in Ecuador. In *Conference Edition: Economic Opportunities for Indigenous Peoples in Latin America*. Washington, DC: World Bank.

Borja-Vega, Christian, Trine Lunde, and Vicente García-Moreno. 2007. Economic Opportunities for Indigenous People in Mexico. In *Conference Edition: Economic Opportunities for Indigenous Peoples in Latin America*. Washington, DC: World Bank.

Bossen, Laurel. 1982. Plantations and Labor Force Discrimination in Guatemala. *Current Anthropology* 23(3): 263–68.

Boston, Thomas D. 2006. Supplier Diversity in the U.S.: A Review of Good Practices. In Claire Nelson and Stacy Richards-Kennedy, eds., *Advancing Equity in Latin America: Putting Policy into Practice*. Washington, DC: IDB.

Boucher, Stephen, Bradford Barham, and Michael Carter. 2007. Are Land Titles the Constraint to Enhance Agricultural Performance? Unpublished.

Bouillón, César, and Mayra Buvinić. 2003. Inequality, Exclusion and Poverty in Latin America and the Caribbean: Implications for Development. Paper presented at the EC/IDB seminar, Social Cohesion in Latin America and the Caribbean, June 5–6, Brussels.

Bourguignon, François, Francisco H. G. Ferreira, and Marta Menéndez. 2003. *Inequality of Outcomes and Inequality of Opportunities in Brazil*. Policy Research Working Paper no. 3174. World Bank, Washington, DC.

Bravo, David, Claudia Sanhueza, and Sergio Urzúa. 2006a. An Experimental Study about Labor Market Discrimination: Gender, Social Class and Neighborhood. Departamento de Economía, Universidad de Chile, Santiago. Unpublished.

———. 2006b. Is There Labor Market Discrimination among Professionals in Chile? Lawyers, Doctors and Business-People. Departamento de Economía, Universidad de Chile, Santiago. Unpublished.

Brown, J. David, John S. Earle, and Almos Telegdy. 2005. *The Productivity Effects of Privatization: Longitudinal Estimates from Hungary, Romania, Russia, and Ukraine*. Working Paper no. 05-121. Upjohn Institute for Employment Research, Kalamazoo, MI.

Brown, J. David, John S. Earle, and Vladimir Vakhitov. 2006. *Wages, Layoffs, and Privatization: Evidence from Ukraine*. CERT Discussion Paper no. 601. Centre for Economic Reform and Transformation, School of Management and Languages, Heriot-Watt University, Edinburgh, Scotland.

Bull, Benedicte. 2006. Social Movements, Political Representation, and Social Inclusion: Experiences from Norway and Latin America. Paper presented at the Workshop for the 2008 Report on Economic and Social Progress in Latin America, June, Washington, DC.

Burchardt, Tania, Julian Le Grand, and David Piachaud. 2002. Introduction. In John Hills, Julian Le Grand, and David Piachaud, eds., *Understanding Social Exclusion*. Oxford, England: Oxford University Press.

Burton, Michael, Richard Gunther, and John Higley. 1992. Introduction: Elite Transformations and Democratic Regimes. In John Higley and Richard Gunther, eds., *Elites and Democratic Consolidation in Latin America and Southern Europe*. Cambridge, England: Cambridge University Press.

Busso, Matías, Martín Cicowiez, and Leonardo Gasparini. 2005. Ethnicity and the Millennium Development Goals in Latin America and the Caribbean. CEDLAS Working Paper no. 27. Universidad Nacional de La Plata, La Plata, Argentina.

Buvinić, Mayra. 2004. Introduction: Social Inclusion in Latin America. In Mayra Buvinić and Jacqueline Mazza, with Ruthanne Deutsch, eds., *Social Inclusion and Economic Development in Latin America*. Washington, DC: IDB.

Buvinić, Mayra, and Jacqueline Mazza. 2005. Gender and Social Inclusion: Social Policy Perspectives from Latin America and the Caribbean. Paper presented at the World Bank conference, New Frontiers of Social Policy: Development in a Globalizing World, December 12–15, Arusha, Tanzania.

Buvinić, Mayra, and Jacqueline Mazza, with Ruthanne Deutsch, eds. 2004. *Social Inclusion and Economic Development in Latin America*. Washington, DC: IDB.

Buvinić, Mayra, Andrew Morrison, and María Beatriz Orlando. 2002. Violencia, crimen y desarrollo social en América Latina y el Caribe. In Carlos Sojo, ed., *Desarrollo social en América Latina: temas y desafíos para las políticas públicas*. San José, Costa Rica: FLACSO.

Buvinić, Mayra, and Vivian Roza. 2004. *Women, Politics and Democratic Prospects in Latin America*. Technical Paper no. WID-108. Sustainable Development Department, Inter-American Development Bank, Washington, DC.

Cacopardo, María Cristina, and Alicia M. Maguid. 2001. Argentina: International Migrants and Gender Inequality in the Labour Market. Paper presented at the 24th General Population Conference, August 18–24, Salvador, Brazil.

Caldeira, Teresa P. R. 2000. *City of Walls: Crime, Segregation, and Citizenship in São Paulo*. Berkeley, CA: University of California Press.

Caldeira, Teresa P. R., and James Holston. 1999. Democracy and Violence in Brazil. *Comparative Studies in Society and History* 41(4) October: 691–729.

Campante, Filipe R., Anna R. V. Crespo, and Phillippe G. Leite. 2004. Desigualdade salarial entre raças no mercado de trabalho urbano brasileiro: aspectos regionais. *Revista Brasileira de Economia* [Graduate School of Economics, Getulio Vargas Foundation (Brazil)] 58(2) April–June: 185–210.

Candelo, Natalia, and Sandra Polanía. 2007. Methodological Steps of an Experimental Design for Measuring Social Capital and Collective Action in Six Latin American Cities. Research Department, Inter-American Development Bank, Washington, DC. Unpublished.

Cappelletti, Mauro, and Bryant Garth. 1996. *El acceso a la justicia: la tendencia en el movimiento mundial para hacer efectivos los derechos.* Mexico City: Fondo de Cultura Económica.

Cárdenas, Juan-Camilo. 2003. Real Wealth and Experimental Cooperation: Experiments in the Field Lab. *Journal of Development Economics* 70(2) April: 263–89.

Cárdenas, Juan-Camilo, Natalia Candelo, Alejandro Gaviria, Sandra Polanía, and Rajiv Sethi. 2006. Discrimination in the Provision of Social Services to the Poor: A Field Experimental Study. Centro de Estudios sobre Desarrollo Económico (CEDE), Universidad de los Andes, Bogotá. Unpublished.

Cárdenas, Juan-Camilo, Alberto Chong, and Hugo Ñopo. 2007. *Basic Experimental Results Measuring Trust, Trustworthiness and Prosociality in Six Latin American Cities.* Working Paper. Research Department, Inter-American Development Bank, Washington, DC. Forthcoming.

Cárdenas, Juan-Camilo, and Elinor Ostrom. 2006. How Norms Help Reduce the Tragedy of the Commons: A Multi-Layer Framework for Analyzing Field Experiments. In John N. Drobak, ed., *Norms and the Law.* New York: Cambridge University Press.

Cardoso, Eliana, and Ann Helwege. 1991. Populism, Profligacy, and Redistribution. In Rudiger Dornbusch and Sebastian Edwards, eds., *The Macroeconomics of Populism in Latin America.* Chicago: University of Chicago Press.

Carnevale, Anthony P., and Stephen J. Rose. 2001. Low Earners: Who Are They? Do They Have a Way Out? In Richard Kazis and Marc S. Miller, eds., *Low-Wage Workers in the New Economy.* Washington, DC: Urban Institute Press.

Carpenter, Jeffrey P., and Juan-Camilo Cárdenas. Forthcoming. Behavioural Development Economics: Lessons from Field Labs in the Developing World. *Journal of Development Studies.*

Carpenter, Jeffrey P., Glenn W. Harrison, and John A. List, eds. 2005. *Field Experiments in Economics.* Research in Experimental Economics. Volume 10. Greenwich, CT: JAI Press.

Carr, Marilyn, and Martha Chen. 2004. *Globalization, Social Exclusion and Work: With Special Reference to Informal Employment and Gender.* Working Paper no. 20. Policy Integration Department, World Commission on the Social Dimension of Globalization, International Labour Office, Geneva.

Carrillo-Flórez, Fernando. 2007. La falta de acceso a la justicia como factor de exclusión social. Office in Europe, Inter-American Development Bank, Paris. Unpublished.

Carter, Miguel. 2003. *The Origins of Brazil's Landless Rural Workers' Movement (MST): The Natalino Episode in Rio Grande do Sul (1981–84). A Case of Ideal Interest Mobilization.* Working Paper CBS-43-2003. University of Oxford Centre for Brazilian Studies, Oxford, England.

Cass, Noel, Elizabeth Shove, and John Urry. 2005. Social Exclusion, Mobility and Access. *Sociological Review* 53(3): 539–55.

Castañeda, Tarsicio, and Kathy Lindert. 2005. *Designing and Implementing Household Targeting Systems: Lessons from Latin America and the United States.* Social Protection Discussion Paper no. 526. World Bank, Washington, DC.

Castillo, Marco, and Ragan Petrie. 2005. Discrimination in the Warplace: Evidence from a Civil War in Peru. Unpublished.

Castillo, Marco, Ragan Petrie, and Máximo Torero. 2007. Ethnic and Social Barriers to Cooperation: Experiments Studying the Extent and Nature of Discrimination in Urban Peru. Georgia Institute of Technology, Georgia State University, International Food Policy Research Institute (IFPRI), and Grupo de Análisis para el Desar-rollo (GRADE). Unpublished.

Cely, Nathalie. 2005. Evaluación y monitoreo del proceso de focalización de los beneficiarios del Bono de Desarrollo Humano. Unpublished.

CERD (Committee on the Elimination of Racial Discrimination). 2003. Reports Submitted by States Parties under Article 9 of the Convention: Seventeenth Periodic Reports of States Parties Due in 2002. CERD/C/431/Add.8. United Nations, International Convention on the Elimination of All Forms of Racial Discrimination, October 16.

Cetrángolo, Oscar, and Juan Carlos Gómez Sabaini, eds. 2006. *Tributación en América Latina. En busca de una nueva agenda de reformas.* Santiago: ECLAC.

Cézar Nunes, Juliana. 2007. Coordenação Nacional de Quilombos pede inclusão de mais estados no Bolsa Família. Agência Brasil, February 18. Available at http://www.agenciabrasil.gov.br/noticias/2007/02/18/materia.2007-02-18.1250341094/view.

Chadwick, Laura, and Gary Solon. 2002. Intergenerational Income Mobility among Daughters. *American Economic Review* 92(1) March: 335–44.

Chong, Alberto, Virgilio Galdo, and Máximo Torero. 2005. *Does Privatization Deliver? Access to Telephone Services and Household Income in Poor Rural Areas Using a Quasi-Natural Experiment in Peru.* Research Department Working Paper no. 535. Inter-American Development Bank, Washington, DC.

Chong, Alberto, and Gianmarco León. 2007. *Privatized Firms, Rule of Law and Labor Outcomes in Emerging Markets.* Research Department Working Paper no. 608. Inter-American Development Bank, Washington, DC.

Chong, Alberto, and Florencio López-de-Silanes. 2005a. Privatization and Labor Policies in Latin America. Inter-American Development Bank. Unpublished.

Chong, Alberto, and Florencio López-de-Silanes, eds. 2005b. *Privatization in Latin America: Myths and Reality.* Palo Alto, CA: Stanford University Press and Washington, DC: World Bank.

Chong, Alberto, Florencio López-de-Silanes, and Máximo Torero. 2007. Back to Reality: What Happens with Workers after Privatization? Inter-American Development Bank, Washington, DC. Unpublished.

Clark, Ximena, Timothy J. Hatton, and Jeffrey G. Williamson. 2003. *What Explains Cross-Border Migration in Latin America?* Discussion Paper no. 2012. Harvard Institute of Economic Research, Cambridge, MA.

CNN (Cable News Network). 2000. Hostage-Taker Shot as Rio Bus Siege Ends. CNN.com, 12 June 2000. Available at http://archives.cnn.com/2000/WORLD/americas/06/12/brazil.hostages/index.html.

Coba, Elena. 2005. *Los pueblos indígenas de Panamá: diagnóstico sociodemográfico a partir del censo del 2000.* Project Document no. 20. Economic Commission for Latin America and the Caribbean (ECLAC), Santiago.

Cohen, Mark A., and Mauricio Rubio. 2007. Solutions Paper: Violence and Crime in Latin America. Paper presented at Consulta de San José, cosponsored by the Copenhagen Consensus Center and the Inter-American Development Bank, October 22–26, San José, Costa Rica.

CONAPRED (Consejo Nacional para Prevenir la Discriminación). 2003. Ley Federal para Prevenir y Eliminar la Discriminación. Capitulo III: Medidas positivas y compensatorias a favor de la igualdad de oportunidades. *Diario Oficial de la Federación* no. 8, 11 June. Mexico City. Available at http://www.conapred.org.mx/index.php.

CONATEL (Consejo Nacional de Telecomunicaciones). 2006. Libro blanco de la Sociedad de la Información. Quito, Ecuador. Unpublished. Available at http://www.conatel. gov.ec/website/conectividad/sociedad/libro_blanco/gobierno_electronico.doc.

Concha-Eastman, Alberto. 2002. Urban Violence in Latin America and the Caribbean: Dimensions, Explanations, Actions. In Susana Rotker, ed., *Citizens of Fear: Urban Violence in Latin America*. New Brunswick, NJ: Rutgers University Press.

Consejo de Seguridad. 2006. Balance de convivencia y seguridad ciudadana: año 2006. Sistema Unificado de Información de Violencia y Delincuencia (SUIVD), Bogotá. Available at http://www.suivd.gov.co/estadisticas/sitio_estadisticas/consejosSe guridad/Balance2006_archivos/frame.htm.

Contreras, Dante, Diana Kruger, and Daniela Zapata. 2007. Economic Opportunities for Indigenous People in Bolivia. In *Conference Edition: Economic Opportunities for Indigenous Peoples in Latin America*. Washington, DC: World Bank.

Contreras, Dante, Jaime Ruiz-Tagle, Paz Garcés, and Irene Azócar. 2006. Socio-Economic Impact of Disability in Latin America: Chile and Uruguay. Departamento de Economía, Universidad de Chile. Unpublished.

Copestake, James, Peter Dawson, J. P. Fanning, Andrew McKay, and Katie Wright-Revolledo. 2005. Monitoring the Diversity of the Poverty Outreach and Impact of Microfinance: A Comparison of Methods Using Data from Peru. *Development Policy Review* 23(6) November: 703–23.

Corak, Miles. 2006. *Do Poor Children Become Poor Adults? Lessons from a Cross Country Comparison of Generational Earnings Mobility*. IZA Discussion Paper no. 1993. Institute for the Study of Labor (IZA), Bonn, Germany.

Corcoran, Mary, and Greg J. Duncan. 1979. Work History, Labor Force Attachment, and Earnings Differences between Races and Sexes. *Journal of Human Resources* 14(1) Winter: 3–20.

Cueto, Santiago, and Walter Secada. 2004. Oportunidades de aprendizaje y rendimiento en matemática de niños y niñas Aimara, Quechua y Castellano hablantes en escuelas bilingües y monolingües en Puno, Perú. In Donald R. Winkler and Santiago Cueto, eds., *Etnicidad, raza, género y educación en América Latina*. Washington and Santiago: PREAL.

Dade, Carlo, and Aleisha Arnusch. 2006. Afro-Latinos, Canada and Poverty in the Americas. Background paper. Canadian Foundation for the Americas (FOCAL), Ottawa.

Dahan, Momi, and Alejandro Gaviria. 2001. Sibling Correlations and Intergenerational Mobility in Latin America. *Economic Development and Cultural Change* 49(3) April: 537–54.

Daude, Christian, Jacqueline Mazza, and Andrew Morrison. 2003. Core Labor Standards and Foreign Direct Investment in Latin America and the Caribbean: Does Lax Enforcement of Labor Standards Attract Investors? Sustainable Development Department, Inter-American Development Bank, Washington, DC. Unpublished.

Daughters, Robert, and Leslie Harper. 2007. Fiscal and Political Decentralization Reforms. In Eduardo Lora, ed., *The State of State Reform in Latin America*. Washington, DC: Inter-American Development Bank and World Bank, and Palo Alto, CA: Stanford University Press.

DAW (United Nations Division for the Advancement of Women). 2004. The Role of National Mechanisms in Promoting Gender Equality and the Empowerment of Women. Report of the Expert Group Meeting, November 29–December 2, Rome.

Dawes, Robyn M., and Richard H. Thaler. 1988. Anomalies: Cooperation. *Journal of Economic Perspectives* 2(3) Summer: 187–97.

de Ferranti, David, Guillermo E. Perry, Francisco H. G. Ferreira, and Michael Walton. 2004. *Inequality in Latin America: Breaking with History?* Washington, DC: World Bank.

de Janvry, Alain, Frederico Finan, and Elisabeth Sadoulet. 2005. *Using a Structural Model of Educational Choice to Improve Program Efficiency*. Working Paper. University of California, Berkeley, CA.

de la Brière, Bénédicte, and Kathy Lindert. 2005. *Reforming Brazil's Cadastro Único to Improve the Targeting of the Bolsa Família Program*. Social Protection Discussion Paper no. 527. World Bank, Washington, DC.

de Soto, Hernando. 2000. *The Mystery of Capital: Why Capitalism Triumphs in the West and Fails Everywhere Else*. New York: Basic Books.

Deaton, Angus. 1992. *Understanding Consumption*. Oxford, England: Oxford University Press.

della Porta, Donatella, and Mario Diani. 1999. *Social Movements: An Introduction*. Oxford, England, and Malden, MA: Blackwell Publishers Ltd.

DEMUS [Estudio para la Defensa y los Derechos de la Mujer]. 2005. National Survey on Exclusion and Social Discrimination. Lima. Available at http://www.pucp.edu.pe/ridei/b_virtual/archivos/Encuesta_discriminacion.pdf.

DeShazo, Peter, and Juan Enrique Vargas. 2006. *Judicial Reform in Latin America: An Assessment*. Policy Papers on the Americas, Vol. 17, Study 2. Center for Strategic and International Studies (CSIS), Washington, DC.

Deutsch, Ruthanne, Andrew Morrison, Claudia Piras, and Hugo Ñopo. 2004. Working within Confines: Occupational Segregation by Gender in Costa Rica, Ecuador, and Uruguay. In Claudia Piras, ed., *Women at Work: Challenges for Latin America*. Washington, DC: Inter-American Development Bank.

DGEEC (Dirección General de Estadística, Encuestas y Censos). 2004. *Paraguay. Resultados finales. Censo Nacional de Población y Viviendas. Año 2002 – total país*. Asunción: DGEEC.

Dowdney, Luke. 2005. Neither War nor Peace: International Comparisons of Children and Youth in Organised Armed Violence. Report. COAV Program. Available at http://www.coav.org.br/publique/media/NewAll.pdf.

Dudzik, Pamela, Ann Elwan, and Robert Metts. 2002. *Disability Policies, Statistics, and Strategies in Latin America and the Caribbean: A Review*. SDS Working Paper. Inter-American Development Bank, Washington, DC.

Dunn, Christopher. 2003. Intergenerational Earnings Mobility in Brazil and Its Determinants. University of Michigan, Ann Arbor, MI. Unpublished.

———. 2004. Intergenerational Transmission of Lifetime Earnings: New Evidence from Brazil. Paper presented at the international colloquium at Cornell University, 75 Years of Development Research, May 9, Ithaca, NY.

Duryea, Suzanne, and María Eugenia Genoni. 2004. Ethnicity, Race and Gender in Latin American Labor Markets. In Mayra Buvinić and Jacqueline Mazza, with Ruthanne Deutsch, eds., *Social Inclusion and Economic Development in Latin America*. Washington, DC: IDB.

Duryea, Suzanne, Amanda Glassman, and Leslie Stone. 2007. Designing Social Programs: Conditional Cash Programs and Underdocumentation. Unpublished.

Duryea, Suzanne, Gustavo Márquez, Carmen Pagés, and Stefano Scarpetta. 2006. For Better or For Worse? Job and Earnings Mobility in Nine Middle- and Low-Income Countries. In Susan M. Collins and Carol Graham, eds., *Brookings Trade Forum 2006: Global Labor Markets*. Washington, DC: Brookings Institution Press.

Duryea, Suzanne, Analía Olgiati, and Leslie Stone. 2006. *The Under-Registration of Births in Latin America*. Research Department Working Paper no. 551. Inter-American Development Bank, Washington, DC.

———. 2007. Underregistration in Latin America: Prevalence and Patterns of Invisibility. Unpublished.

Duryea, Suzanne, and Carmen Pagés. 2003. Human Capital Policies: What They Can and Cannot Do for Productivity and Poverty Reduction in Latin America. In Ana Margheritis, ed., *Latin American Democracies in the New Global Economy*. Coral Gables, FL: North-South Center Press, and Boulder, CO: Lynne Rienner.

Duryea, Suzanne, and Ernesto Schargrodsky. 2006. The Optimal Payment of Welfare Programs: Cash vs. ATM Cards. Inter-American Development Bank, Washington, DC. Unpublished.

———. 2007. Financial Services for the Poor: Welfare, Savings and Consumption. Inter-American Development Bank, Washington, DC. Unpublished.

Echebarría, Koldo, and Juan Carlos Cortázar. 2007. Public Administration and Public Employment Reform in Latin America. In Eduardo Lora, ed., *The State of State Reform in Latin America*. Washington, DC: Inter-American Development Bank and World Bank, and Palo Alto, CA: Stanford University Press.

ECLAC (United Nations Economic Commission for Latin America and the Caribbean). 2000. El desafío de la equidad de género y de los derechos humanos en los albores del siglo XXI. Paper presented at the Eighth Regional Conference on Women in Latin America and the Caribbean, February 8–10, Lima.

———. 2004. Roads towards Gender Equity in Latin America and the Caribbean. Paper presented at the Ninth Regional Conference on Women, June 10–12, Mexico City.

———. 2006a. *Social Panorama of Latin America 2005*. Santiago: ECLAC.

———. 2006b. *Social Panorama of Latin America 2006*. Santiago: ECLAC.

———. 2007. *Cohesión social: inclusión y sentido de pertenencia en América Latina y el Caribe*. Santiago: ECLAC.

Edwards, Sebastian. 1995. *Crisis and Reform in Latin America: From Despair to Hope*. Washington, DC: World Bank.

Edwards, Sebastian, and Guido Tabellini. 1991. *The Political Economy of Fiscal Policy and Inflation in Developing Countries: An Empirical Analysis*. Policy, Research, and External Affairs Working Paper no. 703. World Bank, Washington, DC.

Elías, Julio, Víctor Elías, and Lucas Ronconi. 2007. Determinants of Popularity among Adolescents in Argentina. The State University of New York at Buffalo, Universidad Nacional de Tucumán, San Miguel de Tucumán, Argentina, and University of California at Berkeley. Unpublished.

Elster, Jon. 1985. *Making Sense of Marx*. Cambridge, England: Cambridge University Press.

Elwan, Ann. 1999. *Poverty and Disability. A Survey of the Literature*. Social Protection Discussion Paper no. 9932. World Bank, Washington, DC.

Engel Aduan, Wanda. 2006. Políticas integrales de reducción de la pobreza: el desafío de la efectividad. In Wanda Engel and Carlos Eduardo Vélez, eds., *Políticas efectivas para erradicar la pobreza: desafíos institucionales, de diseño y de monitoreo*. Washington, DC: IDB.

ESA Consultores. 2005. Consideraciones de raza en los Objetivos de Desarrollo del Milenio: el caso de Honduras. Tegucigalpa.

Escobal, Javier, and Carmen Ponce. 2007. Economic Opportunities for Indigenous People in Rural and Urban Peru. In *Conference Edition: Economic Opportunities for Indigenous Peoples in Latin America*. Washington, DC: World Bank.

Escobal, Javier, Jaime Saavedra, and Máximo Torero. 1998. *Los activos de los pobres en el Perú*. Working Paper no. 26. Grupo de Análisis para el Desarrollo (GRADE), Lima.

Espinosa, Isolda. 2005a. *Las Metas del Milenio y la igualdad de género. El caso de Guatemala*. Serie mujer y desarrollo no. 74. United Nations Economic Commission for Latin America and the Caribbean (ECLAC), Santiago.

————. 2005b. *Las Metas del Milenio y la igualdad de género. El caso de Nicaragua*. Serie mujer y desarrollo no. 68. United Nations Economic Commission for Latin America and the Caribbean (ECLAC), Santiago.

European Commission. 2007. Discrimination in the European Union. Summary. *Special Eurobarometer* [TNS Opinion & Social] no. 263/Wave 65.4 (January): 1–36.

Fajnzylber, Pablo, Daniel Lederman, and Norman Loayza. 1998. Determinants of Crime Rates in Latin America and the World: An Empirical Assessment. World Bank, Washington, DC. Available at http://www.worldbank.org/research/conflict/papers/fajnzy.pdf.

Farah, Ivonne, and Carmen Sánchez. 2003. *Bolivia: An Assessment of the International Labour Migration Situation: The Case of Female Labour Migrants*. GENPROM Working Paper no. 1. Gender Promotion Programme, International Labour Organization, Geneva.

Fazio, Maria Victoria. 2007. Economic Opportunities for Indigenous Peoples in Guatemala. In *Conference Edition: Economic Opportunities for Indigenous Peoples in Latin America*. Washington, DC: World Bank.

Ferreira, Francisco H. G., Phillippe G. Leite, and Matthew Wai-Poi. 2007. Trade Liberalization, Employment Flows and Wage Inequality in Brazil. Policy Research Working Paper no. 4108. World Bank, Washington, DC.

Ferreira, Sergio G., and Fernando A. Veloso. 2004. Intergenerational Mobility of Wages in Brazil. Unpublished.

Fields, Gary S. 2000. Income Mobility: Concepts and Measures. In Nancy Birdsall and Carol Graham, eds., *New Markets, New Opportunities? Economic and Social Mobility in a Changing World*. Washington, DC: Carnegie Endowment for International Peace and Brookings Institution Press.

Fields, Gary S., María Laura Sánchez Puerta, Robert Duval Hernández, and Samuel Freije. 2005. Earnings Mobility in Argentina, Mexico, and Venezuela: Testing the Divergence of Earnings and the Symmetry of Mobility Hypotheses. Cornell University, Ithaca, NY. Unpublished.

Figueroa, Adolfo. 2006. *El problema del empleo en una sociedad sigma*. PUCP Working Paper no. 249. Pontificia Universidad Católica del Perú, Lima.

Figueroa, Adolfo, and Manuel Barrón. 2005. *Inequality, Ethnicity and Social Disorder in Peru*. CRISE Working Paper no. 8. Centre for Research on Inequality, Human Security and Ethnicity (CRISE), University of Oxford, Oxford, UK.

Filmer, Deon. 2005. *Disability, Poverty and Schooling in Developing Countries: Results from 11 Household Surveys*. Social Protection Discussion Paper no. 0539. World Bank, Washington, DC.

Finan, Frederico, Elisabeth Sadoulet, and Alain de Janvry. 2005. Measuring the Poverty Reduction Potential of Land in Rural Mexico. *Journal of Development Economics* 77(1): 27–51.

Fleisig, Heywood, Mehnaz Safavian, and Nuria de la Peña. 2006. *Reforming Collateral Laws to Expand Access to Finance*. Washington, DC: World Bank.

Flores Lima, Roberto. 2007. El Servicio de Intermediación Laboral como instrumento de inserción en el mercado laboral en México. Study. Fondo Enlace de Inclusión Social, Inter-American Development Bank, Washington, DC.

Fortin, Nicole M., and Sophie Lefebvre. 1998. Intergenerational Income Mobility in Canada. In Miles Corak, ed., *Labour Markets, Social Institutions, and the Future of Canada's Children*. Ottawa: Statistics Canada.

Franzese, Jr., Robert J. 2002. *Macroeconomic Policies in Developed Democracies*. Cambridge, England: Cambridge University Press.

Frieden, Jeffry. 1991. *Debt, Development and Democracy: Modern Political Economy and Latin America, 1965–1985*. Princeton, NJ: Princeton University Press.

Frieden, Jeffry, Piero Ghezzi, and Ernesto Stein. 2000. *Politics and Exchange Rates in Latin America*. Research Network Working Paper no. R-421. Research Department, Inter-American Development Bank, Washington, DC.

Friedman, Milton. 1962. *Capitalism and Freedom*. Chicago: University of Chicago Press.

Fukuyama, Francis. 1995. *Trust: The Social Virtues and the Creation of Prosperity*. New York: Free Press.

Fundación Mexicana para la Salud and Centro de Economía y Salud. 1998. *Análisis de la magnitud y costos de la violencia en la Ciudad de México*. Working Paper no. R-331. Inter-American Development Bank, Washington, DC.

Gacitúa Marió, Estanislao, and Michael Woolcock, eds. 2005a. *Exclusão social e mobilidade no Brasil*. Brasília: IPEA and Washington, DC: World Bank.

Gacitúa Marió, Estanislao, and Michael Woolcock, with Marisa von Bulow. 2005b. Assessing Social Exclusion and Mobility in Brazil. Unpublished. Translation of Chapter 1 in Estanislao Gacitúa-Marió and Michael Woolcock, eds., *Exclusão social e mobilidade no Brasil*. Brasília and Washington, DC: IPEA/World Bank.

Galasso, Emanuela. 2007. "With Their Effort and One Opportunity": Alleviating Extreme Poverty in Chile. PowerPoint presentation given at the IDB seminar, Policy Seminar with Emanuela Galasso: Evaluation Results of Chile Solidario: With Their Effort and One Opportunity, February 20, Washington, DC. Available at http://www.iadb.org/res/pub_desc.cfm?pub_id=P-865.

Galiani, Sebastián. 2006. Notes on Social Mobility. Universidad de San Andrés, Argentina. Unpublished.

Galiani, Sebastián, Paul Gertler, and Ernesto Schargrodsky. 2005. Water for Life: The Impact of the Privatization of Water Services on Child Mortality. *Journal of Political Economy* 113(1): 83–120.

Galiani, Sebastián, Martín González-Rozada, and Ernesto Schargrodsky. 2007. *Water Expansions in Shantytowns: Health and Savings*. Research Network Working Paper no. R-527. Inter-American Development Bank, Washington, DC.

Galiani, Sebastián, and Ernesto Schargrodsky. 2005. Property Rights for the Poor: Effects of Land Titling. Universidad Torcuato Di Tella, Buenos Aires. Unpublished.

Galiani, Sebastián, and Federico Sturzenegger. 2005. The Impact of Privatization on the Earnings of Restructured Workers: Evidence from the Oil Industry. Forthcoming in *Journal of Labor Research*.

Galindo, Arturo, Alejandro Micco, and Ugo Panizza. 2007. Two Decades of Financial Reforms. In Eduardo Lora, ed., *The State of State Reform in Latin America*. Washington, DC: Inter-American Development Bank and World Bank, and Palo Alto, CA: Stanford University Press.

Galindo, Arturo, and Margaret Miller. 2001. Can Credit Registries Reduce Credit Constraints? Empirical Evidence on the Role of Credit Registries in Firm Investment Decisions. Paper presented at the Inter-American Development Bank Annual Meeting seminar, Towards Competitiveness: The Institutional Path, March 16, Santiago, Chile.

Gamson, William A. 1975. *The Strategy of Social Protest*. Belmont, CA: Wadsworth Publishing Co.

Gandelman, Eduardo, Néstor Gandelman, and Julie Rothschild. 2007. *Gender Differentials in Judicial Proceedings: Field Evidence from Housing-Related Cases in Uruguay*. Working Paper. Universidad ORT Uruguay, Montevideo.

Gandelman, Néstor. 2006. Selection Biases in Sports Markets. Universidad ORT Uruguay, Montevideo. Unpublished.

———. 2007. The Impact of House Titling: Evidence from a Natural Experiment in Uruguay. PowerPoint presentation given at the Inter-American Development Bank seminar, Titling in Latin America: Effects and Channels, March 30, Washington, DC.

Garay, Luis Jorge. 1998. Presentación. In Luis Jorge Garay, ed., *Tomo II – La industria de América Latina ante la globalización: Argentina, Brasil, México, Venezuela: apertura y reestructuración productiva*. Bogotá: Departamento Nacional de Planeación, Colciencias, Consejería Económica y de Competitividad, Ministerio de Comercio Exterior, Ministerio de Hacienda y Crédito Público, and Proexport.

García-Aracil, Adela, and Carolyn Winter. 2006. Gender and Ethnicity Differentials in School Attainment and Labor Market Earnings in Ecuador. *World Development* 34(2) February: 289–307.

Gaviria, Alejandro. 2001. Raza y discriminación en América Latina. Un análisis preliminar basado en el Latinobarómetro. Inter-American Development Bank, Washington, DC. Unpublished.

———. 2005. Movilidad social en América Latina: realidades, percepciones y consecuencias. Facultad de Economía, Universidad de los Andes, Bogotá.

———. 2006. *Movilidad social y preferencias por redistribución en América Latina*. Documentos CEDE no. 002678. Centro de Estudios sobre Desarrollo Económico (CEDE), Facultad de Economía, Universidad de los Andes, Bogotá.

Gavito Mohar, Javier. 2006. Banking the Unbanked: The Experience of Mexico's National Savings and Financial Services Bank (BANSEFI). In Luis Tejerina, César Bouillon, and Edgardo Demaestri, eds., *Financial Services and Poverty Reduction in Latin America and the Caribbean*. Washington, DC: Inter-American Development Bank.

Gill, Indermit, Truman Packard, and Juan Yermo. 2005. *Keeping the Promise of Social Security in Latin America*. Washington, DC: World Bank and Palo Alto, CA: Stanford University Press.

Giugni, Marco G. 1998. Structure and Culture in Social Movement Theory. *Sociological Forum* 13(2): 365–75.

Global Rights. 2005. Brazil: Affirmative Action in Higher Education, 2003–2004. Washington, DC: Global Rights.

Goldstein, Donna M. 2003. *Laughter Out of Place: Race, Class, Violence, and Sexuality in a Rio Shantytown*. Berkeley and Los Angeles: University of California Press.

Gonzaga, Gustavo, Naércio Menezes Filho, and Cristina Terra. 2006. Trade Liberalization and the Evolution of Skill Earnings Differentials in Brazil. *Journal of International Economics* 68(2) March: 345–67.

González, Mary Lisbeth. 2006. Más allá de los promedios: afrodescendientes en América Latina. Los afrohondureños. World Bank, Washington, DC. Unpublished.

González-Eiras, Martín, and Martín A. Rossi. 2007. *The Impact of Electricity Sector Privatization on Public Health*. Research Network Working Paper no. R-524. Inter-American Development Bank, Washington, DC.

Goodin, Robert E. 1996. Inclusion and Exclusion. *Archives européennes de sociologie* 37(2): 343–71.

Gordon, Sara. 2004. Ventajas e implicaciones de una perspectiva de desarrollo basada en los derechos. Paper presented at conference, Derechos y Desarrollo en América Latina: Una Reunión de Trabajo, December 9–10, Santiago, Chile.

Graham, Carol. 2005a. The Economics of Happiness: Insights on Globalization from a Novel Approach. *World Economics* 6(3) July–September: 41–55.

———. 2005b. Insights on Development from the Economics of Happiness. *World Bank Research Observer* 20(2) Fall: 201–31.

Graham, Carol, and Stefano Pettinato. 2001. *Happiness and Hardship: Opportunity and Insecurity in New Market Economies*. Washington, DC: Brookings Institution Press.

Grawe, Nathan D. 2001. Intergenerational Mobility in the US and Abroad: Quantile and Mean Regression Measures. Ph.D. dissertation, University of Chicago.

Guimarães, Roberta de Oliveira. 2006. Desigualdade salarial entre negros e brancos no Brasil: discriminação ou exclusão? *Econômica* [Rio de Janeiro] 8(2) December: 227–51.

Hachen, Jr., David S. 1992. Industrial Characteristics and Job Mobility Rates. *American Sociological Review* 57(1) February: 39–55.

Hall, Gillette, and Harry Patrinos. 2005. Indigenous Peoples, Poverty and Human Development in Latin America: 1994–2004. Report. World Bank, Washington, DC.

Hall, Stuart. 1990. Cultural Identity and Diaspora. In Jonathan Rutherford, ed., *Identity: Community, Culture, Difference*. London: Lawrence and Wishart.

Hanson, Gordon H., and Ann Harrison. 1999. Trade Liberalization and Wage Inequality in Mexico. *Industrial and Labor Relations Review* 52(2): 271–88.

Harrison, Glenn W., and John A. List. 2004. Field Experiments. *Journal of Economic Literature* 42(4) December: 1009–55.

Hashemi, Syed, and Richard Rosenberg. 2006. *Graduating the Poorest into Microfinance: Linking Safety Nets and Financial Services*. Focus Note no. 34. Consultative Group to Assist the Poor (CGAP), Washington, DC.

Haskel, Jonathan, and Stefan Szymanski. 1992. A Bargaining Theory of Privatisation. *Annals of Public and Cooperative Economics* 63(2) July: 207–27.

Haveman, Heather A., and Lisa E. Cohen. 1994. The Ecological Dynamics of Careers: The Impact of Organizational Founding, Dissolution, and Merger on Job Mobility. *American Journal of Sociology* 100(1) July: 104–52.

Heinemann, Alessandra, and Dorte Verner. 2006. *Crime and Violence in Development: A Literature Review of Latin America and the Caribbean*. Policy Research Working Paper no. 4041. World Bank, Washington, DC.

Hernández, Gustavo, Carolina Soto, Sergio Prada, and Juan Mauricio Ramírez. 2000. *Exenciones tributarias: costo fiscal y análisis de incidencia*. Archivos de macroeconomía no. 141. Departamento Nacional de Planeación, Bogotá.

Hernández, Roberto, and Yerina Mugica. 2003. What Works: PRODEM FFP's Multilingual Smart ATMs for Microfinance. Case Study. World Resources Institute, Washington, DC.

Hernández-Jaramillo, Janeth, and Iván Hernández-Umaña. 2005. Una aproximación a los costos indirectos de la discapacidad en Colombia. *Revista de Salud Pública* 7(2): 130–44.

Hernández-Licona, Gonzalo. 2005. *Disability and the Labor Market: Data Gaps and Needs in Latin America and the Caribbean*. SDS Working Paper. Inter-American Development Bank, Washington, DC.

Hernández-Zavala, Martha, Harry Patrinos, Chris Sakellariou, and Joseph Shapiro. 2006. *Quality of Schooling and Quality of Schools for Indigenous Students in Guatemala, Mexico and Peru*. Policy Research Working Paper no. 3982. World Bank, Washington, DC.

Holt, Charles A., and Susan K. Laury. 2002. Risk Aversion and Incentive Effects. *American Economic Review* 92(5) December: 1644–55.

Hooker, Juliet. 2005. Indigenous Inclusion/Black Exclusion: Race, Ethnicity and Multicultural Citizenship in Latin America. *Journal of Latin American Studies* 37(2) May: 285–310.

Hopenhayn, Martín, and Alvaro Bello. 2001. *Discriminación étnico-racial y xenofobia en América Latina y el Caribe*. Serie políticas sociales no. 47. United Nations Economic Commission for Latin America and the Caribbean (ECLAC), Santiago.

Htun, Mala. 2004. Lessons from Gender Quotas. In Mayra Buvinić and Jacqueline Mazza, with Ruthanne Deutsch, eds., *Social Inclusion and Economic Development in Latin America*. Washington, DC: IDB.

———. 2005. Case Study: Latin America. Women, Political Parties and Electoral Systems in Latin America. In Julie Ballington and Azza Karam, eds., *Women in Parliament: Beyond Numbers*. Revised Edition. Stockholm: International IDEA.

Hulme, David, and Paul Mosley. 1996. *Finance against Poverty*. Volume 1. London and New York: Routledge.

IAD (Inter-American Dialogue). 2004. Race Report: Constitutional Provisions and Legal Actions Related to Discrimination and Afro-Descendant Populations in Latin America. Washington, DC: IAD.

IBGE (Instituto Brasileiro de Geografia e Estatística). 2006. *Estatísticas do Registro Civil 2005*. Volume 32. Rio de Janeiro: IBGE.

IDB (Inter-American Development Bank). 1997. *Latin America after a Decade of Reforms*. Economic and Social Progress in Latin America: 1997 Report. Washington, DC: IDB.

———. 1998a. *Facing Up to Inequality in Latin America*. Economic and Social Progress in Latin America: 1998–99 Report. Washington, DC: IDB.

———. 1998b. Institucionalidad para mujer y género en América Latina y el Caribe. Regional Study. Women in Development Unit, Sustainable Development Department, Inter-American Development Bank, Washington, DC.

———. 2000. *Development beyond Economics*. Economic and Social Progress in Latin America: 2000 Report. Washington, DC: IDB.

———. 2001a. *Competitiveness: The Business of Growth*. Economic and Social Progress in Latin America: 2001 Report. Washington, DC: IDB.

———. 2001b. Summary of Proceedings: Towards a Shared Vision of Development: High Level Dialogue on Race, Ethnicity, and Inclusion in Latin America and the Caribbean, June 18, Washington, DC, and Inter-Agency Consultation on Race and Poverty in Latin America Policy Workshops, June 19, Washington, DC.

———. 2003a. *Good Jobs Wanted: Labor Markets in Latin America*. Economic and Social Progress in Latin America: 2004 Report. Washington, DC: IDB.

———. 2003b. Poverty Reduction and Promotion of Social Equity. Strategy document. IDB, Washington, DC.

———. 2004. *Unlocking Credit: The Quest for Deep and Stable Bank Lending*. Economic and Social Progress in Latin America: 2005 Report. Washington, DC: IDB.

———. 2005. *The Politics of Policies*. Economic and Social Progress in Latin America: 2006 Report. Washington, DC: IDB.

———. 2006a. Annual Report of the Social Inclusion Trust Fund. IDB, Washington, DC.

———. 2006b. *Living with Debt: How to Limit the Risks of Sovereign Finance*. Economic and Social Progress in Latin America: 2007 Report. Washington, DC: IDB.

———. 2006c. *Operational Policy on Indigenous Peoples and Strategy for Indigenous Development*. Sector Strategy and Policy Papers Series no. IND-111. Sustainable Development Department, IDB, Washington, DC.

———. 2006d. Profile of Project EC-T1063: Improving Targeting of the Universal Health Insurance Program. Approved September 28, 2006. Available at http://www.iadb.org/projects/Project.cfm?project=EC-T1063&Language=English.

ILO (International Labour Organization). 2004. *World Employment Report 2004–2005: Employment, Productivity and Poverty Reduction*. Geneva: ILO.

INEI (Instituto Nacional de Estadística e Informática). 2006. Resultados de la Encuesta Nacional Continua – ENCO. Primer semestre 2006. Lima.

INSTRAW (United Nations International Research and Training Institute for the Advancement of Women). 2005. Institutional Mechanisms for the Advancement of Women: New Challenges. Progress Report. Available at http://www.un-instraw.org/en/images/stories/Beijing/ institutionalmechanisms.pdf.

IPEA (Instituto de Pesquisa Econômica Aplicada). 2006. Sobre a recente queda da desigualdade de renda no Brasil. Nota técnica. In Ricardo Paes de Barros, Miguel Nathan Foguel, and Gabriel Ulyssea, eds., *Desigualdade de renda no Brasil: uma análise da queda recente*. Volume 1. Brasília: IPEA.

Isaac, R. Mark, and James M. Walker. 1988. Group Size Effects in Public Goods Provision: The Voluntary Contributions Mechanism. *Quarterly Journal of Economics* 103(1) February: 179–199.

Jacinto, Claudia, Cristina García, and Alejandra Solla. 2007. Programas sociales: lógicas desencontradas, abordajes acotados. Paper presented at the Inter-American Development Bank seminar, Advancing Inclusive Policies in Latin America and the Caribbean, March 1, Washington, DC.

Jeter, J. 2003. Affirmative Action Debate Forces Brazil to Take Look in the Mirror. *Washington Post*, June 15.

Kahneman, Daniel, and Amos Tversky. 1979. Prospect Theory: An Analysis of Decision under Risk. *Econometrica* 47(2) March: 263–92.

Karl, Terry Lynn. 1990. Dilemmas of Democratization in Latin America. *Comparative Politics* 23(1) October: 1–21.

Kaufmann, Robert R., and Barbara Stallings. 1991. The Political Economy of Latin American Populism. In Rudiger Dornbusch and Sebastian Edwards, eds., *The Macroeconomics of Populism in Latin America*. Chicago: University of Chicago Press.

Kay, Cristóbal. 1995. Rural Development and Agrarian Issues in Contemporary Latin America. In John Weeks, ed., *Structural Adjustment and the Agricultural Sector in Latin America and the Caribbean*. London: Macmillan.

Ketley, Richard, Ben Davis, and Sarah Truen. 2005. An Inter-Country Survey of the Relative Costs of Bank Accounts. A Study for Finmark Trust. Genesis Analytics (Pty) Ltd., Johannesburg, South Africa.

Kim, Oliver, and Mark Walker. 1984. The Free Rider Problem: Experimental Evidence. *Public Choice* 43(1): 3–24.

Knack, Stephen, and Philip Keefer. 1997. Does Social Capital Have an Economic Payoff? A Cross-Country Investigation. *Quarterly Journal of Economics* 112(4) November: 1251–88.

Kumar, Anjali. 2005. Measuring Financial Access through Users' Surveys: Core Concepts, Questions and Indicators. Paper presented at the joint World Bank/DFID/Finmark Trust Technical Workshop, Defining Indicators of Financial Access, June 14, Washington, DC and London.

Kymlicka, Will. 1995. *Multicultural Citizenship: A Liberal Theory of Minority Rights*. Oxford: Oxford University Press.

La Porta, Rafael, and Florencio López-de-Silanes. 1999. The Benefits of Privatization: Evidence from Mexico. *Quarterly Journal of Economics* 114(4): 1193–1242.

Lam, David, and Robert F. Schoeni. 1993. Effects of Family Background on Earnings and Returns to Schooling: Evidence from Brazil. *Journal of Political Economy* 101(4): 710–40.

Larraín, Felipe, and Patricio Meller. 1991. The Socialist-Populist Chilean Experience: 1970–1973. In Rudiger Dornbusch and Sebastian Edwards, eds., *The Macroeconomics of Populism in Latin America*. Chicago: University of Chicago Press.

Latinobarometer. Various years. Latin American Public Opinion. Available at www.latino barometro.org.

Lazear, Edward P. 1996. *Performance Pay and Productivity*. NBER Working Paper no. 5672. National Bureau of Economic Research, Cambridge, MA.

Legovini, Arianna, César Bouillón, and Nora Lustig. 2005. Can Education Explain Changes in Income Inequality in Mexico? In François Bourguignon, Francisco H. G. Ferreira, and Nora Lustig, eds., *The Microeconomics of Income Distribution Dynamics in East Asia and Latin America*. Oxford, England: Oxford University Press and Washington, DC: World Bank.

Leite, Phillippe G. 2005. *Race Discrimination or Inequality of Opportunities: The Brazilian Case*. Discussion Paper no. 118. Ibero-America Institute for Economic Research (IAI), Goettingen, Germany.

Lémez, Rodolfo. 2005. La integración de las personas con discapacidad en la educación superior en el Uruguay. Report. Instituto Universitario CLAEH, Montevideo.

Lenoir, René. 1974. *Les exclus*. Paris: Seuil.

Levy, Santiago. 2006. Productividad, crecimiento y pobreza en México: ¿Qué sigue después de Progresa-Oportunidades? Inter-American Development Bank, Washington, DC. Unpublished.

Lloyd, Marion. 2004. In Brazil, a Different Approach to Affirmative Action. *Chronicle of Higher Education*, October 29.

Londoño, Juan Luis, Alejandro Gaviria, and Rodrigo Guerrero, eds. 2000. *Asalto al desarrollo: violencia en América Latina*. Washington, DC: Inter-American Development Bank.

Lora, Eduardo. 2001. *Structural Reforms in Latin America: What Has Been Reformed and How to Measure It*. Research Department Working Paper no. 466. Inter-American Development Bank, Washington, DC.

———. 2006. El futuro de los pactos fiscales en América Latina. Paper presented at the Fundación CIDOB seminar, Políticas Económicas para un Nuevo Pacto Social en América Latina, October 6–7, Barcelona, Spain.

Lora, Eduardo, ed. 2007. *The State of State Reform in Latin America*. Washington, DC: Inter-American Development Bank and World Bank, and Palo Alto, CA: Stanford University Press.

Machinea, José Luis, Alicia Bárcena, and Arturo León, coordinators. 2005. *Objetivos de Desarrollo del Milenio: una mirada desde América Latina y el Caribe*. Santiago: ECLAC/United Nations.

Machinea, José Luis, and Cecilia Vera. 2006. *Trade, Direct Investment and Production Policies*. Serie informes y estudios especiales no. 16. United Nations Economic Commission for Latin America and the Caribbean (ECLAC), Santiago.

Maloney, William F. 1999. Does Informality Imply Segmentation in Urban Labor Markets? Evidence from Sectoral Transitions in Mexico. *World Bank Economic Review* 13(2) May: 275–302.

Marconi, Nelson. 2004. Gap between Public and Private Wages and Wages Determination in the Public Sector. *Revista de Economia Política* 24(2) April–June: 257–79.

Marini, Alessandra, and Michele Gragnolati. 2003. *Malnutrition and Poverty in Guatemala.* Policy Research Working Paper no. 2967. World Bank, Washington, DC.

Márquez, Gustavo, and M. F. Prada. 2007. Bad Jobs, Low Productivity, and Exclusion. Research Department, Inter-American Development Bank, Washington, DC. Unpublished.

Márquez, Patricia C. 1999. *The Street Is My Home: Youth and Violence in Caracas.* Stanford, CA: Stanford University Press.

Marshall, Jeffery H., and Valentina Calderón. 2006. *Social Exclusion in Education in Latin America and the Caribbean.* Technical Papers Series. Sustainable Development Department, Inter-American Development Bank, Washington, DC.

Marwell, Gerald, and Ruth E. Ames. 1979. Experiments on the Provision of Public Goods. I. Resources, Interest, Group Size, and the Free-Rider Problem. *American Journal of Sociology* 84(6) May: 1335–60.

Marx, Ive, and Wiemer Salverda, eds. 2005. *Low-Wage Employment in Europe: Perspectives for Improvement.* Leuven, Belgium: ACCO.

Massiah, Ernest. 2004. Disability and Inclusion: Data Collection, Education, Transportation and Urban Development. In Mayra Buvinić and Jacqueline Mazza, with Ruthanne Deutsch, eds., *Social Inclusion and Economic Development in Latin America.* Washington, DC: IDB.

Mauro Machuca, Raúl. 2006. Partidos políticos y financiamiento político. *Economía y Bienestar* 6(10): 9–13.

Mayer-Foulkes, David. 2004. The Human Development Trap in Mexico. División de Economía, Centro de Investigación y Docencia Económicas (CIDE), Mexico City. Unpublished.

Mazza, Jacqueline. 2004. Social Inclusion, Labor Markets and Human Capital in Latin America. In Mayra Buvinić and Jacqueline Mazza, with Ruthanne Deutsch, eds., *Social Inclusion and Economic Development in Latin America.* Washington, DC: IDB.

McAdam, Doug. 1982. *Political Process and the Development of Black Insurgency, 1930–1970.* Chicago: The University of Chicago Press.

———. 1994. Culture and Social Movements. In Enrique Laraña, Hank Johnston, and Joseph R. Gusfield, eds., *New Social Movements: From Ideology to Identity.* Philadelphia: Temple University Press.

McAdam, Doug, Sidney Tarrow, and Charles Tilly. 2001. *Dynamics of Contention.* Cambridge: Cambridge University Press.

McEwan, Patrick J. 2004. La brecha de puntajes obtenidos en las pruebas por los niños indígenas en Sudamérica. In Donald R. Winkler and Santiago Cueto, eds., *Etnicidad, raza, género y educación en América Latina.* Washington and Santiago: PREAL.

McKenzie, David, and Dilip Mookherjee. 2003. The Distributive Impact of Privatization in Latin America: Evidence from Four Countries. *Economia* [Journal of the Latin American and Caribbean Economic Association] 3(2) Spring.

Melo, Alberto. 2001. *Industrial Policy in Latin America and the Caribbean at the Turn of the Century.* Research Department Working Paper no. 459. Inter-American Development Bank, Washington, DC.

Melo, Alberto, and Andrés Rodríguez-Clare. 2007. Productive Development Policies and Supporting Institutions in Latin America and the Caribbean. In Eduardo Lora, ed., *The State of State Reform in Latin America.* Washington, DC: Inter-American Development Bank and World Bank, and Palo Alto, CA: Stanford University Press.

Mesa-Lago, Carmelo, and Gustavo Márquez. 2007. Reform of Pension and Social Assistance Systems. In Eduardo Lora, ed., *The State of State Reform in Latin America.* Washington, DC: Inter-American Development Bank and World Bank, and Palo Alto, CA: Stanford University Press.

Meyer, David S. 2003. *Social Movements and Public Policy: Eggs, Chicken, and Theory.* CSD Working Paper no. 03-02. Center for the Study of Democracy, University of California, Irvine. Available at http://repositories.cdlib.org/csd/03-02.

Meyer, David S., and Nancy Whittier. 1997. Social Movement Spillover. In Doug McAdam and David A. Snow, eds., *Social Movements: Readings on Their Emergence, Mobilization, and Dynamics.* Los Angeles, CA: Roxbury Publishing Company.

Mezza, Víctor. 2004. Bolivia: características sociodemográficas de la población con discapacidad. Paper presented at the ECLAC/IDB Segunda Reunión sobre Estadísticas de Discapacidad en el Cono Sur, October 28–29, Santiago.

Microfinance Information Exchange. Profile for PRODEM Outreach Indicators for December 2006. Available at http://www.mixmarket.org/en/demand/demand.show.profile.asp?ett=149.

Mincer, Jacob. 1974. *Schooling, Experience and Earnings.* Ann Arbor, MI: ProQuest Information and Learning.

Mishel, Lawrence, Jared Bernstein, and John Schmitt. 2001. *The State of Working America 2000–2001.* Ithaca, NY: Cornell University Press.

Mitnik, Pablo A., Matthew Zeidenberg, and Laura Dresser. 2002. Can Career Ladders Really Be a Way Out of Dead-End Jobs? A Look at Job Structure and Upward Mobility in the Service Industries. Paper presented at the APPAM fall research conference, Asking "What If?"—Assessing the Public Policy and Management Implications of Social Science Research, November 7–9, Dallas, TX.

Montaño, Sonia. 2004. Los caminos hacia la igualdad: logros y desafíos. Economic Commission for Latin America and the Caribbean (ECLAC). Unpublished.

Montes, Andrés, and Ernest Massiah. 2002. *Disability Data: Survey and Methods Issues in Latin America and the Caribbean.* SDS Working Paper. Inter-American Development Bank, Washington, DC.

Moreno, Martin, Hugo Ñopo, Jaime Saavedra, and Máximo Torero. 2004. *Gender and Racial Discrimination in Hiring: A Pseudo Audit Study for Three Selected Occupations in Metropolitan Lima.* IZA Discussion Paper no. 979. Institute for the Study of Labor (IZA), Bonn, Germany.

Morris, Aldon D., and Carol McClurg Mueller, eds. 1992. *Frontiers in Social Movement Theory.* New Haven, CT: Yale University Press.

Morris, Felipe, Mark Dorfman, José Pedro Ortiz, and María Claudia Franco. 1990. *Latin America's Banking Systems in the 1980s: A Cross-Country Comparison*. World Bank Discussion Paper no. 81. World Bank, Washington, DC.

Morrison, Andrew, Mayra Buvinić, and Michael Shifter. 2003. The Violent Americas: Risk Factors, Consequences, and Policy Implications of Social and Domestic Violence. In Joseph S. Tulchin, H. Hugo Frühling, and Heather Golding, eds., *Crime and Violence in Latin America: Citizen Security, Democracy, and the State*. Washington, DC: Woodrow Wilson Center Press.

Morrison, Judith. 2006. The Changing Shape of Race and Race Relations in Latin America. In Claire Nelson and Stacy Richards-Kennedy, eds., *Advancing Equity in Latin America: Putting Policy into Practice*. Washington, DC: IDB.

Moser, Caroline, and Cathy McIlwaine. 2000. *Urban Poor Perceptions of Violence and Exclusion in Colombia*. Washington, DC: World Bank.

———. 2001. *Violence in a Post-Conflict Context: Urban Poor Perceptions from Guatemala*. Washington, DC: World Bank.

Moser, Caroline, Ailsa Winton, and Annalise Moser. 2003. Violence, Fear and Insecurity and the Urban Poor in Latin America. Paper for the World Bank Latin American and Caribbean Region Study of Urban Poverty. World Bank, Washington, DC. Unpublished.

———. 2005. Violence, Fear, and Insecurity among the Urban Poor in Latin America. In Marianne Fay, ed., *The Urban Poor in Latin America*. Washington, DC: World Bank.

Mueller, Dennis C. 2003. Interest Groups, Redistribution and the Size of Government. In Stanley L. Winer and Hirofumi Shibata, eds., *Political Economy and Public Finance*. Cheltenham, UK, and Northampton, MA: Elgar.

National Opinion Research Center. Various years. General Social Survey. Inter-University Consortium for Political and Social Research, University of Michigan, Ann Arbor. Available at http://www.icpsr.umich.edu/cocoon/ICPSR/SERIES/00028.xml.

Neumark, David. 1996. Sex Discrimination in Restaurant Hiring: An Audit Study. *Quarterly Journal of Economics* 111(3) August: 915–41.

Ñopo, Hugo. 2004. *Matching as a Tool to Decompose Wage Gaps*. IZA Discussion Paper no. 981. Institute for the Study of Labor (IZA), Bonn, Germany.

———. 2006. *The Gender Wage Gap in Chile 1992–2003 from a Matching Comparisons Perspective*. Research Department Working Paper no. 562. Inter-American Development Bank, Washington, DC.

Ñopo, Hugo, Jaime Saavedra, and Máximo Torero. 2004. *Ethnicity and Earnings in Urban Peru*. IZA Discussion Paper no. 980. Institute for the Study of Labor (IZA), Bonn, Germany.

Núñez, Javier, and Roberto Gutiérrez. 2004. *Classism, Discrimination and Meritocracy in the Labor Market: The Case of Chile*. Working Paper no. 208. Departamento de Economía, Facultad de Ciencias Económicas y Administrativas, Universidad de Chile, Santiago.

Núñez, Javier, and Leslie Miranda. 2007. *Recent Findings on Intergenerational Income and Educational Mobility in Chile*. Working Paper no. 244. Departamento de Economía, Universidad de Chile, Santiago. Available at http://econ.uchile.cl/public/Archivos/pub/75504e79-7bfc-4da9-9843-b4c3b8476f30.pdf.

Núñez, Javier, and Andrea Tartakowsky. 2006. Inequality of Outcomes vs. Inequality of Opportunities in Chile. Departamento de Economía, Universidad de Chile, Santiago. Unpublished.

Ocampo, José Antonio. 2004. Economic Development and Social Inclusion. In Mayra Buvinić and Jacqueline Mazza, with Ruthanne Deutsch, eds., *Social Inclusion and Economic Development in Latin America*. Washington, DC: IDB.

Oliver, Donald H. 2006. Integrating Visible Minority Groups in Canada. In Claire Nelson and Stacy Richards-Kennedy, eds., *Advancing Equity in Latin America: Putting Policy into Practice*. Washington, DC: IDB.

Olson, Jr., Mancur. 1965. *The Logic of Collective Action: Public Goods and the Theory of Groups*. Cambridge, MA: Harvard University Press.

Ordóñez, D., and P. Bracamonte. 2005. El registro de nacimientos: consecuencias en relación al acceso a derechos y servicios sociales y a la implementación de programas de reducción de pobreza en 5 países de Latinoamérica. Report to Technical Cooperation RG-T1082. Inter-American Development Bank, Washington, DC.

Österberg, Torun. 2000. Intergenerational Income Mobility in Sweden: What Do Tax-Data Show? *Review of Income and Wealth* 46(4) December: 421–36.

Ostrom, Elinor. 1998. A Behavioral Approach to the Rational Choice Theory of Collective Action. *American Political Science Review* 92(1) March: 1–22.

Pacari Vega, Nina. 2004. Social Inclusion and Indigenous Peoples' Rights. In Mayra Buvinić and Jacqueline Mazza, with Ruthanne Deutsch, eds., *Social Inclusion and Economic Development in Latin America*. Washington, DC: IDB.

Padilha, José, director. 2002. *Bus 174*. New York: THINKFILM, in association with HBO/CINEMAX Documentary Films.

Pagés, Carmen, Gaëlle Pierre, and Stefano Scarpetta. 2007. Job Creation in Latin America and the Caribbean: Recent Trends and the Policy Challenges. World Bank, Washington, DC. Unpublished.

Pagés, Carmen, and M. F. Prada. 2007. What Drives the Increase of Low-Wage Employment in Latin America? Research Department, Inter-American Development Bank, Washington, DC. Unpublished.

Palfrey, Thomas R., and Jeffrey E. Prisbrey. 1997. Anomalous Behavior in Public Goods Experiments: How Much and Why? *American Economic Review* 87(5) December: 829–46.

Panel on Methods for Assessing Discrimination, National Research Council. 2004. Defining Discrimination. In Rebecca Blank, Marilyn Dabady, and Constance Citro, eds., *Measuring Racial Discrimination*. Washington, DC: The National Academies Press.

Panizza, Ugo G. 1999. *Why Do Lazy People Make More Money? The Strange Case of the Public Sector Wage Premium*. Research Department Working Paper no. 403. Inter-American Development Bank, Washington, DC.

Parker, Susan W., Luis Rubalcava, and Graciela Teruel. 2005. Schooling Inequality and Language Barriers. *Economic Development and Cultural Change* 54(1): 71–94.

Patrinos, Harry. 2000. The Cost of Discrimination in Latin America. *Studies in Comparative International Development* 35(2): 3–17.

Patrinos, Harry, and Vicente García-Moreno. 2006. Salary Gaps between Indigenous and Non-Indigenous Workers in Mexico: Policy Implications. Paper presented at IBERGOP/UDLA/CIDE seminar, Políticas Públicas para Crecimiento y Desarrollo, August 28–29, Mexico City.

Patrinos, Harry, and George Psacharopoulos. 1992. *Socioeconomic and Ethnic Determinants of Grade Repetition in Bolivia and Guatemala*. Policy Research Working Paper no. 1028. World Bank, Washington, DC.

Patrinos, Harry, and Emmanuel Skoufias. 2007. *Conference Edition: Economic Opportunities for Indigenous Peoples in Latin America*. Washington, DC: World Bank.

Payne, J. Mark, and Juan Cruz Perusia. 2007. Reforming the Rules of the Game: Political Reform. In Eduardo Lora, ed., *The State of State Reform in Latin America*. Washington, DC: Inter-American Development Bank and World Bank, and Palo Alto, CA: Stanford University Press.

Payne, J. Mark, Daniel Zovatto G., and Mercedes Mateo Díaz. 2007. *Democracies in Development: Politics and Reform in Latin America*. Washington, DC: Inter-American Development Bank.

Peeler, John A. 2003. Social Justice and the New Indigenous Politics: An Analysis of Guatemala, the Central Andes, and Chiapas. In Susan Eva Eckstein and Timothy P. Wickham-Crowley, eds., *What Justice? Whose Justice? Fighting for Fairness in Latin America*. Berkeley and Los Angeles: University of California Press.

Peixoto, Betânia Totino, Sueli Moro, and Mônica Viegas Andrade. 2004. Criminalidade na região metropolitana de Belo Horizonte: uma análise espacial. Centro de Desenvolvimento e Planejamento Regional (Cedeplar), Belo Horizonte, MG, Brazil. Available at http://www.cedeplar.ufmg.br/diamantina2004/textos/D04A016.PDF.

Pellegrino, Adela. 2002. *Skilled Labour Migration from Developing Countries: Study on Argentina and Uruguay*. International Migration Papers no. 58. International Labour Organization, Geneva.

Peredo, Elizabeth. 2004. *Una aproximación a la problemática de género y etnicidad en América Latina*. Serie mujer y desarrollo no. 53. United Nations Economic Commission for Latin America and the Caribbean (ECLAC), Santiago.

Peres, Wilson. 2005. *El (lento) retorno de las políticas industriales en América Latina y el Caribe*. Serie desarrollo productivo no. 166. United Nations Economic Commission for Latin America and the Caribbean (ECLAC), Santiago.

Pessino, Carola, and Ricardo Fenochietto. 2004. Efficiency and Equity of the Tax Structure in Argentina, Brazil and Chile: Analysis and Policy Considerations. Universidad de Buenos Aires and Universidad Torcuato Di Tella, Buenos Aires. Unpublished.

Peters, H. Elizabeth. 1992. Patterns of Intergenerational Mobility in Income and Earnings. *Review of Economics and Statistics* 74(3) August: 456–66.

Pinker, Steven. 2002. *The Blank Slate: The Modern Denial of Human Nature*. New York: Penguin Group.

Ponce, Juan. 2006. Más allá de los promedios: afrodescendientes en América Latina. Los afroecuatorianos. World Bank, Washington, DC. Unpublished.

Porter, Gordon L. 2001. *Disability and Education: Toward an Inclusive Approach*. SDS Working Paper. Inter-American Development Bank, Washington, DC.

Provoste Campillay, Yasna. 2004. Chile Solidario. Sistema de protección social a las familias más pobres del país. PowerPoint presentation given at the IDB conference, Third Meeting of the Social Policy Monitoring Network, November 22–23, Buenos Aires. Available at http://www.iadb.org/res/seminar_specific.cfm?ev_id=30&sm_id=96.

Putnam, Lara. 2002. La población afrocostarricense según los datos del censo de 2000. Paper presented at symposium, Costa Rica a la Luz del Censo del 2000, August 5–6, San José.

Putnam, Robert D., with Robert Leonardi and Raffaella Y. Nanetti. 1994. *Making Democracy Work: Civic Traditions in Modern Italy*. Princeton, NJ: Princeton University Press.

Rabin, Matthew. 1993. Incorporating Fairness into Game Theory and Economics. *American Economic Review* 83(5) December: 1281–1302.

Ramos, Joseph. 1996. *Política industrial y competitividad en economías abiertas*. Serie desarrollo productivo no. 34. United Nations Economic Commission for Latin America and the Caribbean (ECLAC), Santiago.

Ramos, Silvia. 2006. Youth and the Police. *Boletim Segurança e Cidadania* [Center for Studies on Public Security and Citizenship] 5(12) October: 1–16. Available at http://www.ucamcesec.com.br/arquivos/publicacoes/boletim12web_eng.pdf.

Reiss, Jr., Albert J., and Jeffrey A. Roth, eds. 1993. *Understanding and Preventing Violence*. Washington, DC: National Academy Press.

RENIEC (Registro Nacional de Identificación y Estado Civil). 2005. *Plan nacional de restitución de la identidad: documentando a las personas indocumentadas 2005–2009*. Lima: RENIEC.

Revenga, Ana. 1997. Employment and Wage Effects of Trade Liberalization: The Case of Mexican Manufacturing. *Journal of Labor Economics* 15(3, part 2) July: S20–43.

Riach, Peter A., and Judith Rich. 2002. Field Experiments of Discrimination in the Market Place. *Economic Journal* 112(483): 480–518.

Riaño-Alcalá, Pilar. 2006. *Dwellers of Memory: Youth and Violence in Medellín, Colombia*. New Brunswick, NJ: Transaction.

Ribando, Clare. 2005. Afro-Latinos in Latin America and Considerations for U.S. Policy. CRS Report for Congress. Congressional Research Service, Library of Congress, Washington, DC.

Richards-Kennedy, Stacy. 2006. South Africa's Post-Apartheid Strategy for Black Economic Empowerment. In Claire Nelson and Stacy Richards-Kennedy, eds., *Advancing Equity in Latin America: Putting Policy into Practice*. Washington, DC: IDB.

Robles, Arodys. 1999. ¿Transiciones paralelas o divergentes? Las poblaciones indígenas y no indígenas en América Latina. In Kenneth Hill, José Morelos, and Rebeca Wong, coordinators, *Las consecuencias de las transiciones demográfica y epidemiológica en América Latina*. Baltimore and Mexico City: Johns Hopkins University Press and El Colegio de México.

Roemer, John E. 2004. Equal Opportunity and Intergenerational Mobility: Going beyond Intergenerational Income Transition Matrices. In Miles Corak, ed., *Generational Income Mobility in North America and Europe*. Cambridge: Cambridge University Press.

Roland, Edna. 2001. The Economics of Racism: People of African Descent in Brazil. Paper presented at the International Council on Human Rights Policy Seminar on the Economics of Racism, November 24–25, Geneva.

Ross, Jen. 2007. Chile Kick-Starts Debate on Gender Quotas. *Women's e-News*, February 16. Available at http://www.womensenews.org/article.cfm/dyn/aid/3069.

Rossi, J. 2003. Mecanismos internacionales de protección de los derechos económicos, sociales y culturales. In Víctor Abramovich, María José Añón, and Christian Courtis, eds., *Derechos sociales: instrucciones de uso*. Mexico City: Doctrina Jurídica Contemporánea.

Rotker, Susana, ed. 2002. *Citizens of Fear: Urban Violence in Latin America*. New Brunswick, NJ: Rutgers University Press.

Rubalcava, Luis N., and Graciela M. Teruel. 2004. *The Role of Maternal Cognitive Ability on Child Health*. Research Network Working Paper no. R-497. Inter-American Development Bank, Washington, DC.

Saba, Roberto. 2004. (Des)igualdad estructural. In Jorge Amaya, ed., *Visiones de la Constitución 1853–2004*. Buenos Aires: UCES.

Sadoulet, Loïc. 2006. Savings and Deposit Services for the Poor. In Luis Tejerina, César Bouillón, and Edgardo Demaestri, eds., *Financial Services and Poverty Reduction in Latin America and the Caribbean*. Washington, DC: Inter-American Development Bank.

Salverda, Wiemer, Brian Nolan, Bertrand Maître, and Peter Mühlau. 2001. Benchmarking Low-Wage and High-Wage Employment in Europe and the United States: A Study of New European Datasets and National Data for France, Germany, the Netherlands, the United Kingdom and the United States. European Low-Wage Employment Research Network (LoWER), Amsterdam Institute for Advanced Labour Studies, University of Amsterdam, Amsterdam.

Sanahuja, José Antonio. 2007. La cohesión social en el marco del diálogo político UE-América Latina: visiones y perspectivas desde Europa. Paper presented at the seminar, Exclusión y Fragmentación Social en América Latina—Una Visión desde Europa, Madrid.

Sánchez, Enrique, and Paola García. 2006. Más allá de los promedios: afrodescendientes en América Latina. Los afrocolombianos. World Bank, Washington, DC. Unpublished.

Sánchez, Jeannette. 2006. Inequality, Ethnicity and Social Disorder: The Ecuadorian Case. Paper presented at the Third World Bank Conference on Inequality, June 5–6, Washington, DC.

Sánchez, John. 2005. Afroecuatorianos: invisibilidad, racismo, exclusión y pobreza. Paper presented at the international seminar, Pueblos Indígenas y Afrodescendientes de América Latina y el Caribe, April 27–29, Santiago.

Sánchez, Margarita. 2004. Afro-Latin American Community Development in Honduras and Guatemala. In Mayra Buvinić and Jacqueline Mazza, with Ruthanne Deutsch, eds., *Social Inclusion and Economic Development in Latin America*. Washington, DC: IDB.

Sánchez, Margarita, and Maurice Bryan. 2003. *Afro-descendants, Discrimination and Economic Exclusion in Latin America*. London: Minority Rights Group International.

Sánchez-Páramo, Carolina, and Norbert Schady. 2003. *Off and Running? Technology, Trade, and the Rising Demand for Skilled Workers in Latin America*. Policy Research Working Paper no. 3015. World Bank, Washington, DC.

Schochet, Peter, and Anu Rangarajan. 2004. Characteristics of Low-Wage Workers and Their Labor Market Experiences: Evidence from the Mid- to Late 1990s. Final report prepared for the U.S. Department of Health and Human Services, Office of the Assistant Secretary for Planning and Evaluation. Available at http://aspe.hhs.gov/hsp/low-wage-workers04/.

Scott, Alan. 1990. *Ideology and the New Social Movements*. London: Unwin Hyman.

Secretaría Técnica del Frente Social. 2004. Survey of Perceptions of Racism and Discrimination in Ecuador.

SEDESOL [Secretaría de Desarrollo Social]. 2005. First National Survey on Discrimination in Mexico. Mexico City. Available at http://sedesol2006.sedesol.gob.mx/subsecretarias/prospectiva/subse_discriminacion.htm.

Sen, Amartya. 1999. *Development as Freedom*. New York: Knopf.

Silva Lira, Iván. 2000. *Costo económico de los delitos, niveles de vigilancia y políticas de seguridad ciudadana en las comunas del Gran Santiago*. Serie gestión pública no. 2. United Nations Economic Commission for Latin America and the Caribbean (ECLAC), Santiago.

Smith, Peter H. 2005. *Democracy in Latin America: Political Change in Comparative Perspective*. New York and Oxford: Oxford University Press.

Solano, Elizabeth. 2002. La población indígena en Costa Rica según el censo 2000. Paper presented at symposium, Costa Rica a la Luz del Censo del 2000, August 5–6, San José.

Soruco, Ximena, Giorgina Piani, and Máximo Rossi. 2007. What Emigration Leaves Behind: The Situation of Emigrants and Their Families in Ecuador. Fundación Sur, Cuenca, Ecuador, and Universidad de la República Oriental del Uruguay, Montevideo. Unpublished.

Stefoni, Carolina. 2002. Mujeres inmigrantes peruanas en Chile. *Papeles de Población* [Universidad Autónoma del Estado de México] 33 (July–September): 118–45.

SUIVD (Sistema Unificado de Información de Violencia y Delincuencia). 2006. Estadísticas: caracterización del homicidio en Bogotá. Available at http://www.suivd.gov.co/estadisticas/sitio_estadisticas/1estad.htm.

Svampa, Maristella, and Sebastián Pereyra. 2003. *Entre la ruta y el barrio. La experiencia de las organizaciones piqueteras*. Buenos Aires: Editorial Biblos.

Székely, Miguel, and Marianne Hilgert. 1999. The 1990s in Latin America: Another Decade of Persistent Inequality. Working Paper no. 410. Inter-American Development Bank, Washington, DC.

Taber, Lisa, with Carlos Cuevas. 2004. Integrating the Poor into the Mainstream Financial System: The BANSEFI and SAGARPA Programs in Mexico. In Consultative Group to Assist the Poor (CGAP) and World Bank, *Scaling Up Poverty Reduction: Case Studies in Microfinance*. Washington, DC: CGAP/World Bank.

Tansel, Aysit. 1999. Workers Displaced Due to Privatization in Turkey: Before versus after Displacement. *METU Studies in Development* 25(4): 625–47.

Tarrow, Sidney. 1998. *Power in Movement: Social Movements and Contentious Politics*. Second Edition. New York: Cambridge University Press.

Tejerina, Luis, and Glenn Westley. 2007. Financial Services for the Poor: Household Survey Sources and Gaps in Borrowing and Saving. Inter-American Development Bank, Washington, DC. Unpublished.

Telles, Edward, and Nelson Lim. 1998. Does It Matter Who Answers the Race Question? Racial Classification and Income Inequality in Brazil. *Demography* 35(4): 465–74.

Tenjo Galarza, Jaime, Rocio Ribero Medina, and Luisa Fernanda Bernat Díaz. 2004. Evolution of Salary Differences between Men and Women in Six Latin American Countries. In Claudia Piras, ed., *Women at Work: Challenges for Latin America*. Washington, DC: Inter-American Development Bank.

Thomas, Sue, and Susan Welch. 2001. The Impact of Women in State Legislatures: Numerical and Organizational Strength. In Susan J. Carroll, ed., *The Impact of Women in Public Office*. Bloomington: Indiana University Press.

Thorp, Rosemary. 1998. *Progress, Poverty and Exclusion: An Economic History of Latin America in the 20th Century*. Washington, DC: Inter-American Development Bank.

————. 2007. The Historical Roots of Social Exclusion in Latin America. Paper presented at workshop, Exclusión y Fragmentación Social en América Latina: Una Visión desde Europa, February 23, Madrid.

Tilly, Charles. 1978. *From Mobilization to Revolution*. Reading, MA: Addison-Wesley.

————. 2004. *Social Movements, 1768–2004*. Boulder, CO: Paradigm.

Torero, Máximo, Eduardo Nakasone, and Lorena Alcázar. 2006. Provision of Public Services and Welfare of the Poor: Learning from an Incomplete Electricity Privatization Experience in Rural Peru. Inter-American Development Bank, Washington, DC. Unpublished.

Torero, Máximo, Jaime Saavedra, Hugo Ñopo, and Javier Escobal. 2004. An Invisible Wall? The Economics of Social Exclusion in Peru. In Mayra Buvinić and Jacqueline Mazza, with Ruthanne Deutsch, eds., *Social Inclusion and Economic Development in Latin America*. Washington, DC: IDB.

Townsend, Peter. 1979. *Poverty in the United Kingdom: A Survey of Household Resources and Standards of Living*. Berkeley and Los Angeles: University of California Press.

Tsakloglou, Panos, and Fotis Papadopoulos. 2001. *Identifying Population Groups at High Risk of Social Exclusion: Evidence from the ECHP*. IZA Discussion Paper no. 392. Institute for the Study of Labor (IZA), Bonn, Germany.

UNICEF (United Nations Children's Fund). 2005. *The 'Rights' Start to Life: A Statistical Analysis of Birth Registration*. New York: UNICEF.

Universidad Nacional de Tres de Febrero. 2006. Más allá de los promedios: afrodescendientes en América Latina. Resultados de la prueba piloto de captación en la Argentina. World Bank, Washington, DC. Unpublished.

Van Cott, Donna Lee. 2005. *From Movements to Parties in Latin America: The Evolution of Ethnic Politics*. New York: Cambridge University Press.

Vega, Gabriela. 2006. Comments at the Inter-American Development Bank seminar, Right from the Start: Registration, Identity and Development in Latin America and the Caribbean, February 2, Washington, DC.

Verdisco, A., V. Calderón, and J. H. Marshall. 2004. Social Exclusion in Education in Latin America and the Caribbean. Inter-American Development Bank, Washington, DC.

Wendel Abramo, Helena. 2004. Políticas de juventud en Brasil: nuevos tiempos, nuevas miradas. In Elisabet Gerber and Sergio Balardini, eds., *Políticas de juventud en Latinoamérica: Argentina en perspectiva*. Buenos Aires: Facultad Latinoamericana de Ciencias Sociales (FLACSO) and Fundación Friedrich Ebert.

Wiesner, Eduardo. 2003. *Fiscal Federalism in Latin America: From Entitlements to Markets*. Washington, DC: Inter-American Development Bank.

Wodon, Quentin. 2001. Income Mobility and Risk during the Business Cycle: Comparing Adjustments in Labour Markets in Two Latin-American Countries. *Economics of Transition* 9(2) July: 449–61.

Wolff, Jonas. 2007. (De-)Mobilising the Marginalised: A Comparison of the Argentine Piqueteros and Ecuador's Indigenous Movement. *Journal of Latin American Studies* 39(1) February: 1–29.

Woolcock, Michael. 2005. Calling on Friends and Relatives: Social Capital. In Marianne Fay, ed., *The Urban Poor in Latin America*. Washington, DC: World Bank.

World Bank. 2005. The Gap Matters: Poverty and Well-Being of Afro-Colombians and Indigenous Peoples. Report. World Bank, Washington, DC.

———. Various years. World Development Indicators Online. Available at http://dev data.worldbank.org/dataonline/.

World Commission on the Social Dimension of Globalization. 2004. *A Fair Globalization: Creating Opportunities for All*. Geneva: International Labour Office.

Yashar, Deborah J. 2005. *Contesting Citizenship in Latin America: The Rise of Indigenous Movements and the Postliberal Challenge*. New York: Cambridge University Press.

———. 2006. Indigenous Politics in the Andes: Changing Patterns of Recognition, Reform, and Representation. In Scott Mainwaring, Ana María Bejarano, and Eduardo Pizarro Leongómez, eds., *The Crisis of Democratic Representation in the Andes*. Stanford, CA: Stanford University Press.

Yinger, John. 1986. Measuring Racial Discrimination with Fair Housing Audits: Caught in the Act. *American Economic Review* 76(5) December: 881–93.

Index